The Last Empress

Painting of Empress Alexandra, 1896.

THE
LAST EMPRESS

*The Life and Times of
Alexandra Feodorovna,
Tsarina of Russia*

Greg King

A Citadel Press Book
Published by Carol Publishing Group

A Citadel Press Book
Published by Carol Publishing Group
Citadel Press is a registered trademark of Carol Communications, Inc.
Editorial Offices: 600 Madison Avenue, New York, N.Y. 10022
Sales and Distribution Offices: 120 Enterprise Avenue, Secaucus, N.J. 07094
In Canada: Canadian Manda Group, One Atlantic Avenue, Suite 105, Toronto, Ontario M6K 3E7
Queries regarding rights and permissions should be addressed to Carol Publishing Group, 600 Madison Avenue, New York, N.Y. 10022

Carol Publishing Group books are available at special discounts for bulk purchases, for sales promotion, fund-raising, or educational purposes. Special editions can be created to specifications. For details, contact: Special Sales Department, Carol Publishing Group, 120 Enterprise Avenue, Secaucus, N.J. 07094

Manufactured in the United States of America

10 9 8 7 6 5 4 3 2 1

Library of Congress Cataloging-in-Publication Data

King, Greg.
   The last empress : the life and times of Alexandra Feodorovna, Tsarina of Russia / by Greg King
     p. cm.
   "A Citadel Press book."
   ISBN 0-8065-1761-1
   1. Alexandra, Empress, consort of Nicholas II, Emperor of Russia, 1872–1918. 2. Empresses—Russia—Biography. 3. Russia—History—Nicholas II, 1894–1917. I. Title.
DK254.A5K56   1994
947.08'3'092—dc20
[B]   93-45737
                                                CIP

To Russ

Without friends, no one would choose to live,
though he had all other goods.

—Aristotle

Contents

25   To Fall Asleep Forever in Your Arms   /   183
26   Spala   /   194
27   1913   /   200
28   Summer of War   /   209

Part Four: Sister Alexandra (1914–17)   219

29   Russian Slaughter   /   221
30   Sister Alexandra   /   229
31   The Shadow of Rasputin   /   236
32   "For Baby's Sake"   /   244
33   The Ruin of the Government   /   251
34   Autumn of Delusions   /   256
35   December Nightmare   /   264
36   The Palace Revolution Proposal   /   274
37   Revolution   /   283
38   Abdication   /   290

Part Five: Alexandra Romanova (1917–18)   301

39   Prisoners   /   303
40   Royal Betrayal   /   311
41   Exile   /   318
42   Siberian Winter   /   326
43   "God's Will"   /   333
44   The House of Special Purpose   /   342
45   The Last Days of the Romanovs   /   354
46   The End of the Romanovs   /   363
47   The Secret of Koptyaki Forest   /   371
     Epilogue   381

     Acknowledgments   /   393
     Source Notes   /   397
     Bibliography   /   413
     Index   /   421

T HE LIFE OF THE LAST Empress is clearly divided in two epochs, and she has to be judged as if she were two different women.

The first woman is a wife, a mother and a spouse offering controversial advice in matters which were properly not of her concern. The second woman appears as soon as the Tsar abdicates, lives through humiliations and constant fear and by a calvary road arrives at the Ipatiev House cellar.

The one characteristic common to the two women is the Empress's passionate love of her husband. The first woman is open to the most severe criticism; the second woman is admirable.

—From a letter by Prince Nicholas Romanoff to the author

Preface

Alexandra Feodorovna, consort of Nicholas II, the last
tsar of Russia, has been the subject of an immense body of literature. As
one of the principal figures in the final drama of the Russian Empire and
the subsequent Revolution, she has been studied, analyzed, criticized,
and condemned for three-quarters of a century. Perhaps no other
woman in twentieth-century history has been so maligned, so misunderstood, and held partially responsible for such a momentous event as
the Russian Revolution.

History has painted her as a shy, headstrong young woman who,
once married to Tsar Nicholas II, lost all sense of balance: She became a
haughty prude, isolating her family to the detriment of Russian society
as a whole and the prestige of the Romanov family in particular. Her
failure to attend to her duties as tsarina lost for Alexandra all public
sympathy. When her last child and only son, Tsarevich Alexei, was
found to have hemophilia, she was so crushed that she became a religious fanatic, allowing herself to fall under the evil influence of the notorious Rasputin. In the years of the First World War, his domination
over her was so great that it was Rasputin—drunken, lecherous, barbaric, and fraudulent—who ordered the destinies of imperial Russia,
while the tsarina, his adoring devotee, practically compelled her weak
husband to fulfill them. Together she and Rasputin marched hand in
hand in bringing about the fall of the Russian Empire. Alexandra,
naively blind to the end, continued to believe, against all evidence, that
she and her husband were beloved of the people, and when the Revolution came, few mourned her fall from grace and subsequent death.

Seventy-five years after her death, Alexandra continues to fasci-
nate, a measure, no doubt, of her complexity and nearly incomprehensible character. That she remains very much an enigma is not for lack of
evidence of her life and thought. Alexandra left a wealth of letters and
diaries, spanning over thirty years; members of her family recalled her
life and times in their memoirs; her friends wrote defenses praising her,

while her enemies blamed her for the fall of the Romanov dynasty. No matter how many books are written featuring Alexandra as either their subject or as a secondary figure, there seems to be little agreement among their authors as to her role in Russian society, the degree of influence on her husband, and the question of Rasputin's influence over her.

For a woman of such notoriety and supposed power, Alexandra has been the sole subject of only two serious biographical works.* In 1928, Alexandra's former lady-in-waiting Baroness Sophie Buxhoeveden wrote something close to an official life, using documents held in Alexandra's family's collection and drawing upon her own experiences at the court. This biography, however, suffered from the author's apparent biases toward her subject arising from closeness to her in real life.

In 1961 came E. M. Almedingen's thoughtful *The Empress Alexandra*—the first work which attempted to examine the tsarina's life against the backdrop of her times and to interpret her character from an unbiased position. While an improvement on the previous works, this book sacrificed thoroughness and Alexandra's personal life to the larger picture of the disintegration of Russian society as a whole. For example, Alexandra's first twenty-two years are dealt with by Almedingen in less than a dozen pages, and the concentration in the remainder of the book is on a clear, concise presentation of the factors which influenced the tsarina's life in Russia but not necessarily her reactions to them or, indeed, why she reacted in the manner she did.

Robert K. Massie's *Nicholas and Alexandra*, while not a work dealing solely with the tsarina, did much to humanize the imperial couple and focused on their great love story as a counter to the decline of the Russian Empire. Massie applied to Alexandra a balanced understanding which had, up to that point, been lacking; and yet, like previous works, it missed much important detail in her life, being necessarily divided in its focus.

Other writers—both historians and biographers—have generally judged Alexandra harshly. A typical example comes from Edward Crankshaw's otherwise excellent work *The Shadow of the Winter Palace*, which is worth quoting at length, for it illustrates what seems to be history's pervasive verdict on the tsarina:

> Alexandra, if not an imbecile, was politically and socially
> illiterate, dominating him [the tsar] and towards the end forcing

---

*For practical purposes I do not include in this number the works of Princess Catherine Radziwill, which were clearly written as accusatory materials, or the books by Anna Vyrubova and Lili Dehn, which served the reverse.

upon him calamitous decisions. . . . She convinced herself, not
without grounds, that the court was corrupt and corrupting, and
with it the whole bureaucratic system; it was on the rather shakier
grounds that she convinced herself that she and she alone
understood the holy inwardness of the Russian peasant and
that virtually the whole of educated society was engaged in a
conspiracy to set barriers between Nicholas and his people. She
trusted nobody and believed the worst of anyone who sought to
advise or influence her husband. . . . The harm she did by causing
Nicholas to leave St. Petersburg . . . by cocooning him in her
claustrophobic apartments, visited only by inferior hangers-on
. . . helping him to pretend that he was indeed the autocrat and
father of his people, was past all computing.[1]

Here, in a few sentences, Crankshaw has demonstrated his own prejudices against Alexandra quite clearly while at the same time encapsu-
lating all of the animosity toward her which has grown over the years.
He certainly is not alone in his judgment of Alexandra; but is the portrait the correct one?

What has emerged from my own fifteen-year study of this controversial woman is that nearly all previous accounts of her life must be
disregarded in an attempt to understand her. While I do not pretend to
know the entire truth about Alexandra Feodorovna, I have come to believe that the key to understanding her character—and thus her role as
tsarina and her part in the fall of the Russian monarchy—lies not in the
twenty-two years she spent in Russia as tsarina but rather in the previous twenty-two years, when she was a princess of the small grand
duchy of Hesse and By Rhine in Germany. These years of her life—so
important in understanding how she became the woman she did and
why she fell under the influences which eventually dominated her—
have, as I explained earlier, been largely ignored. Yet here, as a girl and
a young woman, we can see Alix, as she was then, already closing herself off from society and unfamiliar people, already impressing those
around her as a tragic figure, already susceptible to an extreme religious exaltation—all of which would later be manifested more strongly,
and unfortunately to greater effect, once she became tsarina.

The disintegration—and that is, in truth, what it was—of the tsarina as the years went by—from the isolation from society to the influence of Rasputin and finally the political domination of her husband—
all are rooted in her formative years. She entered Russia as one of
Queen Victoria's enlightened and democratic granddaughters; scarcely
ten years later, her belief in the institution of autocracy had surpassed
that of her husband. Her entire nature changed—or seemed to

change—with each passing year. But in her childhood and teenage years, Alix of Hesse already possessed in her character the seeds of her own destruction: her fatalism, her overwhelming religious convictions, and her susceptibility to grandeur and opulence.

Thus, in this biography of the tsarina, I have dealt extensively with her formative years. If, at times, the reasoning does not seem immediate, I ask the reader's indulgence, for much of what Alexandra experienced in her childhood only came to be relevant once she sat on the Russian throne at the side of her husband. Along with other writers and historians, I have puzzled over her actions and responses, trying to interpret them in light of what we know of her character. In some cases, where we have little primary evidence, it has been impossible to second-guess Alexandra; at other times and with other circumstances— such as her relationship with Rasputin during the First World War—I have added my own interpretation to those of my predecessors.

And so here, in these pages, we have the story of Alexandra Feodorovna, the last tsarina of Russia. It is a story often told—of her tragic childhood, her happy married life, her son's tragic illness, her alienation from society, her relationship with Rasputin, and her ultimately terrible death. But I think the story told here goes further than any other toward understanding and making understood this important and controversial woman.

Author's Note

THE USE OF THE TITLES *Tsar, Tsarina, Emperor,* and *Empress* can be confusing. Until 1721, all Romanov rulers used Tsar, a title derived from Caesar. Peter the Great, enamored of all things Western, officially adopted the title *Gosudar Imperator* (Sovereign Emperor), which was the correct form of address until the end of the Romanov dynasty in 1917. Even so, the sovereign was commonly referred to as Tsar and his wife as Tsarina, although her title was Empress. Nicholas II, himself a Slavophile, preferred the more ancient form Tsar, while Alexandra preferred Empress. I have used both forms of address throughout this book. The heir to the throne held the title *Tsarevich* until 1721, when it became *Tsesarevich*. Most writers have continued to spell it as Tsarevich, which I have chosen for this book.

When Alix was born in 1872, she was styled "Her Grand Ducal Highness," taking her rank from her father, Prince Ludwig of Hesse and By Rhine. Alix became Alexandra Feodorovna upon her conversion to Orthodoxy in 1894.

There may be some confusion as to the spelling of names mentioned herein. Alexandra's father, Grand Duke Ludwig of Hesse and By Rhine, for example, is called by the German rendering of his name rather than the English "Louis"; this is not always the case, however. Alexandra's brother-in-law, Prince Louis of Battenberg, is referred to using the English form, partially to avoid confusion with Ludwig and also because much of his life was spent in England.

The transliteration of Russian names has followed the Library of Congress method with certain exceptions. All proper names have been rendered in English; thus, "Paul" for "Pavel" and "Serge" for "Sergei." The name of Alexandra's son has been rendered as "Alexei," however, rather than the more commonly Western "Alexis."

A word, too, about dates. In Russia, until the Bolshevik Revolution, the Julian, rather than the Gregorian, calendar was in official use. As a result, dates in the nineteenth century were twelve days behind

xv

those of Europe; in the twentieth century, they were thirteen days behind. For example, Nicholas II abdicated on 2 March 1917 according to
the Russian calendar but on 15 March according to Western dates. I
have, without exception, followed the Gregorian calendar and rendered dates in Western fashion. Even so, a note of caution should be
sounded: Some writers dated their diaries and letters with the Western
style even before the Revolution, and this could not always be determined.

PART ONE

Princess Alix

(1872–94)

1

An English Princess

SHE WAS AMBITIOUS. She was loved. She was hated. She was sensitive. She was strong. She was weak. She was charming. She was cold. She was proud. She was common. She was intelligent. She was narrow-minded. She was shy. She was warm. She was hysterical. She was a saint. She was a wife, a mother, and an empress. Above all, she was misunderstood. She was a woman who would change the course of modern history.

Alexandra Feodorovna was not born a Russian. Yet she was capable of being more patriotically Russian than any of her husband's subjects. She was not brought up in the Orthodox faith. Yet she was possessed of more religious fervor than most who had been born into the Russian church. She cared little for politics. Yet she found in it her *raison d'être* as the years went by. She loved her husband passionately. Yet she found in him an outlet for her ambitions through which she ultimately came to control the destinies of the Russian Empire. Later in her life, she was known as Your Imperial Majesty. Her friends called her Alexandra Feodorovna. To her family, she was Alicky or Sunny. But she came into the world as Alix of Hesse, the product of a fateful marriage some ten years prior to her birth.

On that cold, windswept first day of July 1862, Alix's parents—Princess Alice of Great Britain and Prince Ludwig of Hesse—were married in a private, sad little ceremony at Osborne House on the Isle of Wight, Queen Victoria's summer home.

Such an event should have been celebrated with due pomp. Indeed, there had been plans for a London wedding in the Chapel Royal of St. James's Palace, but the death of the prince consort only six months before brought gloom to the ceremony. Instead of a chapel there was a dining room—hastily converted by the erection of an altar. The bride's mother, Queen Victoria, draped herself in black for the service, and every aspect of the day reflected her intense grief at the loss of her beloved husband. Princess Alice, in a dress of white satin covered with flounces of Honiton lace, and Prince Ludwig exchanged vows kneeling before a Winterhalter portrait of the royal family painted in 1846. From the portrait the prince consort gazed at the spectacle, his outstretched hand seeming to point toward the chair which his widow occupied. The bride's brothers and sisters wept openly through the service, and afterward the groom's parents expressed sympathies to the queen while the archbishop wiped tears from his eyes.[1] The whole affair had gone off badly. It had been no real wedding. Rather, the ceremony possessed all the elements of mourning—weeping family members, a widow dressed in black, and the stifling atmosphere of a house dominated by a feeling of overwhelming, absolute grief. "Alice's wedding," the queen noted, "was more like a funeral."[2]

There was no honeymoon. The family gathered on the Italian portico to see the newlyweds off. A four-horse brougham carried Alice and Ludwig away from Osborne. As they left, the sky opened up, and a threatening storm finally broke over the island. It was a fitting start to one of the most tragic royal families in all of history.

Nineteen years earlier Queen Victoria had given birth to Princess Alice. A birth caused the queen immense difficulty, and the result was none too pleasant. She thought most babies "frightful" and "quite repulsive." There were few pretty babies, and ugly ones were "nasty objects."[3] The queen had to draw on her reserves of patience in dealing with her children. She could blame one of them for nearly anything; when her mind was set, she refused to retreat. Yet there was another side to the queen. Once, at a state dinner, she was seated next to a deaf admiral. The talk switched from his ship to his sister without his realizing it, and Victoria laughed hysterically when he told her he intended to have the latter's bottom scraped.[4]

Prince Albert had come across the Channel from Coburg to capture the heart of this difficult and passionate woman. She found in him a glorious example of all that was good in life, and their children were molded to follow in his footsteps. He was a true Renaissance prince—studying, designing, observing, and teaching. It was he who organized the first exhibition of British goods and technology at the Crystal Palace in 1851. But the queen could not see past his outstanding qualities to the other, darker side of his character. The prince was shy and nervous in public. The English, on the whole, disliked him, finding him too German and too domineering. His nervousness kept him pacing the halls of the palace long after all others had retired. As a parent, he believed in absolutes, and so dominated his children as he himself had been dominated by his own tutor.

Alice was one of nine children, a number with which Queen Victoria was pleased. Vicky, the eldest daughter, was so precocious that by the age of three she was fluent in French, German, and English.[5] Bertie, the Prince of Wales, rebelled against his strict training for the throne by becoming the antithesis of what his father stood for—gay, uncontrollable, and loose. Alfred resented Bertie to the extent that the two eventually had to be separated. Arthur played with soldiers, and Leopold suffered from hemophilia. Helena and Louise were, in kindly terms, plain and unattractive, while the baby of the family, Beatrice, spent her childhood under the burden of her mother's excessive mourning.[6]

Alice and Bertie shared a close relationship, for they were both regarded as disappointments within the royal family. Alice's problem lay in her appearance—her father regularly referred to her as "poor dear Alice."[7] Her features were fine but were lost in a face which by no stretch of the imagination could be considered beautiful. Her sense of independence caused the royal family much worry; she visited hospitals, helped the poor, and studied anatomy, which the queen thought "disgusting."[8] Still, she was less a problem than her elder brother, as the queen noted in a letter to Vicky, who had married the crown prince of Prussia: "Dear, good Alice has improved so much. She has a sweet temper, is industrious and has made good progress. She takes lessons of an evening with Papa, who says she is very attentive, whereas Bertie is stupid and inattentive."[9]

When Alice was seventeen, the queen decided that it was time for her daughter to marry. The royal houses of Europe promised a suitable husband, and the queen, an incurable matchmaker, was beside herself with delight at choosing a mate for her daughter. Alice's sister Vicky had found the best match with the crown prince of Prussia, so she herself would have to settle for a less illustrious position. When the time did come, Victoria turned quite naturally to one of the small, independent duchies scattered across the lands bordering the Baltic, which were traditionally the breeding grounds for the children of sovereigns.

Her choice fell on Hesse, a small grand duchy, cut in half by the Rhine River. It was ruled by the oldest Protestant dynasty in the world. The Hesse family counted among their ancestors St. Elizabeth of Hungary; Mary, Queen of Scots; and Emperor Charlemagne. In the palace decked with the red-and-white Hessian flag, many a royal marriage had been arranged. The sister of the reigning grand duke at this time was Empress Marie Feodorovna of Russia, and the family's blood ties with other ruling houses were equally strong. Even today it survives: there is a higher percentage of Hessian blood in the British royal family than any other.[10]

At the head of the family was Grand Duke Ludwig III. Six feet ten inches tall, the grand duke had been twice married but had yet to produce an heir.[11] His younger brother Karl expected to inherit the throne. Prince Karl had, in 1836, wed Princess Elizabeth of Prussia, who bore him four children: Ludwig, Heinrich, Anna, and Wilhelm. It was upon the young prince Ludwig, handsome, polite, inoffensive, that the queen centered her hopes for Alice's future. Having selected the potential groom, Victoria invited Ludwig to England for Ascot Week in June 1860.

What Alice saw in Ludwig was a new face, an attractive one. Her cloistered existence in her mother's palaces had kept her exposure to the opposite sex reduced to a handful of servants and family. Ludwig was the first eligible young man with whom she was allowed to spend any time. She fell, quite simply, in love with him at first sight. After he had left, Alice confessed her feelings to a friend, who wrote: "She talked almost exclusively of her anxieties and sufferings from her excessive love for Prince Louis of Hesse-Darmstadt. He is now the 'one being,' the only man she ever did, shall, can or will ever love. . . ."[12]

Six months later, Prince Albert took Ludwig aside during a visit and told him that he should propose to Alice that evening.[13] Alice accepted, and the queen was overjoyed.

A year later, the queen's joy turned to worry. In the midst of the wedding preparations, Prince Albert fell ill. He refused to eat; in a dressing gown, he shuffled from room to room, coughing. By the first week of December, gastric fever had set in, and Albert was confined to bed.[14] Victoria refused to believe that the matter was serious. She regarded the illness as having been brought on solely through worry about the recently exposed indiscretion of the Prince of Wales with a young actress named Nellie Clifton. Too late, the queen realized that her husband really was ill. On 14 December 1861, the prince slipped into a coma and died. The queen's hysterical screams echoed throughout the huge sprawl of Windsor Castle.

Alice was eighteen years old when her father died. The queen lay immobile on her bed except for frequent trips to the room where her husband had died, and it was left to the young princess Alice to arrange the funeral. Prince Albert lay in the Blue Room, dressed in an overcoat of blue.[15] He clutched a photograph of the queen in his stiff fingers.[16] Screaming, weeping, the queen covered his cold face with kisses and grasped at his clothing before the body was taken away.[17]

It was, in fact, Queen Victoria's endless obsession with her dead husband which led to the wedding the following summer. Albert had given the match his blessing; Albert had planned the ceremony; he had designed the bride's gown. Therefore, the wedding would proceed. But not as a public celebration—the queen would have none of that. So the wedding party retreated to gloom-ridden Osborne House, to engage in worshipful homage to the memory of the prince consort as much as to witness the nuptials.

Life in Darmstadt, the capital of Hesse, proved far different from Alice's expectations. Her early years of marriage were shattered by the actions of Prussia and its chancellor, Otto von Bismarck. Prussia, ruled by the Hohenzollern family, was the largest and most powerful of the loosely federated German states. Disagreements became wars, and family differences took the form of political support for opposing armies. The inevitability of Prussian domination, according to Bismarck, needed to be sped along. He found a convenient excuse in the Baltic duchies of Schleswig-Holstein-Sonderburg-Augustenburg.

What Bismarck wanted and what he got was a simple military exercise for Prussia. On the death of King Friedrich VIII of Denmark, Chancellor Bismarck "invited" the duchies to join the Prussian nation. The question of to whom they properly belonged had never been legally established, but the duchies declined Bismarck's offer in favor of an association with Denmark. But the population, said Bismarck, spoke German, not Danish. The new king of Denmark, Christian IX, declared that the duchies were inseparable from his country, in violation of a previously arranged treaty. Duke Friedrich of Augustenburg believed that his family held the rights to govern the duchies and even proclaimed himself king of Schleswig-Holstein-Sonderburg-Augustenburg.

Alice was placed in a peculiar position. Her husband believed in the rights of the duke of Augustenburg. Her brother Bertie had married Princess Alexandra of Denmark, a daughter of King Christian IX, and the pair naturally supported the Danish view. Alice's sister Vicky, wife of the crown prince of Prussia—as well as Queen Victoria herself—took the side of Bismarck.[18]

Bismarck eventually persuaded Austria to join in attacking the duchies; Schleswig-Holstein-Sonderburg-Augustenburg before long were firmly Prussian. Bismarck, in token gratitude, gave a small section to Austria. But this section lay smack in the middle of Prussian territory, and Austria naturally objected. They turned the matter over to the Frankfurt diet for consideration, but the diet shocked everyone by suggesting that the duchies should revert to the rule of the duke of Augustenburg. The diet voted for the mobilization of the Federal German army. Bismarck took this move as a sudden declaration of war and ordered the Prussian army to march into those states which opposed his policies. Two days later, the Prussians occupied Hanover, Saxony, and Nassau.[19]

Alice was one of many women who waved their husbands off to war as Ludwig took up his position as Commander of the Hessian cavalry. Hesse was utterly unprepared for war. Alice tore up sheets to be used as bandages and wrote to the queen asking for extra linen from Osborne and Windsor.[20] She saw the need for nurses and founded the Central Ladies' Union to help train them; she herself took classes so that she could assist in the military hospitals.

The war went on for seven weeks. At the Battle of Königgrätz the Austrians suffered a terrible defeat, and Prussia emerged victorious. Their army crossed the Hessian frontier and swept through Darmstadt, confiscating what they pleased and paying for nothing at all. Princess Alice wrote to her mother the queen:

> The Prussians marched in this morning, their bands playing and making as great a demonstration as they could. . . . I do not know where dear Louis is now. Please God he is safe, but the anxiety is fearful. . . . We must get the gracious permission of the Prussians for anything we want, we smuggle people without things with difficulty out of town, if we want anything, but the Prussians watch so well, to prevent our communicating with our troops or with anywhere outside, that we are complete prisoners. This goes so far we have difficulty in getting any decent meat, or the common luxuries of life, for the Prussians devour everything. . . .[21]

The armistice placed Hesse under the virtual control of Prussia. In 1871, after the Franco-Prussian War, Hesse lost what little independence it still held when it was forcibly incorporated into the newly formed German Empire ruled by the Hohenzollerns of Prussia.

Incorporation meant impoverishment for the duchy. As an indemnity the country had to pay a huge amount in addition to losing most of its revenue-producing lands. Alice was forced by circumstances to draw up a family budget. When she married Ludwig, she brought with her a dowry of thirty thousand pounds, but this, as well as most of her husband's private fortune, was consumed by the building of a new residence in Darmstadt. She had to let some of her servants go and alter her plans for hiring new ones. She wrote to her mother: "We must live so economically—not going anywhere or seeing many people, so as to be able to spare as much a year as we can. . . . We have sold four carriage horses and have only six left to drive with now, two of which the ladies constantly want for theatres, visits, etc., so we are rather badly off in some things."[22]

In 1876, Alice asked her mother if she could stay at Buckingham Palace for two nights on her way to Balmoral, the queen's castle in Scotland. She traveled with only two people, a colonel and his wife who lived in Darmstadt. But Queen Victoria said no, it would be too much trouble. Alice was forced to say that she had no other choice—she could not afford to pay for hotels. A courtier suggested that the queen could pay the bill for the hotel, to which Victoria replied that she would have to know how many nights were in question. Alice cabled back two or three; the queen said she would have to think the situation over. In the end, Alice tired of begging. She traveled alone, unattended and staying in cheap hotels.[23]

The wars and financial hardships took their toll on the marital relationship, which was perhaps inevitable as Alice and her husband were so entirely different. She was temperamental, he shallow. She was sensitive and emotional; he, gruff and reserved. Whereas Alice was an intellectual, Ludwig was childlike and unassuming. Ludwig tried to act British, wearing Norfolk jackets and speaking English, but his heavy accent gave him away. Through careful affectation Ludwig hoped to fool others into thinking he was the perfect English gentleman. But the queen found the game— her son-in-law's attempts to lay claim to a heritage he did not possess— particularly distasteful. He liked to talk about British politics, a subject forbidden among the royal family, and whenever he brought up the topic, the queen began to cough nervously. One unimpressed dinner companion later wrote: "Louis's English and whole conversation consists in: `You have in your country a—a what you call—ah—so. Like what you call—Alice! Alice! *Was herst ein wohlengeblandersuhe* ? Fog. Ah, so, yes. A fog, which makes what you call—ah—Alice! *Was ist geblandesbend*? Dark, yes, dark.'"[24]

Where Alice prided herself on being well read, Ludwig, according to his uncle Alexander of Battenberg, "reads as little as possible and never writes at all," although he did note that his nephew was "very fond of sherry and horses."[25] The marriage suffered because of these differences. What Alice needed was an emotional and intellectual equal, someone in whom she could confide her hopes and fears; but Ludwig was not such a man. Of their love there can be no doubt, but the union was far from untroubled. During the war over the duchies, when Ludwig was away, Alice wrote to him, "How I miss you—day and night— I cannot tell you, darling husband—and how I wish I could talk to you. I kiss your dear picture when I get up and wish it could speak. It is so lonely in bed when you are not with me. . . ."[26] Ten years later, however, the picture was far different. After an argument with her husband, Alice joined her mother at Balmoral Castle in Scotland. When Ludwig wrote to her daily, Alice answered him with a sad and illuminating letter:

> It is kind of you to write so often and it gives me such a pleasure,
> but darling Louis, if the children wrote me such childish letters—

only short accounts—of where and what else they had eaten or where they had been, etc., and nothing else, no opinions, observations and remarks, I should be surprised—and how much more so when *you* write like that.

There has never been any lack of love—only with time, the disillusion became harder to bear. . . . I longed for a real companion, for, apart from that, life had nothing to offer me in Darmstadt. I could have been quite happy and contented living in a cottage, if I had been able to share my intellectual interests and intellectual aspirations with a husband whose strong, protective love would have guided me round the rocks strewn in my way by my own nature, outward circumstances and the excess of my opinions.

So naturally I am bitterly disappointed with myself when I look back and see that in spite of good intentions, and real effort, my hopes have nonetheless been completely shipwrecked—and this realization, my darling, often makes me unjust towards you—for one carries the blame for everything in one's self—I know that *now*. It always grieves me, too, to see how you can have been disappointed—for the fault is *mine*. But let us go on helping each other—honestly—we cannot let ourselves be paralyzed by the past—and there is nothing I want but to make your life happy and to be useful to you.

I have tried again and again to talk to you about more serious things, when I felt the need to do so—but we never met each other—I feel that true companionship is an impossibility for us—because our thoughts will never meet. There are so many things that are necessary to me, of which you know nothing, but which, at my age, form a part of my personality, and make up my life. You would laugh, you would not understand it, if I expressed what I think and feel. I shall never forget your *great* goodness, nor that you are still so fond of me—and I love you too so very much, my darling husband, that is why it is so sad to feel that our life is nevertheless so incomplete and sometimes so difficult. But you are never intentionally to blame for this—I *never* think that, *never* . . . .[27]

Later, Alice was able to write to Ludwig, "I am not blind to my faults. But I think I can say that we did not choose badly then and that we are a very happy couple."[28]

Despite her efforts to adjust to her new country and position, Alice still felt herself an outsider. The twelve-year-old daughter of Prince Alexander of Battenberg, Princess Marie, later said: "She was a forcigner, come from distant England, and as I soon remarked, did not fit in at all with the Darmstadt connections. I often felt very sorry for her, she was so kind and so congenial to us, more so than our Hessian relations, and in a different way . . . [she] was a most attractive and arresting personality; her voice, particularly, and her pretty mouth with its even teeth, aroused my admiration. . . ."[29]

The unhappiness—in both the marital relationship and life in Darmstadt—began to reflect itself in Alice's personality. More and more often she was prone to fits of melancholy and suffered from nervous attacks, alternating with exhaustion and bouts of sickness. Her health steadily declined, although much of the problem seems to have been psychosomatic: "When she had nothing special to take her mind off life at its most ordinary," wrote Noel Gerard, "the aches and pains appeared to be at their worst."[30]

Complicating health matters even further was the fact that in the first ten years of her marriage Alice had given birth to five children, one every other year. The eldest, Victoria, had come in 1863; she was followed by Elizabeth—Ella—in 1864; Irene in 1866; Ernest Ludwig in 1868; and Friedrich Wilhelm—Frittie—in 1870. Since nurses and nannies were expensive, Alice cared for the children herself when they were born or, later, was assisted by a very small—by royal standards—staff.

In December 1871, Alice's brother Bertie, the Prince of Wales, fell ill with typhoid. She rushed to his home in Norfolk, Sandringham House, where he lay dying. Day by day the doctors saw him slipping away, but Alice stayed by his side and—along with his wife, Alexandra—nursed him back to health. By the time Bertie was out of danger, Alice was an emotional and physical wreck. She lay on a couch for days, unable to sleep. Her health was bad, she was three months pregnant, and she feared that the atmosphere might somehow affect the life of her unborn child. As she felt the baby kick, Alice wrote, "I think the child is coming to life. If only this does not harm it."[31]

2

A June Baby

ALICE'S NEW BABY—a healthy girl with dark, shining eyes, a tiny head topped with a curl of reddish-gold hair, and small, finely formed features—was born on 6 June 1872, at the height of the sweltering German summer. She was christened on her parents' wedding anniversary, 1 July, and given the complex string of names favored by the period: "'Alix' we gave for 'Alice' as they murder my name here: 'Alice' they pronounce it, so we thought 'Alix' could not so easily be spoilt," her mother wrote to Queen Victoria.[1] The choice of names was, by this time, becoming something of a family tradition, for the queen had declared that all of her descendants should bear either the name Victoria or Albert in memory of the royal couple. So Victoria was added to Alix. Helena, Louise, and Beatrice were the baby's English aunts, Alice's sisters. And so it was Her Royal Highness the Princess Alix Victoria Helena Louise Beatrice von Hesse and By Rhine who was sprinkled with holy water at her christening. This tiny descendant of Emperor Charlemagne and Mary, Queen of Scots, had an illustrious group of godparents: the future King Edward VII of England and his wife; the future tsar Alexander III of Russia and his wife; Princess Beatrice of England; the duke of Cambridge; and the landgrave of Hesse.

From her earliest days Alix lived in a succession of palaces, castles, hunting lodges, and shooting camps scattered through the pleasant Hessian countryside. On the banks of the nearby Rhine, in the depths of the dark pine forests and atop low mountains overlooking golden meadows, the family had a number of homes. There was a hunting lodge called Seeheim and a very eerie Gothic castle known as Kranichstein.

Darmstadt, the capital of Hesse, was a town of modest size. Typical of hundreds of medieval German cities, Darmstadt rose and twisted around narrow cobbled streets and squares. Its romantic buildings, carved with rococo details and overlooking splashing fountains, evoked the Germany of Goethe, lost in dark antiquity. One of Alix's homes captured this sense of the past perfectly. The old *Schloss* was actually two buildings: one, a new, plainly decorated wing facing out onto the Marktplatz; the other, a castle bristling with gables and towers, surrounding small courtyards, and arcades beneath the clock turret that chimed the hour to all Darmstadt. Although the family owned all these homes, Alix really grew up at the New Palace, in the center of the town.

The New Palace—it had been built only six years before Alix was born—sat in a huge park, which had once been a botanical garden, surrounded by a tall iron fence. Elm, linden, and chestnut trees shaded gravel paths which skirted the lake and flower gardens and led up the sloping lawns to the house. Alice had chosen a style she knew from her childhood days at Osborne—Italianate—and the house was constructed accordingly, with French doors opening to loggias and terraces. The rooms, planned for comfort, had high ceilings and walls hung with portraits of Queen Victoria, Prince Albert, and King George III and sketches of Windsor, Osborne, and Balmoral.[2] Peculiarly, Alice furnished her palace with selections from Maples in London. Maples specialized in elegant but inexpensive machine-made pieces, the kind of items with which any middle-class Briton might furnish a home.

Alix's first years were uneventful, and she appears to have had a relatively happy babyhood. "Baby is like Ella, only smaller features, and still darker eyes," her mother wrote. "She is a sweet, merry little person, always laughing and a dimple in one cheek, just like Ernie." By the time of her sister Marie's christening in 1874, Alix was regularly called Sunny, due to her cheerful nature. "Sunny in pink was immensely admired," her mother reported.[3] Later, she added that her little girl was fast growing up: "Sunny is the picture of robust health."[4] Queen Victoria tried sketching "dear, beautiful, amusing little Alix" but was forced to report that she "sat very badly."[5]

When Alix was still a very young girl, her great-aunt Empress Marie Alexandrovna of Russia, who had been born a princess of Hesse, paid a visit to Darmstadt with her husband, Alexander II. With her she brought a maid of honor, Baroness Anne Pilar von Pilhau. When the imperial visitors arrived at the New Palace, all of the children, smartly dressed in new frocks and sailor suits, waited in a line to greet them. When the empress reached Alix, she pointed at the girl and turned to Baroness von Pilhau, saying, "Kiss her hand. That is your Empress-to-be."[6]

However improbable the story may have been, it is but one of many concerning Alix which would later circulate at the Russian court at the time of her engagement to Tsarevich Nicholas. Another told of how, when Alix and her sisters, as young girls, were walking in Richmond Park outside of London, they happened upon an old gypsy woman. The girls had their palms read, giggling over the predictions for Victoria and Irene. But when the old woman came to Alix and Ella, she grew troubled and announced that both sisters would marry in a distant country and that both would be unhappy.[7]

Whatever its truth, the story captures the early sense of tragedy which soon began to surround Alix. The first blow was the death of her brother Frittie, who suffered from the dreaded disease hemophilia. The defective genes which caused the illness to manifest itself in Queen Victoria's descendants had sprung up suddenly, although Alice must have known that it was a possibility; her own brother Prince Leopold also suffered from hemophilia. When he was two, Frittie cut his ear; the blood flowed until the poor child's hair was matted with it. A year later, on a late May morning, the little prince burst into his mother's bedroom at the New Palace. Alice sat at the piano playing Chopin's "Funeral March."[8] She watched as Frittie raced across the floor to a bow window overlooking the gardens. When he reached the frames, he put out his hands to stop himself, but on this morning the windows were unlatched, and the frames gave way. Frittie tumbled out the window to the stone terrace some twenty feet below. Alice screamed and ran down the stairs to the crumpled body of her son. He was still alive. At first it was thought that he would recover, for the doctors could find no serious damage. But bleeding on the brain had begun, and by nightfall Frittie was dead.[9]

For the rest of her childhood the shadow of Frittie's death hung over Alix. She herself had never really known him, but Princess Alice made certain that he was not forgotten. For Alix and her family there were annual visits to the crypt where Frittie's body lay. Alice spoke endlessly of being reunited in heaven with her child and of the judgment of God, sowing deep seeds of fatalism in her young daughter's mind. To the queen, Alice wrote: "In the midst of life we are in death. . . . Our whole life should be in preparation and expectation for eternity."[10] And Ernie, by the age of four, was already exclaiming, "We must all die together," and dreaming of his dead brother in heaven calling to him, which Princess Alice thought most touching.[11]

Although cloaking herself in grief, Princess Alice was looking ahead with higher expectations to her children's educations. To the queen she outlined her unusual philosophy: "What you say about the education of our girls I entirely agree with and I strive to bring them up totally free from pride of their position which is nothing save what their personal worth can make it. . . . I feel so entirely as you do on the difference of rank and how important it is for Princes and Princessess to know that they are nothing better or above others and of being an example: good and modest. This I hope my children will grow up to be."[12]

Alice and Ludwig, in an era of servants and nannies, were far more attentive parents than most royal couples. So many royals were the most neglectful parents owing to their obligations outside the house, and most of the children were brought up very differently from the manner in which Alix was raised. Frances Donaldson writes:

> All upper class children were reared in isolation from their parents, whom in many families they saw once, at the most twice, a day, when they had been specially dressed and prepared to meet them. It was quite common for their parents to be uneducated in child care and subject to the conventions of the time. The only obvious difference between the routine arrangement for royal children and those for hundreds of others throughout the land was that when they were dressed and taken to the drawing room to meet their mother, she was usually attended by a lady-in-waiting.[13]

The legendary, historic nanny of upper-class England was brought across the Channel to reign in the nurseries of the New Palace in the person of Mrs. Mary Anne Orchard. Her role was all-important. Mrs. Orchard woke Alix each morning; got her bathed and dressed; sent her off to her mother's room to say good morning; taught her Bible lessons and told her bedtime stories; listened to her joys, and gave comfort in her sorrows—in short, what Princess Alice should have and would have done had she not been a royal princess with limitations on her time.

Mrs. Orchard, or Orchie, as the children called her, had several nursery maids under her. The children must have been terrors, for they went through a rapid succession of nannies before finding Orchie. With explicit instructions from Princess Alice, Orchie ruled the nursery with an iron fist. The children had to get up early, for lessons began promptly at seven. Breakfast at nine was hearty: porridge, sausages, and cold meats. Such food was not uncommon. Orchie favored simple, uncomplicated fare: Lunches and dinners, more likely than not, included beef, rice, boiled potatoes, and baked apples.[14]

The early lessons were quite easy—reading or drawing with Orchie or Princess Alice—followed by play with Ernie or little Marie, whom the family called May. Alix loved animals from an early age, riding through the park at the New Palace in a pony cart, accompanied by a liveried footman who led the horse. As she grew, Shetland ponies gave way to swift and sturdy horses, which Alix rode gracefully. There was also a pet fox who smelled none too pleasant, a wild boar, rabbits, guinea pigs, and pet sheep.[15]

In 1877, Alix's father became Grand Duke Ludwig IV of Hesse. She saw her mother much less now, for the additional duties as First Lady of the land took up more and more of her time. Under Alice's guidance Darmstadt came to be a center of enlightenment and romantic thought. She argued religion with her controversial friend David Strauss, much to the anger of the conservative Lutherans; John Ruskin often stayed at the New Palace, as did Thomas Carlyle and Alfred Tennyson, and Alice even played duets on the piano with Johannes Brahms.[16] These extra activities took their toll on Alice. The depression and the periods of illness increased as the duties came down upon her. Gerard Noel writes: "Perhaps it would have been impossible for her not to inherit the kind of melancholy whose chief antidote was a tendency to dominate others when there was no one capable of satisying her own latent desire to be dominated. To this must be added the fatalism allied to intelligence from the Prince Consort."[17]

There is much here in the life of the mother which would later be repeated in her daughter. The psychological pressures, the strains of her position, the melancholy temperament, would all be passed on to a greater degree to Alix. In 1878, Princess Alice wrote to the queen: "I don't think you know quite how far from well I am, and how absurdly wanting in strength. . . . I am good for next to nothing. . . . I have never in my life been like this before. I live on my sofa and see no one and yet go on losing. . . ."[18]

Alice was less and less a part of Alix's life. She was increasingly gone from the palace. When she was home, she spent her days in bed, suffering from exhaustion. She had never really recovered from the death of her son before her eyes four years earlier, and the children felt it keenly. Alix saw far more of Orchie than she did of her mother, and when Princess Alice was with her daughter, she spoke of heaven and death and meeting others in the next world—hardly comforting words from a mother to a six-year-old girl. The seeds of tragedy were already being planted; it would take a lifetime for them to come to fruition.

Alix spent the summer of 1878 traveling with her parents, sisters, and brother Ernie. Their visits took them to palaces and castles across Europe, inhabited not by distant crowned princes but by aunts, uncles, and cousins. In England, the Hessians stayed with Queen Victoria before moving on to Compton Place, the seaside home of the duke and duchess of Devonshire, near Eastborne. Here Alix learned to play tennis amid the cool breezes which swept in from the Channel. Before returning to Darmstadt they stayed with the duke and duchess of Baden on the Baltic and romped with their German cousins on the beach. No sand castles for these royal children—the Hessians and their Hohenzollern cousins fought over the colored pebbles on the beach: the Hessians for white and red, to make their father's flag, and the Hohenzollerns for yellow and red, representing the Prussian standard.[19]

While in England, a tragedy occurred which Princess Alice took as an ill omen. On 8 September 1878 the paddle steamer *Princess Alice* struck another ship while cruising on the Thames and sank with a loss of over six hundred lives. The ship had been named for her, and Alice was convinced that it foretold a tragedy in her own life.

Back home in Darmstadt the children fell into their autumn routine. On 5 November, Victoria, the eldest daughter, was reading *Alice in Wonderland* to her sisters and brother. She did not feel at all well. When she complained of a sore throat and a fever, Princess Alice called in the family doctor. On examining Victoria, he discovered that she was suffering from diphtheria. Immediately the New Palace was put under quarantine. By the eleventh, Victoria was out of danger, but the very next day, Alix fell ill. Her mother wrote to the queen: "This is so dreadful, my sweet, precious Alicky so ill. At three this morning Orchie called me, saying she thought the child was feverish; complaining of her throat. I went over to her, looked into her throat, and there was not only spots, but a thick covering on each side of her throat of that horrid white membrane."[20]

Alix was quickly followed to the sickbed by May, Irene, Ernie, and the grand duke himself; only Ella did not catch it, and she was sent away. The illness was severe—several times the children came close to death. All Alice could do was go from room to room, nursing, holding hands, and dampening foreheads with a cold cloth.

May died on the night of the sixteenth. Heartbroken as she was, Princess Alice decided to keep the news from her children until they were well. But Ernie kept asking after his sister and, much to his mother's anguish, sent all sorts of books and presents to her.[21] When she could stand it no longer, Alice told him that May had died; then, in an effort to comfort him, she bent over Ernie and received from him what Disraeli, the British prime minister, later described as the "kiss of death."[22] Ernie was soon out of danger, but Alice, worn out by nursing her family, began to fall ill. After the first week of December, there was no doubt: Princess Alice had diphtheria. Queen Victoria was stunned, writing, "Oh! It surely cannot be true! She will never have the strength to get through it."[23]

For days, the doctors hovered over her bed, trying to work a miracle on the princess; the queen sent over her own personal physician to assist. But their efforts were in vain. Day by day Alice grew worse. Her temperature rose and fell, making her delirious for short periods of time. She began to have visions of her father, Frittie, and May standing together in heaven to welcome her. On 13 December there was a turn for the worse. The following morning, before she lapsed into a coma, Alice whispered, "May . . . dear Papa."[24] And, indeed, it was the seventeenth anniversary of the prince consort's death. At seven-fifty that morning, Alice died. She was thirty-five.

The family was devastated. "I wish I had died instead of her," exclaimed her brother Bertie upon learning of the news.[25] Queen Victoria was shaken, writing, "That this dear, talented, distinguished, tenderhearted, noble-minded, sweet child, who behaved so admirably during her father's illness, and afterwards, in supporting me and helping me in every possible way, should be called back to her father on this very anniversary of his death, seems almost incredible and most mysterious."[26] The people of Darmstadt were silent and respectful as the coffin was taken from the palace to the chapel in the Old Schloss , accompanied by a procession of mourners bearing flaming torches. The following day, they filed past the casket, which was draped with a Union Jack. Flowers scented the air: From the Court Theatre, with which Alice had been involved as patron, came a large wreath"; a peasant woman sent a garland of rosemary and two little orphan girls whom she had once befriended sent a crumpled bunch of violets."[27] Later, Alice was buried in an elaborate tomb designed by Joseph Edgar Boehm; it showed a reclining Princess Alice holding the dead May in her arms.[28]

The children did not attend the funeral. They watched, faces pressed against the cold, frosted windows of the palace as their mother was carried away into the December twilight. To them, Queen Victoria sent a glum and sorrowful letter:

> Poor Dear Children, for I write this for you all—you have had the most terrible blow which can befall children—you have lost your precious, dear, devoted Mother who loved you—and devoted her life to you and your dear Papa. That horrid disease which carried off sweet little May and from which you and the others recovered has taken her away from you and poor old Grandmamma, who with your other kind Grandmamma will try and be a mother to you. Oh! Dear Children, dearest beloved Mama is gone to join dear Grandpapa and your other dear Grandpapa and Frittie and sweet little May where there is no more sorrow or separation. I long to hear every detail. Poor dear Ernie, he will feel it so dreadfully. May he and dear Papa not suffer from this dreadful blow. Try and do everything to comfort and help poor dear Papa. God's will be done. May He support and help you all. From your devoted and most unhappy Grandmamma, VRI.[29]

3

Childhood

THE CHRISTMAS TREE stood in regal splendor in the center of the white and gold ballroom of the New Palace. From its branches hung gilded apples, nuts, and wooden ornaments carefully carved by the finest craftsmen.[1] The aroma of the wax candles on the tree mingled with that of the evergreen boughs which hung about the room. Small tables, draped in white cloth, held the presents of the Hessian royal family. Only this year there were two fewer tables set out on the parquet floor.

The family was ripped apart with grief. Alix, at the age of six, was left motherless. Her sister May was also gone. Alone, ignored, not fully understanding what had happened, Alix watched Orchie break down time after time, running off to the bathroom, unable to hide her own grief. Each day brought new snowstorms which whipped against the windows of the palace, new winds which howled through the desolate corridors. In the cold, empty nursery, there was only loneliness for Alix; even her toys had been burned as a precaution against the disease.[2]

Eventually, the tears stopped, and Alix rebounded from the tragedy with the energy of youth. For while her mother and her sister were gone, all else remained the same. In the New Palace there were the same servants, nannies, and cooks as had been there before. Her family, too, compensated for their loss by becoming that much closer, forming a tightly knit, loving circle to provide emotional support.

The suggestion that her mother's death changed Alix's life forever needs to be looked at if only because it has been so often repeated that it is now firmly part of that gray area from which legends emerge. Those who look for an insight into Alix's character invariably return to 14 December 1878. In truth, however, her mother's death did not destroy Alix. It only added to the preoccupation with death which surrounded her from the first years of her life. Her mother's death, it is said, made her cold, insensitive, and withdrawn. This simply is not true. Even as a little girl she was obstinate, wayward, and willful. Anything said to her—even in jest—could touch a nerve, but she never showed it.[3] Overly sensitive, she had inherited her mother's moody, melancholy temperament, which later made her seem cold, introspective, and haughty. The visit she made each year to Frittie's tomb, the constant mourning, the talk of death and heaven—all of these things influenced Alix's mind-set long before her mother's death. Hers was a family preoccupied with gloom and the hereafter: The queen mourned Albert to the grave and loved to dwell on the morbid details of her daughter's passing; Alice never let her children forget their dead brother and questioned why God had punished her. To this indulged grief, the family now added another monument: When Queen Victoria visited Darmstadt in April 1880, she was quite pleased to see that her daughter's bedroom had been left exactly as it was on the morning that she died, the bed draped in black crepe.[4] Queen Victoria was very concerned that her family should continue to mourn those who had died. When Alix's uncle Leopold, the duke of Albany, died in 1884, the queen felt that the Hessians had not expressed quite enough grief over his passing. She wrote: "I thought Ernie and Alicky would write to me. Dear Uncle loved them, as he did you all, so much and Alicky was such a pet. I *hope* they feel what a loss he is to them too?"[5]

It was a solitary existence for a child of six, and it is hardly surprising that Alix later developed into a woman who seemed cold and withdrawn. Her childhood left her unable to reconcile the pleasant side of her character with the darkness which she had inherited and in which she had been raised by her mother. She studied the same lessons with the same tutors, took the same holidays, and was influenced by the same morbid and fatalistic forces which had always been present. She was later haunted not by her mother's death in December 1878 but by all that had gone before that cold, bleak midwinter day.

More important than the six years spent with her mother were the twenty-two years Alix had with her grandmother Queen Victoria. When the queen wrote that her grandchildren should look upon her as a mother, it was not idle talk. Alix spent a considerable part of her childhood at the queen's homes in England and was guided into womanhood by her grandmother, who lectured her on being a dutiful princess.

The queen was sixty when her daughter died. Albert had been dead nearly twenty years, yet the mourning continued. At Osborne, Windsor, and Balmoral, everything remained exactly as it had been when he died; nothing had been changed. The prince's clothes still hung in his closets, his bed was turned down each night, and the chamber pot in his room was scrubbed every morning. The prince's writing pens lay on his desk where he had left them, and his walking sticks stood in readiness—everything continued as if he lived. When the queen retired at night, she clutched her dead husband's nightshirt between her hands; above her hung a wreath and a portrait of her husband on his deathbed. For the rest of her life she wore mourning. To Alix, Grandmamma was an imposing lady of somewhat large girth, encased in black silk which rustled with every movement. Atop her graying hair, which she wore pulled back into a tiny bun, was a widow's cap of white tulle with a long veil. A ring on her finger carried the image of the prince consort, a picture also contained in the locket she wore around her neck. She smelled vaguely of orange blossoms, from her favorite perfume.[6]

Morbid, regal, and domineering to most of her family, the queen was, above all else, a friend and counselor to Alix. When they were together, the queen gave her granddaughter all manner of advice, from how to do the *cercle*—walking around a room, talking to pieces of furniture as if they were people to improve her social graces—to the proper way to sit when wearing a court dress. Above all, etiquette was emphasized, along with the idea of *noblesse oblige*, that with royal rank came social responsibilities.

The royal residences of England became Alix's second homes. It was usual for her to spend a few weeks of the summer at Osborne House, perched on a bluff above Cowes and overlooking the Solent off the Isle of Wight. In the summer Osborne came alive: Bed after bed of exotic roses burst into bloom; gardeners trimmed the acres of lawns which sloped down to the sea and the shrubs which bordered them; and above the tops of the magnolia, cedar, fir, and pine trees the royal standard would rise on the Italianate flag tower to signal that the queen had arrived. Carriage after carriage, bringing members of the royal family, suite, and household, rolled through the high iron gates and under the porte cochere.

Everything at Osborne celebrated Victoria and Albert: above every doorway in the house, carved into overmantels and keyholes and crowning valances, were the entwined initials *V* and *A*. Albert himself had helped design the house, with its corridors in bright Renaissance colors, elaborate plaster moldings, and ceilings held up by gilded marble columns. The house teemed with reminders not only of the prince consort but of Alix's mother as well: portraits, busts, photographs, even Princess Alice's tiny hands and feet at the age of one, which had been modeled from life. Osborne, in fact, overflowed with statuary. Once, members of the queen's suite accidentally knocked a bust from its stand, prompting the mistress of the house, fearful of her young grandchildren, to issue an order that "they must not touch the statues and certainly must not play with them."[7]

Afternoon teas at Osborne took place in the Swiss Cottage, a prefabricated kit bought by Prince Albert, and Alix sat in the chair which her mother had used. At playtime, Alix climbed the fortifications and redoubts of the Albert Barracks, the children's fort where her mother had played. Other English toys at playtime strongly reflected the queen's prejudices. At Buckingham Palace there was a full-sized toy lion with a crank attached to its tail. When the tail was turned, the lion opened his mouth and swallowed a model of a Russian soldier.[8]

Visited far more frequently was Windsor Castle, nestled in the rolling Berkshire hills west of London. The children loved to explore its corners and towers and the battlements and balconies overlooking the Thames and Eton beyond. The rooms were a succession of brilliant achievements: large chambers hung with watered silks in green, crimson, and white, carved and gilded woodwork; and painted ceilings high above the parquet floors. One room, the Grand Corridor, often became a playground for the Hessian children on the long, rainy afternoons. "There were lovely corners and curtains behind which one could hide and leap," Alix's sister Victoria recalled. "Our wild romps . . . were often interrupted by one of the pages bringing a message from the Queen that she would not have so much noise."[9]

In the summer, when the heat was at its most unbearable, the queen and her family dined out-of-doors at Frogmore House, a short distance below the castle and next to the royal mausoleum, where Prince Albert lay entombed. Otherwise, Alix and her family would assemble in the State Dining Room to attend the arrival of the queen. A band waiting under an awning on the terrace for her entrance on the arm of an Indian attendant would strike up the national anthem as the queen slowly made the rounds of the room and took up her place at the long table. Because the dining room was a considerable distance from the kitchens, the food often arrived cold. Even had it been warm, dinner would not have been very appetizing, according to Alix's sister Victoria. She later recalled "awful bread and butter puddings without a raisin" and "stodgy tapioca puddings full of lumps."[10]

But to Alix the favorite of all the queen's homes was Balmoral. Nestled snugly amid the Cairngorms in the Scottish Highlands, Balmoral was a fairy-tale castle, built as recently as 1855 and partially designed, of course, by Prince Albert in a style he remembered from his childhood days in Germany. Being so far north, the castle was at its best only in the summer, when the surrounding hills were awash in color, the heather came into bloom, and the breezes blowing through the Dee Valley were still warm. Even in the late summer a dense early-morning frost covered the huge lawns.

Behind the Gothic façade, with its eighty-foot-high tower and arched windows, were rooms designed strictly for comfort, unadorned and carpeted in simple tartan patterns. Lord Archibald Roseberry once said that he thought the drawing room at Osborne must have been the ugliest one in the world until he saw the one at Balmoral.[11] Bedrooms were at a premium, and Alix often had to share not only with her sisters but her cousins as well. One of these cousins, Princess Marie Louise of Schleswig-Holstein, was the same age as Alix, and the two quickly became good friends, hiking over the mountains and fishing in the River Dee.

There were other cousins as well; on the British side alone Alix could count twenty-eight. It is hardly surprising that Grand Duke Ludwig termed this extended family "the Royal Mob."[12] Chief among them were the children of the Prince and Princess of Wales—Eddy, George, Louise, Victoria, and Maud. Eddy, who was heir presumptive to the British throne, was the leader of the group, and Alix and her cousins followed him over the hills and through the forests on long walking expeditions. A small shop near Balmoral sold sweets and was, more often than not, their destination; later, the two women who ran it taught Alix how to make scones.[13]

One outcome of these lengthy and frequent visits was Alix's excellent education. The queen carefully supervised her granddaughter's schooling, and the tutors were required to write reports every month to Victoria on Alix's progress. The queen, in turn, gave unsolicited advice on every subject: what books should be read, what courses studied, what subjects pursued, which pieces of music learned. In this respect, Alix was being guaranteed a substantive education; it was certainly a change from the usual Victorian routine. Most girls' educations were concerned only with singing, dancing, and learning the rules of proper etiquette.

Alix's tutor, an eccentric Englishwoman named Margaret Hardcastle Jackson, was responsible for a good deal of her independent thinking. Unlike her mother, Alix cared little for social work but recognized that helping the unfortunate was something that came with the rank of princess. This is not to say that the problems of the poor did not occupy her thoughts, but it was a curious, almost preoccupied concern, resulting more from a sense of duty than a genuine interest. Alix's first consideration—and the one area in which she was radically different from most of her family—was the role of women in society. And it was in this area that Miss Jackson was to have her most lasting influence.

Because she was stubborn and willful, Alix could never tread the path of Victorian submission which women of society were expected to walk. Even from her earliest years, Alix knew her mind, and once she had made it up, she stuck to her beliefs without a hesitation of self-doubt. Therefore, when Miss Jackson began to couple the ideas of women and politics together in the schoolroom, Alix quickly absorbed the controversial theories without a question. To Alix, the point was only obvious: Her grandmother was the most powerful monarch in Europe.

She was a good student. Her memory was excellent, and she was quite willing to study hard. By the time she was fifteen Alix had completed most of her lessons in history, literature, geography, arithmetic, and languages. She spoke German and English equally well. German was the language of her country; English, her natural language. But she found French difficult and always hesitated when using it.[14] Alix loved music, especially that of Wagner, and was taught to play the piano by the director of the opera at Darmstadt. At the piano she was brilliant but very self-conscious. On one occasion Queen Victoria made her play before a roomful of suite and guests at Windsor Castle. She complied but did so in torment.[15] She was a fairly good artist, with a skill for watercolors, and, like all other proper girls of the Victorian era, very handy with a needle.

Between school and holidays in England, Alix spent many of her childhood days at her father's new hunting lodge. The grand duke already had a castle, the brooding and somber Kranichstein. But following his wife's death, the grand duke purchased a new retreat called Wolfsgarten. Sitting on top of a small hill in the forest between Darmstadt and Frankfurt, the lodge commanded a view of the rolling hills and the Rhine beyond. The gardens were filled with lovely pergolas covered with ivy and roses, and in the center of the courtyard was a carved fountain. The house itself was nothing palatial, a two-story affair in rose-colored brick with low wings at each side, but the interior was apparently something of a shock. Lord Henry Ponsonby recalled rooms with deep blue walls, trimmed in green, with red furniture, all hideously modeled on the current trend, art nouveau. He termed the lodge "a Swiss cottage . . . in *Faust*."[16]

At Wolfsgarten, Alix was frequently visited by her British cousins. The children of the Prince and Princess of Wales came often, as did her playmate Marie Louise. Even as a child, Marie Louise recognized her cousin's darker side. "Alix," she said, "you always play at being sorrowful; one day, the Almighty will send some real crushing sorrows and then what are you going to do?"[17]

Less welcome was the son of the crown prince and princess of Prussia, Alix's cousin Wilhelm. Cousin Willy had been born with a deformed arm, and he compensated for this by generally behaving rudely and selfishly. He would order his cousins to play tennis and then throw down his racket in the middle of the game, demanding to row or ride and expecting everyone involved to follow his wishes. When he tired, he ordered his cousins to sit around him while he read aloud from the Bible.[18]

Wilhelm was in his late teens when most of these visits occurred. Cousin Willy was passionately in love with Ella, Alix's sister. He was nineteen and a student at Bonn University when this desire overwhelmed him; he later admitted that he spent most of his time writing love poetry to his cousin instead of studying.[19] Ella was only fourteen; she thought Wilhelm absolutely horrid. Nevertheless, she was far too kind to be outwardly rude to him, and he followed her everywhere. When she sat, Willy sat. And when she spoke, he stared at her in awe. After she was married to Grand Duke Serge of Russia, Wilhelm refused to speak to Ella in private, only forcing himself to converse with her in polite terms during unavoidable public functions. Even so, he always remained in love with her.

In the spring of 1884, Alix's sister Victoria married her cousin Prince Louis of Battenberg. There was an awful scandal at the time involving the grand duke of Hesse and a woman variously described as kind and beautiful by some and by Queen Victoria as "depraved" and "scheming."[20] The lady in question, Alexandrine de Kolemine, was the thirty-year-old former wife of a Russian diplomat who had been posted to the Hessian court. Ludwig had taken Madame de Kolemine as a mistress a few years after his wife's death. "We quite liked the lady, who was full of attentions toward us," recalled Alix's sister Victoria, and there was no resentment over her place in the grand duke's household.[21] But no matter how acceptable she might have been as a mistress, Madame de Kolemine could never be the grand duke's wife; she was not only divorced but Russian Orthodox as well. But marriage was precisely what the grand duke had in mind, and worse yet, he intended it to take place under the worst of circumstances: at the same time as his daughter's wedding.

Everyone was convinced that there was going to be a terrible row over the situation, for Queen Victoria was attending her granddaughter's wedding in Darmstadt and the situation in the New Palace was volatile. The queen had not been told of her son-in-law's impending wedding. Sir Henry Ponsonby, her private secretary, wrote: "The Grand Duke has behaved very badly in not telling the Queen before she came to Darmstadt because it places her in a most awkward position. If she goes away it will create a scandal, if she remains it will look as if she has approved the marriage."[22]

No one knew exactly when the grand duke intended to marry; there were vague rumors, but it seems that Ludwig told no one until the day of the actual ceremony. But with the threat hanging over the household, it was decided that the queen had to be told. The problem was that no one wanted the job, and it fell to Victoria to inform her grandmother of her father's intentions. The queen was furious. She declared that if Ludwig married "such a person," it "would lower him so much that I could not have him so near as much as before." The queen continued to record her protests in a letter to Victoria:

> He cannot say that this intended union is for the sake of his Children or for his country—it would be the very reverse of *both*, it can only be for what *he thinks* (and I am afraid he is much mistaken) will be for his *own* personal happiness. It will do him immense harm in his own country—in England he will lose the position he held and enjoyed and I could *not* defend such a choice. If dear Papa should feel lonely when you three elder are married—I should say nothing (tho it must pain me) if he chose to make a morganatic marriage with some nice, quiet, sensible and amiable person—who would at any rate command the respect of us all as well as of his country. But to choose a lady of another religion who has just been divorced—who no doubt has tried to obtain Papa's sympathy as well as admiration, would, I fear, be a *terrible mistake* and one which he would soon repent of, when *too late*.[23]

But all of this talk was to no avail: The grand duke was still determined to marry Madame de Kolemine. The only question was when. Victoria was so worried that on the morning of her own wedding, 30 April, she lay in bed in a fit of nerves.[24]

Victoria's wedding went off without a hitch, except that the bride was seen to be limping from a twisted ankle, the result of an attempted jump over a large coal scuttle some days before.[25] But the grand duke's marriage was foremost in everyone's minds, although, according to Ponsonby, they all "went about pretending they knew nothing about it. The great marriage ceremony of Prince Louis and Princess Victoria was duly performed, and then came the thunderclap. The grand duke married Mme. Alexandrine de Kolemine *the same evening!*"[26]

In fact, the wedding was a virtual secret. Before it took place, the grand duke gathered his children together and told them that they were to have a new mother, then disappeared into a drawing room to celebrate the match, which was performed by the Hessian prime minister in the presence of only two witnesses. The grand duke and his new wife were forced apart immediately after the service when the rest of the family discovered it had taken place.

Chaos erupted in the New Palace. All of the members of the Prussian royal family in attendance were at once ordered home by the emperor himself. The grand duke was horrified at the reaction his wedding evoked. Alix herself had little idea of what was happening, but her tutor, Miss Jackson, was in a panic, declaring that Madame de Kolemine must be sent back to Russia at once.[27]

There was never any question as to what the grand duke would have to do: The whispered asides and secret talk about an annulment made the choice quite clear. On this point the queen was firm and asked her son the Prince of Wales to inform his brother-in law of the decision. The wishes of the family came before those of the grand duke, he said. "We are," commented Bertie, "a very strong family when we agree."[28] The grand duke dutifully said good-bye to his new wife and commenced proceedings for an annulment, and Queen Victoria, in a fit of rage over the whole incident, said good-bye to the grand duke and returned to England.

More excitement was to follow. No sooner had Victoria married than Ella became engaged to Grand Duke Serge of Russia. Such an event called for pomp as only the Romanovs could dispense it, and therefore the wedding was to take place in their capital, St. Petersburg. Of course, Alix and her family would attend. On a warm June evening in the summer of 1884, Alix boarded a train and set off into the night for the land of the tsars. She did not know it then, but it was on this trip to Russia that Alix would meet her future husband.

4

Imperial Russia

ALIX WAS ONLY TWELVE when she made her first visit to Russia. She had studied its history in the course of her education, yet it remained veiled, to most of Europe a land still shrouded in mystery. But her family ties with the Romanovs were strong. A distant and ancient relative, Countess Wilhelmina of Hesse, had married Tsar Paul; the sister of Alix's great-grandmother had wed Tsar Alexander I; her great aunt Marie had been the wife of Tsar Alexander II; and now Ella was on her way to Russia to add her name to the growing list of Hessian princesses who found husbands in this strange and forbidding land.

Ella was, at twenty, stunningly beautiful, with golden hair and dark eyes. Her agreeable personality accorded with her looks. Serge contrasted sharply with his fiancée. The third son of Tsar Alexander II, the grand duke was tall and slim, with dark eyes and a pointed beard. Serge had the reputation of a political reactionary, and his curious private life earned him both the fear of Russia's liberals and the mistrust of most of the Romanov family. He took strange pride in knowing that he was regarded as a tyrant. This was a side of Serge which Alix never saw; she adored the grand duke, and the pair could often be found together, collapsed in laughter. She made an easy target for his jokes, and Serge could greatly embarrass her by reminding Alix in front of others that he had watched her bathing naked as a baby.[1]

The train journey took three days. Alix had never been so far from Darmstadt or so far north. The air grew cooler the farther east the train went, following the rugged shore of the German and Polish provinces on the Baltic. The land quickly became a long succession of lakes, swamps, and dark forests of pine and birch.

No one knew better than the Romanovs how to put on a spectacle. When the train bearing the Hessians pulled into the main station at St. Petersburg, flags waved, brass bands played, and thousands of people cheered. Ella entered the capital riding in a gilded state coach drawn by eight white horses and led by footmen in powdered wigs, scarlet livery, and silk stockings.

The Hessians were lodged at Peterhof, the imperial summer palace on the shore of the Gulf of Finland. This proved to be an eye-opening experience. Alix had grown up surrounded by splendor; her visits to Queen Victoria had shown her the particular luxury in which sovereigns lived. But in Russia magnificence had been replaced with gaudy ostentation. The palace at Peterhof was a perfect example of this: built by Peter the Great and enlarged by Empress Elizabeth, the palace stretched for six hundred feet along the crest of a hill, punctuated with gilded columns, baroque decorations, and golden domes. At one end was a church capped with five cupolas; at the other, the Coat of Arms Wing, so called for its six hundred pounds of gilt decorations.[2] It was a dazzling introduction to the world of imperial Russia.

Many of Alix's relatives had traveled to Russia for the wedding. She met many of them for the first time, a head-turning parade of princes and princesses, grand dukes and archdukes, royal and serene highnesses. Her godparents, Tsar Alexander III and his wife, Marie Feodorovna, presided over this royal gathering, holding court in their splendid palace by the sea.

The tsar was a giant of a man, six feet six inches tall, with a gruff manner that masked a warm heart and dislike for all pomp and ceremony. He was unbelievably strong, bending iron pokers in half and ripping packs of playing cards to amuse his children. Once, at a state dinner in the middle of some trouble between Russia and Austria in the Balkans, the Austrian ambassador hinted that his country might be forced to mobilize two or three army corps. At this, the tsar calmly picked up a silver fork, twisted it around into a knot, and threw it across the table at the startled ambassador, saying, "That is what I am going to do to your two or three army corps."[3]

Marie Feodorovna, the tsar's wife, was the complete opposite of her husband. Petite, with dark hair and sparkling eyes which were always moving to take everything in, Marie loved balls, pomp, and gossip. Her position as tsarina gave her endless opportunities to indulge these pleasures. At the age of forty-four, she wrote, "I danced and danced. I let myself be carried away."[4] She had not originally been engaged to Alexander, expecting, instead, to marry his elder brother Tsarevich Nicholas. When Nicholas died before the wedding took place, Alexander assumed his brother's place not only as heir to the throne but as future husband to Marie as well. Surprisingly, theirs was a love match from the beginning, and Alexander III was probably the first Russian tsar to be both a good husband and father.

Their son, Tsarevich Nicholas, sixteen years old and disarmingly charming and handsome, was Alix's second cousin. They were both descended from a common great-grandfather, Ludwig II of Hesse, Alix through her father and Nicholas through his grandmother Marie, who was Ludwig's daughter and had married Alexander II. With his light brown hair, deep blue eyes, and unassuming manner, Nicholas was popular with his cousins. That one day he would become tsar of Russia after his father seemed not at all to occupy his thoughts. On 8 June 1884 he recorded their first, momentous meeting: "We met Uncle Gega's [Grand Duke Serge Alexandrovich] beautiful fiancée Ella, her sister and brother. The whole family dined at half-past seven. I sat next to little twelve-year-old Alix, and I like her awfully much."[5]

The days at Peterhof leading up to the wedding were leisurely, filled with long walks through the park and carriage rides along the shore of the Gulf of Finland. It was a romantic setting: formal gardens dotted with gilded statuary and laced with graveled walks which led to the sea and fountains which glistened in the distance. They were so far north that even at midnight the sky was awash with blues and pinks and the brilliant light of the aurora borealis.

Ella married Serge in the white-and-gold chapel of the Winter Palace in St. Petersburg. She wore a Russian court dress of silver tissue, with a long train and jewels which had belonged to Catherine the Great. During the service, Alix, wearing a dress of white muslin with roses in her hair, stood to the side of the altar. Nicholas stared at her throughout the service, overwhelmed by her beauty.[6]

It is said that during this visit the tsarevich fell hopelessly in love with Alix. Certainly her own feelings were somewhat more ambiguous, for she was but a twelve-year-old schoolgirl enjoying a first crush. Her diary contains no hint of the blossoming romance, although she filled its pages with girlish drawings of herself as a bride. Nevertheless, as Nicholas noted, at every occasion Alix "was sure to sit at my side. We played and ran in the garden. Alix and I exchanged flowers."[7] In another entry, the tsarevich wrote: "Alix and I were writing our names on the back window of the Italian House (we love each other)."[8] It is doubtful that Alix was as certain of her feelings as Nicholas's diary entry seems to indicate. What is certain is that the tsarevich, on one of their strolls about the grounds, presented Alix with a small brooch. She accepted it, but later, perhaps feeling it somehow improper to have taken such an expensive gift, Alix pressed it back into Nicholas's hand during a party.[9]

Whatever her feelings may have been in 1884, by the time of her next visit to Russia, in 1889, Alix was no longer a schoolgirl with unknown thoughts but rather a radiantly beautiful seventeen-year-old princess with a mind of her own. Nicholas had changed as well: He was now twenty-one, an officer in the guards, and cut a sleek figure in his uniform. It was the first time that the pair had met as adults.

If there was a time and a place more romantic than late sunsets and twilight drives at Peterhof, it was the dead of winter in St. Petersburg—the time of the "season", when society went to balls and parties and held midnight sleigh races by the light of flaming torches. St. Petersburg was magical, at its best, in the winter.

It was a city built on water, sliced in half by the mighty Neva River, which in winter froze and became a playground for skaters St. Petersburg spread out over nineteen islands, linked by bridges and ribboned with canals. Narrow streets twisted along the canals, lined with baroque palaces in delicate shades of aqua, green, yellow, pink, and crimson, their elegant gardens covered over beneath the snow. The atmosphere in the capital of imperial Russia changed according to the season: In summer, when the great families deserted their mansions for summer villas, the city was empty, quiet, at rest. But in winter the city came alive, bristling with carriages, the broad expanse of the Nevsky Prospect—the city's main thoroughfare—crowded with couples wandering arm in arm from store window to store window, walking to the great opera houses or concert halls to nestle in the warmth of a plush velvet seat as waves of music floated over them and on into the night. With the first frosts, the statuary in the Summer Garden disappeared for the winter into wooden plankings set up around the marble, fountains were turned off, and the imperial parade ground—the *Champs de Mars*—became a vast, empty field, surrounded by a dismal mist rising from the canals. The city disappeared beneath the snow, colors fading and then mingling together in a gray slush. Above was a sky capped with a hundred gilded onion domes and crosses, rising over the city, which sparkled and shone beneath the white powder of a northern winter.

Alix, Ernie, and Grand Duke Ludwig came to St. Petersburg to stay with Ella and Serge. As soon as he could get away from his duties in the army, Tsarevich Nicholas visited the Belosseilsky-Belossievsky Palace, where his aunt and uncle lived. Both Ella and Serge favored a match between Alix and Nicholas and did everything within their power to influence the young lovers.

Ella led the younger Romanovs on sleigh rides, followed by an escort of brightly costumed Cossack Guards. They spent their days sledding on icy hills. These were not mere mounds of snow but wooden structures some fifty feet high covered with layers of snow and then watered so that ice would freeze them over, providing a fast run for sledding. This activity was so popular that it continued after the sun had set to the light of huge bonfires.[10] From their sleds they pelted each other with snowballs before rushing back to Ella's palace for tea.

At night, St. Petersburg society went to the Mariinsky Theatre to see the ballet. From the imperial box, draped with blue-and-gold curtains, rows of white and gilded loges stretched around the interior to the stage. These boxes were high prizes, being passed from father to son so that the theater was nearly always booked on a permanent basis. The seats bristled with young girls in elegant gowns and soldiers in uniform, with gold braid and epaulets denoting rank in the hierarchy of the Russian army. The air smelled faintly of leather, wood, cigarette smoke, and flowers that decorated the intimate reception rooms behind the boxes, where the theatergoers retired between acts to smoke, chat, and exchange the latest gossip.[11] On nights when there was no ballet or theater there were usually grand balls.

St. Petersburg took its parties quite seriously, one hostess vying with the next to give the most elegant and expensive fetes. The season began on New Year's Day and continued until Lent, a hedonistic two months. In the darkness of the capital, brightly painted *troikas* carried the partygoers from street to street, racing over bridges and along frozen canals, to arrive at one of the palaces lining the Neva River, depositing them at the entrance, where they walked across a crimson carpet set out on the snow and climbed a set of marble steps into the warmth of the mansion.

A ball meant long hours underneath the gilded ceilings of St. Petersburg's palaces. The night passed as a succession of extravagant scenes. The crowd sank into bows and curtsies as princes and grand dukes entered the room, the silk of the ladies' gowns rustling while the gold aiguillettes and shoulder cords on the uniforms sparkled in the light. The ladies wore court gowns of silk and velvet, with long trains trimmed with sable fur, diamond tiaras holding long veils of tulle atop their heads. The weight of this outfit was staggering. Yet the ladies were more fortunate than members of the Hussar Guard, who had to wear elkskin breeches. One man recalled: "It was essential that the breeches should not have the slightest crease. To attain this result they were dampened, smeared with soap, and put on— after taking off the pants if I may venture to say so. The operation called for the services of a couple of vigorous soldiers."[12]

During the evening, servants in livery carried silver trays from which guests selected glass after glass of champagne, vodka, and rare Crimean wines. They danced across the sweep of the ballroom floor to the music of Tchaikovsky, Rimsky-Korsakov, and Borodin in the soft light of hundreds of glittering candles in silver-and-crystal chandeliers. At midnight, overcome with hunger, they rushed to tables overflowing with thousands of fresh flowers, shipped through the snow from the tropical Crimea. Waiters handed around trays of stuffed eggs, caviar, lobster, delicate French pastries, sturgeon, smoked salmon, mushrooms in cream sauce, salted cucumbers, cold tongue, ice creams, and fresh fruits.

Sometime after four or five in the morning, before the sun rose on the snowy horizon and filtered its rays across the golden domes of the St. Petersburg churches, the partygoers departed. They wrapped themselves in heavy coats of mink and fox to guard against the cold, said good-bye to their hosts, and climbed into their carriages to the light of blazing torches. Through the empty streets they raced, "down the Neva embankment past the black and menacing façades of the hulking buildings, the broad Neva, a frozen desert of ice, the gas lamps in the *Champs de Mars*, golden halos in the murk, exhausted, excited, champagne still bubbling in their heads and their hearts beating fast."[13]

One of the most famous balls ever given in St. Petersburg was hosted that winter by the tsar and tsarina. On a cold, snowy morning, the bodies of Crown Prince Rudolf of Austria and his mistress Mary Vetsera were found in the Hapsburg hunting lodge known as Mayerling. Sometime during the night, after the two had made a suicide pact, the crown prince shot Mary Vetsera, then blew off the top of his own head. It was customary, on the death of a member of a royal family, for European courts to go into mourning. But several years before, when a Romanov prince had died, the Austrians had held a great fete as planned. Remembering this snub, the empress declared that her ball would take place as planned but asked her guests to come in black. Thus was born the celebrated *bal noir*.[14] On the night of the ball, the three-hundred-room Anichkov Palace blazed with light. In its silk, velvet, and damask-lined rooms, fires burned in the porcelain stoves to keep out the cold.

Alix stayed in Russia through the early weeks of spring as the snow began to melt and the ice on the Neva thawed. Grand Duchess Marie Pavlovna (the younger) later recorded this magnificent sight: "Dull, cracking noises rose from the depths of the ice; rifts appeared here and there, disclosing black water. Soon, the river was furrowed by gaps which kept widening. Immense pieces of ice broke away with a crash and whirled down stream, obstructing the current. They smashed against each other with a dry sound, turned, climbed one upon another. The river swelled, the turbulent water, muddy and yellowish, swept its burden at full speed towards the sea."[15]

The last Sunday before Lent was *La Folle Journée*, and Tsarevich Nicholas gave a special ball for Alix at the Alexander Palace at Tsarskoe Selo, some fifteen miles south of the capital. The rooms were filled with roses and orchids, scenting the air with their delicious odor. Knowing how shy Alix could be with strangers, Nicholas invited only a small number of personal friends, younger members of the Romanov family, and his fellow officers from the army. At this intimate party, Alix and Nicholas again danced the entire evening together, until, at the stroke of midnight, Lent called an end to the festivities.[16]

Lent meant daily religious services. Alix went with the imperial family to the magnificent penitential masses and matins at St. Isaac's Cathedral, the third largest domed church in the world. Spread over three acres, the cathedral rose to a golden dome, beneath which stood, surrounded by columns of granite, a two hundred-foot *iconostasis*, a jeweled altar screen of marble and malachite studded with diamonds and pearls. According to legend, some sixty thousand men died of lead poisoning gilding the cathedral dome. After the rush of carnival, Alix must have been happy to bask in the cool marble interiors of St. Petersburg's great cathedral. Finally, at the end of six weeks, Alix and her family returned to Darmstadt.

The following summer, Alix returned to Russia. She did not go to St. Petersburg, but rather to Moscow, to stay with Ella and Serge at their country estate of Ilinskoe, on the banks of the Moscow River. A long journey over straight, sandy roads took her past fields of wheat, still green with early summer, and into a deep pine forest. At the fringe of the forest, the carriage swung into a small village, crossed a wooden bridge, and then drove through the gates of the estate. At the end of a long avenue of lime trees, the roofs of Ilinskoe came into view, and then the house itself, a large, square oak structure skirted with balconies.[17]

Alix and Ella went rowing on the river or picnicking in the depths of the forest. Lounging in the shade of the pine trees, they dined on caviar, smoked salmon, cold game, and vegetables, followed by fresh berries, which they had found in the woods. In the afternoons they visited Arkhangelskoe, the nearby Youssoupov estate, to play lawn tennis with the glamorous circle which revolved around the elegant house. The countryside was beautiful, and by the end of the summer, the harvest was ripe, the air was sweet, and the long fields of hay were ready for mowing. One man recalled those halcyon days many years later: "It was a beautiful sight to see the mowing in the sunset by the river; the meadows were of an intense soft green; the sky all fleecy and golden to the west, and black with a great thunder cloud, over the woods to the east, lit up with intermittent summer lightning. The mowers were all in different coloured shirts—scarlet, blue, white and green. They mowed till the twilight fell and the thunder clouds got near to us. . . ."[18]

At the end of the summer, the peasants in the village at Ilinskoe held a fair, and Alix and Ella visited the small patch of tents and stalls hung with brightly colored fabrics. The contrast between the elegant, jeweled women of St. Petersburg and the coarse peasants of Ilinskoe quickly brought the two worlds of imperial Russia into focus: on the one hand, elegant society; on the other, those who had nothing but who outnumbered the aristocracy seventeen to one. They trudged through the dusty streets of the village, old toothless women in rags, men in blouses and trousers, children covered with dirt, laughing and playing in the roadway. Gypsies danced in the square to the music of the balalaika or the accordion, their voices growing louder with each drink. When Ella's carriage passed them, the peasants fell to the ground, bowing their heads to the dirt as a sign of respect.

Nicholas did not come to Ilinskoe that summer; royal engagements kept him away. During this visit, Alix came to know the countryside of Russia, the long fields and deep forests, the simple peasants who bowed to her yet smiled their toothless grins as she passed. She never forgot these golden days at Ilinskoe; four years later, this summer would return to Alix, convincing her that she truly belonged in Russia.

5

A Princess at Home and Abroad

O<small>N A SWELTERING</small> English summer day in June 1887, Queen Victoria celebrated fifty years on the throne of Great Britain. There had been no great public ceremony in Great Britain since the death of the prince consort. The magnificent spectacle of the Golden Jubilee gave a dull Victorian London a chance to dust off uniforms, ball gowns, and carriages that had long been stored away. Such an event called for the full participation of the royal family, including Alix, who came to England with her father, sister Irene, and brother Ernie especially for the occasion.

They stayed at Buckingham Palace during Jubilee Week. Also lodged behind its ugly Victorian façade were not only members of Alix's family from all over Europe but such exotic royalties as the maharajah of Cooch Behar and Her Majesty Queen Kapiolani of Hawaii.[1] The entire week leading up to the great jubilee service at Westminster Abbey was filled with parties, receptions, and balls, all presided over by the elderly queen.

On the morning of the great day itself, Alix climbed into a semi–state landau beneath the portico of Buckingham Palace and rode down the Mall, through Trafalgar Square and Whitehall to the Abbey. Accompanying her was an escort of the Household Cavalry—the Life Guards, the Royal Horse Guards, and the Royal Dragoons—all in brilliant scarlet or gold tunics, white breeches, and black boots, with golden helmets whose plumes waved in the breeze. Flags and bunting fluttered in the wind, and brass bands struck up "God Save the Queen" in salute every few hundred yards along the route. It must have been quite a sight to an impressionable girl of fifteen.

Inside the medieval, soaring church, below the arched ceiling and magnificent stained-glass windows, the royal family walked down the long carpet from the west door, under the organ screen, and past the carved choir stalls to the high altar. Trumpets echoing their fanfares sounded loudly throughout the Abbey, punctuated with the rolling melodies of the choir and organ as they performed a great *Te Deum* in celebration of the jubilee. The subject of all this devotion sat on a gilded chair, a tiny woman wrapped in black satin, while her family fell to their knees to pray for her long life and lustily sang the national anthem.

This was the first big royal occasion in which Alix had been directly involved. Two years before, she had acted as a bridesmaid to her aunt Beatrice at the latter's wedding to Prince Henry of Battenberg; but that wedding was held at a small country church on the Isle of Wight and was a very private affair. True, there had been magnificent balls and receptions on her first visit to Russia when Ella married Serge, but Alix had been watching through foreign eyes as the exotic spectacle of imperial Russia passed before her. At the jubilee, she saw firsthand the adoration surrounding her own family. Never before had the mixture of devotion, pageantry, and opulence given such an intoxicating glimpse into the world of royalty and power.

The contrast between the crowds in London during Jubilee Week and the New Palace at Darmstadt must have seemed especially apparent when Alix returned home. Not only were Victoria and Ella gone, but in 1888, Irene was wed to Prince Heinrich of Prussia, whose brother was the despised Cousin Willy from Alix's childhood. There was quite a bit of opposition from Queen Victoria to the match on the grounds that Irene and Heinrich were too closely related: the pair were first cousins whose maternal grandparents were double cousins, and they shared paternal grandparents as well.[2] All objections aside, the pair were determined and wed in Berlin as Heinrich's father, Emperor Friedrich Wilhelm III of Germany, lay dying of throat cancer. Two weeks later, the emperor was dead—his son and heir, the new kaiser Wilhelm II, having all but snatched the crown as his father breathed his last.

At the age of sixteen Alix was given her own lady-in-waiting. Now that she was the only daughter left in the New Palace, Queen Victoria expressed the hope that she would "*not be left* to Miss Jackson *alone*, with her bad health, hard ways and crabbed, bad temper. It would ruin Alicky. Someone must be found for her, younger, softer, brighter, else her life all alone will be utterly miserable." She suggested Gretchen von Fabrice—"such a very nice person"—who was governess to the children of Alix's aunt Helena.[3] Soon Miss von Fabrice was safely installed as Alix's lady-in-waiting. A lady-in-waiting's chief duties were secretarial and ceremonial, but as Alix was too young to play a big part in the complicated day-to-day mechanisms of the court, Gretchen von Fabrice served as more of a companion than anything else. Together the pair studied lessons for Alix's confirmation into the Lutheran church.

In the Victorian age, confirmation was a must for any girl who hoped to enter society; without being confirmed, she would be hard-pressed to be presented at any European court. Confirmation was looked upon as the coming of age of a young lady, celebrated as much for its social benefits as for its religious implications. The Royal Mob, for the most part, regarded religion and its practice as a virtue and an expected duty, but not necessarily as a commitment to a way of life. Few of the family understood their beliefs. In this, Alix was far different.

She studied hard for her confirmation, spending long hours kneeling in prayer in the shadows of the New Palace. Perhaps because her childhood had been darkened by thoughts of death and heaven, Alix had always been introspective. Like Princess Alice, she pondered the past, searching for meaning and purpose. In the church these spiritual ideals were fulfilled. Alix accepted the Lutheran doctrines and, in return, felt herself accepted wholeheartedly into a larger, higher, and more meaningful existence than her daily life at the New Palace. This religious faith would become, in time, a protected fortress that no invader could penetrate.

Following her confirmation, Alix had her formal presentation to Darmstadt society. Many a Victorian girl suffered through the anxiety that she would fail to create a good impression and thus avoid attracting suitors. One lady wrote: "Unless a girl was quite exceptional . . . her fate was decided by her first impact on society. Anyone who failed to secure a proposal within six months of coming out could only wait for her second season with diminishing chances. After the third time there remained nothing but India as a last resort before the specter of the Old Maid became a reality."[4]

Alix may not have placed all of her matrimonial hopes on her presentation, but she certainly worried a good deal over the event itself. Her father went to enormous expense in giving a spectacular ball at the New Palace. Hundreds of guests were invited, and the palace blazed with light to welcome them—aunts, uncles, cousins. Even Ella and Serge came from Moscow just for the event. In the dim light of the candles burning in the crystal chandeliers, Alix, on the arm of her father, swept down the staircase of the palace to greet the guests. She wore a white gown covered with tulle, with bunches of lilies of the valley on her dress and in her hair.[5] Moving from room to room that night, Alix evoked the sad image of her late mother to the ladies of Darmstadt society who waited to welcome her as their new leader.

Alix now assumed the duties of a princess of Hesse. She acted as her father's hostess, giving small dinner parties and receptions, teas for the less fortunate, and elaborate balls for society. At one, she decided upon a Renaissance theme and came costumed accordingly in a dress of pale green velvet with high collar and full sleeves piped with silver cord and set off by the emeralds she wore around her neck and in her hair.[6] Despite the magnificent life she was beginning to lead, Alix continued to sympathize with the poor of Hesse, and she contributed large sums of her own to local charities.

As a young lady she traveled frequently. In 1890, with her father, she journied to Malta. Her brother-in-law Prince Louis of Battenberg was stationed there, commissioned to the torpedo cruiser HMS *Scout*, and Victoria had taken a house on the island. Malta was fairly desolate and hot, but the English who lived there were determined to transplant their culture as nearly as possible. On sunny afternoons they gathered to watch polo matches and bet on horse races; at night they danced at parties and balls. It was a new experience for Alix, who found the extreme heat unbearable. Nevertheless, she enjoyed herself immensely and was, in turn, highly popular with Louis's fellow officers. The commander's flag lieutenant, a Scot named Mark Kerr, was put in charge of the guests, and Alix became quite attached to him, jokingly referring to the handsome young man as "my Malta aide-de-camp."[7] The sailors arranged many special excursions and dinner parties to keep Alix entertained, although their commander was a bit cautious lest they become overenthusiastic in their pursuits.

Three years later, Alix returned to the warm climate of the south, this time on a visit to Italy. First, she went to Florence to stay with Queen Victoria, who liked to holiday in the warmer climates of southern Europe. Alix was fascinated by the ancient city and spent her days touring its sites, then moved on to Venice. She walked the cool marble halls of the palaces and museums and explored the many canals from a gondola, basking in the Adriatic breezes that swept the city. She fell in love with the architecture and the works of Botticelli and Michelangelo. When it was time to return to Germany, Alix wrote to a friend that she feared she would always long to come again.[8]

Back in Darmstadt, Alix was hosting a luncheon for her father one day when he suddenly collapsed at the table. Ludwig had been unwell for some time; in 1892, he was diagnosed as having heart trouble. But no one had expected a heart attack. Alix refused to let him go; she sat by his bed day and night, waiting for a faint glimmer of recognition, the merest sign. But the grand duke never recovered consciousness and died on 13 March 1892. He was fifty-five.[9]

Queen Victoria was—as usual—overwhelmed, writing to her granddaughter Victoria, "This is too terrible. . . . It adds to *my quite overwhelming* grief to think of your distress and of poor dear Ernie and Alix alone—*Orphans*. . . . It is *awful!* But I am *still there* and while I live Alicky, till she is married, will be *more* than *ever my own child*."[10] Ernie succeeded his father as the grand duke of Hesse at the age of twenty-three.

Alix was desolate with grief. After her father's death, she lay in her bed for weeks, weeping hysterically, refusing to eat at all. Everything reminded her of her loss—every photograph which she saw, every letter which she read, brought forth a new rush of tears. Her father's death struck deep at the sense of security in her family which Alix had relished since her mother's death. His passing left a deep void in her life. She filled her grief with religion and developed an obsessive need for her brother. Alix was on the verge of having a nervous breakdown; Queen Victoria, once again coming to her granddaughter's rescue following a death in the Hessian family, hastily sent for Alix, who spent the rest of the year with her.[11]

During her time with the queen, Alix accompanied her grandmother on many of her rare public appearances, including a tour of the Welsh mining districts. Although she wore an elegant dress and hat, Alix jumped from the carriage and insisted on being lowered into the grimy shafts so that she could see firsthand the working conditions of her grandmother's subjects. Queen Victoria must have been pleased with this young woman over whom she had exercised so much influence. Alix had been shaped by her years with the British royal family. She did not yet realize it, but plans were under way to make her one of its most powerful members.

Princess Alix at eighteen had blossomed into a beautiful young lady. Tall and thin, with large, luminous blue-gray eyes, she was immensely proud of her golden hair, which she wore coiled atop her head with a fringe across her forehead; when it was unbound, she could easily sit on it. Her outstanding features were a long, well-shaped neck and shoulders. Her skin was pale, her complexion the English "peaches and cream." She blushed beautifully, hiding her delight behind a shy smile. Contemporary accounts convey more of her natural beauty than any photograph. Anna Vyrubova, who met her at the turn of the century, described her like this: "Tall she was, and delicately, beautifully shaped, with exquisite white neck and shoulders. . . . Her complexion was clear and rosy as a little child's. The empress had large eyes, deep grey and very lustrous."[12] Alix rarely smiled in public, but when she did, according to one lady, "it lit up her face, it turned her mouth into a flower, it did something unforgettable to her beautiful eyes."[13]

Her education had left her a well-informed, if not a particularly brilliant, young woman. Her choice of literature reflected the somewhat middle-class upbringing all of the children shared in the New Palace: Alix's favorite author was the vapid and florid Marie Corelli. But in this Queen Victoria shared her opinion. The queen once remarked that one day Marie Corelli would rank among the greatest writers in the world, a sentiment to which the queen's daughter Vicky, the Empress

Friedrich of Germany, replied that Marie Corelli's works were "trash."[14] Along with her taste in reading materials, Alix's fashion sense remained solidly middle class. She disliked fussy clothing and rarely wore when she was younger anything but the simplest dresses of muslin and silk, and almost always in the same color: mauve. It was, in fact, her favorite color, but one from which, due to Victorian custom, she could not escape. According to the stiff etiquette of the day, mourning had to be worn for a full year following the death of any member of one's family. For the first six months, nothing but black was allowed. But for the last term, half-mourning could be worn—white, gray, or mauve.[15] With such an extended family, Alix was nearly always in mourning for some relative. It is perhaps revealing that even in her later years Alix chose to surround herself with a color that she must certainly have associated with death.

Queen Victoria found Alix to be "dear and good and clever."[16] And, indeed, among her family, she was. But Alix never felt at ease with those whom she did not know. She had never developed any social skills despite the supervision of her grandmother. And she never mastered doing the *cercle* and thus found social conversation a burden and an ordeal. This, in turn, led to the widely held belief that Alix was haughty and cold. With her family, she could be fun-loving, joining in all of their games and laughing uncontrollably. But never in public. She had no sense of balance and thus could never understand that she might give offense with a frown or a worried look of the eye.

Alix was highly emotional, but it was an emotion tempered with her mother's melancholy. She found comfort in her religion, and this made her all the more reserved, all the more guarded over her every action. She visited the wards of the Darmstadt hospitals, as her mother had done, but with none of the feeling or grace so essential for a life of public service. She was also less sensitive to others than her mother had been, particularly in recognizing their perceptions of her.

Despite her shortcomings, Alix was an undeniably attractive candidate as a wife. Her family background was impeccable, her looks elegant, even ethereal. She would make one prince a perfect wife and consort. And one woman in Europe, Queen Victoria, knew who that man was to be.

For years, Grandmamma had planned what courses Alix would study, what books she would read, what pieces of music she would play on the piano, where she should holiday. An incurable matchmaker, the queen had long ago decided whom Alix would marry. She was to be the wife of her cousin Prince Eddy and become, successively, the duchess of Clarence and Avondale, the Princess of Wales, and the queen of Great Britain and empress of India.

6

The Duke of Clarence and Avondale

A CHILL NORFOLK WIND from the sea swept through Sandringham House all day long; outside, gusts of snow pounded against the windows of the rambling, red-brick mansion. The sky was gray and threatening, heavy with the white powder covering the broad lawns and drives which curved up to the house. The bare, gnarled fingers of the leafless trees reached into the darkening sky as evening approached, and puffs of smoke choked from the tops of the chimneys rising from the slate roofs. Slowly, as darkness crept over the land, the windows of the big house were filled with light. Servants hurried from one room to another, building up fires, clearing away the remains of the afternoon's tea, drawing the heavy curtains across the French doors opening to the terraces.

Upstairs, in a cramped room, lay Prince Albert Victor Christian Edward, the duke of Clarence and Avondale and heir presumptive to the British throne. Prince Eddy was dying. A week earlier he had come down with pneumonia; his coughs and gasps of breath filled the silent bedroom. Around his bed stood his family: the Prince of Wales, his father, looking on nervously; his mother, the Princess of Wales, beside him in a chair, holding his hand; George, his brother, and his three sisters. A fire burned in the grate, and the room was insufferably hot. Doctors came and went all through the night, his family drifted in and out, but along with his mother, one figure remained constant: the sad girl in the corner of the room who was Prince Eddy's fiancée. The snow continued on through the night, and the wind whistled on mournfully, rattling the windows of the sickroom. Then Prince Eddy began to scream out in pain. His family knew that the end was near.

Prince Eddy had been born in the second week of January 1864 at Frogmore House in Windsor Home Park. He was two months premature. This almost certainly had something to do with his seemingly arrested mental condition as he began to grow up. His tutor, John Neale

42

Dalton, tried to break through the mental barriers in his pupil's mind; after eight years, however, Dalton was forced to report to the Prince of Wales that Eddy "fails, not in one or two subjects, but in all." There seemed to be no reason for this, Dalton explained, other than the "abnormally dormant condition of his mind," which prevented Eddy from devoting "his attention to any given subject for more than a few minutes consecutively."[1] And, again, Dalton states: "[Eddy] sits listless and vacant, and . . . wastes as much time in doing nothing as he ever wastes. . . ."[2]

His childhood must have been an unhappy one, for he hardly saw his parents. His father, the Prince of Wales, was a wayward husband and an inattentive father, spending more time gambling or with his mistresses than with either his wife or his children. Eddy's mother, the beautiful Princess Alexandra, ignored by her husband and rapidly going deaf, was a doting but often indifferent mother. As a result, their children grew up undisciplined and ill-mannered. Prince Eddy, as the future king of England, needed to possess exceptional abilities; it was his misfortune that he shone in neither social skills nor in educational capabilities.

His education was a constant battle and had to be abandoned—at least temporarily—in favor of the possible benefits of a naval existence. Both Eddy and his brother George trained as cadets and then joined the crew of HMS *Bacchante* on a three-year cruise. The Prince of Wales hoped that the discipline of the navy would strengthen Eddy's weak character. But the cruise had quite the wrong effect on the prince, and Dalton again had to report to the Prince of Wales that his son had learned nothing except activities of "a dissolute nature."[3]

Upon completion of his naval term, Prince Eddy's formal education resumed. He entered Trinity College, Cambridge, as an undergraduate. The prince might have stood a fair chance at Cambridge had his father not made the unfortunate choice of James Kenneth Stephen as his son's tutor. Stephen was a scholar and a poet of some repute; he was also a mentally disturbed homosexual who may well have influenced the prince under his care to carouse with him at all hours of the night.

Cambridge failed to instill in Prince Eddy a love of intellectual pursuits, and so he was sent to join the army. On 17 June 1885, His Royal Highness the Prince Albert Victor of Wales was commissioned in the Tenth Hussars Cavalry Regiment, of which his father was colonel in chief.

In 1888, Eddy was twenty-four years old. Of him at this time, James Pope-Hennessy has written:

[Eddy] was a thin young man, slightly taller than his brother and his sisters, with brown wavy hair that had started to recede, an oval face, an aquiline nose, large, gentle, doe-like eyes, and a buoyant little cavalry mustache which was waxed and turned up at the ends. His neck was astonishingly long—"a neck like a swan"—as one of his family termed it; when not in uniform he was thus obliged to wear an unusually high starched collar, and from this necessity there arose his nickname of "Collars and Cuffs"—a nickname which his father, the Prince of Wales, who dearly loved to tease Prince Eddy, would recommend to child members of the Royal Family, "Don't call him Uncle Eddy, call him 'Uncle Eddy Collars and Cuffs.'"[4]

There was much speculation concerning the prince's private life not only among the royal family but also by the public as well. It was widely rumored that the prince was a homosexual, perhaps influenced by his tutor James Kenneth Stephen. It is known that Eddy frequented a certain male brothel at 19 Cleveland Street whose patrons were young, aristocratic scions of society. Among those the police discovered in a raid on the Cleveland Street premises was Lord Arthur Somerset, a friend of Eddy's. Somerset, in danger of being prosecuted for his activities, had to quickly flee the country. Like so much of Eddy's life, his involvement in the Cleveland Street club remains, for the most part, surrounded by a cloak of mystery and silence.

In the early morning hours of 31 August 1888, a worker returning home in Whitechapel, a slum area in the East End of London, saw a woman lying in the gutter. Such a sight was not uncommon in Whitechapel; the area teemed with thousands of cheap prostitutes who staggered drunkenly through the streets, and the man assumed that another must have passed out in the roadway. But when he got closer, he found that the lady was not drunk but dead. It was not until the police arrived that they discovered the cause of her death; shining their lights upon her, they saw that her clothing was soaked with blood. The prostitute, Polly Nichols, had been strangled, her throat slashed and her body disemboweled.

For the next nine weeks Whitechapel was rocked by the bizarre slayings of four other area prostitutes: Annie Chapman, Elizabeth Stride, Catherine Eddows, and Mary Kelly. The savagery of the attacks increased with time. Annie Chapman was found with her head almost severed from her body, disemboweled and with her intestines thrown over her shoulder. Stride and Eddows were murdered on the same night; the killer was apparently interrupted with Stride and sought out a second victim, Eddows. The following day, a piece of her kidney arrived at a London hospital, along with a letter headed "From Hell" and signed "Jack the Ripper."

With Mary Kelly's death the killings stopped. Jack the Ripper was never caught. But over the last hundred years, an extraordinary rumor—that Prince Eddy was Jack the Ripper—has gained much attention. It has long been intimated that the prince suffered from syphilis of the brain, contracted, it is said, during his cruise around the world. The gradual decline in mental stability which would result from the disease is said to have triggered the Whitechapel murders. A man who saw Mary Kelly with her killer described the man as being of medium height, with brown hair, a small waxed mustache, well dressed, and wearing long collars and cuffs. From this description, it is said that Eddy could be identified as the murderer. Eddy had watched deer being dressed, and from this he is alleged to have gained the anatomic knowledge demonstrated by the Ripper. His tutor at Cambridge, James Kenneth Stephen, is alleged to have written several of the Ripper letters received by various newspapers. It also appears suspicious that nearly all of the vital evidence concerning the Jack the Ripper case was either suppressed or later burned, as if the police wished to avoid disclosing the truth.

The story that Eddy was the Ripper must stand or fall on the evidence of his whereabouts at the time of the murders, and here there seems conclusive proof that he could not have been the killer, for he was in Scotland on two of the nights in question and at Sandringham at the time of the last murder. Nevertheless, other theories have linked the prince to the killings, claiming that he had fathered a bastard child with a servant girl and that the murders were designed to cover up this fact.[5] It must be said, however, that no firm evidence has yet come to light indicating the prince's involvement in any way with the murders.

What is certain is that the prince, with the rumor and innuendo surrounding his name, was the object of controversy within his family. A future king of England could not be dragged through any public scandals; his father had already been the subject of such disasters, and the wayward Eddy further threatened the stability of the British throne at a time when the royal family could ill afford any further humiliations. Queen Victoria thought that Eddy needed a stabilizing influence, a wife, and that Alix would provide the encouragement necessary for the prince's uncertain future.

As early as 1887, the queen was writing to Victoria: "As Irene has been lost to us here—and I must tell you, who have so much influence with Papa and generally in the family, that my heart and mind are bent on securing dear Alicky for either Eddy or Georgie. You must prevent *further* Russians or other people coming to snap her up."[6] But if the queen was trying to encourage her granddaughter, Alix's family appears to have been against the match. "I find the idea of Eddy's marrying Alix quite dreadful—first cousins it is best to avoid—but the chief objection is that he does not look overstrong and is too stupid," Ella wrote to Ernie. "England with such a husband is not at all a place for Alix. I long to have her as happy as are we three."[7]

Once the idea of marriage to his cousin was proposed to him, Eddy went along with it. He fancied himself desperately in love with Alix; in any case, he was far too weak to go against the wishes of his powerful grandmother. In 1889 the queen summoned Alix to Balmoral. Prince Eddy was also staying at the castle. He took his cousin on carriage rides and escorted her on walks over the hills, waiting for the right moment to ask the important question. We do know that Prince Eddy proposed, because Alix rejected him. It is not hard to imagine her reasons. Eddy must have seemed a disappointment to her. Pope-Hennessy has described him as "backward and utterly listless. He was self-indulgent and not punctual. He had been given no proper education and as a result he was interested in nothing. He was as heedless and aimless as a gleaming goldfish in a crystal bowl."[8]

Eddy was crushed. He wrote plaintively to his mother, "I don't think she knows how much I love her or she could not be so cruel."[9] The queen was also concerned, for the prince was making an awful fuss about being rejected. "If only poor Eddy (who is so devoted to Alicky) I felt had decided what to do or not to do about Alicky . . . " she wrote.[10]

In a series of letters to Victoria, the queen expressed her concern and continuing hope that all would be resolved between her grandchildren: "And now let me say a word about Alicky. Is there *no* hope about Eddy? She is *not* nineteen—and she should be made to reflect seriously on the folly of throwing away the chances of a very good husband, kind, affectionate and steady and of entering a united happy family and a very good position which is second to *none in the world*. Dear Uncle and Aunt [the Prince and Princess of Wales] wish it so much and poor Eddy is so unhappy at the thought of losing her also. Can you and Ernie not do any good? What fancy has she got in her head?"[11]

When this approach did not overcome Alix's objections, the queen again wrote to Victoria: "It is most sad about Alicky and Eddy. We still have a faint, lingering hope that she *may* —if he remains unmarried, after all when she comes to reflect and see what a sad and serious thing it is to throw away such a marriage with such a position, and in such an amiable family in her Mother's country—where she would be received with open arms—and change. Moreover Eddy is not stupid, is very good, affectionate and a good looking young man."[12]

Eventually, even the queen gave up on the match. A year later, in May 1890, she wrote: "I fear all hopes of Alicky's marrying Eddy is at an end. She has written to tell him how it pains her to pain him, but that she cannot marry him, much as she likes him as a cousin, that she knows she would not be happy with him and that he must not think of her. . . . It is a real sorrow to us . . . but . . . she says—that if she is forced she will do it—but that she would be unhappy and he too. This shows great strength of character as all of us wish it and she still refuses the greatest position there is."[13]

Eddy was hurt by this final rejection but soon recovered and fell in love with Princess Helene, the daughter of the pretender to the French throne, Louis, Comte de Paris. Prince Eddy was desperately in love with Helene, and Queen Victoria and the Princess of Wales both encouraged the couple in their romance. They ignored the insurmountable issue of religion: Helene was a Catholic, and Eddy, under the Act of Settlement, could not wed her unless he either gave up the throne or she changed her religion. Helene was willing enough, but her father refused to allow her to convert. When the matter came to the attention of Pope Leo XIII, he threatened to excommunicate Helene for even considering marriage to a "heretic." Against his wishes, Eddy had to give Helene up.

In 1891, Eddy finally discovered a woman agreeable to his family and to the idea of marrying him. She was Princess Victoria Mary of Teck, a distant cousin who was always called May. The country celebrated the engagement, but those in the know had a different view. One society lady wrote: "The newspapers are twaddling and *asinine* over this desperate love match and the attachment of years triumphing over all obstacles. Columns of *rot*. How Princess Helene must laugh in her sleeve as she reads of this long devotion. And Princess Alix of Hesse, too."[14]

The date for the wedding was set for the last week of January 1892. In the weeks preceding the marriage, the engaged pair, along with Eddy's entire family, retreated to Sandringham in Norfolk, the home of the Prince of Wales. Eddy had not been well for some time, but after a few days spent shooting in the chill Norfolk wind and snow, he developed a persistent cough. His appetite failed, and soon, on the orders of the family doctor, Eddy was confined to bed with a diagnosis of pneumonia.

He grew worse each day. With the coming of night, Eddy's temperature rose and fell. He began to shout at the top of his lungs—about his horses, his regiment, his friends, and his grandmother the queen, interrupted by his hoarse cries of "Helene! Helene!" echoing throughout the big house.[15] The queen sent her personal physician to Sandringham, but he could do nothing. As the hours slipped into each other, Eddy's screams rose in agony. The Princess of Wales sat by her son's bed, while May hovered like a shadow in the corner of the room. On 14 January 1892, Eddy, with a sigh and a shallow breath, died. He was twenty-eight.

Eddy was buried on a snowy day at Windsor Castle. His oak coffin, covered with a Union Jack, was escorted by members of his old regiment, the Tenth Hussars, into St. George's Chapel for a very short and somber funeral. Alix, veiled in black, watched as the body of the man who had once wished to make her the queen of England was carried past her for the last time. Eddy was later interred in a magnificent tomb of marble and alabaster in the Albert Memorial Chapel, Windsor. On his coffin, at the funeral, lay two bouquets: Princess May's unused bridal wreath of orange blossoms, placed there by the Prince of Wales, and a large band of *immortales* with a single word inscribed on a ribbon: "Helene."[16]

Above left. Hessian Royal Family Group. *Standing, left to right:* Prince Ernest, Princess Alice, Prince Ludwig, Princess Elizabeth (Ella). *Sitting, left to right:* Princess Irene and Princess Victoria. Around 1875. (*Broadlands Archives*) *Above right.* With Queen Victoria at Windsor Castle, 1879. *Left to right:* Princess Victoria, the queen, Princess Alix, and Princess Elizabeth. (*Broadlands Archives*)

The children of Princess Alice and Prince Ludwig of Hesse and by Rhine, around 1876. *Standing, in back:* Prince Ernest and Princess Elizabeth. *Sitting, left to right:* Princess Irene, Princess May, Princess Victoria, and Princess Alix. (*Broadlands Archives*)

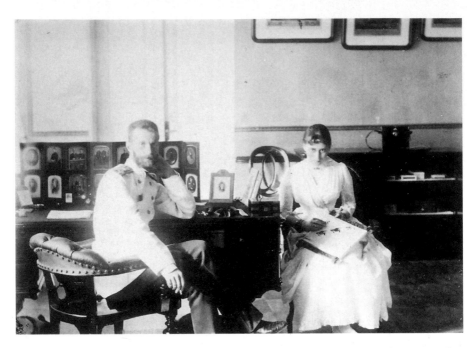

Grand Duke Serge Alexandrovich and his new wife Elizabeth Feodorovna at his summer estate, Ilinskoe, outside of Moscow, 1884. (*Broadlands Archives*)

Above left. Family group taken at Darmstadt, 1890. *Seated, left to right:* Grand Duke Serge Alexandrovich of Russia, Grand Duchess Elizabeth Feodorovna of Russia, and Grand Duke Ludwig of Hesse. *At rear:* Prince Louis of Battenberg and his wife, Princess Victoria. (*Broadlands Archives*)   ***Above right.*** Alix, Ella, and Ernie, St. Petersburg, 1889. (*Broadlands Archives*)

Princess Alix, 1888.
(*Broadlands Archives*)

Peterhof Palace seen from the end of the
Grand Cascade, photograph circa 1900.
(*Broadlands Archives*)

The Winter Palace, seen from Palace Square, circa 1900.

Tsarevich Nicholas Alexandrovich, around 1890.

HRH Prince Albert Victor, the Duke of Clarence, 1890.

Princess Alix of Hesse, 1894, engagement photograph.

Tsar Nicholas II, in the uniform of an imperial falconer, 1894.

Tsarevich Nicholas, in hussar uniform, and Princess Alix of Hesse. Engagement photograph, 1894. (*Broadlands Archives*)

Dowager Empress Marie Feodorovna of Russia, 1895.

Tsarevich Nicholas, Princess Alix, Grand Duke Ernest Ludwig, and Princess Victoria Melita (Ducky), Darmstadt, 1894. (*Broadlands Archives*)

Top. The tsar and tsarina reviewing the Railway Corps at Sevastopol in the Crimea, 1898.
Center. The New Palace at Alexandria, Peterhof, circa 1900. (*Broadlands Archives*)
Bottom. The Catherine Palace at Tsarskoe Selo, circa 1900.

Top. Tsar Nicholas II and his son, Tsarevich Alexei, reviewing soldiers at Ropsha, near Peterhof, 1909.

Center. Tsarevich Alexei (*third from right*) with some ship's boys, Finland, 1912. The big sailor at the left is the tsarevich's bodyguard Derevenko.

Bottom. Tsar Nicholas II with a stag, Spala, Poland, 1912.

Above left. The imperial family after the christening of Grand Duchess Anastasia, July 1901. *Left to right:* Grand Duchesses Tatiana and Olga, the tsar with Grand Duchess Marie, and the tsarina holding Grand Duchess Anastasia Alexandra is still in mourning for her grandmother Queen Victoria, who died six months previously. (*Broadlands Archives*)
Above right. Tsarina Alexandra, 1902.

Above left. Grand Duchess Elizabeth Feodorovna, 1901. (*Broadlands Archives*) *Above right.* Tsarina Alexandra holding her son, Tsarevich Alexei, after his christening, August 1904.

lowered, gave to her whole figure a maidenly shyness that
made it wonderfully attractive.[11]

Waiting, in glittering stoles of silver and copes and miters studded
with diamonds, the elderly, white-haired priests stood at the doorway.
Slowly, they set off down the aisle of crimson, swaying back and forth
with each step, sparkling in the candlelight. Alexandra and Nicholas
followed down the length of the white-and-gold chapel, smiling to family and friends who packed the room. Step by step, Alexandra made her
way, her face all but hidden in the cocoon of veil cascading from the diamonds atop her head, her train and robes flowing in layers of silver tissue and brocade, her jewels flashing light with each move, each turn, as
she floated across the red carpet while the glorious harmonies of the
gathered choirs filled the room, lofting up to the gilded and domed ceiling, where cherubs danced in the blue sky of heaven. A few more steps
and she and Nicholas stood on the dais beneath the dome, flanked by
huge bowers of orchids and lilies, surrounded by family, facing the
iconostasis, the jeweled altar screen, which glittered in the dim light of
the votive candles.

A priest handed Alexandra and Nicholas lighted tapers, then presented a silver tray, upon which rested the two wedding rings. Slowly,
the elderly metropolitan of St. Petersburg made the sign of the cross
over them, announcing, "The servant of God, Alexandra, betroths herself to the servant of God, Nicholas." The bride and groom exchanged
the rings three times, a sign of recognition of the Holy Trinity, while
priests chanted and swung golden censers of incense. Once the wedding rings had been exchanged, Alexandra and Nicholas knelt as the
choir thundered into the Seventy-Seventh Psalm, a strange and somber
selection for a wedding.

Alexandra and Nicholas exchanged their wedding vows. She
promised to love, honor, and obey; he, to cherish and worship. Whereas
she made her responses in a low but firm voice, the tsar had to be
prompted several times by the priest. Two golden crowns were blessed,
then held over the heads of the bride and groom and again exchanged
three times in recognition of the Trinity. Hand in hand, Alexandra and
Nicholas circled the altar three times, then knelt for prayers. On rising,
they kissed a golden cross and an icon, and shortly after one in the afternoon, Alexandra became Her Imperial Majesty the tsarina Alexandra
Feodorovna, empress of Russia.

Watching the couple leave, everyone was struck by how obviously in love they were. George, duke of York, wrote: "I think Nicky is
a very lucky man to have got such a lovely and charming wife and I
must say I never saw two people more in love with each other."[12] They

walked back through the palace to the Malachite Drawing Room, where they posed for wedding photographs and received the family. As a wedding gift, Nicholas gave his new wife a round crown of diamonds, pearls, and sapphires.[13] Alexandra changed out of her gown into the silver traveling dress, and together she and Nicholas climbed into a carriage and left for the ride back to the Anichkov Palace.

They stopped at the Cathedral of Our Lady of Kazan and went inside to pray before a famous and much-revered icon. As soon as they emerged from the church the crowd erupted, screaming, cheering, even singing "God Save the Tsar." Overwhelmed, Nicholas ordered that the soldiers lining the route be removed so that the people could surge forward around the carriage for a better view, a move which the correspondent of the French newspaper *Journal des Débats* called "a daring and beautiful gesture."[14]

There had been no time to plan for a honeymoon; Alexandra and Nicholas spent their first married night together in his mother's palace, in the tsar's childhood bedroom. At the front door of the Anichkov Palace, Marie Feodorovna, now the dowager empress, welcomed her son and his bride with the Russian greeting of bread and salt. Alexandra and Nicholas spent the evening answering the many telegrams which had poured in from around the world. After dinner with Alexandra's brother Ernie, the pair retired, early, as Nicholas explained, "because Alix had a headache."[15]

Before she went to bed, Alexandra wrote in her new husband's diary, "At last united, bound for life and when this life is ended, we meet again in the other world and remain together for eternity. Yours, yours."[16] The following morning, she recorded, "Never did I believe there could be such utter happiness in this world, such a feeling of unity between two mortal beings. I love you—those three words have my life in them."[17]

PART TWO

Empress of Russia

(1894–1905)

12

Her Imperial Majesty

ALEXANDRA CAME TO THE THRONE of imperial Russia at the age of twenty-two. It was an extraordinary position in which to be at such a young age. With her marriage came the title "Imperial Majesty, Tsarina of all the Russias," and the advantages and trials associated with it.

The position of tsarina was what the title holder made of it. There were no official responsibilities accompanying the office; principally, the lady was supposed to be a leader of St. Petersburg society. This involved taking the lead in fashion, giving an endless round of parties and receptions, and enjoying the prerogatives of the wife of the most powerful monarch in the world. This generally frivolous view of public responsibility had been the rule rather than the exception among most of Russia's empresses. Their attitudes ranged from indifference to joyous extravagance in the execution of their duties. Marie Feodorovna, for example, loved to cover herself in jewels and entertain at magnificent balls until the early-morning hours, much to the distaste of Alexander III, who hated all pomp and ceremony.

There was much speculation as to what the new reign would bring. Some hoped for civil reforms; others dreamed of a glorious era for the arts and sciences, a revival of all that was good in Russia. As far as the role of tsarina was concerned, most hoped for a leader of society who would glory in her position and set the tone for the most brilliant reign of any Russian tsar. There was every expectation that Alexandra would be a successful and highly popular empress. In time, most hoped that she would fulfill these expectations. She had a number of advantages: She was young and beautiful, the sister of the popular Grand Duchess Serge, with a reputation for being high-minded, intelligent, and artistic. She also, at the beginning of the reign, had public sympathy on her side, arising from her unfortunate entry into the country and the circumstances surrounding her marriage to the tsar.

Alexandra was of a different mind. Her natural inclination was to avoid society as much as possible. She must have realized, however, that such a move on the part of the tsarina would be unwelcome and could only attract criticism of her and her position. She had no choice. At her husband's side she would stand through official receptions, speeches, meetings with local officials, reviews of troops, inspections of hospitals, and society balls. She would encourage her husband in the execution of his duties, aid in the upholding of his prestige and position as autocrat of all the Russias, and act as his representative in the best manner she knew how. But despite her eventual interpretation of her duties as tsarina, Alexandra never came to appreciate or enjoy them, and this distaste was constantly displayed to the public. However, in marrying Nicholas, Alexandra had accepted not just a man but also a way of life.

It was a lifestyle that must have dazzled and at the same time be-witched Alexandra. Her daily existence constantly reminded her of the magnificent wealth of the Romanovs. Her husband was undoubtedly the richest man in the world, with assets close to $20 billion. He held more than $1 billion in private gold reserves alone, owned jewels, had interests in timber and mining ventures, and had a total of 150 million acres in his own name and millions of dollars in foreign banks.[1] The Winter Palace in St. Petersburg was the chief residence, supplemented by two palaces at Tsarskoe Selo, three at Peterhof, two at Livadia in the Crimea and the Kremlin in Moscow. Aside from these main residences, there were smaller palaces: the Anichkov Palace, Elagin Palace, and Gatchina in or near the capital; the Petrovsky and Neschensky palaces in Moscow; three hunting compounds in Poland comprising thousands of acres, several hunting lodges in Finland; four imperial yachts and two imperial trains. The cheap holidays at second-rate seaside resorts, shared ponies, and welcome checks from Queen Victoria of her child-hood must have been quickly forgotten by Alexandra, replaced by the Byzantine opulence of the Russian court.

Gone, too, were the trappings of her position as a princess of Hesse and the Rhine. Her new, full title reflected the dramatic changes. Officially, and only on the most sacred of ceremonial occasions, such as her wedding, coronation, or funeral, she was Her Imperial Majesty the Tsarina Alexandra Feodorovna, Empress of Russia, Grand Duchess of Smolensk, of Lithuania, Volhynia, Podolia, and Finland, Princess of Estonia, Livonia, Courland, and Semigalia, Bialostock, Karelia, Tver, Yougouria, Perm, Viatka, Bulgaria, and other countries; Grand Duchess of Lower Novgorod, of Tchernigov, Riazan, Polotsk, Rostov, Yaroslav, Belozero, Oudoria, Obdoria, Condia, Vitebsk, Mstislav, and the North; August Consort of the Sovereign of Cartalinia, Iveria, Kabardinia, Armenia, Turkestan; Heiress of Norway, Duchess of Schleswig-Holstein,

Storman, the Ditmars, and Oldenburg, of the House of Romanov-Hol-stein-Gottorp.[2] She automatically became the Deputy Grand Master of the Imperial Order of St. Catherine upon her marriage and was, by virtue of her position, entitled to wear the decorations and ribbons of the Imperial Orders of St. Anna, St. Alexander Nevsky, and the White Eagle.[3]

But during the first days of Alexandra's married life, the dramatic wealth and plethora of titles must have seemed nonexistent. Alexandra and Nicholas had not been able to plan for either a honeymoon or a first residence. Their first home was six cramped rooms in the Anichkov Palace, the residence of the dowager empress. Although Alexandra must have been uncomfortable with the situation, there was little she could do; rooms were being redecorated in the Winter Palace and the New Palace at Peterhof, but until they were done, she would have to make the best of the domestic arrangements. "I cannot yet realize that I am married, living here with the others, it seems like being on a visit," Alexandra wrote somewhat bitterly to her sister.[4] Yet she seems to have been happy enough, writing to Queen Victoria, "I never can thank God enough for having given me such a husband, and his love for you touches me also so deeply, for have you not been as a mother to me since beloved Mama died?"[5] Still, the pressures were beginning to tell, as Alexandra revealed in a letter to her brother-in-law Prince Louis of Battenberg:

> My thoughts are much with you and Victoria and I wonder when
> we shall meet again and when all our nice plans of seeing you at
> Malta are at an end as, alas, now Nicky will not have much
> liberty. Poor boy—he has to work so much and I am sure you,
> who were forced to sit writing away so many hours in London
> will understand how tiring it is. And the great responsibilities. He
> receives people and visitations all the morning and sometimes
> even after luncheon and then has to read through useless papers
> so that we have little free time together.[6]

Not only did Alexandra live with her husband and her mother-in-law; she also shared rooms with the tsar's sixteen-year-old brother, Michael, and his twelve-year old sister, Olga. Many years later, Olga said of Alexandra:

> She was absolutely wonderful to Nicky, especially in those first
> days when he was crushed by his responsibilities. Her courage
> undoubtedly saved him. No wonder Nicky always called her
> Sunny, her childhood name. She undoubtedly remained the only

sunshine in the ever-growing darkness of his life. I had tea with them often. I remember Nicky coming in tired, sometimes irritable, his mind in a maze after a day crowded with audiences. Alicky never said a wrong word or did a wrong thing. I loved to watch her tranquil movements. She never resented my being there.[7]

Alexandra's days were endless, ordered in the same manner. Bored, lonely, and out of touch, she waited in her sitting room for the few minutes that Nicholas could share with her between audiences with officials. She did not know her suite at all, since they had been appointed by the dowager empress. Her only friend was Mrs. Orchard, who had come from Darmstadt to stay with her. Alexandra was still learning Russian, and this prevented any meaningful conversation with any of the servants. French was the official language of the court; although she spoke it, Alexandra was so uncomfortable doing so that she rarely used it. No one at court spoke German in everyday use; this meant that Alexandra could converse only in English with other members of the imperial family and those few court officials who were proficient enough to stutter through a conversation. She was virtually cut off from society, but this was just one of many problems she encountered.

The chief problem was the dowager empress, Marie Feodorovna. She was more than just a difficult mother-in-law; she was spiteful, jealous, and, like her son, obstinate. She had just lost her husband; now Alexandra had taken her son away from her. Marie Feodorovna resented her daughter-in-law as a German from Hesse, even though her own mother, Queen Louise of Denmark, was a daughter of the landgrave of Hesse. It is true that the dowager empress had wished her son to marry someone other than Alexandra, a fact which certainly did nothing to endear her to her daughter-in-law. But as long as her daughter-in-law shared her house, Marie Feodorovna would exert all of her authority. And her authority was considerable.

According to the strict protocol of the Russian court, a dowager took precedence over a reigning empress. The rule was usually not put into force, as empresses tended to retire from public life upon the deaths of their husbands. But Marie Feodorovna was still youthful, filled with energy, and in no mood to disappear behind a black veil. As soon as the period of mourning was over, the dowager empress returned to her former glory, giving parties and hosting balls. At public functions she, not Alexandra, walked first, on the tsar's arm; her daughter-in-law followed on the arm of the young grand duke Michael. To Marie Feodorovna, it seemed only natural, but Alexandra resented the public snub.

One of the first conflicts between Alexandra and her mother-in-law involved the official Orthodox liturgy, said at every mass across the country. Although it was customary for the names of both the tsar and tsarina to be coupled in the liturgy, Marie Feodorovna insisted that her name should immediately follow that of her son in the prayers for the imperial family, thereby displacing that of the reigning tsarina. Alexandra was furious. To counter her mother-in-law's pettiness, the tsarina turned the matter over to the Holy Synod, the ministry of religion, for a ruling. The minister of religion duly assured the new tsarina that her name should precede that of the dowager empress, as the consort of the tsar, but both Alexandra and Marie Feodorovna remained bitter over the encounter.[8]

But it was the incident with the crown jewels which caused the biggest rift. It was the custom for a dowager to hand over certain pieces of the imperial jewels to a reigning tsarina. But Marie Feodorovna loved to cover herself in diamonds, pearls, emeralds, and sapphires. The necklaces and tiara meant too much to her to part with, even though by protocol they belonged to Alexandra. Instead, she turned over to Alexandra some hundred-year-old tiaras and earrings and necklaces which had belonged to Catherine the Great and were too uncomfortable for Marie Feodorovna to wear. Alexandra was deeply hurt. Nicholas asked his mother to hand over the main jewels, but the dowager empress refused. When she heard this, Alexandra was not only hurt but angry. She knew just how to retaliate. Saying that she no longer cared about the jewels, Alexandra told Nicholas that even if the dowager empress gave them to her, she would now refuse to wear them. The tsar passed this along to his mother, who realized that Alexandra would, by tradition, have to wear the jewels on state occasions. Sensing a scandal, Marie Feodorovna hastily sent the jewels to Alexandra. Sure enough, Alexandra soon wore them, but everyone knew what had happened. Alexandra was convinced that the humiliation had been intentional and thereafter only spoke to Marie Feodorovna of generalities, in polite but distant terms.[9]

Alexandra certainly felt that her husband was being used by his mother for her own political ambitions. There is a story which illustrates the apparent jealousy on the part of the new tsarina. In the early days of her marriage, Alexandra produced a series of caricatures, done in her idle hours. One depicted her husband sitting in a baby chair, with his mother standing over him, scolding the tsar for refusing to eat from a plate which she had handed him. Alexandra should have been more discreet. The drawing passed from hand to hand in the court, scandalizing nearly everyone and alienating Alexandra and Marie Feodorovna from the very first days of the marriage.[10]

The dowager empress later complained of her daughter-in-law, "She never tells me what she does, or what she intends to do; when we are together she speaks of everything in the world except herself. I would be happy if she would throw off this reserve for once."[11] But Marie Feodorovna also contributed to the silence. The problem was that Alexandra and Nicholas had no dining room of their own; they took meals with the dowager empress. At table, Alexandra sat between mother and son, ignored by both. Marie Feodorovna, insulted by her daughter-in-law, rarely tried to include her in the conversation. Nicholas was too weak to stand up for his wife, and so Alexandra sat in silence until the meal was over. Years later the tsar's sister Olga said: "I still believe that they had tried to understand each other and failed. They were utterly different in character, habits and outlook. . . . My mother did like gossip. Her ladies did not take kindly to Alicky from the very beginning. There was such a lot of tittle-tattle about Alicky's jealousy over my mother's precedence. . . . So poor Alicky could not have been very happy. But I never heard her complain. . . .[12]

Domestic tensions eased when, at the beginning of the new year, Alexandra and Nicholas moved to their apartments in the Winter Palace. No palace in Europe was as large or quite as brilliant. It was so large, in fact, that once an entire peasant family was found to be living in a few rooms on the top floor. The husband, who worked at the palace as a servant, had brought his entire family with him, as well as pet dogs and a cow for fresh milk. They were only discovered when the smell became unbearable.[13]

It is said that Louis XIV disliked the Palace of Germain-en-Laye because from its tall windows he could see the towers of St. Denis, the burial place of the kings of France. Like the Bourbons, the Romanovs, from the windows of the Winter Palace, saw their own eventual tomb, the Cathedral of the Fortress of Peter and Paul, across the gray expanse of the Neva River.

The imperial family did not live in the splendid halls and reception rooms, richly decorated with French furniture and Gobelin tapestries. Rather, Alexandra and Nicholas selected rooms of moderate proportions and doubtful taste. The tsar had a Gothic study, a billiard room, and a swimming bath—all decorated in heavy, dark paneling. Alexandra's drawing room, filled with potted palms and chintz fabric, was typical of the prevailing *bourgeois* tastes. In one of the many coincidences connecting her to the doomed French queen, Alexandra hung their bedroom with silk copied from the walls of Marie Antoinette's rooms at Fontainebleau Palace.[14]

Up to six thousand people worked and lived in the Winter

Palace whenever the imperial couple were in residence. Of these, almost two hundred were members of the suite—seventy-three generals and seventy-six extra aides-de-camp, fifteen members of the imperial family, seventeen princes not of imperial birth, seventeen counts, nine barons—and they were just the members of the tsar's entourage.[15]

The move to the Winter Palace officially signaled the beginning of the season in St. Petersburg. The capital was a shock to Alexandra, who was used to the quiet dignity and public reserve of both Germany and England. Russians were excessive in all respects; in the money they spent on balls, jewels, and palaces; in the practice of their religion, where the faithful sought out God in everything, including the occult and spiritualism; and in sexuality, where affairs were public and homosexuality among the young aristocrats was flaunted.

St. Petersburg did not appeal to Alexandra. She was shocked by its love affairs, the gossip, the idleness of the ladies. "Most Russian girls seem to have nothing in their heads but thoughts of officers," she complained.[16] Anna Vyrubova later wrote: "The Empress, coming from a small German court where everyone at least tried to occupy themselves usefully, found the idle and listless atmosphere of Russia little to her taste. In her first enthusiasm of power she thought to change things a little for the better. One of her early projects was a society of handiwork composed of ladies of the court and society circles, each one of whom should make with her own hands three garments a year to be given to the poor."[17]

Unfortunately, the ladies of St. Petersburg were not interested in the proposal, declaring that they had no time for such rubbish. Deeply hurt, Alexandra nonetheless felt it was her duty to remain at her husband's side throughout the long balls which they hosted at the Winter Palace.

But the imperial balls, despite their magnificence, only served to further alienate the tsarina from the affections of society. According to tradition, Alexandra and Nicholas opened a ball with the polonaise. However, far from enjoying the dance, Alexandra moved slowly from room to room on her husband's arm, walking in an almost studied and awkward fashion, her head dropping to a slight bow with each step, a smile rarely crossing her face, an unbecoming red flush spreading over her features. In the reception lines, she stood silent, never speaking more than a word or two of welcome to her guests. Occasionally, her eyes darted down the line to see how many more waited to be greeted. Her hand hung clumsily in the air, waiting to be kissed. She made no effort to hide the fact that she found the ball an ordeal. Impressions were mixed. One woman later wrote:

. . much of her beauty comes from exquisite colouring and . . . there is about her a subtle charm impossible to picture and difficult to describe. She is very tall and very slender, yet most finely proportioned. Her features are almost Greek in their regularity, and the natural expression of her face struck me at once in a singularly wistful and sweet sadness that never went quite away even when she smiled. Her hair is strikingly beautiful and luxuriant, long, heavy, glossy, and brown-gold in colour. Her eyes are large, soft, lustrous grey-blue, with long lashes.[18]

But most ladies of St. Petersburg society were left with the impression of "her timidity and the exceedingly melancholy expression of her eyes."[19] As early as her first reception, Alexandra failed to win over society. The wife of General Bogdanovich noted after meeting her: "The new Tsarina is not friendly."[20]

Alexandra was terrified of the unknown surroundings and people, fearful of the slightest mistake. After her first ball, she admitted that she would have liked nothing better than to have sunk beneath the floors. Alexandra had no opportunity to make friends, as she had to leave her guests after only a few minutes. One observer wrote: "She . . . did not seem to possess the talent of drawing people to her. She danced badly, not caring for dancing, and she certainly was not a brilliant conversationalist. . . . She had red arms, red shoulders, and a red face which always gave the impression that she was about to burst into tears. . . . Everything about her was hieratic, to the very way she was dressed in the heavy brocade of which she was so fond, and with diamonds scattered all over her, in defiance of good taste and common sense."[21]

Alexandra was in an impossible situation. She could not break protocol and chat freely with her guests, for her shyness prevented it. Instead, she said nothing, giving the impression of aloofness and pride. She rarely smiled, never laughed in public, and kept a firm distance between herself and her husband's subjects. Her Victorian morality caused Alexandra to cross off name after name from potential guest lists; anyone with the slightest scandal attached to his name was no longer welcome at imperial functions. This went for members of her husband's family as well.

Society fought back. They called Alexandra prim and dull, provincial, uninteresting, and haughty. There is a story which captures the battle between tsarina and society perfectly. At one ball, Alexandra spotted a young woman whose décolletage she considered too low. A lady-in-waiting was dispatched to the woman, saying, "Madame, Her Majesty wishes me to tell you that in Hesse-Darmstadt, we don't wear our dresses that way."

"Really?" the woman replied, at the same time pulling the front of her dress still lower. "Pray tell Her Majesty that in Russia, we *do* wear our dresses this way."[22]

Such displays undoubtedly angered Alexandra, and the insult was made even worse by the popularity of the dowager empress. At every ball, every dinner, every reception, Alexandra believed herself persecuted, whispered about behind her back, mocked, hated, and compared unfavorably to her mother-in-law. Alexandra resented not only Marie Feodorovna's charm and wit on public occasions but also the thinly veiled animosity radiating from her mother-in-law. Alexandra made almost no effort to win over the affection of society, but Marie Feodorovna also encouraged the rift by continuing to gossip about her daughter-in-law. The dowager empress had lived in Russia for seventeen years before coming to the throne; Alexandra had barely a month between the time of her arrival and her marriage. Alexandra knew better than to publicly criticize "Mother dear," and Marie Feodorovna knew nothing of her daughter-in-law's character. But the tsarina's aunt, the Empress Friedrich of Germany, wrote to Queen Victoria that "Alix is very imperious and will always insist on having her own way; she will never yield one iota of the power she will imagine she wields. . . ."[23]

There is an often-repeated story that illustrates the contrast between Alexandra and Marie Feodorovna. Once, when Alexandra was expecting a baby, she and Nicholas traveled on the imperial train south to the Crimea. Because she was not well, the tsar gave orders that there were to be no receptions along the way. In spite of this, groups of peasants gathered in their Sunday best next to the platform at a small rural station. The grand marshal of the imperial court urged Alexandra and Nicholas to go to the windows and show themselves. When she heard this suggestion, Alexandra was furious that the tsar's orders had not been followed. She did not care that the people had been standing overnight to catch a glimpse of them; they had ignored the wishes of the tsar. Nicholas went to the window despite his wife's anger, and the crowd went wild with joy.[24] But Alexandra refused to open the curtains at her sitting-room window at all. When the dowager empress heard this, she was beside herself with anger, writing: "If she were not there Nicky would be twice as popular. She is a regular German. She thinks the Imperial Family should be 'above that sort of thing.' What does she mean? Above winning the people's affection? . . . Nicky himself has all that is required for popular adoration; all he needs to do is to show himself to those who want to see him. How many times I have tried to make it plain to her. She won't understand; perhaps she hasn't it in her to understand. And yet, how often she complains of the public indifference toward her."[25]

With each party, each dinner, each reception, the gulf between tsarina and society widened. With each stumble, each mistake by Alexandra, the criticism grew louder, the gossip more bold. Hurt and insulted, Alexandra stopped entertaining. The dinners, receptions, and balls ceased, and one by one the lights in the Winter Palace went out, leaving its marble halls, and society, in darkness.

13

The New Reign

PRESIDING OVER THE EMPIRE in the first turbulent years of his reign, Nicholas experienced the growing influence of his wife. At the beginning of his reign, the tsar had given way to his mother, perhaps recognizing that the years she had served on the throne next to his father had left her with valuable insight into the political affairs of the country. Unfortunately, the dowager empress proved too dominant a force, a force which Alexandra would not tolerate.

Very early on, the tsar struck everyone as impressionable. The head of the court chancellery, Alexander Mossolov, later wrote that Nicholas had

> . . . an unshakable faith in the providential nature of his high office. His mission emanated from God, for his actions he was responsible only to his conscience and to God. In this view the Empress supported him with intense conviction. Responsible only to his conscience, his intuition, his instinct—to that incomprehensible thing which in our days is called the subconscious, and of which the notion did not exist in the Sixteenth Century when the Tsars of Muscovy forged for themselves an absolute power. Responsible to the elements that are not reason and at times are contrary to reason. Responsible to imponderables; to the mysticism that steadily increased its hold over him. . . .[1]

That the tsar believed himself selected by God is without question. But in carrying out that role, he relied not only on his own conscience but also on the people surrounding him. Alexandra quickly managed to displace nearly all of the tsar's trusted advisers in an effort not only to assist her husband in his duties but also to isolate him from those elements she considered harmful to the serenity of their happy married life.

There is one characteristic indication at the beginning of the tsar's reign of the power and influence which Alexandra would later come to wield. Ignored by society, she turned instead to the political arena and began to concentrate her energies on assisting her husband. It was an isolated incident but one which came to be widely known among St. Petersburg society, further alienating her from the public.

It was customary, on the accension of a new sovereign, for various groups of representatives to make addresses of support and loyalty to the throne. Among these groups were the local zemstvos, small bodies of provincial officials from across the country. One such group of representatives, the Tver Zemstvo, sent a congratulatory message to the tsar which included the following passage:

> We earnestly believe that during your reign the rights of individuals as well as those of already existing representative bodies, will be protected permanently and energetically.
>
> We expect, Gracious Sovereign, that these representative bodies will be allowed to voice their opinions in matters in which they are concerned, in order that the expressions of the needs and thoughts, not only of the representatives of the administration, but also of the whole Russian nation, might reach the throne.[2]

Such a declaration was a clearly aimed threat to the autocratic powers of the tsar. On 30 January 1895, Nicholas II received the members of the Tver Zemstvo—along with representatives of zemstvos nationwide—in the Winter Palace. Each group presented to the tsar a congratulatory speech and, in turn, was addressed by Nicholas. When the Tver Zemstvo delegates delivered their message, the tsar answered them with a carefully worded statement in which he chided them for their "senseless dreams of the participation of the Zemstvos' representatives in the affairs of internal administration." To make his point quite clear, he added, "I shall maintain the principle of autocracy just as firmly and unflinchingly as it was preserved by my unforgettable dead father."[3]

The tsar's speech came as a shock to nearly everyone. Many people had believed and hoped that Nicholas would reverse the trend toward reactionary conservatism that had been a hallmark of his father's reign. After the speech, Princess Catherine Radziwill happened to meet Constantine Pobedonostsev, the tsar's former tutor. Naturally, their conversation turned on the tsar's address.

"I suppose they are saying I advised the tsar to utter these ridiculous words?" Pobedonostsev remarked.

"Of course," answered Radziwill.

"Well," the man replied, "I thought that I should at least have been given credit for a certain amount of intelligence and common sense. . . ." Pobedonostsev continued:

> No one believes more firmly than I do that autocracy is the only possible government for this country, but there is an abyss between that and advising the tsar to wound public sentiment to the quick. Besides, I don't believe in doing anything that is useless. When the late Emperor succeeded his father, the country stood on the brink of disorder, anarchy and ruin. Assassination had become almost normal; Nihilism was fast gaining mastery of the situation, and our so-called Liberals would never have been able to control it. Something had to be done to show Russia and the world that we still had a sovereign endowed with a strong will and a firm hand. That was why I advised Alexander III to issue the manifesto declaring his intention to uphold autocratic government. But what was necessary in 1881 is certainly not needed in 1895. Our country is prosperous, it is at peace, Nihilism has been destroyed. What earthly reason was there suddenly to hurl a threat at the head of the entire nation? No, I have nothing to do with "senseless dreams." Even if I had drawn up a speech on these principles, I would never have expressed myself in such crude terms. My advice was to say nothing except commonplace in receiving the deputations, and the Emperor had promised to confine himself to the obvious. I was as amazed as anybody else when I heard this evening what had taken place in the Winter Palace, amazed and horrified!

"But," asked Radziwill, "who could have advised the Emperor to do such an unfortunate thing?"

"Have you not guessed? Of course it is the young Empress."

"She?" Radziwill exclaimed. "What does she know about Russia or what ought to be said to the Russian people?"

"Precisely!" Pobedonostsev replied. "She knows nothing. But she thinks she knows everything, and above all else is pursued by the idea that the Emperor does not assert himself sufficiently, that he is not given all she thinks he ought to receive. She is more autocratic than Peter the Great, and perhaps as cruel as Ivan the Terrible. Hers is a small mind that believes it harbours a great intelligence."[4]

Alexandra gradually came to believe that her ability to understand the political situation in the country surpassed that of her husband. There is a story that on one occasion Alexandra sat defending her views with Prince Peter Sviatopolk-Mirsky. The tsarina told him that the common people loved the tsar and that only the intelligentsia wanted a change in the autocratic system. "Yes," the prince replied, "that is true enough but it is the intellectual class that makes history everywhere while the masses are merely an elemental power; today, they massacre the revolutionary intellectuals, tomorrow they may loot the tsar's palaces."[5]

The turn of the century found the Russian Empire on the brink of profound industrial changes and social unrest. Most European nations had developed their technology slowly; as a result, the people had learned to adjust to it. Russia enjoyed no such breathing space. The twentieth century was abruptly thrust upon an eighteenth-century society. A backward and ignorant people was faced with twentieth-century opportunities and problems without the means to cope with them. A class that had never before existed in Russia, a working class, was suddenly created. While thousands of jobs were created, the necessary laws—limits on the workday, standard wage scales, child-labor laws, and safe conditions—did not exist. This resulted in worker unrest, and revolt quickly followed.

Most of these workers came from the countryside, peasants discontented with their rural existence and optimistic about the opportunities awaiting them in the cities. These peasants had lived lives of intense poverty in the little provincial villages and hamlets scattered across the country.

Russian peasants remained mysterious figures to most who lived in Moscow or St. Petersburg. Many, Alexandra included, chose to believe in the often-propagated myth of the contented peasant happily toiling away in an idyllic countryside. To Alexandra, these peasants represented the "true" Russia, those nameless millions who adored the tsar and would sacrifice their lives for his happiness. Her views came from experience: she had met and seen peasants on her visit to Ilinskoe, outside Moscow, in 1890. She saw their humble but clean villages, children playing with simple toys while the men and women plowed the fields, fed the animals, and celebrated religious holidays with colorful fairs. This picture was true enough for those peasants fortunate enough to be attached to a great estate like Ilinskoe or the Youssoupovs' Arkhangelskoe. But farther out in the provinces, the picture was not so pastoral.

Most peasant villages were far from clean: Dusty roads were lined with crudely built log huts, lacking windows and proper ventilation, standing every few feet along the stretch of the village. Small patches of gardens planted with vegetables surrounded these dwellings. There were rarely fenced pastures: Cows, chickens, and pigs wandered through the streets. The smell, as a result, was nearly unbearable. There was no thought as to proper sanitation: Communal water supplies were shared by both peasants and animals. Waste ditches ran from hut to hut, along the street, often ending in the water supply itself. As a result, disease was rampant. Typhoid, malaria, cholera, tuberculosis, diphtheria, dysentery, and internal parasites were all common, depleting the village population every year.

Not surprisingly, these peasants were crude, illiterate, and disgruntled. To escape the desolation of their lives, they often resorted to drink; alcoholism was the common bond among many village inhabitants. Cheap vodka flowed like water in these towns. Dispossessed, without hope, these peasants lived their short lives largely ignored by the bureaucratic system of provincial authorities. And the system was so antiquated, so complex, and so filled with holes that it often created victims of those it was designed to help. Even in the larger rural cities, oversight resulted in tragedy. In 1901, for example, newspapers reported the death of a young teacher in the province of Novgorod. She had died of starvation when local authorities forgot to pay her salary for two months.[6]

In Russia, the imperial family, the nobility, the military, and the church owned nearly everything. What remained to be divided up was scarce. The workers who left the countryside to earn a living in St. Petersburg or Moscow had nothing. They lived for the most part in wooden barracks owned by the factory, which extracted up to half of their monthly wage as payment for room and board. After working twelve-, fifteen-, or eighteen-hour shifts each day, the workers returned to their barracks—to rooms with no windows, no sanitation, and floors that were covered with water and crawling with cockroaches and spiders. One 1903 report told how "the workers, all greasy, in soot covered rags with a thick layer of grime and dust, swarm like bees in the extremely dirty and congested quarters. A repulsive smell hits you as soon as you try to approach. . . ."[7]

As bad as factory conditions were, the workers who found employment there were more fortunate than the thousands who came to the cities in search of a better life and instead found poverty and starvation. The worst center of the dispossessed, the most notorious slum in all of Russia, was the Khitrovka District in Moscow.

Khitrovka sprawled on the banks of the Yauza River near the Kremlin. The smell was repulsive: A mix of stale beer, urine, vomit, and feces flowed through the streets. Drunken men lay on the street corners, prostitutes prowled the market, and child beggars pleaded for alms. Nearly every other building was a whorehouse or a tavern. Like a magnet, Khitrovka drew together the worst elements in the city: alcoholics, whores, beggars, theives, murderers. The streets teemed with crime: Police were so fearful of their own safety that they would not venture into the district after nightfall.

In these surroundings, screams and cries for help went unnoticed. People were killed in broad daylight in front of witnesses; every morning, the police gathered up the corpses—men stripped of their clothing by thieves; prostitutes beaten, raped, and killed; children dead from starvation.

The people of Khitrovka survived largely on crime. Young girls were sold by desperate mothers at the open marketplace for as little as fifty rubles; drunken ten-year-old prostitutes plied their trade, and babies were rented to beggars to arouse sympathy. Infants often died from such abuse, but enterprising mothers continued to make capital: Dead infants were sources of income to beggars. Children were deliberately starved to make their pitiful cries of hunger all the more realistic. If they survived, these children often went on to become whores or thieves themselves.[8]

Although Khitrovka was the most dramatic example of the squalor which engulfed many of those living in Moscow or St. Petersburg, its conditions, in lesser form, were repeated in many towns and led in turn to the unrest which tore the country apart. Workers' strikes were quickly and brutally put down by the army, but dissent continued. Students in both Moscow and St. Petersburg took up the political banner on behalf of the workers. To their demands for the workers, they added one of their own: a Constitution and an elected assembly. Political violence erupted. The minister of the interior, Dimitri Sipiagin, was shot by a revolutionary; a year later, the provincial governor of Ufa was assassinated. Growing rebellion promised to turn the country upside down.

The turn of the century also brought with it more violence directed toward Russian Jews. Persecution of the Jews was one of the hallmarks of imperial Russia. Since Catherine the Great had established the infamous Pale of Settlement, most Jews had lived in southwestern Russia. By the end of the nineteenth century, however, many had moved to the larger cities; they were allowed into universities and the lower orders of the civil service. Still, most faced seemingly insurmountable prejudice. Most Orthodox Russians regarded them as Christ killers; when one of his ministers suggested to Alexander III that some of the legal barriers facing Jews be removed, the tsar replied, "We must never forget that it was the Jews who crucified our Lord and spilled His precious blood."[9] This kind of attitude produced the horrible pogroms which swept the country during the reigns of both Alexander III and Nicholas II, the most infamous of which occurred in the Bessarabian capital of Kishinev in 1903. The Kishinev pogrom, if not officially sanctioned by the Russian government, was allowed to occur with the complicity of numerous high ranking officials, perhaps even the minister of the interior himself.

Vladimir Ulyanov was familiar with the harsh realities of political violence. In 1887, his elder brother, Alexander, was caught trying to plant a crude bomb with which he hoped to kill Alexander III. The attempt failed, and Alexander was hanged. Although he confessed the crime to his brother and warned him against becoming involved, his death had a profound effect on the boy, who grew up to be known as Lenin.

Lenin grew up in a pleasant provincial town on the Volga River. He was not of peasant stock. His father, Ilya, was a director of schools for the province and later became an actual councilor of state, a lesser rank of hereditary nobility.[10] After his brother's death, Vladimir entered Kazan University as a law student and was quickly expelled for participating in demonstrations. He began to study Marx and found that socialism could be a viable form of government, according to the author of *Das Kapital*, if only its structure were properly organized. This Vladimir decided to do, and his goal became the overthrow of the tsarist regime, to be replaced with a Communist state. He went to St. Petersburg, where he began to spread his gospel. But the police caught him, and he was sentenced to Siberian exile.

Contrary to popular conception, Siberian exile, at least for Lenin, was not unpleasant. The worst result was that he had to move to the village of Shushenskoe, near Mongolia. Other than the remoteness, life was comfortable. A Siberian exile could move about freely, live anywhere in the prescribed village, have his own money, and do whatever he pleased with his time. Lenin took a thousand rubles with him into exile; his early days were spent reading and duck hunting.[11] Joining him soon after his arrival was a heavy, unpleasant woman by the name of Nadezhda Krupskaya, whom Lenin had known in St. Petersburg. Political convictions rather than love brought them together, and in 1898 they married. No romantic illusions for these two: Lenin and his new wife spent their honeymoon translating *The Theory and Practice of Trade Unionism* by Sidney and Beatrice Webb.[12]

In time, the pair moved to Western Europe, where Lenin tried to organize groups of fellow socialists dedicated to the overthrow of the Russian monarchy. He disliked the acknowledged leader in exile of the Russian revolutionary movement, George Plekhanov, finding him too moderate. In 1903, the Social Democratic party, exiled Russian monarchists, held a conference to discuss unity. Lenin had risen to the very pinnacle of the party, dividing his followers from those of Plekhanov, who found him too abrasive and authoritarian. The conference was called to resolve the party differences. Instead, the group broke in half. The vote eventually came down to a power struggle between Plekhanov and Lenin. With the votes cast, Lenin won a narrow majority. Promptly, Lenin renamed his party with a name symbolic of their majority—the Bolsheviks.[13]

14

The Crown of Blood

A VISITOR TO MOSCOW in May 1896 was met with a dazzling sight: freshly painted and whitewashed buildings capped with
multicolored tile roofs and hung with white, blue, and red Russian Tricolor flags and bunting, strings of electric lights, and evergreen boughs;
Turks in black fezzes, Persians with white turbans and gowns; hussars
in gold-and-white cloaks and plumed caps, and cossacks in long red
coats with black hats and shining sabers; wide avenues lined with elegant, colonnaded mansions, decorated with flags, bunting, and baskets
of spring flowers pouring their aromas into the sky; and, emblazoned
on every doorway, over every window, and atop steeply pitched roofs,
the initials *H* and *A* for Nicholas and Alexandra in the Cyrillic alpha-
bet.[1] The city eagerly awaited the coronation of Tsar Nicholas II.

St. Petersburg was supreme over Moscow in all things but one: religion. For over seven hundred years, Moscow had been the citadel of
Russian Orthodoxy, the city of "forty times forty" churches, the "Third
Rome," dominated by tall onion domes, glistening gold, blue, and
white, and capped with a forest of crosses gathering up the prayers of
the faithful and sending them toward heaven. A coronation was not
merely the crowning of a sovereign; it was the physical and spiritual an-
nointing, at the hands of metropolitans and bishops, of God's representative on earth. Its traditions dated back hundreds of years, and each
coronation not only relied on these but also renewed them as living witnesses to the power of Orthodoxy. As such, a coronation was a supreme
celebration of the Russian church, with all of its pomp, power, and
majesty vested in the person of the tsar.

Tradition ruled every aspect of the ceremony. Alexandra and
Nicholas were not even allowed to enter Moscow until the day before
the actual ceremony. They stayed at the Petrovsky Palace on the edge of
the city, praying and fasting in preparation for the ceremony, while
pages in medieval uniform read out the proclamation of the tsar "to the
good people of Our Former Capital" that the date for the coronation

had been fixed for 26 May 1896. It had been thirteen years since the coronation of Tsar Alexander III, and thousands of foreign guests as well as Russians from all parts of the empire jammed into the city. They staked out claims on seats in special wooden stands built along the processional route, in windows, and doorways, or on balconies and rooftops of buildings lining the streets. Enterprising owners rented out windows and balconies overlooking the processional route for as much as five hundred rubles.[2] Every day, bells pealed from the spires of Moscow's churches, choirs sang "God Save the Tsar," cannons boomed, and cossacks galloped through the gaily decorated avenues.[3]

On 25 May, the imperial family entered Moscow in a magnificent state parade. Hundreds of thousands of people waited for the smallest glimpse, the merest smile, from the gentlemen in uniform and ladies in carriages as they passed through the streets. Also watching, for the slightest suspicious movements, were hundreds of security men, guarding against the revolutionaries. One observer later recalled:

> From time to time a superior officer was seen on horseback, passing from one place to another, and saying, as the occasion demanded, a word or two to another officer on duty. Then again, a member of the high clergy appeared, and, robed in cloth of gold, entered the chapel, from the steps of which he was to greet the two sovereigns. Or again, a Cossack of the escort in his red uniform went to and fro, looking for somebody who was not to be found, or a court official with a cocked hat decked with white plumes, and in his hand a stick surmounted by a knot of pale blue ribbon, disposed the various deputations massed at the entrance of the chapel, or gave a direction to the choristers standing in their long tunics of raspberry red, braided with gold. It was a never ending pleasure to look upon this varied sight, so quaint and so unlike anything one had ever seen before; and when at length the first gun was fired announcing that the cortege had left the Petrovsky Palace outside the town . . . expectation became so intense that it was almost painful.[4]

The sun was brilliant, passing its bright rays over all in a blanket of glitter; from the helmets and cuirasses of gold worn by the Imperial Guard Cavalry to the long red coats and black hats of the Cossack Guards; the gold-braided uniforms of Moscow's nobility; the polished wood of the instruments carried by the court orchestra; the silver trumpets of the imperial hunt; and the red velvet knee breeches and white silk stockings of the imperial footmen.[5]

Atop a white horse, like a conquering hero, rode the tsar, in military uniform, his right hand frozen in salute. The imperial family followed in ascending order of rank: princes and princesses of the royal blood; serene and royal highnesses and grand dukes and duchesses. Alexandra rode in a gilded state carriage, with side panels painted by Watteau and lined with velvet brocaded with *point d'espagne* lace in gold. It was drawn by eight white horses in harnesses of red Moroccan leather with white stitching. The saddles of the outriders, of the same material, had stirrups of chased and gilded bronze, and the saddle blankets were of gold lace with the imperial arms embroidered on them. Each horse had a plume of white ostrich feathers.[6] The ride was none too pleasant, as the carriages were uncomfortable, terribly stuffy, and without springs, so that every bump caused Alexandra to jolt. In the best of circumstances the ride was unenviable; in the armor, as the family called their court regalia, it was a nightmare.[7] Alexandra, dressed that day in a long white gown sewn with jewels which made it even heavier, suffered through the unbearable miles of the route as the sun beat down mercilessly. Eventually, her carriage reached the sixty-five-foot-high, fifteen-foot-thick red-brick walls of the Kremlin and disappeared through the Spassky Gate.

Following a special *Te Deum*, the imperial family retired to the Grand Kremlin Palace to rest. Alexandra entered the Kremlin not as a minor German princess, as she had on her visit to Ella in 1890, or as a Russian grand duchess for the funeral of a dead monarch, but as a mighty empress. Within these walls, the strange and tragic history of the Romanovs had been played out along with the triumphs of Peter the Great and Catherine the Great. When she went to bed that night, it was with the knowledge that on the following morning, and in the footsteps of three hundred years of Romanovs, she, along with her husband, would be consecrated, crowned, and revered as God's chosen to rule Russia.

She awoke on 26 May 1896 to a sunlit morning. The golden rays streamed in through the tall, arched windows of her bedroom, shining upon the blue silk-lined walls and crystals dangling from the chandeliers. After completing her toilette, Alexandra began to robe herself in her coronation gown.

She wore a Russian court dress of silver brocade over silver tissue, with a wide skirt which opened at the front to reveal the inner dress. The tight bodice and short sleeves were heavily ornamented, sewn with seed pearls and mirror jewels and silver thread. A fifteen-foot train, also sewn with jewels and rich embroidery, fell from her waist.[8] Her hair was done in twin side curls, and around her neck she wore a single strand of pink pearls. Across her breast was the red ribbon of the Order

of St. Catherine, held in place by a diamond-studded star.[9] The coronation involved a ceremonial robing and crowning of the tsarina, and the
mantle and the crown had been brought from the armory to the private
apartments so that Alexandra and Nicholas could practice before the
actual event. Nicholas wrapped the robe around her shoulders, and
Alexandra practiced fastening the clasps. To rehearse the moment of
crowning, she knelt in front of her husband. As Nicholas placed the
crown atop her head, a hairdresser stepped forward and inserted a diamond hairpin to hold the crown in place. The pin went in too far, and
Alexandra cried out in pain.[10]

   Out French doors, preceded by priests in golden vestments and
miters with huge diamonds, members of the imperial family, the diplomatic corps, and the dowager empress, Alexandra and Nicholas
walked, stepping into the bright sunshine. Slowly, arm in arm, they
walked down the famous Red Stairway, the scene of so much turbulent
Romanov history; here Peter the Great had seen many of his family
thrown onto the pikes of the palace guard below during a revolt, and
Alexander I had marched to celebrate Russia's triumph over the French
army in 1812. Grandstands filled with the invited lined all sides of the
cobbled square below, and a long red ribbon of velvet carpet stretched
from the Palace of Facets to the doors of the Cathedral of the Assumption, where the service would take place. At the bottom of the staircase,
Alexandra and Nicholas stepped under an enormous canopy of gold
cloth with yellow, white, and black ostrich feathers gathered at the corners and at the top and held aloft by sixteen generals.[11] In measured
steps, Alexandra and Nicholas walked between a guard of honor composed of the imperial cavalry, resplendent in red, white, and gold uniforms with silver helmets topped with the Romanov double-headed
eagle, following the crimson carpet to the door of the cathedral. At the
door, priests annointed them with holy oil before Alexandra and
Nicholas stepped into the dim interior.
   The Cathedral of the Assumption was not as large as St. Isaac's or
Kazan Cathedral; only two thousand people could stand within its
walls. Five hundred years old, the church was entirely decorated with
frescoes and icons studded with diamonds and gold, which, in the light
of thousands of votive candles, flashed and sparkled. Five golden
domes rose from the painted ceiling, allowing shafts of light to penetrate the stone walls. A choir, robed in silver and blue, sang old Russian
hymns. At the front of the cathedral, beneath a heavy purple canopy,
was the dais, covered in crimson carpet. The crowns, scepter, orb, and
mantles all rested on golden pillows before the *iconostasis*. The two
coronation chairs sat on smaller steps. Nicholas sat on the seventeenth-

century diamond throne of Tsar Alexei I, encrusted with 870 diamonds. Alexandra sat beside him on the solid-ivory throne of Ivan the Great.[12]

The ceremony lasted five hours. After a long mass, the tsar stood on the dais and recited the Nicene Creed in a loud voice. The tsar was then invested with the regalia: the orb, the scepter, and the chain of the Order of St. Andrew. Nicholas knelt before the metropolitan and recited the words of the coronation oath, beginning with "God of Our Fathers and Lord of Mercy, You have chosen Me to be Tsar and Judge over Your People." As he rose, the choir burst into the hymn *Thee, O Lord, We Praise*.[13]

Annointed with holy oil, the tsar was finally proclaimed "Nicholas II, the Rightful and Only Emperor and Autocrat of all the Russias." For the only time in his life, the tsar entered the sanctuary to celebrate the mass as a priest of the Orthodox church. As he walked up the steps to the *iconostasis*, the chain of the Order of St. Andrew slipped from Nicholas's shoulders and crashed to the carpet with a thud. Only a few people had seen the incident, and they were later sworn to secrecy to avoid superstitious talk.[14]

By tradition, a tsar crowned himself, thereby attesting that his power came not from man or the church but from God himself. Nicholas had wished to use the eight-hundred-year-old cap of Monamakh, weighing two pounds. But the tradition of the ceremony made this impossible, and the tsar was forced to crown himself with the imperial state crown, weighing nine pounds.[15] Made for Catherine the Great, the crown was shaped like a miter and topped with a cross of diamonds and an uncut ruby; around the arches were set forty-four inch-wide diamonds surrounded by smaller diamonds and thirty-eight pink pearls.[16] First, Nicholas placed it atop his own head, then removed it and touched the tip to Alexandra's forehead, thus signifying that her power as tsarina came from neither God nor the church but from the graces of the tsar himself.[17] Once the crown had been replaced atop his own head, Nicholas carefully set a second, smaller crown of two thousand diamonds in gold atop Alexandra's curled locks.[18] One observer called her "by far the most beautiful" woman present. "As she stepped upon the dais, the color in her cheeks was high and her eyes were filled with that shyness or melancholy which her pictures have made familiar. . . . She looked more like Iphigenia going to the sacrifice than the queen of the most powerful empire in the world. . . ."[19] Robed now in their brocaded mantles of cloth-of-gold edged with ermine, Alexandra and Nicholas walked to their thrones, where they sat on chairs of ivory and diamonds to receive their homage as the mightiest couple in the world, crowned with the most magnificent jewels, surrounded by endless yards of their imperial robes gathered on the steps of the dais, in a cathedral packed with thousands who swore allegiance to them—Nicholas Romanov and the former Princess Alix of Hesse and By Rhine—the last tsar and tsarina of all the Russias.

They walked out of the cathedral into the bright afternoon sunshine, across the cobbled square, up the Red Stairway, and onto a balcony. Turning to the crowd, they bowed three times. Thousands of voices shouted cheers and the bells of the Kremlin churches pealed, announcing that a new tsar had been crowned.

Seven thousand guests attended the coronation banquet that night. In addition to the grand dukes, princes, and ambassadors, one room in the palace was specially reserved for simple Russians. They were there by hereditary birthright, all being descended from persons who had at one time saved the life of a Russian sovereign.[20] This very fact attested to the terrible uncertainty surrounding the life of a Russian tsar. On the tables stood illuminated parchments, rolled and tied with silk cords. Inside was the menu: borscht, pepper pot soup, turnovers filled with meat, steamed fish, spring lamb, pheasants in cream sauce, salad, asparagus, sweet fruits in wine, and ice creams.[21]

Alexandra and Nicholas dined alone, under a golden baldachin draped with cloth-of-gold and surrounded by carved and gilded cherubs, in the Throne Room of the Palace of Facets. Foreign guests watched from a tiny window set high up in the frescoed wall; only Russians could take part in the actual ceremony. But all through the meal, princes and ambassadors bowed before the dais and drank a toast to the health of the newly crowned sovereigns.[22]

The coronation ball followed. It took place in the enormous Hall of the Order of St. George in the Grand Kremlin Palace, with its dazzling white-and-gold walls, inlaid parquet floors, crimson draperies, and six newly electrified chandeliers blazing with over five hundred bulbs each. Music filled the hall as the guests waltzed past the enthroned tsar and tsarina. Alexandra wore her coronation gown, covered in splendid jewels. Atop her head she wore a diadem of pearls and diamonds made especially for the event by jeweler Kurt Hahn, with matching earrings, collar, and necklace. The diamond chain of the Order of St. Andrew was draped about her shoulders, and the red ribbon of the Order of St. Catherine stretched across the bodice of her dress, nearly hidden beneath the bow brooches and order stars and insignia. Around her waist, Alexandra wore a thick band of thousands of diamonds, which flashed fire with every breath.

At ten in the evening Alexandra and Nicholas stepped out onto the balcony of the Grand Kremlin Palace, overlooking the Moscow

River, as hundreds of guests pressed against the windows of the galleries and halls inside. A boom, then the sky exploded with brilliant oranges, reds, and greens. In the light of the fireworks, Alexandra was handed a large bouquet of roses on a silver tray; when she picked up the flowers, she set off a hidden switch which sent a signal to the Moscow Power Station. At once, thousands of tiny electric lights all across the city—lining streets, surrounding windows and doorways, creeping across rooftops and the onion domes of churches, sparkling in the spring foliage of the trees—flickered on.[23] Long after the imperial ball ended and Alexandra and Nicholas had gone to bed, the city continued to glow as Moscow sparkled with the coronation celebrations.

Four days later, a gigantic coronation feast for the common people was planned in a field outside Moscow. Known as Khodynka Meadow, the field was a military exercise ground crossed by a number of trenches, pits, ravines, and abandoned wells.[24] The choice was, like all aspects of the coronation, a matter of tradition: Alexander III's coronation feast had taken place here; in any case, it was the only place in the vicinity which could hold the expected masses.

While crowds were gathering at Khodynka, the tsar and tsarina attended a gala performance of Michael Glinka's *Life for the Tsar* at the Bolshoi Theatre. The theater had been refurbished at a cost of some 50,000 rubles; the imperial box, enlarged to seat sixty-three guests.[25] The tsar, tsarina, and their guests settled back in their comfortable armchairs to enjoy the spectacle of this most patriotic of all Russian operas.

At Khodynka cartloads of enamel mugs, stamped with the imperial seal, waited, along with free beer, at one end of the field, to be given away in celebration. On the night before the feast, people began to crowd onto the field; a wooden rail was all that separated them from the carts of mugs and beer at the end of the meadow. When dawn came, nearly half a million people could be seen. Most were peasants, their eyes glued to the spot where the gifts waited. Only sixty men had been detailed to guard the crowd; with apprehension, their commander watched the crowd grow as the night progressed. Finally, at dawn, he sent for reinforcements, hoping that they would arrive before the ten o'clock distribution time.[26] What happened next is not known, but in all probability a rumor went through the crowd that there were fewer carts of gifts than were expected. At once, the crowd of 500,000 surged forward. Those at the front stumbled and fell into the ditches and pits; at the rear, unaware of this, people pushed harder and harder. There was simply no stopping them. Down they went—into wells, holes, and trenches: mothers clutching children, husbands holding wives; faces, arms, legs, ground and trampled into the dirt, feet scurrying over their backs, screams and moans rising from the field. It was all over in fifteen minutes.[27]

In the early-morning light, the meadow looked like a battlefield. Bodies—faces turned black or blue and clothing covered in blood—lay everywhere.[28] The screaming, crying, and angry shouts continued for hours. The official count set the number of dead at 1,429; thousands more were seriously wounded.[29] The cartloads of mugs and beer stood untouched next to the pavilions where the feast was to have taken place.

Later that morning, Alexandra and Nicholas arrived at the field. The Russian Tricolor of white, blue, and red fluttered over the pavilions in the light summer breeze as the beautiful melodies sung by the Moscow Conservatory floated over the remaining crowd. But no matter how bright the sun, how beautiful the songs, there was no masking the atmosphere of horror which hung over the proceedings.

Alexandra and Nicholas were shaken. They spent the afternoon visiting the city hospitals, going from ward to ward, comforting the wounded. Both declared that they could not possibly attend the ball being given that night in their honor by the French ambassador. This upset a good many people. Thousands had been spent by the French government to ship silver plate and tapestries from Versailles and over 100,000 roses from the south of France, all for the occasion.[30] The tsar's four uncles, Vladimir, Alexei, Serge, and Paul, all insisted that it was diplomatically necessary for the couple to attend to avoid an incident. Nicholas considered this and decided that they would attend. They arrived noticeably upset; Alexandra's eyes were red and swollen from crying.[31] Together Alexandra and Nicholas led the first dance, exchanging pleasantries with the diplomatic corps and drinking champagne. One observer called it "the saddest ball ever given."[32] Serge Witte, the minister of finance, attended the ball and confronted Grand Duke Serge Alexandrovich, governor-general of Moscow, voicing the opinion that the festivities should have been canceled. However, according to Witte, Serge informed him that the "Tsar did not agree with this view" and that Nicholas felt nothing should "darken the coronation holiday."[33] Others at the ball made their feelings known to all. Grand Dukes Alexander, George, Nicholas, and Michael Michailovich attended the ball but left en masse when the dancing began. Grand Duke Alexei Alexandrovich watched them leave and muttered with disgust, "There go the four Imperial followers of Robespierre."[34] Arriving back at the Kremlin, Alexandra dropped into a chair and sobbed uncontrollably.[35]

Khodynka was an avoidable tragedy. At Alexander III's coronation feast, thirty-two persons had been crushed to death at Khodynka

Meadow. But the organizers of the 1896 festivities ignored the difficulties and past warnings. Blame fell on both Count Vorontsov-Dashkov, the minister of the imperial court, and Grand Duke Serge, governor-general of Moscow. Vorontsov-Dashkov, in charge of the coronation festivities, tendered his resignation from the imperial court, and the tsar accepted it. But the grand duke, who had been responsible for security arrangements and was more obviously at fault, was saved through the intervention of Alexandra, his sister-in-law, a political involvement on her part which did little to endear her to the public.

The tsar and tsarina tried to make amends by paying 1,000 rubles to the family of each victim out of their own fortunes. But it was a gesture which came too late. Unaware of the tsar's and tsarina's true feelings, Moscow was stunned. The tragedy of Khodynka was soon eclipsed by tales of the insensitive tsar and tsarina dancing and drinking while hundreds of their subjects suffered and died. The superstitious took it as an ill omen for the new reign. And while the tsar was blamed for his lack of judgment, Alexandra came to be despised as heartless. To the common people she soon became known as *Nemka*—the German bitch.

15

The Imperial Progress

O<small>N</small> 27 A<small>UGUST</small> 1896 there was a great flurry of activity at the Vienna train station. Flags and bunting fluttered in the warm wind, while the sun beat down on an orchestra playing military marches. Nervous soldiers in tall, white-plumed hats marched up and down the siding impatiently, and plainclothes police scurried about, shouting orders to everyone to stay away. Slowly, with steam billowing from its engine, the imperial train bearing the tsar and tsarina of all the Russias pulled up at the station platform as the band intoned the national anthem and children sang "God Save the Tsar."

The journey to Austria was the first of the imperial progresses which Alexandra and Nicholas, as newly crowned sovereigns, made to their fellow European monarchs. For the visit to Emperor Franz Joseph, the beautiful and sad Empress Elizabeth had come specially to meet Alix and Nicholas. Franz Joseph and Elizabeth were perhaps the most tragic of all European monarchs. They had lost their only son, Crown Prince Rudolf, when he shot both himself and his mistress at the Hapsburg hunting lodge of Mayerling; Franz Joseph's brother Maximilian had been crowned emperor of Mexico, then deposed and subsequently executed at the hands of revolutionaries; Elizabeth's sister Sophie had been engaged to a favorite cousin, King Ludwig II of Bavaria, who went mad and drowned himself in the waters of an Alpine lake; and Sophie was later to die in a charity bazaar fire in Paris. These tragedies deeply affected Elizabeth, and she retreated from the world, draping herself in black and closing out both her husband and society. She refused to participate in the dazzling Hapsburg court. It was therefore a great honor when Elizabeth declared she would abandon her retirement to meet the new Russian sovereigns.

The Austrian stay was short, only two days, but it marked Alexandra's first state visit as empress of Russia. The only inconvenience was caused by Franz Joseph's refusal to alter his daily schedule. The emperor regularly rose at four in the morning and retired at seven, so that dinner, as a consequence, was always served at the unfashionable hour

of five in the afternoon. Franz Joseph refused to deviate from this, and the great state banquet at the Hofburg in honor of the tsar and tsarina took place according to the emperor of Austria's peculiar dining schedule.[1] Empress Elizabeth appeared in a plain black gown, her seemingly eternal beauty all but upstaging her younger guest. The two empresses sat side by side at a table decked with hundreds of gray edelweiss. Although it was a charming display, court gossip had it that two men had died picking the Alpine flowers from the mountain peaks to decorate the banquet table for the Russian sovereigns.[2]

From Vienna the tsar and tsarina traveled to Breslau to attend the German summer army maneuvers with the kaiser. Cousin Willy, especially, was delighted to receive the new Russian sovereigns, since he himself felt that he had had a hand in the match. He also brought his wife, Dona, the kaiserin, whom the tsar thought ugly and Bismarck once called "the cow from Holstein."[3] Alexandra's sister Irene and her husband Heinrich were also at Breslau, however, and the family reunion must have helped sweeten the days with the dreaded kaiser. At one reception, Alexandra met Princess Daisy of Pless, who wrote, "The tsarina looks very healthy and has a most charming and clever face with deep blue eyes and low, straight eyebrows; her head is small and her hair brushed up from her forehead, only a few curls in the temples, and just twisted up in back; she has loads of lovely diamonds and great big sapphires."[4] Before they left Breslau, an event occurred which many took as an ill omen. While the imperial train was sitting at a siding waiting to leave, Prince I. Lobanov, the minister of foreign affairs, collapsed and died. After Germany and a short family holiday in Denmark, the tsar and tsarina boarded their new yacht, the *Standart*, and sailed to Scotland for the highlight of the trip, a stay with Queen Victoria at Balmoral Castle.

In pouring rain, the *Standart* anchored at Leith. The Prince of Wales, Uncle Bertie, met Alexandra and Nicholas to escort them on their railway journey to Ballatar. On a station siding, when they arrived, stood the duke and duchess of York, George and May; the duke of Cambridge; and a guard of honor of the Black Watch, in regimental kilts. The drive to the castle through the wet night took almost an hour, so that by the time they arrived, Alexandra and Nicholas were almost frozen. Scots Greys, Balmoral Highlanders, and the men of the Crathie and Ballatar Volunteers walked beside the carriage, holding huge torches which spewed their fiery ashes into the dark sky. On the hills along the way huge bonfires blazed, and the queen's pipers blew out music which filled the valley.[5] As they approached the castle, Alexandra and Nicholas could see the queen standing under the porte cochere, silhouetted against the glow of the lights blazing inside the house.

Balmoral, although a relatively large house, did not possess the rooms to house the Russian suite, who found themselves in newly constructed round huts of stone, resembling grain storehouses. Still, those who found lodging on the estate were more fortunate than those who ended up in farmhouses and inns some distance away, unable to understand the language of their Scottish hosts and themselves not being understood.

Victoria was overjoyed with the reunion and spent her days chatting with Alexandra about her life in Russia. Nicholas, on the other hand, found himself entrapped by Uncle Bertie, who deemed it necessary to go shooting every day. The weather for most of the visit was awful, with wind and rain and even sleet. Day after day, as his wife sat comfortably inside the warm castle, the tsar traipsed over the rough hills in search of a stag. Nicholas was even more upset by the fact that, despite his best efforts, he could not seem to shoot anything.[6] Uncle Bertie liked to talk politics and favored an Anglo-Russian alliance which he hoped to influence through the close family ties between the Saxe-Coburg-Gothas and the Romanovs.

It was during the Balmoral visit that Alexandra and Nicholas joined in the celebrations for the seventy-seven-year-old queen who, one day in September, had become the longest-reigning British monarch. Family parties gave way to the famous Ghillies' Ball, held for the servants and staff at Balmoral in the castle ballroom and attended by the entire royal family. Alexandra, having grown up around Queen Victoria, was accustomed to these somewhat peculiar affairs. She joined in the Scottish reels, decked in the royal family's Balmoral tartan and wearing gorgeous jewels which, the queen noted, were "all her own property."[7] To Nicholas, on the other hand, dancing with the wives of gamekeepers must have seemed a bit awkward, but he did so, even sporting a kilt for the occasion as he and his wife twirled on the ballroom floor to the accompaniment of pipers. One day, Alexandra and Nicholas marched up and down the terrace with the queen for the benefit of a moving-picture camera.[8] The days at the castle passed all too quickly for Alexandra, who was reliving the happy days of her childhood summers in the Highlands. "It has been such a very short stay and I leave dear, kind Grandmama with a heavy heart," she wrote.[9]

Alexandra aroused much interest from the British press, particularly where her fashion sense was concerned. The *Graphic* reported:

> Charming and graceful as the Russian Empress is, it is hoped that she is not going to set the fashion for us. . . . She alighted from one sea voyage in a pale blue dress, fawn mantle trimmed with white ostrich feather collar and a bonnet of white and blue. Another long railway voyage was set forth upon in a light pink silk gown

and a delicate heliotrope mantle and white bonnet. Going on the same journey, the Duchess of Connaught wore "a real English costume"—a dark brown tweed tailor-made dress and coat.[10]

From Scotland the tsar and tsarina traveled to France, Russia's only European ally, for a full state visit. The French were so concerned about cementing the bonds of a Franco-Russian alliance that they went to great lengths to assure a favorable impression. Specially designed artificial chestnut blooms were wired to thousands of trees lining the route which the tsar would take through Paris, and more than 900,000 visitors alone poured into the capital to see the Russian sovereigns.[11] Alexandra had, surprisingly, never been to Paris and was eager to visit.

The tsar and tsarina arrived by train at Passy Station, to the sound of "God Save the Tsar" and the "Marseillaise." They rode into Paris in an open carriage, between lines of soldiers stationed at intervals every few yards. Security was tight, for on the last visit of a Russian tsar, Alexander II, an anarchist had tried to assassinate him. One million people waited along the route for a view of the carriage as it drove to the Elysée Palace, where Alexandra and Nicholas met the French president, Felix Faure. That night, there was a glittering state banquet in honor of the visiting sovereigns.

On the first morning of the visit, Alexandra and Nicholas toured the magnificent Paris Opera House. The following day, they visited Notre Dame, the Panthéon, and Invalides, to gaze upon Napoleon's tomb. That afternoon, they helped lay the cornerstone of the Pont Alexandre III across the Seine, being constructed in memory of the tsar's father. On the third day, they were rushed through the wonders of the Louvre.

On the fourth day, with the trees just beginning to explode with rust and gold, Alexandra and Nicholas drove to the Palace of Versailles. They wandered through the empty marble rooms where the sun king had once lived; since the Franco-Prussian War, the rooms had been empty of their gilded furniture and paintings, as if they had been abandoned. As night fell and the shadows lengthened over the formal gardens, the famous Versailles fountains suddenly burst into life, splashing forth their colors at the special request of the Russians. Once night had fallen and the rooms of the palace glowed with light, Sarah Bernhardt began a poetry reading in honor of the Russian sovereigns. When the evening's entertainment had come to an end, Alexandra retired to the rooms that had been set aside for her use. In these richly decorated chambers, preserved as they had been when Marie Antoinette used them, Alexandra went to sleep—beneath the damask canopy of the doomed queen's bed.[12]

16

An Enchanted Fairyland

Fifteen miles south of St. Petersburg, behind high iron gates, gilded and capped with double-headed eagles, lay eight hundred acres of paradise known as Tsarskoe Selo, the tsar's village. Tsarskoe Selo was an oasis on the edge of swamps and forests unfit for habitation, an artificial setting carefully created and nurtured for nearly two centuries by a succession of Russian rulers. Because it was so close to the capital, it made an ideal summer residence for the imperial family. Alexandra and Nicholas loved its feeling of seclusion and peace and selected the Alexander Palace there as a first home. After the 1905 revolution, they rarely lived anywhere else.

Tsarskoe Selo was the first town in the empire to receive a railway link to the nearby capital; from the tsar's private station, with its tall, peaked roofs, the main boulevard sliced through the village, lined on each side with large mansions belonging to the great Russian families at court. A gilded fence and Egyptian-style gates marked the main entrance to the imperial park. On the other side of that fence, hand-smoothed walks wound over and around the lush green lawns, past bridges, fountains, and obelisks. Gleaming white pavilions crowned artificial mounds; fragrant gardens planted with roses and lilacs alternated with elaborate parterres in golden box and topiary. A Chinese village for aides-de-camp, with brightly painted and gilded dragons perched menacingly on the rooftops, sat across a lake from a small granite pyramid which served as a tomb for the favorite dogs of Catherine the Great. An artificial lake, which could be emptied and filled like a bathtub, was dotted with baroque and Turkish follies. In the middle of these peaceful acres of carefully manicured lawns and gardens stood two palaces, some five hundred yards apart: the magnificent two hundred-room Catherine Palace, gleaming white, blue, and gold, and the yellow-and-white Alexander Palace.

Alexandra had first visited the Alexander Palace in 1889, when Nicholas gave a special dance there in her honor. Perhaps it was for this reason that out of all the country palaces which were at her disposal, she selected the Alexander Palace as her home. It was among the smaller of the suburban palaces, with only a hundred rooms. The Italian architect Giacommo Quarenghi had designed a two-story, Palladian neoclassic structure. Long wings stretched out from a domed, semicircular portrait gallery on the northern side, joining at the front of the courtyard in a huge colonnade of Corinthian columns. Unlike the nearby Catherine Palace, with its exuberant baroque details, the Alexander Palace relied on simplicity and the cleanness of its lines for its splendor.

There were five main entrances to the Alexander Palace, all situated on the southern side, facing the lake. A sixth entrance led from the domed Portrait Gallery on the northern side, at the end of a long, formal *allée* which cut through the park. The Portrait Gallery, with screens of neoclassic columns and enormous gilded bronze chandeliers, centered on the two-story domed bow. The imperial family lived in the west wing of the palace, away from the magnificent state apartments, with their gleaming parquet and marble floors, gilded woodwork, and *trompe l'oeil* ceilings. They were guarded by four gigantic Abyssinian footmen attired in gold embroidered jackets, scarlet trousers, white turbans, and curved shoes. "They were not soldiers," wrote Anna Vyrubova, "and they had no function except to open and close doors and to signify by a sudden, noiseless entrance into a state apartment that one of Their Majesties was about to appear."[1]

The private apartments were quite unremarkable. Alexandra had set out to copy rooms she remembered from her childhood at the New Palace, Wolfsgarten, Osborne, and Windsor. As a result, the chambers were furnished with English chintzes and potted palms and looked positively middle class. Prince Felix Youssoupov later wrote: "In spite of its modest size, the Alexander Palace would not have lacked charm had it not been for the young Empress's unfortunate 'improvements.' She replaced most of the paintings, stucco ornaments and bas-reliefs by mahogany woodwork and cosy-corners in the worst possible taste. New furniture by Maples was sent from England and the old furniture was banished to storerooms."[2]

The furniture was a memory from childhood. Princess Alice had furnished the New Palace in Darmstadt with pieces from Maples Department Store in London. Instead of using the exquisite French and English antique pieces at her disposal from the collection of Catherine the Great, Alexandra furnished her home by mail order, with machine-made assembly-line couches, tables, and chairs.

The central block of the palace contained several drawing rooms named after their principal colors, red and green, as well as galleries. A

Tapestry Room, hung with Catherine the Great's magnificent Gobelin silks, opened to the Jacaranda Room, with fine, highly polished woodwork. The State Library housed some five thousand volumes, all encased in monumental, ornately carved cabinets. The State Dining Room, a large chamber with deep pile carpets and velvet brocade draperies, was located in the east wing, followed by the service rooms and pantries.

Set at the northwestern corner of the palace, the Corner Salon, dominated by a large state portrait of Alexandra by Friedrich August von Kaulbach and a companion bust by the sculptor Marcus Antokolsky, marked the entrance to the family's apartments. In one corner, above a gilded console, hung a Gobelin silk tapestry of the doomed Marie Antoinette and her children, a rather tactless gift from the French government. This room opened to the Maple Room, a former dancing hall which had been divided to form two apartments. At one end of the room, a low balcony, with art nouveau decorations and posts, led to the second floor. Specially designed cabinets in this room held Alexandra's collection of Fabergé Easter eggs and objets d'art . The tsar's formal Audience Chamber, the other half of the dancing hall, had a specially coved and vaulted ceiling, designed to magnify Nicholas's merest inflection into an awe-inspiring bellow. From these rooms, a long central corridor spanned the wing. On the western side were Alexandra's rooms; on the east, those of the tsar. The Large Study was decorated in dark blue silk hangings and mahogany panels, the stucco ceiling supported by marble columns topped with bronze capitals. Nicholas's own study was a relatively small room, paneled in dark wood and dominated by a large, elaborately carved desk covered in family photographs and surrounded with chairs upholstered in green leather. This opened to the tsar's dressing rooms and the dayroom for his aide-de-camp. Beyond this lay perhaps the biggest surprise: a large indoor swimming pool filled with salt water and enclosed behind the classical windows of the palace façade. On the opposite side of the corridor, the Palisander Room, named after its woodwork, served as a semiformal reception room for the imperial family. This opened directly to the most famous room in the entire palace, Alexandra's Mauve Boudoir, overlooking the park.

The Mauve Boudoir was appropriately named. The walls were covered in mauve moiré silk, decorated in a pattern of roses. Everything—carpets, draperies, furniture, even the roses, lilacs, and orchids in the Chinese and Sévres vases on its tables—was mauve. It was Alexandra's obsession. She loved this room and lay on a flowered chaise looking out from her private balcony for hours. An art nouveau–styled cozy corner ordered from Maples in London sat next to the white upright piano, draped in a mauve cover dripping with fringe. Screens and potted palms helped divide the room, defining the areas where the tsarina's ladies-in-waiting sat reading while in attendance. Above the chaise, a large icon of the Virgin Mary stared down. A portrait of Princess Alice faced a large framed photograph of Queen Victoria on a nearby table, and the walls were covered with family photographs, religious icons, and pictures of Hessian and English scenes.[3] Most visitors regarded the room as an ugly yet comfortable retreat.

Next to the Mauve Boudoir were the tsarina's dressing rooms. Closets and cabinets were filled with rows of dresses, all wrapped in covers, and racks of shoes; drawers held silk blouses, packed in tissue, and hundreds of handkerchiefs and pairs of gloves neatly folded; boxes of the latest hats, with feathers and flowers and lace; and chests containing hairpins and brushes and bottles of her favorite perfume, Rose Blanche.[4] The empress's mistress of the robes, Princess Marie Golitsyn (later replaced by Princess E.A. Naryshkin), oversaw the personal staff. First maid Marie Mouchanow assisted Alexandra each day with her clothing, helped by eight undermaids.

Alexandra disappointed many in the capital, for her fashion sense left something to be desired in the eyes of society. She dressed for her own comfort, and although she patronized the most prestigious couturiers of the day, she took little interest in current trends. Each season, she ordered fifty new dresses from Paquin or Worth in Paris.[5] Alexandra constantly made additions to her wardrobe when she found a gown whose style she particularly liked; as a result, the tsar paid clothing bills of up to 10,000 rubles a month. When she had married, her entire trousseau consisted of mourning and half-mourning clothes, so that she came to the throne with no clothing appropriate to her station. Alexandra favored flowing silk dresses of white, cream, or mauve, covered in lace and worn with large, wide-brimmed hats trimmed with ostrich feathers made by Bertrands, a French firm which had an outlet in St. Petersburg. Her stockings of silk and lace were manufactured by Swears and Wells in London. Her shoes were low-heeled, in suede and leather, and she always carried a parasol as protection against the sun.[6] She disliked many of the famous fashions of the day, finding the "hobble skirts" an impossible nuisance.

"Do you really like this skirt?" she once asked Lili Dehn, the wife of an officer on the imperial yacht *Standart* .

"Well, Madame, it's the fashion," replied Lili.

"It's no use whatever as a skirt," Alexandra shot back. "Now, Lili, prove to me that it is comfortable—run, Lili, run—and let me see how fast you can cover ground in it."[7]

Along with the clothing from Paris, Alexandra also ordered gowns from the capital's leading fashion queen, Madame Brissac, who made a huge fortune from the outrageous prices she charged her clients. Everyone complained, but there was nothing they could do. Once, however, at a fitting with Alexandra, Madame Brissac confided, "I beg Your Majesty not to mention it to anyone but I always cut my prices for Your Majesty." The truth came home, however, when Alexandra's sister-in-law Olga told her what Madame Brissac had related to her: "I beg Your Imperial Highness not to mention these things at Tsarskoe Selo but I always cut my prices for you."[8]

Her jewels were stored in special boxes and trays built into the walls of the dressing room. She had at her disposal the richest collection of jewelry in the world—tiaras, necklaces, earrings, bracelets, brooches, rings, stomachers, crowns, and collars. Each year, Nicholas added to this with a special gift, usually commissioned from Fabergé or Bolin, which had standing orders to reserve the best specimens for the tsarina. Of all jewels, pearls were Alexandra's favorites: She loved to drape herself in ropes of the finest matched freshwater pearls, worn with brooches and stud earrings set in platinum. Despite her well-known battle to obtain the crown jewels from the dowager empress, Alexandra rarely wore them. When she did, she liked to use every piece, a display which Grand Duchess Marie Pavolvna, wife of Grand Duke Vladimir, characterized as *"un gout de parvenue."*[9]

In the morning, Alexandra ate her favorite breakfast of eggs and crisp bacon in the boudoir. Following this, she read or wrote, drinking her favorite tea—"very strong and bitter"—and smoked her delicate French cigarettes.[10] Her choice of reading material ranged from romantic novels to the latest works on science. She found history boring but always had the latest works on astronomy, mathematics, and philosophy. Her private confessor argued in vain against her reading Charles Darwin's *Origin of Species*, which she frankly admitted was one of her favorites.[11] Before she dressed for the day, Alexandra wore a Japanese kimono and lay on her chaise, reading and writing. Curled against her was Eira, her pet Scottish terrier. The dog was none too popular with most people: He had the rather nasty habit of darting from underneath chairs and tables, snapping at people's heels. But Alexandra doted on him, even carrying him to the dinner table.[12]

After breakfast, Alexandra sometimes took an early-morning walk around the park, dressed in a short sable jacket if the weather was bad.[13] The walks continued through the autumn, until the snows of winter came to Tsarskoe Selo. Then, as dead leaves floated on the ponds, the boats on the lake were locked away in the boathouse, and the marble statues were covered with wooden planking to protect them against the frosts.[14]

On days when there were no official engagements, Alexandra sat

at her white-and-gilt desk in her library, working on papers and correspondence with her ladies-in-waiting and her private secretary, Count
A. Lambsdorff (later replaced by Count Rostaslav). In the afternoon, if
he was free, the tsar might collect her for a ride in his favorite motorcar,
a Delaunay-Belleville.[15] Or if the tsar was busy, Alexandra would take
a carriage ride. A shining black landau, with two footmen in blue livery
and tall hats and a very fat coachman covered in medals, rolled up in
front of the Alexander Palace, and Alexandra climbed aboard. Trotting
behind on a horse was a member of the Cossack Guard.[16] Alexandra
could never escape the intense security of the Russian court. Detectives
were stationed along the route, behind every bush and tree. And, if
Alexandra stopped to speak with anyone along the way, the moment
the carriage rolled away, a policeman, notebook in hand and pencil
poised, appeared, asking, "What is your name and what reason had
you for conversation with Her Imperial Majesty?"[17]

Being surrounded by servants and guards was a part of life once
Alexandra became tsarina. Five thousand infantrymen alone guarded
Tsarskoe Selo, supplemented by the Cossack Guards, complete with
scarlet tunics and swinging sabers, patrolling the perimeter of the park
on horseback. A thousand more servants, to operate the telephones,
shine the imperial silver, clip and arrange the flowers, cook and clean
and serve and wait on other servants, worked inside the Alexander
Palace. The courtiers were often eccentric. One of the tsar's favorites
was a prince named Vladimir Orlov. Orlov was so fat that when he sat
he could not see his knees; when he could no longer mount a horse for
reviews, he ran alongside the tsar's horse, puffing heavily.[18] Another
man, Count Vladimir Fredericks, was chief minister of the imperial
court. Because of his advanced age, Alexandra and Nicholas referred to
him as "the old man." In turn, Fredericks called the couple "*mes en-
fants*"; he was the only court official allowed to do so.[19]

Alexandra always changed for dinner, even if there were no
guests. In the evenings, Alexandra and Nicholas might attend a play or
concert. Every year, the entire *Ring* cycle by Richard Wagner was performed at Tsarskoe Selo, at the special request of the empress, who
loved the music of the German composer.[20] Tea at eleven signaled the
end of the day. In her dressing room, Alexandra removed the golden
hairpins which kept her long hair coiled atop her head. A maid brushed
her hair for half an hour, after which she tightly plaited and bound it
with silk ribbons to match the tsarina's nightgown.[21] Alexandra disliked lingerie of silk.[22] Instead, her nightgowns were of fine linen or
batiste, ornamented with Valenciennes and Mechlin lace. Alexandra
once told her first maid, Marie Mouchanow, that indulging in beautiful
lingerie was one of her greatest pleasures.[23]

Alexandra and Nicholas shared the same bedroom, a rarity for sovereigns. Their twin brass bedsteads were at one side of the room, in a curtained alcove, the walls of which were hung with hundreds of icons. Usually they went right to sleep. The exceptions were the nights they made love, for their relationship was intensely physical and passionate, or when she sat propped up on pillows, reading the latest English romance novels and crunching on English biscuits, much to the chagrin of the emperor.[24]

Almost directly above the bedroom were the nurseries. These rooms were light and airy, hung with flowered cretonne and furnished with polished lemonwood.[25] They were constantly in use, for during the first seven years of her marriage, Alexandra had given birth, in rapid succession, to four children. In reality, her only obligation as tsarina was to produce a male heir to the throne. And, in this, Alexandra had failed, for her four children—Olga, born in 1895; Tatiana, in 1897; Marie, in 1899; and Anastasia, in 1901—were girls.

Six months after her marriage Alexandra was pregnant with her first child. "It has become very big and kicks about a good deal inside," Nicholas wrote in amazement.[26] Both Alexandra and Nicholas hoped for a boy; the birth of a tsarevich directly to a reigning sovereign would be the first since the eighteenth century. They decided that if the baby were a boy, he would be called Paul. This worried the dowager empress; the only other Romanov tsar named Paul was the mad son of Catherine the Great, whose legitimacy was never established and who was murdered in a conspiracy involving his own son. Hearing the suggested name, Marie Feodorovna wrote: "The name for the future baby seems to be well chosen, though Paul for the first somehow frightens me a little; still, there is time to talk. . . . It is understood, isn't it, that you will let me know as soon as the first symptoms appear? I shall fly to you, my dear children, and shall not be a nuisance, except, perhaps, by acting as policeman, to keep everybody else away."[27]

Shortly after one on the morning of 15 November 1895, Alexandra went into labor. It was agonizingly long, nearly twenty hours. Finally, at nine in the evening, she gave birth to a daughter.

Grand Duchess Olga Nicholaievna was a fat, fair baby; at birth, she weighed ten pounds. A golden coach bore her to her christening ceremony in the chapel of the Catherine Palace. Olga lay on a golden cushion, covered with a mantle of cloth-of-gold. Her godmothers included Queen Olga of Greece and the dowager empress, who held the baby during the service, this great-granddaughter of Queen Victoria and four times great-granddaughter of Catherine the Great.

Alexandra fed and bathed Olga herself, knitting endless stacks of socks and sweaters under the watchful eyes of Mrs. Orchard, who had come from Darmstadt to supervise the nurseries at Tsarskoe Selo. "It is a radiantly happy mother who is writing to you," Alexandra declared to her sister Victoria a month after Olga's birth. "You can imagine our intense happiness now that we have such a precious little one to care for and look after."[28]

Alexandra was a doting mother. Convention had not changed since her own childhood, especially for royal mothers. Nannies and nurses were still expected to act as secondary mothers, with children kept from their parents' presences behind the green baize doors of the nursery wing. Queen Victoria herself was a less than enthusiastic and active mother, while Princess Alice had virtually withdrawn from her family's company at the time of her death in 1878. Alexandra, however, relished motherhood. With each new child, she moved the baby's bassinet into her bedroom; she never thought of ringing for servants in the middle of the night when one of the babies needed changing. She delighted in dressing her children up in matching outfits—frilly dresses trimmed in lace and sailor suits and caps—and in recording their lives with her Kodak camera.

Less than six months after Olga's birth, Alexandra was again pregnant, at the time of the coronation. The newspapers in St. Petersburg began to hint that the tsarina was expecting, and even Queen Victoria wrote to Alexandra's sister Victoria to discover the truth.[29] But within a matter of days the pregnancy had come to an end: Following the stress of the coronation, Alexandra suffered a miscarriage and lost the baby.[30]

Her pregnancy in 1897 with Tatiana was difficult; Alexandra was ill, confined to bed for seven weeks, and was so weak, in fact, that she had to use a wheelchair to get about.[31] The dowager empress wrote to the tsar: "She ought to try eating raw ham in bed in the morning before breakfast. It really does help against nausea. I have tried it myself and it is wholesome and nourishing, too. . . . It is your duty, my dear Nicky, to watch over her and to look after her in every possible way, to see that she keeps her feet warm. . . ."[32]

The entire nation hoped for a tsarevich. When Tatiana was born, Alexandra was beside herself with worry, saying, "My God, it is again a daughter! What will the nation say?"[33]

The next pregnancy, two years later, was less difficult, although Nicholas was forced to inform his mother, "Alix does not go driving anymore, twice she fainted during mass. . . ."[34] Later, he wrote, "The nausea is gone. She walks very little, and when it is warm sits on the balcony. . . . In the evenings, when she is in bed, I read to her. We have finished *War and Peace*."[35] Alexandra prayed for a boy, but, she wrote to Victoria, "I never like making plans. . . . God knows how it will all end."[36] It ended with the birth of yet another daughter, Grand Duchess Marie.

During this pregnancy, a crisis arose which forcefully reminded Alexandra of the need to produce an heir. When Nicholas assumed the throne, his younger brother George received the title of tsarevich, heir to the throne, until such time as the tsar should have a son. In 1899, George died. The next in line to the throne, Nicholas's brother Michael, was only twenty-one. Before any formal arrangements could be made, the tsar fell ill with typhoid. He was so ill that it was believed that he might die. The dynastic question then became of primary importance. During the tsar's illness, Alexandra refused to let anyone near him, nursing her husband herself. Nicholas was too ill to attend to state matters, and members of the government protested, saying that certain decisions had to be made. Serge Witte, among others, proposed making Michael regent until such time as the tsar recovered. In this, he was supported by the dowager empress. Alexandra believed that they were plotting to remove her husband from the throne. Witte pressed the question, saying that if the tsar died, some arrangement would have to be made. He suggested making Michael regent for the tsarina's unborn child if it turned out to be a boy. Alexandra herself felt that if her husband died and she then gave birth to a boy, she should be made regent. No one in the government wanted this, and Witte tactlessly told her so. Alexandra was afraid that Michael, encouraged by his mother and Witte, was trying to snatch the throne from her husband.

The tsar eventually recovered, but Alexandra felt certain that his family had been involved in plotting against him. The baby turned out to be Grand Duchess Marie, and the question of the succession remained unresolved. But after this, the title of tsarevich did not pass to Michael as the heir presumptive, as the laws dictated. Witte believed that this was due to the influence of the tsarina, who still believed that her brother-in-law had acted out of greed. Apparently she must have convinced the tsar of this, for he refused to grant Michael the title which George had held. Coincidentally, ministers in the government noted that papers sent to the tsar at this time began to come back across their desks with notations in the tsarina's hand.[37] It seems that the tsarina had succeeded in convincing the tsar of his family's duplicity, and he began turning to her for political advice.

The 1899 crisis and the birth of yet another daughter devastated Alexandra. She was the empress of Russia, married to the man she loved, surrounded by palaces and jewels, yet the one thing she most wanted, the simplest wish, a son, something nearly every other woman could offer her husband, was continually denied her. A year after Marie's birth, Alexandra was again pregnant. She prayed for, hoped for, a boy but feared the worst. People openly remarked on her inability to produce a son and Alexandra longed to silence her critics. But there was to be no tsarevich for Alexandra this time: On 18 June 1901 she gave birth to a fourth daughter, Grand Duchess Anastasia.

17

The Turn of the Century

THE WINTER SKY OVER Osborne Bay was dark and threatening. Waves crashed endlessly against the rocky beach, spitting foam and spraying mist into the cold wind. High on a bluff, overlooking the Solent and the English Channel, Osborne House was grimly silent. Lights burned on through the night in this Italian Renaissance palace, greeting the comings and goings of princes and princesses. Upstairs, in her bedroom, Queen Victoria lay dying.

The day before, the kaiser had arrived at Cowes. He greeted his Uncle Bertie, the Prince of Wales, with a kiss on the cheek, and said, "I should like to see Grandmama before she dies, but if that is not possible I shall quite understand."[1] Despised by nearly all of the British royal family for his arrogant and offensive manner, for once the kaiser was silent as he followed his uncle through the town and up the winding road to the gates of the great house. Now he sat on his grandmother's great bed, beneath its canopy of chintz specially selected by Prince Albert, who had, in fact, designed the house. The old queen gazed at those who gathered around her. They stood in the shadows of the room, staring at the old lady in white who lay cradled in the kaiser's one good arm. On the other side of the bed hung a black wreath and a portrait of her husband, Albert, on his deathbed. For two and a half hours, Willy held the queen as she lapsed in and out of consciousness. At the last, Victoria opened her eyes and gazed at her son the Prince of Wales, the object of so much of her scorn during the past half century. She whispered but one word—"Bertie"—his name, before she closed her eyes for the last time. Surrounded by her family and her dogs, her white hair losely framing her small, round face, the queen died. It was 6:30 P.M., 22 January 1901—the end of an era.

Alexandra was devastated by the death of her beloved grandmother. Just a year before, in the summer of 1900, the queen had invited her granddaughter to come and stay with her at Windsor Castle. Alexandra wrote: "How intensely I long to see her dear old face, you can imagine; never have we been separated so long, four whole years, and I have the feeling as though I should never see her any more. Were it not so far away I should have gone off all alone for a few days to see her and left the children and my husband, as she has been as a mother to me, ever since Mama's death twenty-two years ago."[2]

On a bitterly cold day in February, the dead monarch was buried by her son and successor King Edward VII in a solemn and grand ceremony in St. George's Chapel, Windsor Castle. That afternoon, Queen Victoria was laid to rest beside her beloved Prince Albert in the mausoleum which she herself had designed at Frogmore. According to her last request, her wedding veil had been placed atop her white hair and smoothed round her tiny body as it lay in the coffin. At last, she was reunited with her husband.

On the same day that the queen was buried a thousand miles away, Alexandra knelt on a velvet cushion in the Anglican Church of St. Petersburg to pray for her grandmother's soul. As the bishop intoned the prayer for the dead, her emotions overwhelmed her, and the tsarina of all the Russias broke down and sobbed before the eyes of the diplomatic corps, a startling gesture to those who believed her cold and unfeeling.[3] She could not go to Windsor for the funeral, as she was pregnant with Anastasia at the time and travel was considered too dangerous. To her sister Victoria she wrote: "How I envy you, being able to see beloved Grandmama being taken to her last rest. I cannot believe she is really gone, that we shall never see her any more. It seems impossible. Since one can remember, she was in our life, and a dearer, kinder being never was. The whole world sorrows over her. England without the Queen seems impossible."[4]

Alexandra was inconsolable. The queen had never been able to entirely set her mind at ease with regard to her granddaughter's Russian marriage, but as long as she lived, Victoria made certain that Alexandra knew precisely what the English view of the world situation was and expected her to follow her advice. As traditional enemies, the tension between Russia and England had been eased somewhat with Alexandra's marriage to Nicholas, as it guaranteed an English voice at the Russian court in the person of the tsarina. Alexandra, in turn, had relied on her grandmother's constant stream of advice to help her adjust to her position. Even when the two disagreed, as often happened in the queen's declining years, Alexandra always gave her grandmother's advice much thought; she respected the queen more than anyone else. But throughout their differing opinions and all of the political considerations, the family ties remained strong. Had the queen lived for another five years, perhaps, she would have been able to offer her granddaughter practical and enlightened advice to help her deal with the turmoil which plagued Russia. As it was, Alexandra was left on her own, with no one to support her opinions or argue with her against them. The death of Queen Victoria, who despised Russia, could not have come at a worse time either for the country she hated, or for its restless, ambitious, and narrow-minded tsarina.

In the last few weeks of September 1903, Alexandra took a long holiday. She packed up a dozen suitcases and trunks, loaded a retinue of household ladies and staff onto the imperial train, and along with Nicholas, set off for Darmstadt. Crammed on board, at the tsar's insistence, was the whole of the Russian imperial choir. The entire entourage steamed off for the wedding of Princess Alice of Battenberg, Alexandra's niece, to Prince Andrew of Greece.

They stayed at Wolfsgarten. Princess Alice was Victoria's eldest daughter (and the future mother of Prince Philip, the present duke of Edinburgh). All of Alexandra's family were there for the wedding: Ella and Serge, Irene and Heinrich, and the bride's parents Victoria and Louis, with all of their children, including a rather too boisterous three-year-old Prince Louis, later Lord Mountbatten. But all eyes were on Ernie, whose marriage to Ducky had collapsed earlier in the year.

Ernie and Ducky had never really been happy, and despite Queen Victoria's matchmaking, the marriage was a disaster from its very first days. Ernie was artistic and sensitive, loving uniforms and flowers and the arts. He had made Darmstadt into a German cultural center, but without the help of Ducky, who found him effeminate and boring. They remained together for the sake of the queen and for their only child, a daughter called Elizabeth. In 1903, just weeks after the Greek wedding, the child died while on a visit with Alexandra and Nicholas at a hunting lodge in Poland. Ducky no longer had any reason to remain in a loveless marriage, and she left Ernie, determined to get a divorce. After the divorce, Ernie remarried, this time happily, to a woman with the rather complex name of Eleonore, princess of Solms-Hohensolms-Lich, and the pair had two children, George, born in 1906, and Louis, born in 1908. Ducky, meanwhile, had fallen in love with the tsar's cousin Grand Duke Cyril, who was at this time presumably third in line to the throne. The pair wed, illegally, for the tsar, according to the law, had to approve the marriages within his own family. When Cyril did not seek the tsar's consent and went through with the ceremony, Alexandra and Nicholas were furious. As Tsarina of Russia, Alexandra would be forced to receive her former sister-in-law as well as Grand Duke Cyril, since both were prominent members of the Romanov family. In retaliation, the tsar stripped Cyril of his offices and honors and banished him and

Ducky from Russia. In 1909, after much family pressure, Nicholas relented and allowed the pair to reside in Russia, and the lost honors were restored. But the tsar refused to grant recognition to the marriage, and neither he nor Alexandra would receive the scandalous lovers.

With such domestic worries, the wedding between Alice and Andrew was almost overlooked. Because Alice was a Protestant and Andrew Greek Orthodox, three ceremonies took place—the two religious services as well as a simple civil ceremony. Alice was deaf and had to lip-read to follow the service, but she could not do so in Greek and was left confused and unsure of what was happening. When the priest asked her if she was marrying Andrew of her own free will, she replied, "No." The priest ignored the slip and moved on to the next question: Had Alice promised her hand to another? Unaware of her first mistake, she smiled at Andrew and loudly answered, "Yes."[5] The family, grouped around the altar, collapsed in laughter, leaving Alice to wonder if she had missed the joke.

The wedding reception followed in much the same manner. Fearful of young children racing about, the aged grand duchess Vera of Württemberg had secured her diamond tiara to the top of her head with a piece of elastic. But she had neglected her eyeglasses; a relative promptly knocked them off. Unable to see anything but a blur, the old lady grabbed her handbag and swung it with a vengeance at anyone who passed near her, hitting several innocent people squarely in the face.[6]

When the newly married couple departed, the tsar goaded the rest of the family into showering them with rice, rose petals, and satin slippers. The Wolsely car, a wedding gift from Alexandra and Nicholas, carried Alice and Andrew through the center of Darmstadt, crowds cheering them on their way. Alexandra was standing with the rest of the family at the palace gates when she spotted her husband pushing his way through the crowd. He turned and yelled, "Come along, we can catch them again!"[7] Dashing madly through the streets, chased by the police, who were sure that he was going to be shot, Nicholas caught up with the car just as it turned the corner. He threw an entire bag of rice straight into Alice's face, followed by a satin slipper, which she caught. Leaning over the back of the car, Alice hit the tsar on the head with it, shouting, "You're a stupid old ass!"[8] When Alexandra finally caught up with him, Nicholas was collapsed in the middle of the road, bent over with laughter.[9]

Deaths, marriages, and scandals marked the turn of the century among Alexandra's family, but in her country a cultural and social revolution promised new and dramatic changes in Russian society. The full weight of the upheavals would have a profound effect on the course of Russian history.

The greatest of all Russian arts, the ballet, reached its zenith in the years surrounding the turn of the century. Marius Petipa reigned supreme as the choreographer of the Russian Imperial Ballet, blending the classical music of Tchaikovsky's *Swan Lake, Sleeping Beauty,* and *The Nutcracker* with the elegant, unparalleled forms of Kschessinska, Vyaschaslav Nijinsky, Tamara Karsavina, and Pavlova. The results captivated the art world, yet Serge Diaghilev found the style too conservative. Within a decade, his famous *Ballet Russe* would sweep across Europe, with Nijinsky in top form, dancing to the music of Igor Stravinsky against a backdrop reflecting the art nouveau tastes of the painter Michel Fokine.

Russian literature had finally come of age in the works of Anton Chekhov, Maxim Gorky, and the symbolists Andrei Bely and Alexander Blok. Constantine Stanislavsky's Moscow Art Theatre performed the works of the great Russian writers, sparing no detail in the total performance: real trees for the forest scenes, barnyard animals for the peasant village, and fires burning in the onstage fireplaces to heat the drawing rooms of the main characters. No singer was more revered than Feodor Chaliapin, who dominated the stage of every opera to which he lent his superb basso. After years of domination by Western painters, Russians began to appreciate the subtle detailing in Valentin Serov's works of shadow and light, the depth of a canvas by Ilya Repin, the harmony in the paintings of Michael Vrubel; a few years later, Marc Chagall began his studies in St. Petersburg under the master Leon Bakst. Music exploded. Rimsky-Korsakov himself conducted the St. Petersburg Symphony while giving lessons to Stravinsky and Serge Prokofiev. But perhaps the sublime artist of those years was Peter Carl Fabergé, the jeweler to the Russian imperial court.

No palace or country house in Russia—and, in time, across Europe—was complete unless its tables sported Fabergé photograph frames encrusted with pearls and diamonds; snuff boxes enameled with delicate scenes of Moscow or St. Petersburg; cigarette cases of silver and gold, engraved with family crests; or Fabergé desk sets, clocks, and bell pushes to summon the servants. His reputation earned Fabergé an international clientele, among them the kings of Great Britain, Denmark, Greece, and Norway. But it is for his famed imperial Easter eggs that Fabergé is best remembered.

Each year at Easter, according to Russian custom, members of the court exchanged small enamel eggs as gifts. Tsar Alexander III first commissioned Fabergé in 1884 to create a similiar present for his wife

Marie Feodorovna. What Fabergé produced was a remarkable work of art: a plain white eggshell of silver, which broke in half to reveal a golden interior. Tucked into this tiny gift was a golden cockerel with ruby eyes which came apart to disclose another surprise inside: a replica of the imperial crown. Nicholas II continued the tradition in his reign, ordering two eggs a year, one for his wife and one for his mother. They were magnificent, their design left solely to Fabergé himself. One year, Alexandra received an egg enameled in gold and decorated with tiny double-headed Romanov eagles; when she broke the shell in half, a miniature golden replica of the coronation coach rolled out, complete in every detail, down to the folding steps which gave access to the interior. In the years that followed, Alexandra might receive an egg in pink and blue or silver, covered with diamonds and pearls, inlaid with traceries of silver or platinum or gilded and covered with the lightest, most delicate fretwork of chased gold. Within the shell, she might find a miniature portrait of the tsar or their children, awaiting the press of a button before it sprang through the top of the egg, or a golden model of a favorite palace. An egg with a clock face revealed its surprise at the stroke of the hour: A golden bird, enameled in yellow and green, which rose from the top of the egg, bobbed its head, flapped its jeweled wings, and disappeared back inside the shell.

On 4 February 1903 the last great ball of imperial Russia took place. It was the Medieval Ball at the Winter Palace, and all of the guests came costumed as sixteenth-century Russian nobility. Alexandra herself designed the clothes which she and Nicholas wore. The tsar dressed as Alexei I, in a robe of raspberry and white; he wore Alexei's crown and carried his staff, items brought from the Kremlin armory especially for the event. Alexandra's dress, patterned after one worn by Alexei's wife Marie Miloslavskaya, was of gold brocade sewn with emeralds and pearls.[10] Around her neck, she wore a Fabergé creation crafted specially for the dance: a necklace whose centerpiece was a 159-carat cabochon sapphire.[11] They paraded through the halls of the enormous palace, Alexandra in her golden dress glittering with jewels, while outside, on the cold, snowy streets, the factory workers froze and starved to death. It was a strange spectacle. As the imperial family of Russia celebrated the magnificent dances and costumes of their sixteenth-century ancestors,their empire was about to slide down a precipice.

18

"A Small, Victorious War"

O<small>N THE NIGHT OF</small> 6 F<small>EBRUARY</small> 1904, Alexandra and Nicholas drove to the Mariinsky Theatre in St. Petersburg to attend a performance of the opera *Rusalka*. As they entered the blue-and-gold imperial box, the crowd turned its eyes on them and sang "God Save the Tsar." Four thousand miles away, Admiral Eugene Alexeiev, the Russian viceroy and commander in chief of the empire's forces in the Far East, sat in a room in his palace above Port Arthur, safely snuggled in a chair, reading a book and enjoying a cigar.[1] Shortly after half-past eleven, he heard low noises in the dark harbor below; thinking nothing of them, Alexeiev returned to his reading. At the same hour as the guns began to thunder in Manchuria, Alexandra and Nicholas left the theater and raced through the snow in a gilded sleigh, surrounded by galloping cossacks, across bridges and canals to the Winter Palace. They were just climbing into bed when a knock sounded on the door and a page handed the tsar a cable. That same night, the Japanese admiral Togo had destroyed the Russian Pacific Fleet at Port Arthur. His torpedo boats hit three ships, including the pride of the Russian navy, the month-old *Tsarevich*. The Russo-Japanese War had begun.

Up until 1898, Russia's only Pacific port had been Vladivostock, which was locked in ice a quarter of the year. Three years previously, Japan had invaded several territories Russia had always longed for; chief among them was the fortress and seaport of Port Arthur in Manchuria. Six days after the occupation of Port Arthur, the Russians lodged a formal complaint, stating that Japan's actions "constituted a perpetual menace to the peace of the Far East."[2] Unwilling to confront the enormous Russian army at this time, Japan retreated from Port Arthur and went back to their own shores. Russia was able to extract a ninety-nine-year lease on Port Arthur from the Chinese government in 1898.

With the lease came the Liaotung Peninsula, jutting into the sea between the Manchurian mainland and Korea. The Russians ran a spur of railway track from Port Arthur through Mukden to Harbin, into the Chinese Eastern Railway and finally connecting with the Trans-Siberian. After they had finished laying down the tracks across Manchuria, the Russian workers and guards remained behind. Two years later, the Boxer Rebellion broke out in Peking. As members of the Chinese Nationalist Society attacked foreigners in the capital of China, the tsar ordered Russian troops into Manchuria. Even after the Boxer Rebellion had ended, the troops stayed. Slowly, they began to colonize Korea.

A private company, the Yalu Timber Corporation, was formed. Secretly financed by the Russian government, the company's main purpose was to smuggle Russian soldiers, disguised as workmen, into Korea. The tsar approved of the plan. But Japan was soon aware of the situation and sent their statesman Ito to St. Petersburg to try to negotiate a settlement. But Ito was not received by any official, and his requests for an audience were ignored. He eventually left Russia in despair.

All the while, Kaiser Wilhelm II encouraged his Cousin Nicky in his imperialistic Asian policy. Wilhelm wrote endless letters to the tsar which spoke of Russia's "Holy Mission" in Asia and of the threat of the "yellow peril." One such letter read:

> Clearly it is the great task of the future for Russia to cultivate the Asian continent and to defend Europe from the inroads of the Great Yellow Race. In this you will always find me on your side, ready to help you as best as I can. You have well understood the call of Providence . . . in the defense of the Cross and the old Christian European culture against the inroads of the Mongols and Buddhism. . . . I would let nobody try to interfere with you and attack you from behind in Europe during the time you were fulfilling the great mission which Heaven has shaped for you.[3]

In Russia, it was always assumed that if the situation did come to war, the tsar's soldiers would win easily. Talk and boasts ran high in the marble palaces along the Neva; armchair generals bragged of Russia's great strength and the weakness of the Japanese. It was said that the Russian army would not even have to fire a shot to win the war; all they would have to do to annihilate the Japanese "monkeys" was throw their caps at them. Popular though this talk was, it greatly overestimated Russian military strength. Some people were ignorant of the facts; others openly welcomed the idea of a war to distract attention from Russia's internal problems. Among this latter group was Vyascheslav Plehve, the minister of the interior, who, worried about the rebellions and strikes cropping up throughout the country, thought that "a small, victorious war to stem the tide of revolution" would be a godsend.[4]

On New Year's Day, 1904, Alexandra and Nicholas hosted the annual diplomatic reception at the Winter Palace. While waiting to be presented to the tsar and tsarina, the ambassadors chatted among themselves about Russian militarism and the coming war with Japan. As champagne was plucked from silver trays, the boasts grew louder, the threats of retaliation bolder. The tsar himself found the Japanese ambassador, Shinchiro Kurino, and talked to him in humiliating tones of Russia's patience and her strength. A month later, the Japanese government broke off diplomatic relations with the Russian Empire and recalled Kurino.[5]

Within a few days, Japan had launched her surprise attack on the Russian fleet at Port Arthur. The beginning of the war was marked with intense patriotic fervor. On the day after the attack at Port Arthur, thousands marched to the Winter Palace, where the tsar and tsarina appeared on the balcony. "Everyone was mixed together—generals and tramps marched side by side, students with banners and ladies, their arms filled with shopping. Everyone was united in one general feeling. Everyone sang."[6]

From the beginning of the Russo-Japanese War, Alexandra was active. Her first order was that the social season be canceled; wartime was not meant for parties and balls. Instead of receptions, Alexandra filled the galleries and drawing rooms of the Winter Palace with long tables. Each day, she moved from table to table, supervising the war work. Ladies sewed and knitted all day long and ripped up sheets to be used as bandages and sent them off to the Red Cross. Alexandra sat beside them, picking up a needle, and did her part for the war effort. But this was no palace free-for-all; only the ladies of high society and their staffs came and sat with Alexandra at the tables. Even in war, decorum had to be maintained.

When she was not supervising workshops at the Winter Palace, Alexandra stood at her husband's side in St. Petersburg's railway stations, watching the soldiers go off to war. A brass band played rousing military music while the tsarina passed out holy images to the soldiers who knelt before her. They boarded trains which steamed off on the track of the Trans-Siberian. Everything the Russians sent to the war— every soldier, every gun, every scrap of food—traveled on a single line some four thousand miles long. The Japanese were only two hundred miles away from the fighting in Korea. Worse still, for a hundred miles near Lake Baikal, there was no railway track at all. It had never been finished. All Russian transport had to be unloaded, packed on sleds, and dragged up and down hills for three days, then reloaded at the other end.

Although it began with patriotic fervor, the war soon lost public support. Unrest turned into violence directed against anything official. Plehve, the minister of the interior, was perhaps the most hated man in Russia, and it was inevitable that dissatisfaction with the war would eventually be directed against him. In July 1904, Plehve was assassinated. Dr. E. J. Dillon of the London *Daily Telegraph* wrote:

> Suddenly, the ground before me quivered, a tremendous sound, as of thunder, deafened me, the windows of the houses on both sides of the broad street rattled and the glass of the panes was hurled on to the stone pavement. A dead horse, a pool of blood, fragments of a carriage and a hole in the ground were part of my rapid impressions. My driver was on his knees devoutly praying and saying that the end of the world had come. I got down from my seat and moved toward the hole, but a police officer ordered me back, and to my question replied that the Minister, Plehve, had been blown to fragments. . . .[7]

The government began to disintegrate as the war continued. The British chargé d'affaires in St. Petersburg wrote:

> Each minister acts on his own doing as much damage as possible to the other ministers. . . . It is a curious state of things. There is an Emperor, a religious madman almost—without a statesman, or even a council—surrounded by a legion of Grand Dukes, thirty five of them and not one at war . . . with a few priests and priestly women behind him. No middle class . . . an underpaid bureaucracy living, of necessity, on corruption. Beneath this, about 100 million people gradually becoming poorer and poorer as they bear all the burden of taxation, drafted into the army by the thousands. . . .[8]

Witte, the minister of finance, had predicted in a conversation with the tsar that "an armed struggle with Japan . . . would be a great disaster. . . ." It would, he said, certainly provoke "the latent dissatisfaction of our domestic life" to political violence.[9]

The Russian army had 3 million men against Japan's 600,000, but only 133,000 Russian soldiers were actually in Korea.[10] The Russians' hopes rested with their navy, the third largest in the world after England and France. Admiral Stephan Markov, the admiral in charge of the fleet, attempted to sail his flagship, the *Petropavlovsk*, into safer waters.

The ship steamed out of Port Arthur straight into a Japanese mine and sank with a loss of over seven hundred men, including Markov.

Throughout the fall of 1904 the Japanese advanced toward Port Arthur. The combat was hand to hand, from hill to hill. Russian losses were terrible, but the troops fought against the onslaught of the Japanese until they could continue no longer. In January 1905, Port Arthur fell to the Japanese. The loss of this prized port had a demoralizing effect on the soldiers. Desertions became commonplace. In the frozen winter, the soldiers who remained huddled around small fires, wrapped in tattered blankets, and ate if and when food arrived. A story told by Countess Marie Kleinmichel illustrates the disillusion of the army and the indifferent leadership of the officers. A colonel and his wife and children sat in their private compartment in a train bound for the war. An officer knocked on the door to let the colonel know that his 120 men had been crammed into a cattle truck so small that they could neither sit nor lie down. The car was only intended for a third of the men. They did not even have water to drink. The colonel said he would see to the matter shortly and dismissed his officer. An hour passed. The officer returned to the compartment, saying that although the colonel might be pleased with his private compartments, his men were being treated like animals. The colonel immediately arrested his officer for insubordination, in response to which the man released a torrent of verbal abuse on his senior. The colonel promptly drew his sword and struck the man with it, slicing deep into an artery. When the troops learned what had happened, they broke loose from their prison car, stormed into the colonel's private compartment, and in front of his horrified wife and children, drenched the colonel in kerosene and burned him alive.[11]

The kaiser urged the tsar to send the Russian Baltic Fleet halfway around the world to do battle with the yellow peril. After much thought and consultations with the admiral in charge of the fleet, Zinovii Rozhdestvensky, the tsar decided to send it off to war. It was a last-ditch effort—all Russian hopes centered on the fleet's mission being victorious. As if to emphasize this, all of Rozhdestvensky's ships had been personally blessed by the tsar; each carried Nicholas's portrait and a special icon sent by the tsarina; and even the huge guns had been individually sprinkled with holy water.[12]

The fleet steamed through the Baltic and into the North Sea. The Russians, suspecting another Japanese surprise attack like that of Port Arthur, were on the lookout. They had even gone so far as to hire a certain Captain Hartling to keep an eye on the waters. With his nine boats and enormous expense account, Captain Hartling chose to sit in his hotel suite in Copenhagen, sending off false reports to the effect that the

North Sea was crawling with Japanese torpedo boats, further fueling Russian paranoia.[13]

One night, as the Fleet sailed through the North Sea near Dogger Bank, a lookout on the *Kamchatka* spied a ship through the fog. Having no doubt that it was a Japanese vessel, the lookout rang the bridge. Nearly the entire crew and officers on the *Kamchatka* were drunk; the captain staggered to the bridge and ordered guns trained through the fog. Almost three hundred shells flew through the night, punching into a tiny British fishing trawler.[14]

Hearing the guns echoing in the night, other Russian ships began to fire. Shells crashed into several fishing boats, killing two men. In the silence that followed, the Russians soon discovered their mistake; rather than pick up survivors, Rozhdestvensky ordered his ships full steam ahead. Meanwhile, two Russian ships, the *Aurora* and the *Dimitri Donskoy*, were engaged in their own battle. Each thought that the other was a Japanese ship. The *Dimitry Donskoy* fired six shells into the *Aurora*, injuring several of its crew and blowing off the chaplain's hand.[15]

England was outraged. The tsar was in no mood to apologize, and it was only after the British government dispatched a cruiser detachment in hot pursuit of the Russian Baltic Fleet that Nicholas, unwilling to fight a sea battle with anyone other than Japan, relented and agreed to turn the matter over to arbitration by the International Court at The Hague.[16] Russia eventually paid over sixty thousand pounds in damages.[17]

On the afternoon of 27 May 1905 the Russian Baltic Fleet steamed into the Strait of Tsushima off Korea in columns led by eight battleships. The Japanese admiral in charge, Heihachiro Togo, had placed his ships in a semicircle at the mouth of the strait.[18] When the Russians sailed toward them at two o'clock in the afternoon, Togo ordered his men to fire. Shells hit the Russian fleet from three sides, ripping their hulls apart; the barrage lasted for three-quarters of an hour. The Russians lost twenty major warships, and over forty-three hundred sailors were killed.[19]

The war with Japan was as good as over. In less than an hour, the yellow peril had put an end to Russia's hopes of a holy victory in Korea. There was no more army, soldiers had deserted by the thousands, and the Russian Imperial Fleet lay beneath the waters off Korea.

The peace conference in Portsmouth, New Hampshire, was hosted by President Theodore Roosevelt. To negotiate the terms, the tsar sent Serge Witte. On Nicholas's instructions, Witte presented the Japanese with an ultimatum: Accept Russia's terms for peace or continue the war. Although the Japanese approached the proceedings as victors, the tsar knew that financially they were in no shape to continue the conflict. Angry with this diplomatic coup but having no alternative, Japan reluctantly agreed to the Russian demands.

The Treaty of Portsmouth awarded some advantages to Japan but extracted no great penalties from Russia. Japan gained Port Arthur, the Southern Manchurian Railway, the southern part of Sakhalin Island, and recognition of the preponderance of her interests in Korea.[20] But these Japanese gains were minor losses by Russia in view of the fact that they were the only ones Japan made. Russia still held northern Sakhalin, a territory Japan had been most insistent on possessing; most of her territorial gains and advantages in the Far East remained intact; and she did not have to pay an indemnity because Japan had actually started the war. When these terms were revealed in Japan, angry crowds swept through the streets in protest, so great was the insult.

In fifteen months, Japan—barbaric, pagan Japan—had brought the mighty Orthodox Russian Empire to its knees. Defeat was humiliating. A quarter of the men sent to Korea never returned, and the Russian Imperial Navy lay sunk and abandoned. The war seemed a personal loss to the tsarina. When the cable announcing the destruction of the fleet at Tsushima arrived, she broke down and cried for hours, so severe was this blow to her.[21] Defeat meant disgrace for the autocracy. The country erupted in chaos, and Russia was plunged into a full-scale revolution.

19

Bloody Sunday

THE SIXTH OF JANUARY 1905 was extremely cold in St. Petersburg. Snow fell heavily, scattering a thick blanket of white across the baroque palaces and gilded domes of the city's churches. Priests in golden vestments marched along a red carpet laid out across the snow, swinging silver crosses and censers of incense and chanting ancient words of blessing. The tsar followed to the edge of the quay lining the frozen Neva River. A golden canopy rose above a hole chopped in the ice. A priest dipped a cross into the cold water, blessing it, and brought it up. On the other side of the Neva, the guns of the Fortress of Peter and Paul were ready to fire their salutes at the ceremony of the Blessing of the Waters. The sound of cannon fire rent the sky. Then disbelief on the faces of the priests and the tsar as a shell from the fortress slammed into the red-carpeted square. Pieces of pavement flew through the air, striking a policeman on guard duty. Disbelief turned to horror as a second shell struck the Admiralty Building across the square. People ran, peasants, court officials, and members of the police spreading in all directions. A third report from the fortress hit the columned red façade of the Winter Palace. Alexandra stood behind a tall window in the Winter Palace, next to her mother-in-law. She wore a white court gown and diamond tiara. With terror, she saw the first shot land a few yards from her husband. Panic and confusion followed, and as the halls of the palace filled with worried officials, a second gun boomed out, followed by a third. Suddenly, the marble floor rocked from beneath the tsarina's feet, the glass windows exploded, and part of the exterior wall of the palace collapsed into rubble. Both Alexandra and Marie Feodorovna were covered with shattered glass and dust from the rubble, but they were unhurt. "I knew that somebody was trying to kill me," the tsar later said. But he stayed in his position throughout the shelling, saying, "What else could I do?"[1]

It was a miracle that the only injury of the entire day was that suffered by the policeman. An official investigation into the shots fired on

Epiphany Day, 1905, concluded only that someone must have accidentally placed live shells in the cannon instead of the usual blanks.
Whether intentional or accidental, the shots turned out to have been the
first ones of the 1905 revolution.

A young priest of thirty-two years, Father George Gapon fancied
himself a leader among men. Not only was Gapon a priest, he was also
a paid police informer. He had created a union, the Assembly of Russian Factory and Plant Workers, to petition for better living and working
conditions and as a result had become immensely popular among the
poor of St. Petersburg.[2] Gapon's idealism showed itself when he told
workers that the tsar was not responsible for Russia's misfortunes but
rather the factory owners and their fellow capitalists. If only the Little
Father knew how his subjects really lived, the priest argued, Nicholas
would help them.

Gapon presided over nearly a quarter million workers in St. Petersburg at the height of the war with Japan. On 16 January 1905, in the
same week that Port Arthur fell, workers at the Putilov Ironworks went
out on strike over a minor dispute; within five days, over 150,000 workers, all members of Gapon's union, had left their posts to join in.[3]

The priest spent the next week visiting the workers, going from
hut to hut, sewer to sewer, through snow and slush. What he saw convinced him that something had to be done: children, malnourished and
sick, lying in "beds" of straw and rags; men and women clad only in
woolen tatters, bent low over open fires to keep warm; dead infants hidden away under a chair or a table. And everywhere disease and hunger.
To each, Gapon said the same thing: On the next Sunday, he would lead
a march of thousands of workers to the Winter Palace. Once there,
Gapon would go to the tsar on the balcony and present him with a petition calling for a constituent assembly, universal manhood suffrage,
universal education, separation of church and state, an income tax,
amnesty for all political prisoners, a minimum wage, and an eight-hour
workday.[4] If the tsar did not respond, the petition said, "we shall die,
here, on this square, before your palace."[5]

The government, under the leadership of the minister of the interior, Prince Sviatopolk-Mirsky—who had replaced the assassinated
Plehve—had expected discontent. In anticipation of this, the minister
drafted a decree for reforms which Nicholas signed to appease those
planning to march for change. What the people got instead of the expected reforms was minor: government insurance of workers, less government interference, and the easing of legal positions for national and
religious minorities.[6] The march remained scheduled.

Sviatopolk-Mirsky ordered reinforcements called in and gave the order that under no circumstances should the workers be allowed to reach the Winter Palace. Soldiers shipped into the capital were stationed at strategic points leading to the Palace Square. The tsar was not told of the plan until Saturday night. The workers believed he would be in St. Petersburg as usual; but the season had been called off because of the war, and, with the growing unrest in the capital, the imperial family was only safe at Tsarskoe Selo or at Peterhof. Nicholas grappled with the idea of meeting the marchers but decided eventually that it was best not to encourage them in their hopes.

Sunday morning, 22 January 1905, was cold and clear in St. Petersburg. The air hung heavy, ominously, over the drifts of snow that had collected along the avenues and canals of the city. St. Petersburg was frozen, its streets hushed; the only sound to be heard was the constant tolling of church bells in the tall golden spires, calling the faithful to prayer. An icy wind howled through the narrow back streets as factory workers gathered and prepared to march. They followed each other expectantly, in a generally cheerful mood, wearing their best coats and hats, carefully sewn with muslin patches to keep out the cold. Muffled and wrapped, they carried icons, religious banners, and portraits of the tsar. Small clusters of workers grew into crowds, then swirling masses, as they neared the Winter Palace. Gapon marched on; it was nearly two o'clock, the time when all the groups would converge in the square. The workers sang hymns and "God Save the Tsar."[7]

The long red façade of the Winter Palace loomed through the fog as the 200,000 workers marched toward their destination. At one end of the square, a line of Preobrajensky Guards stood rigid across the snow, blocking access to the palace. They had been told that the workers wanted to murder the imperial family and destroy the Winter Palace.[8] Blank volleys fired into the air by the soldiers left the workers confused. Instead of turning back, they pressed forward, across the white square toward the line of armed men. More shots into the air, blank, followed by live rounds. Then one soldier after another lowered his rifle and shot into the crowd. In the minutes that followed, bullets ripped through men, women, and children, banners, icons, and portraits of the tsar, splattering the white snow with red. Crying, screaming, and moaning rose over the square. The massacre of 22 January 1905—"Bloody Sunday"—was over.

The official number of dead was set at ninety-two; the wounded, at several hundred.[9] The real numbers were much higher, as many more workers had been shot all around St. Petersburg as they tried to reach the Winter Palace. Ninety-two or nine hundred, St. Petersburg was shocked. Gapon survived the massacre; in a statement from his secret hiding place, he called the tsar a "soul murderer," soaked in "the innocent blood of workers, their wives and children."[10] Although the tsar fired Sviatopolk-Mirsky, blame ultimately fell back on to the throne. The imperial family's image was not helped at all by the unbelievably callous statement of Grand Duke Vladimir to newspaper reporters in London. Asked about the tragedy, the grand duke stiffened, coldly stating, "We prevented the assemblage."[11]

Alexandra was stunned. She could not turn to Nicholas for comfort, for the tsar himself was deeply depressed. Instead, she poured out her feelings in a lengthy letter to her sister Victoria:

> You understand the crisis we are going through. It is a time full of trials indeed. My poor Nicky's cross is a heavy one to bear, all the more as he has nobody on whom he can thoroughly rely and who can be a real help to him. He has had so many bitter disappointments, but through it all he remains brave and full of faith in God's mercy. He tries so hard, works with such perseverance, but the lack of what I call "real men" is great. Of course they must exist somewhere, but it is difficult to get at them. The bad are always close at hand, the others through false humility keep in the background. We shall try to see more people but it is difficult. On my knees I pray to God to give me wisdom to help him in his heavy task. I rack my brain to pieces to find a man and cannot; it is a despairing feeling. One is too weak, the other too liberal, the third too narrow-minded and so forth. Two very clever men we have and both are more than dangerous and unloyal. The Minister of the Interior is doing the greatest harm— he proclaims grand things without having prepared them. It's like a horse that has been held very tight in hand, and then suddenly one lets the reins go. It bolts, falls, and it is more than difficult to pull it up again before it has dragged others with it into the ditch. Reforms can only be made gently with the greatest care and fore-thought. Now we have precipitately been launched forth and cannot retrace our steps. All these disorders are thanks to his unpardonable folly and he won't believe what Nicky tells him, does not agree with his point of view. Things are in bad state and it's abominably unpatriotic at the time when we are plunged into war to break forth with revolutionary ideas. The poor workmen, who had been utterly misled, had to suffer, and the organizers have hidden as usual behind them. Don't believe all the horrors the foreign papers say. They make one's hair stand on end—foul exaggeration. Yes, the troops, alas, were obliged to fire. Repeatedly the crowd was told to retreat and that Nicky was not in town (as we are living here this winter) and that one would be

forced to shoot, but they would not heed and so blood was shed. On the whole 92 killed and between 200–300 wounded. It is a ghastly thing, but had one not done it the crowd would have grown colossal and 1,000 would have been crushed. All over the country, of course, it is spreading. The petition had only two questions concerning the workmen and all the rest was atrocious: separation of the church from the state, etc., etc. Had a small deputation brought, calmly, a real petition for the workmen's good, all would have been otherwise. Many of the workmen were in despair, when they heard later what the petition contained, and begged to work again under the protection of the troops. Petersburg is a rotten town, not one atom Russian. The Russian people are deeply and truly devoted to their Sovereign and the revolutionaries use his name for provoking them against landlords, etc., but I don't know how. How I wish I were clever and could be of real use. I love my new country. It's so young, powerful and has so much good in it, only utterly unbalanced and childlike. Poor Nicky, he has a bitter hard life to lead. Had his father seen more people, drawn them around him, we should have had lots to fill the necessary posts; now only old men or quite young ones, nobody to turn to.[12]

Clearly, at the time of Bloody Sunday, Alexandra believed that she had a duty to her husband—to guide him in the execution of his duties. Alexander III had not done enough to ensure that his son would have men to rely on, Alexandra said; therefore, it was up to her to help Nicholas in the difficult situation. Daily, she "prays to God to give me wisdom"—on her knees, even—and "racks her brain" to help her husband make political judgments and choose his ministers.

It is an important point, for it has always been assumed that the tsarina took no active role in political affairs until the First World War. But the evidence suggests that the reverse may well have been true, that Alexandra did, in fact, exert her considerable weight in certain matters. Certainly, as she withdrew from society and society from her, she turned to the tsar for company and protection, in turn isolating him more and more. In this closed family setting, it would be unrealistic to suppose that her opinions and views were not made known to Nicholas. And, equally, he in turn was less exposed to outside opinions. Under such circumstances, Alexandra's influence became formidable.

Her influence on the tsar was rooted not, as one might expect, in the experience of her childhood but in the summer of 1894, when she was lectured on the Russian autocracy by Ella's husband, Grand Duke Serge. It was from Serge that she learned the principles of autocracy and the mystical nature of the tsar's office.[13] In the two years that followed, she seemingly underwent a conversion to the most conservative, narrow-minded viewpoint imaginable. By the time of her visit to Balmoral in 1896, Alexandra had become absolutely convinced of the necessity of maintaining and preserving the autocracy.[14]

She came to the throne of imperial Russia with a political heritage deeply rooted in the constitutional monarchy of England. Even in Hesse, her father and brother had few real political prerogatives. In Russia, however, the tsarina was married to a man regarded as semidivine, and she herself was revered and exalted. It proved a tragically impressionable experience for her. As a girl, she had seen the pomp and glamour and devotion surrounding her own family, but it paled in comparison to Russia. The palaces, the jewels, the homage, the Orthodox church, the Byzantine opulence of the Russian court—all slowly influenced Alexandra's point of view from her first days as tsarina.

Queen Victoria had anticipated this. In 1884, when Ella married Grand Duke Serge, the queen expressed the hope that "darling Ella won't be spoilt by all this admiration and adulation and all of this glitter of jewelry and grandeur."[15] The queen recognized the impact the atmosphere of the Russian court could have on her granddaughters, and her worst fears became a reality in Alexandra's life.

As the years went by, Alexandra's ideas changed. She developed an increasingly isolated and reactionary view of the situation in Russia. She never forgot her English heritage. But to the tsarina, England eventually came to mean summer holidays at Osborne and Windsor, family dinners in London, and picnics at Balmoral, not, as M. E. Almedingen has pointed out, the liberalism of "Whitehall or Westminster."[16]

Her belief in the autocracy as an institution established by God was very real. With these thoughts in mind, Alexandra quickly forgot the realities of popular monarchy, the need to win the people's support and affection. She firmly believed that "true" Russians already loved the imperial family merely by virtue of their position. She did not understand that it was still necessary, if not to win popular support, then certainly not to alienate it. She once wrote to Queen Victoria, "Russia is not England. Here it is not necessary to make efforts to gain popular affection."[17] It was, for the tsarina, a convenient point of view, for she always felt ill at ease trying to charm strangers. Her self-imposed isolation, coupled with the increasingly reactionary stances which she took, made Alexandra into a dangerous influence on her husband. Ideas of enlightenment and reform found no place in her body of reason. To her, aristocratic privilege was justified by the position in which they had been placed by God. Any attempt to intrude on that privilege was regarded as an attack on a system ordered by God for the preservation of the Russian state.

Alexandra's views on Russia were clearly ill conceived and unrealistic. At the time of Bloody Sunday, her failure to understand the political and social realities of the country led to clearly delineated lines of "us" and "them," a firm belief that "real" Russians lived not in the cities but in the provinces, happy, prosperous peasants toiling contentedly and slavishly devoted to their sovereign. She would soon see this last illusion shattered.

20

1905

Iт was THREE O'CLOCK on the afternoon of 17 February 1905 when Grand Duke Serge Alexandrovich, Alexandra's brother-in-law and Nicholas's uncle, left his apartment in the Kremlin, boots clicking swiftly down the marble hall. He was in a foul mood. It was just three weeks after Bloody Sunday. Following in the wake of the St. Petersburg massacre, Moscow had erupted in violence. Students marched and rioted at Moscow University, and thousands filled the streets, shouting angry antiwar, antimonarchist slogans. As governor-general of Moscow, the grand duke had watched helplessly as unrest overtook the former capital. Faced with this failure to control the situation, Serge had resigned his post. He climbed into an antique German carriage, lined in gray silk, and set off across the square to attend his last official meeting.[1]

Serge Alexandrovich had always been among the most hated of all the Romanov family. The general public despised him for his cold, reactionary manner, and Serge took a kind of perverse pride in knowing how detested he really was. Although he himself opposed any form of liberalism, Serge reserved his most vehement hatred for Russian Jews. He was determined to rid Moscow of all Jews. In 1891, Serge was appointed governor-general of Moscow. "My brother Serge does not want to go to Moscow before the Jews are cleaned out," Alexander III allegedly told his minister of the interior, Ivan Durnovo.[2] Serge's first official act was the expulsion of some twenty thousand Jews from Moscow. He followed this with a new law, outlawing the common practice of Jews taking Christian names during the course of their educations.[3] He forbade any new Jewish immigrants to take up residence in Moscow; the only exception to this law was young Jewish girls, who Serge decreed could live in the city as long as they listed themselves officially as prostitutes.[4]

Serge was not without his supporters. Moscow conservatives admired his strength in dealing with the city's internal strife. It has even been suggested that he was actually under the influence of powerful political forces against which he was impotent and that these forces were responsible for the policies which made Serge so unpopular.[5] None of the evidence available seems to support this view, however, and certainly, in the eyes of the public, it was the grand duke who assumed total blame for the repressive measures he instituted.

His own family also regarded Serge with disgust. The grand duke liked to wear corsets, and younger members of the family always tried to touch the stays through Serge's tunic, which annoyed him immensely.[6] Vain, narrow-minded, and insensitive, he was long whispered to be a sadist—or worse, a homosexual—in the bedroom.[7] Alexander Mossolov, the head of the imperial chancellery, wrote that "his private life was the talk of the town."[8] His marriage to Ella was not a happy one, and the pair lived virtually separate lives. He once forbade Ella to read *Anna Karenina*, fearing that it would incite her to curious and unnatural thoughts.[9] "How can you bear it?" Alexandra allegedly once asked her sister. But Ella's only response was "He is my husband."[10] Whatever the truth, most of the Romanovs regarded Serge with suspicion and mistrust. "Try as I will," wrote Grand Duke Alexander Michailovich, "I cannot find a single redeeming feature in his character. . . . Obstinate, arrogant, disagreeable, he flaunted his many peculiarities in the face of the entire nation, providing the enemies of the regime with inexhaustible material for calumnies and libels."[11]

Serge had always been a prime target for the revolutionaries of Moscow, and it is perhaps surprising that he continued, in the face of the terrible chaos spreading over the city, to drive about with only an ordinary escort. On the fateful afternoon of 17 February 1905, Ella said good-bye to her husband and returned to her rooms in the Kremlin. Serge had not been gone for more than a few minutes when a tremendous explosion rattled the windows of the palace. Ella guessed at once what must have happened. She screamed, "It's Serge!" and rushed out into the courtyard.[12]

Running across the square, she gradually came upon splinters of glass and wood and steel, then pieces of cloth still burning from the explosion. A bit farther on lay her husband's leg, with the foot some distance away in the crimson snow. The other foot, still in the leather boot, led the way to the wreckage of the carriage itself. In the pile of smoldering wood lay what was left of Serge, a terrible bloody mess missing its limbs. Nothing much remained of the grand duke's head except for a few bones which protruded through what little flesh was left and his eyes, which stared vacantly.[13] Ella watched as the guards scurried about from piece to piece, trying to gather what remained of the grand duke. Her only thought, or so she later wrote, was "Hurry, hurry, Serge hates blood and mess."[14] With her own hands, the grand duchess picked up some of the bigger pieces from the snow and placed them in the folds of her dress. By the time the square had been cleaned of its gruesome sight, Ella's silk dress was covered in her husband's blood. The force of the blast had been so strong that some of the grand duke's fingers, with their rings still on, were later discovered on a rooftop some distance away from the Kremlin.[15]

Alexandra was horrified at the news and wanted to start at once for Moscow to be with her widowed sister. But the tsar declared this too dangerous, and she remained in the safety and seclusion of Tsarskoe Selo. Nicholas himself was apparently not overwhelmed with grief at his uncle's death, if Prince Friedrich Leopold of Prussia is to be believed. The prince was staying with the tsar and tsarina at the time of the assassination. He assumed that the banquet that evening would be called off. But when he entered the reception room, he saw the tsar and his cousin Sandro, Grand Duke Alexander Michailovich, sitting on a couch, tickling each other and trying to push one another onto the floor amid howls of laughter.[16]

After the grand duke's funeral, Ella went to see his assassin in prison. The man, Ivan Kaliaev, was a social revolutionary. When the grand duchess entered his cell, he asked her, "Who are you?"

"I am the widow of the man you killed," she answered. "What led you to commit this crime?"[17] The pair spoke at length; Ella did not, however—as has often been alleged—offer to plead with the tsar for Kaliaev's life. She told her sister Victoria, "I have nothing to do with earthly justice. It was his soul and not his body I was thinking of."[18] Kaliaev told the grand duchess that his death would aid the revolutionary cause. And Kaliaev did die: He was executed by hanging. On the appointed day, he was led up the scaffold steps, his head covered with a hood and a noose placed around his neck. At a signal, the floor dropped out from the scaffold, and Kaliaev shot downward—only to land on the ground, where he regained his balance and stood wondering what had happened. Officials quickly cut the rope to its proper length, and again Kaliaev climbed the scaffold steps to be hanged, this time successfully.[19]

Ella made a controversial decision after her husband's death: She sold all of her possessions and, with the money, built a convent and hospital on the banks of the Moscow River. After many years of fighting with the Holy Synod, she was granted the right to become its abbess and founded the Convent of St. Mary and St. Martha. Perhaps the empty years with Serge had helped prepare her for a life filled not with earthly goods but with spiritual ideals. With a devotion which earned her the reputation of a saint, Ella wore the robes of her sisterhood and worked tirelessly on behalf of the sick and the poor. Her commitment was total; she even sold her wedding ring.[20]

A short time after Bloody Sunday, the rest of Russia erupted in violence and anarchy. Some 500,000 workers from all across the country were on strike. The armies deserted, the navies mutinied, the peasants revolted, and the revolutionaries plotted. In St. Petersburg food supplies ran short, hospitals closed, and electrical plants were abandoned. By night the city was dark and lifeless; by day, thousands marched, waving red flags and shouting antitsarist slogans.

No part of the country was immune from the chaos. Along the Black Sea, the sailors of the battleship *Potemkin* threw their officers overboard and cruised up and down the coast firing on the towns until they eventually ran out of fuel. In central Russia, angry peasants stormed the great country houses and murdered their landlords. Students in both St. Petersburg and Moscow provoked the cities to unrest. The country was in the midst of a full-scale revolution. Alexandra and Nicholas remained at Tsarskoe Selo, unable to leave their own palace for fear of assassination.

The tsar responded by calling out his soldiers to put down the rebellions. But the army was sadly depleted; the Russo-Japanese War had taken a heavy toll. Still, peasant revolts were dealt with ruthlessly, and the tsar reported to his mother that "many seditious bands have been dispersed, their homes and property burnt." Thousands were killed. As historian W. Bruce Lincoln has noted, "No Romanov before Nicholas II had ever crushed his subjects on such a massive national scale."[21] Even so, the revolution continued.

At the end of September and the beginning of October, a new wave of strikes broke out in both Moscow and St. Petersburg. Railway workers virtually cut off communication and transportation by their walkouts. There were more demonstrations—workers and students marching in the streets—and by the middle of October it was obvious that the situation could not continue.

There seemed to be only two ways out of the crisis: crush the revolt, which meant a military dictatorship, or grant a Parliament and Constitution. The tsar himself was said to have favored a military dictatorship under the leadership of his cousin Grand Duke Nicholas Nicholaievich, known to the family as Nikolasha. But when the grand duke got wind of this, he drove out to Tsarskoe Selo, pushed his way into the tsar's study, and threatened to shoot himself on the spot unless the tsar granted considerable reforms.[22]

Serge Witte, the tsar's prime minister, continually urged the granting of concessions. To many, it seemed inevitable and the only way out of the crisis, but the tsar was reluctant to part with his auto-cratic powers. "I shall never, under any circumstances," the tsar once told Witte, "agree to a representative form of government because I consider it harmful to the people whom God has entrusted to my care."[23] On another occasion, Nicholas had told Prince Sviatopolk-Mirsky, "I maintain autocracy not for my own pleasure, I act in its spirit only because I am convinced that it is necessary for Russia. If it were for myself, I would gladly be rid of it."[24] Witte met with the tsar on 22 October and advised him to grant a Parliament and a Constitution. It is apparent that Nicholas spoke with Alexandra at some length that evening, for the next day, Witte was called back, to meet with both sovereigns and explain the proposals for the tsarina's benefit. Given her views—expressed previously on the subject—it is unlikely that Alexandra was sympathetic to Witte's program. But the tsar, faced with no alternative, finally broke down and bowed to pressure. On 30 October 1905 he signed an imperial manifesto creating a Constitution and an elected Parliament. The manifesto promised freedom of conscience, speech, assembly, and association. That evening, one of the tsar's staff found him at his desk, crying. "Don't leave me today," Nicholas said. "I am too depressed. I feel that in signing this act I have lost the crown. Now all is finished."[25]

The October Manifesto paved the way for a great democratic experiment in Russia. While it did not specifically use the word *constitution*, the manifesto effectively ended the autocratic rule of the Romanovs. Even so, the tsar remained the most powerful constitutional monarch in the world. So ambiguous was the delineation of power that the 1906 *Almanach de Gotha* referred to Russia as a constitutional monarchy ruled by an autocrat.[26]

The opening session of Parliament, called the Duma, took place, oddly enough, in the throne room of the Winter Palace, the sanctum sanctorum of the autocracy. More than one observer was struck by the fact that on a similiar May morning in 1789, Louis XVI had opened the Estates General at Versailles. The tsar, tsarina, and dowager empress all paraded into the room wearing brocaded mantles and ceremonial clothing. Slowly, the tsar made his way to the throne, preceded by pages in livery carrying velvet cushions on which rested the regalia: the imperial state crown, the orb, and the scepter, all visible symbols of the autocracy. From the dais, the tsar read the speech inaugurating the Duma. To the minister of finance, Vladimir Kokovstsov, it was a strange scene:

> The entire right side of the room was filled with uniformed
> people, members of the State Council and, further on, the Tsar's

retinue. The left side was crowded with the members of the Duma, a small number of whom had appeared in full dress, while the overwhelming majority . . . occupying the first places near the throne were dressed, as if intentionally, in workers' blouses and cotton shirts, and behind them was a crowd of peasants . . . some in national dress, and a multitude of the clergy.[27]

The room was filled with hatred. Both Alexandra and Marie Feodorovna fought back tears as the tsar read his speech ending the autocracy. One guest recalled that the tsarina "appeared as cold and disdainful as usual; she seemed bored more than anything else, and scarcely noticed the low salutations with which the imperial party was greeted when they came into the room."[28] The minister of the imperial court, Count Vladimir Fredericks, later declared, "The deputies, they gave one the impression of a gang of criminals who are only waiting for a signal to throw themselves upon the ministers and cut their throats. What wicked faces! I will never again set foot among those people!"[29]

21

The Birth of an Heir

WHEN ALEXANDRA GAVE BIRTH to a third daughter, Grand Duchess Marie, in 1899, Nicholas was so overcome with disappointment that he had to walk in the park before he could face his wife.[1] The tsarina, in the first ten years of her marriage to Nicholas, gave birth to four daughters—Olga, Tatiana, Marie, and Anastasia. But as the wife of the tsar of all the Russias, she had not gratified the expectations of the nation: A tsar must have a son to succeed him to the throne.

It had not always been so. By the time of Nicholas's reign as tsar, the imperial crown no longer passed through the female as well as the male line. This was the direct result of the bad relationship between Catherine the Great and her only son, Tsar Paul. Paul so hated his mother that one of his first acts upon her death had been to strike down the law of primogeniture and replace it with the Salic law, whereby all females were barred from ever holding the Romanov throne unless all legitimate male descendants were dead. This meant that if Alexandra could not produce a son, the throne would not pass to her daughters but to the tsar's brother and thence to his uncle and cousins.

Alexandra grew frantic and began to clutch at straws. Just after the turn of the century, a number of wandering pilgrims and holy men and women all made their way to the Alexander Palace at the request of the tsar and tsarina. Many of these so-called religious figures were clearly charlatans but had impressed various religious leaders enough to be brought to the attention of the imperial couple. It should not be surprising that Alexandra and Nicholas turned to such people for comfort; wandering holy men and women were condoned and even encouraged by the Orthodox church, which taught that miracles and the power of prayer were active forces working within a twentieth-century world.

Among the first of these spiritual advisers was a peasant woman known as Matronushka the Barefooted. She was a retarded peasant of nearly eighty who was said to predict the birth of a male heir to the throne. Another woman, Daria Ossipova, was an epileptic who fell into fits and shouted predictions to the tsar and tsarina. According to one source, Alexandra was terrified by her displays and soon sent her away.[2] A third, more disagreeable figure was Mitia Koliaba. Koliaba was a deaf-and-dumb peasant who was said to have the special gift of direct communication with God. He was an epileptic and during a seizure was apparently overcome with religious hysteria. The experience was made even worse by the fact that Koliaba was a cripple and had two stumps in place of his arms, which he waved wildly in the air when in one of his fits, accompanied by "horrible sounds" uttered in "painful gasps" and a terrifying howling and spitting. One man, who suffered through such a display of divine revelation, later wrote, "One had to have extremely strong nerves to endure the presence of this imbecile."[3]

Alexandra eventually fell under the influence of two individuals known to be practitioners of the occult: Grand Duchesses Militza and Anastasia. Both were daughters of King Nicholas I of Montenegro, and both had married cousins of Tsar Nicholas II, Militza to Grand Duke Peter Nicholaievich and Anastasia to Peter's brother Nicholas Nicholaievich. Socially prominent, the sisters led the mystical elements of society through the adventures of seances and table rapping.

In 1900, Militza told Alexandra of a French mystic and clairvoyant, a man named Philippe Nazier-Vachot. Nazier-Vachot had previously worked as a butcher's assistant in Lyon but turned to faith healing in the hope that it would prove a more profitable profession; three times he was arrested for practicing medicine without a license. But Militza, no doubt, skipped over these unpleasantries and developed glowing reports for the tsarina. On a state visit to France in 1901, she arranged for Nazier-Vachot to be presented to the tsar and tsarina. They met with him at Compiégne. He made such an impression on the imperial couple that when they returned to Russia they requested that he accompany them as a doctor attached to the court.

This presented numerous problems. First, there were doubts as to Nazier-Vachot's reputation; the tsar and tsarina seemed not to care about the warnings issued by the French government on this account. But in order for Nazier-Vachot to take up an official position at court, he had first to be granted a medical degree. Requests through discreet channels in the French government met with firm resistance. Eventually, the tsar was able to convince his minister of war to grant the Frenchman a position as a doctor of military medicine, despite the fact that Philippe had never had any medical training. Credentials in hand, Nazier-Vachot promptly journeyed to St. Petersburg.

Some of the powers claimed by Nazier-Vachot were truly incredible. Once, according to his biographer, the little Frenchman calmed the seas to provide a more comfortable voyage for the imperial yacht. Even more miraculous were his claims of invisibility. Once, in the Crimea, Prince Felix Youssoupov met Grand Duchess Militza driving with a strange man. Youssoupov bowed to her, but the grand duchess ignored him and drove on. A few days later, when asked why she had not responded, Militza declared that Youssoupov could not possibly have seen her, because she was with Nazier-Vachot, "and when he wears a hat he is invisible and so are those who are with him."[4]

Although there is no evidence that Alexandra ever believed in this nonsense, she did consult Nazier-Vachot because it was said that he could control the sex of an unborn child. In 1902, it was rumored that Alexandra was again pregnant. Nazier-Vachot is said to have confirmed that the baby would be a boy. But Alexandra never gave birth.

Two differing views have been advanced to explain what happened next. Several contemporary sources indicate that Alexandra had suffered a false pregnancy brought about by the power of suggestion. This version has been widely repeated in many accounts. But there also exists evidence that the tsarina had indeed been pregnant and had suffered a miscarriage. Baroness Sophie Buxhoeveden, Alexandra's chief lady-in-waiting, hinted in her book that this was the case, and Maurice Paléologue, the French ambassador in St. Petersburg, even gives the date for the miscarriage: 1 September 1902.[5]

Whatever the truth of the 1902 pregnancy, a year later Nazier-Vachot again declared that the tsarina was expecting. This came as news to her, and Alexandra called in the imperial physicians. The doctors, after an examination, found no sign of a pregnancy, and Nazier-Vachot was sent packing, but not before he pronounced that God would send Alexandra a new friend to help her through her troubles.[6]

Although the advice of the Montenegrin sisters had thus far only led to trouble, Alexandra again consulted them. They suggested that she ask for the intercession of Seraphim, an old hermit who had lived and died in poverty in Sarov and who had a reputation as a holy man. But, Militza said, the one thing which Alexandra must do in order to obtain Seraphim's intervention was to convince the Holy Synod of the hermit's sainthood. Pobedonostsev, the tsar's old tutor and now minister of religion, was called in and told to arrange for the canonization. He protested, saying that such a step required years of investigation. But Alexandra angrily interrupted him, saying that "everything is within the Tsar's power, even to the making of saints."[7]

Although Seraphim was generally regarded as a holy man, there was a great public outcry when Alexandra began to push for his canonization. He had died in 1833. As a prerequisite for the canonization, the Orthodox church required some outward sign of holiness; a major test was the preservation of the remains of the candidate in question. In Seraphim's case, the outcry was all the more violent because when the coffin was opened the body was in an advanced state of decomposition. This failed to deter Alexandra and Nicholas. When Bishop Anthony of Tambov spoke out against the proposed canonization, the tsar sent him to Siberia.[8] The public outcry forced Metropolitan Anthony of St. Petersburg to formally declare in a Holy Synod announcement that the state of Seraphim's remains was not essential to the question of his alleged sainthood, thereby contradicting hundreds of years of official Orthodox canon law.[9] In the end, Alexandra had her way, and Seraphim was canonized in a great ceremony in Sarov. That same night, Alexandra quietly slipped down to the Sarovka River and bathed in its waters, feeling certain that this would help her conceive.[10] Sure enough, within a few months, Alexandra was again pregnant.

Friday, 12 August 1904, was a hot summer day at Peterhof, where Alexandra and Nicholas were in residence. At noon, the imperial couple sat down to luncheon. Alexandra had very little appetite and could barely finish her soup. When she could wait no longer, Alexandra excused herself and went to her bedroom. The doctor was called in and alerted the tsar that his wife was not suffering merely from indigestion. That afternoon, at a quarter past one, Alexandra gave birth to a son. "Oh, it cannot be true! It cannot be true!" Alexandra sobbed. "Is it really a boy?"[11]

In St. Petersburg the guns of the Fortress of Peter and Paul fired a salute of three hundred rounds. Across the country, church bells rang out, cannon roared, and people rejoiced. The new baby was the first male heir born to a reigning sovereign since the seventeenth century.

His Imperial Highness Alexei Nicholaievich, Sovereign Heir and Tsarevich, Grand Duke of Russia, Hetman of All Cossacks, Knight of the Order of St. Andrew, Head of the Siberian Infantry, of the Horse Battalion Infantry, and of the Cadet Corps, was a fat, fair little baby with deep blue eyes and golden curls. His parents called him Alexei after the second Romanov tsar, the father of Peter the Great. When they were permitted, the four little grand duchesses tiptoed into the nursery next to the tsarina's bedroom and peered into the brass crib that held their new brother.

The christening of this little prince took place in the Peterhof Church on a rainy Wednesday afternoon in late August. For the event, many European royalties gathered; even the eighty-seven year-old great-grandfather of the new tsarevich, King Christian IX of Denmark, came to Russia. The tsarevich's godparents included Kaiser Wilhelm II, King Edward VII, Grand Duke Ernest Ludwig of Hesse, and his grandmother the dowager empress.

Alexei lay on a pillow of cloth-of-gold, covered with the heavy cloth-of-gold christening mantle lined in ermine. Princess Marie Golitsyn, a lady-in-waiting who, by tradition, carried all imperial babies to the baptismal font, also bore Alexei to the church. Because of her advanced age, special precautions had to be taken to ensure that she would not fall and drop the tiny infant. Attached to the pillow on which Alexei lay was a golden band slung around the princess's shoulder; even the shoes which she wore were fitted with rubber soles to prevent slipping.[12]

As the princess walked up the aisle to the baptismal font, the crowd looked on in admiration at the fat little prince kicking on the pillow. The four sisters giggled in delight as their brother passed them by; only the parents were absent, according to an Orthodox custom. The service itself was performed by elderly Father Yanishev, the former confessor to the imperial family who had taught Alexandra the Orthodox catechism. He took the prince from the pillow, held him up for all to see, and pronounced over the baby the name of Alexei.[13] Yanishev dipped the tsarevich bodily into the font, and Alexei screamed in response. When the service was over, the parents rushed to the church; both were sure that between the aged princess and the elderly priest, someone would drop their son. That afternoon, Alexandra and Nicholas received guests in a drawing room at Peterhof. She lay on a couch, smiling at the tsar, who stood nearby.[14]

The tiny prince captivated all those who saw him. "How beautiful he was, how healthy, how normal, with his golden hair, his shining blue eyes, and his expression of intelligence so rare for so young a child," wrote Anna Vyrubova.[15] Pierre Gilliard first met Alexandra and Alexei when the baby was just eighteen months old. He wrote: "I could see she was transfused by the delirious joy of a mother who had at last seen her dearest wish fulfilled. She was proud and happy in the beauty of her child. The Tsarevich certainly was one of the handsomest babies one could imagine, with lovely fair curls, great grey-blue eyes under the fringe of long, curling lashes and the fresh pink colour of a healthy child. When he smiled, there were two little dimples in his chubby cheeks."[16]

The proud parents never missed an opportunity to show off their new son. When the tsar met Alexander Mossolov, the head of the court chancellery, he dragged the man off to the nursery, saying, "I don't think that you have yet seen my dear little Tsarevich. Come along and I will show him to you."

"We went in," records Mossolov. "The baby was being given his daily bath. He was lustily kicking out in the water. . . . The Tsar took the child out of his bath towels and put his little feet in the hollow of his hand, supporting him with the other arm. There he was, naked, chubby, rosy—a wonderful boy."

"Don't you think he's a beauty?" asked the smiling Nicholas. The next day, the tsar informed Alexandra that "yesterday I had the Tsarevich on parade before Mossolov."[17]

The joy was temporary. Six weeks after Alexei's birth, he began to hemorrhage from the navel. The doctors applied bandages to the gurgling blood as the horrified parents watched. After two days, the bleeding stopped. But for the next few months Alexandra lived in terrible fear. She watched as her beloved son grew and began to crawl and walk. When he tumbled, his arms and legs were covered with dark blue bruises. Alexei cried out in pain as, beneath his skin, the blood refused to clot and instead formed horrible swellings. There was no longer any doubt. The tsarevich had hemophilia.

Alexandra had always known that hemophilia was a possibility. Indeed, it ran in the British royal family. When Queen Victoria gave birth to a hemophiliac son, Prince Leopold, she protested that "this disease is not in our family."[18] This sudden appearance of the defective genes, known as spontaneous mutation, only served to highlight the uncertainty surrounding the disease. Although transmitted by mothers to their sons, hemophilia is, nearly without exception, a male disease. Even so, it does not always strike each male child of a hemophiliac carrier: Of Queen Victoria's four sons, only Prince Leopold suffered from it. There is no way of knowing if a girl whose mother had a hemophiliac son is herself a hemophiliac carrier until she has her own children. Two of Queen Victoria's daughters, Alice and Beatrice, had hemophiliac sons. In turn, two of Alice's daughters, Irene and Alix, had hemophiliac sons. In fact, Irene's youngest son, Heinrich, died at the age of four, only a short time before Alexei was born. Through Queen Victoria, the disease came to the royal houses of Britain, Germany, Spain, and Russia.

No tragedy affected Alexandra as deeply as her son's hemophilia. Wars, political struggles, and family deaths could be relegated to the past, but not so the tsarevich's illness. Alexandra lived through its realities daily, experienced its terrible uncertainty every hour, every day, for the rest of her life. She could never forget it. Her son's hemophilia became a presence in her life, affecting her decisions and dictating her attitudes. It was not, for her, merely an illness; it became an active force working within her son.

The tragedy of the tsarevich's hemophilia was compounded by the secrecy which surrounded the Russian court. Cloistered at Tsarskoe Selo, both Alexandra and Nicholas believed that what went on behind the palace walls was their own private family business. They did not seem to understand that they and their children were public figures, subject to speculation and rumor. The wall that went up around the imperial family alienated them from public affection. This self-imposed isolation was damaging enough; but the tsar and tsarina made a fatal mistake regarding their son's illness, a decision which kept the tsarevich's hemophilia a secret. Russia was denied the knowledge of the heir's affliction. When Alexei was sick, it was said that he had a sprained ankle or a cold. When Alexandra had to appear in public, her face was tightly set, masking the terrible anxiety she felt for the son she left behind. Since no one knew that her grave expression came from worry over her son, many of the public took her appearance for haughtiness. In time, rumors about Alexei began to circulate: It was said that he was an epileptic, deformed, or retarded.[19] Denied a true understanding of the situation at Tsarskoe Selo, the public's love for the imperial family quickly turned to apathy and, with time, to hatred directed against the tsarina. The louder the rumors and criticism, the higher the walls of secrecy surrounding the imperial family. Tragedy built upon misunderstanding and the shadows of public indifference lengthened over the imperial park at Tsarskoe Selo.

PART THREE

The Starets

(1905–14)

22

Holy Russia

ALEXANDRA WAS THIRTY-TWO YEARS OLD when she gave birth to the tsarevich. His first hemorrhage marked the turning point in her life as tsarina. Her existence became a series of constant worries over narrowly avoided accidents and tragedies which were always feared and awaited with a dreaded uncertainty. Members of the Romanov family who knew of the tsarevich's disease could offer Alexandra little in the way of sympathy, as most of them had been banished from imperial court functions due to scandals and rumors, and disliked the tsarina intensely. The rest of the country did not know what was wrong with the tsarevich. Instead, Alexandra turned to the ancient center of Russian life and unity, the Orthodox church. She found in its passionate faith both comfort and understanding.

The Russian Orthodox church began in 988. Grand Duke Vladimir of Kiev, ruler of ancient Rus, selected the Eastern faith for his people and proceeded to baptize them in the waters of the Dnieper River. In 1054, the Orthodox church, in a conflict over the correct form of worship and the supremacy of the Roman pope, broke away from the West, and thereafter Constantinople became the center of the Orthodox world. The church was so separated from the happenings in Europe that it experienced the effects of neither the Renaissance nor the Reformation. In 1453, Constantinople fell to the Turks; a hundred years later, Moscow gained its own patriarch and the title of "the Third Rome."

In the seventeenth century, the Russian Orthodox church was plunged into a schism. The liturgy at the time contained several errors and the patriarch, Nikon, set about reforming the church, changing, for example, the number of fingers which the faithful should extend when crossing themselves.[1] The corrections may have been minor, but to certain members of the Orthodox church, they meant the difference between salvation and damnation. Consequently, a number of so-called Old Believers split from the established church and formed their own reclusive communities. Some believed that the tsar at the time, Peter the

Great, was the Antichrist. Rather than submit to a ruler they considered under the control of the devil, some twenty thousand Old Believers voluntarily burned themselves alive for their faith in a six-year period.[2]

The Old Believers were schismastics, not heretics, but with time small groups broke away from the communities, establishing sects like the *Khlysty*, who believed in masochistic beatings and whippings as a form of religious worship, and the *Skopsty*, religious castrates. Sectarians quickly became a notorious fact of life in Russia, and with the passage of time, their numbers only increased. There is a story which tells of a sectarian peasant named Kovalev who, on learning that a census was to be taken, declared that the Antichrist wanted a list of the damned. He set about digging graves for himself and his family. He was able to bury his wife and children alive before fellow sectarians interrupted his work. They, too, wished to die. Kovalev helped kill twenty of his comrades before himself committing suicide and falling into his own grave. This event took place not in the seventeenth century, but, extraordinarily, in 1897, in the third year of Nicholas II's reign.[3]

For Alexandra, the decision to convert to Orthodoxy had not been an easy one. But once it was made, she came to embrace the church with all the fervor of a convert. In time, she became so absorbed in the church and its ritual that to many she appeared overzealous in the practice of her religion. In fact, she was merely following the customs which the Orthodox church dictated. She devoutly lit candles, prayed before icons, bowed to priests, and observed feast and fast days. To the aristocracy of St. Petersburg, who had been raised in the church and took much of their religion for granted, this devotion seemed absurd. But Alexandra had been determined from the first not only to understand the church's teachings but also to put them into practice no matter how strange they may have seemed.

She had always been easily impressed by pomp and splendor, and in the Orthodox church this side of her nature was fulfilled. The Russian church was an enormous contrast to the Lutheran beliefs which Alexandra had been taught. It had none of the Lutheran austerity. Alexandra had joined a church of metropolitans in copes and stoles and priests in black chanting in the incense-filled shadows; of richly decorated palaces dedicated to the worship of God, filled with glittering icons and frescoes; of *Te Deums* and litanies sung by robed choirs; and of saints, miracles, and holy men.

Alexandra's religious views remain something of an enigma. Few writers have attempted to understand her motivations and thoughts. Based on appearances, most of St. Petersburg took her to be fanatical. Her propensity toward holy men was highly criticized at court. Yet she once angrily told one official, "These people speak to my heart and to the depth of my spirit more than the officials who come to see me clad in rich robes or silk. When I see a metropolitan dressed in a swishing soutane enter my palace, I ask: What is the difference between him and the elegant folk of high society?"[4]

One of the few clues to Alexandra's beliefs is a small book called *The Friends of God*. She once gave it to Anna Vyrubova to read, but the tsarina's friend could not make sense of it.[5] But this book is the key to understanding the tsarina's beliefs.

The Friends of God was a medieval religious movement. They believed that both suffering and humility were necessary for salvation. Suffering, according to the Friends, was not a sign that God had abandoned one but that he was showing favor. Through such trials, the seeker could come to appreciate his position in relation to God. Many of God's favorites, the Friends believed, were those who had suffered the most. Along with suffering, lack of pride was important in the quest for salvation. One might be filled with sin and yet obtain salvation before the man who believed himself to be pure. The Friends of God strongly criticized the upper classes, who piously attended masses and outwardly observed all the signs of propriety while at the same time committing sin in secret. The lower classes, on the other hand, made no such pretense at righteousness; they admitted their shortcomings, and in recognizing their sins, they stood closer to God than the mighty aristocracy.

Such a belief in the simple purity of the lower classes influenced the Friends to find in the common people the true voice of God. Certain people of this order were more blessed because of their humility. If a peasant was filled with sin, he was also closer to God because of his recognition of this sin. Among such people were to be found leaders in the quest for salvation, men blessed by God to help others. A man so called was likely to be a peasant, to be reviled by others as a sinner, and to himself be a mixture of sin and religious piety. But if one found such a Friend to lead one through life, the quest for salvation was assured as long as the seeker did not waver in his or her support.

Such a philosophy struck a deep chord within Alexandra. She at times believed that her faith was inadequate in itself to reach God and that the intervention of others was necessary on her behalf. It was a belief which the Russian Orthodox church endorsed. The church was filled with wandering holy men rumored to have the ear of God. They were *stranniki*, some of whom journeyed on religious quests, while others may have been escapees from their own brutal existence. There were also monks in the church who lived their lives as spiritual guides to the powerful. Called a *starets*, such a man was thought to not only heal the spirit but also to interpret the will of God to those seeking answers. Prayers were directed at saints and icons or sometimes channeled through those men who claimed such powers. Although such men operated on the fringes of established Orthodoxy, they were recognized as being, if not official representatives of the church, then certainly of their faith. Under these circumstances, it is not surprising that Alexandra should have believed in men such as Mitia Koliaba, Nazier-Vachot, and later, Rasputin.

When, six weeks after Alexei's birth, Alexandra learned of her son's hemophilia, her first reaction may have been disbelief. But soon she not only accepted his disease but found the strength to combat it through her faith in the church. She devoted herself to praying for her son's health. In the Feodorovsky church in the park at Tsarskoe Selo, she had a small chapel built in the crypt.[6] Hour after hour, Alexandra knelt on the cold stone floor, alone in the flickering shadows, begging for the life of her son and repeating over and over, "God is just."[7]

When the doctors could no longer offer hope, Alexandra turned to the church. Her brother-in-law wrote that she "refused to surrender to fate. She talked incessantly of the ignorance of the physicians. She professed an open preference for medicine men. She turned toward religion and her prayers were tainted with a certain hysteria. The stage was ready for the appearance of a miracle worker. . . ."[8]

The "miracle worker" came to the Alexander Palace on 14 November 1905. On that day, Grand Duchess Militza brought with her a simple Siberian peasant who would change the course of Russian history. That man was Gregory Rasputin.

23

Rasputin

Tʜᴇ ᴠɪʟʟᴀɢᴇ ᴏғ Pᴏᴋʀᴏᴠꜱᴋᴏᴇ sat perched on the banks of the Tura River, the main line of communication and travel in the Siberian province of Tobolsk. It was a village of little importance, which was reflected in its narrow, dusty streets, small peasant cottages of rough, unpainted logs, and the manner of its citizens. Pokrovskoe was a village of farmers tending their animals on the edge of the Siberian taiga. Shaped by their surroundings, the people of Pokrovskoe were deeply religious, conservative, and coarse.

It was in Pokrovskoe, sometime in the 1860s or early 1870s, that Gregory Rasputin was born. The exact date of his birth is not known. Just as little is known about his birth, there is next to nothing on record of Rasputin's early life. His father, Efimy Rasputin, had at one time been a coachman in the imperial mail, although apparently he was dismissed for drunkenness and is said to have turned to horse stealing.[1]

The earliest story concerning Rasputin, and one which must be treated with the greatest caution, tells of a gift of prophecy. According to the story, Rasputin, then a small boy, was in bed, ill with a high fever, when a group of villagers came to his father's house to discuss the theft of a horse. The animal had belonged to one of the poorer peasants, and the men were furious, horse stealing being regarded as a capital offense in Siberia. As the men spoke, Gregory listened, sat up in his bed, and pointed to one of the startled peasants, declaring that he was the thief. Quickly, Rasputin's father stepped in, saying that his son could not be held responsible for his words due to the fever. But several of the peasants were suspicious of the accused man's actions. Following him to his house, they saw the suspect lead the stolen horse from his barn and set it free. They beat the peasant quite severely and recaptured the horse for return to its owner.[2]

As he grew up, Rasputin began to acquire the reputation of a rake. He took a job as a supply carrier, traveling from town to town by wagon. These frequent journeys opened up an entirely new sphere of activity to Rasputin. In these secluded villages he discovered pretty, voluptuous peasant girls not adverse to accepting his advances. He was direct, grabbing chests and undoing buttons, and was frequently kicked and bitten.[3] But many of the girls did not resist, and Rasputin's name soon became infamous in Tobolsk Province.

One of his trips took Rasputin to Verkhoturye Monastery. Gregory was so fascinated by what he found at Verkhoturye that when he was later sentenced for stealing some fence posts from a neighbor, he asked that as his punishment he be sent to the monastery rather than prison. He stayed on for several months. For it was at the monastery that two heretical sects had chosen to live, the *Khlysty* and the *Skopsty*. The *Khlysty*, as mentioned earlier, believed in wild beatings as a form of religious worship. At times, and within some of the groups, these rituals ended in sexual intercourse practiced by the participants. Some of the *Khlysty* members believed that only in this way could they reach God: first, sin had to be committed, then confessed, in order for God to hear their prayers.[4] This belief in the use of "sin to drive out sin" was not the only perverse philosophy Rasputin learned at Verkhoturye. There was another sect, the *Skopsty*, whose beliefs the peasant later came to relate as his own. The *Skopsty* believed that after a period of deprivation and study it was possible to attain the nature and omnipotence of God. They came to interpret this as meaning that whatever the sins one might commit, a person could not be judged because he was beyond earthly judgment. They also held that chastity was "the sin of pride" and thus it was wrong to remain chaste in order to present a holy image.[5]

Rasputin's own religious beliefs are somewhat difficult to delineate. He tended to assimilate the beliefs of others and reinterpret them as his own perverse theology. When he returned to Pokrovskoe, he was certainly surrounded by an aura of holiness, although it is not known how much of this new image may have been carefully crafted for the benefit of his impressionable friends. He soon discovered a woman who did not fear the challenge of being his wife, and the pair married sometime after 1890.[6] In later years, when she learned of her husband's sexual exploits, Praskovie Dubrovina never complained, saying, "He has enough for all."[7] She bore Rasputin four children, two boys and two girls. One son died in infancy; the other was retarded. But the two girls, Maria and Varvara, grew up quite normally and later lived for a time with their father in the capital.

In time, Rasputin found it difficult to make a living as a somewhat heretical village holy man. His neighbors believed that he was a member of the *Khlysty* sect, and eventually these rumors reached the village priest, who lodged a formal complaint with the archbishop of Tobolsk

Province. It was only the first of the many allegations which were to surface about Rasputin's involvement with the group. The charge was false; while Rasputin certainly seemed to be fascinated by the sect and eventually borrowed some of their theological ideas as his own, he was never a *Khlyst*. But the allegations were harmful in themselves no matter what the truth behind them.

One day, while working in the fields, Rasputin claimed to have seen a vision. According to Gregory, the Virgin Mary came out of the sky, dressed in magnificent robes, and told him to become a pilgrim. Whether Rasputin actually saw something or merely suffered a hallucination is beside the point; the fact is that he said he sincerely believed he had been visited by the Virgin Mary. Rasputin's father regarded this suspiciously, saying, "Gregory has turned a pilgrim out of laziness."[8] But there is no reason to believe that Rasputin did not enter into his journey sincerely.

According to Gregory, the Virgin Mary told him to walk to the Holy Land. Rasputin walked for some two thousand miles; he finally ended his journey in Greece, at the monastery at Mount Athos. During that time, Rasputin certainly underwent a change. When he returned to Pokrovskoe his manner was entirely different. "His conversation," writes Alex De Jonge, "was desperately hard to follow, for he often spoke in riddles, accompanied by strings of spiritual adages and half-remembered passages from the scriptures."[9] When he spoke, Gregory displayed his greatest gift, the ability to manipulate the people around him.

Perhaps the largest contradiction in Rasputin's character was his sensuality, which he frequently used to achieve his goals. One of his favorite activites was sleeping with one or more naked women or having them wash his sexual organs as a test of his self-control. In later years his carnal appetites were enormous, yet there is no evidence that he ever regarded the apparent contradiction between flesh and spirit with any puzzlement.

When living conditions in his own village grew disagreeably stagnant, Rasputin left on another pilgrimage. Two of the many legends surrounding Rasputin spring from this second journey. It has been said that the villagers of Pokrovskoe gave Gregory "Rasputin" as a nickname. In fact, it had always been his surname, probably derived from the Russian *raspute* meaning a fork in the road, and not *rasputstvo*, debauchery, as has been claimed.[10] Another misconception is that Rasputin was a starets, a monk who wandered the country, helping and guiding others and praying for their souls. A true starets lived an austere, religious life, devoid of the sexuality which was a hallmark of Rasputin's ministry. Rasputin was simply a wandering peasant in search of adventure and his own salvation. Again, it is difficult to say with any certainty what Rasputin's genuine religious concerns may have been.

In 1903, Rasputin arrived in St. Petersburg. The picture is well known. He has been described as

> ... in his early thirties, broad-shouldered, of average height. He dressed roughly in loose peasant blouses and baggy trousers tucked into the top of heavy, crudely made leather boots. He was filthy. He rose and slept and rose again without ever bothering to wash himself or change his clothes. His hands were grimy, his nails black, his beard tangled and encrusted with debris. His hair was long and greasy. Parted loosely in the middle, it hung in thin strands to his shoulders. Not surprisingly, he gave off a powerful, acrid odour.[11]

The writer is Robert K. Massie. The picture has become a part of the Rasputin legend. But how accurate are these descriptions? Colin Wilson takes exception to the entire portrait and writes the following defense of the peasant:

> Several writers have mentioned Rasputin's fondness for the *banie* or steambath, so it is unlikely that he smelt vilely. . . . The rest of the picture presents a completely misleading description of Rasputin as a barbaric drunkard and rapist. His daughter Maria, who lived with him in Petersburg during the years of his greatest influence, records that he began to drink too much only in the final years of his life. He never at any time drank vodka but was fond of sweet wine; in earlier years he was able to drink large quantities of this without showing any sign of it. He was fond of sex, but seems to have had no difficulty in finding fashionable ladies and actresses to share his bed.[12]

The true Rasputin legend really began when he arrived in the capital in 1903. In St. Petersburg he found a mass of elegant, jeweled women, proper on the exterior but longing for something new and daring on the inside. When the strange, mysterious peasant appeared in the elegant drawing rooms, he was backed by the city's most prestigious ecclesiastical hierarchy, Father John of Kronstadt and the Inspector of the St. Petersburg Theological Academy, Archimandrite Theophan. In turn, Theophan introduced the peasant to Bishop Hermogen of Saratov, a much-revered priest in the Orthodox church. It was not unusual for a simple peasant to attract such attention in the capital. Wandering men of God frequently caught the eye of this or that priest, bishop, or prince, who would then display them to his society friends. It was, however, unusual for such exalted church officials to take an interest in a peasant, and this in turn gives an idea of the presence Rasputin must have possessed. Of the clergy who received him, perhaps none was as influential as Father John of Kronstadt, who was responsible for St. Andrew's Cathedral at the naval base outside of St. Petersburg. Father John was one of the most gifted and inspirational of the Orthodox clergy and had served as personal confessor to several members of the imperial family. His popularity caused many Orthodox faithful to flock to him to confess their sins personally. Due to their large numbers, Father John developed a new form of the sacrament: He gathered his congregation together and listened while they all shouted out their sins at the same time.[13] Father John died in 1908, five years after Rasputin came to the capital and before the most notorious period of his St. Petersburg existence; in 1964, he was canonized by the Russian Orthodox Church Outside Russia.

The impressions of society toward Rasputin were vastly different. Some women looked to him for rough, sensual pleasures, which, apparently, if the stories about Rasputin are to be believed, he was only too happy to supply them with. Men looked to him for spiritual guidance and, later, power. Others, offended by his crude manner and lack of humility, called him a fake and accused him of trying to obtain personal power through his society contacts. At least two socially prominent members of the aristocracy, the Grand Duchesses Militza and Anastasia, were impressed enough with Rasputin to bring him to the attention of the tsar and tsarina. As they were the same two sisters who had recommended Nazier-Vachot to Alexandra, it is perhaps surprising that the tsar and tsarina consented to receive him at all. But when Rasputin appeared at the Alexander Palace, he also carried an important backing from Archimandrite Theophan, who, according to one story, told the imperial couple the following:

> Gregory Efimovich is a peasant, a man of the people. Your Majesties will do well to hear him, for it is the voice of the Russian soil which speaks through him. . . . I know his sins, which are numberless, and most of them are heinous. But there dwells in him so deep a passion of repentance and so implicit a trust in divine pity that I would all but guarantee his eternal salvation. Every time he repents he is as pure as the child washed in the waters of baptism. Manifestly, God has called him to be one of His Chosen.[14]

Thus, with such an impressive introduction, Rasputin came to the Alexander Palace, and history.

Alexei was just over a year old when Rasputin first appeared at the Alexander Palace. Hemophilia automatically placed limits on the kind of life Alexei would be able to lead. From the beginning Alexandra decided that he needed bodyguards, and two huge, burly sailors from the imperial navy, Andrei Derevenko and Clementy Nagorny, were assigned to protect him from any injury. "Derevenko was so patient and so resourceful, that he often did wonders in alleviating the pain," wrote Anna Vyrubova. "I can still hear the plaintive voice of Alexei begging the big sailor, `Lift my arm,' `Put up my leg,' `Warm my hands,' and I can see the patient, calm-eyed man working for hours to give comfort to the little pain-wracked limbs."[15]

Even though he was surrounded by bodyguards, accidents were inevitable. When Alexei was three, a blow to his face closed both of his eyes, turning them purple and causing great pain. As he grew older, Alexandra tried to impress on Alexei that he must be careful, even when he played. The tsarevich had a playroom filled with expensive toys and numerous pets, including a spaniel named Joy and a donkey called Vanka. But even with his attacks, Alexei was a growing boy. He had a specially designed tricycle, a bicycle being considered too dangerous; yet he longed for the real thing. "Can't I have my own bicycle?" he would plead. "Alexei, you know you can't," Alexandra would reply. "May I please play tennis?" "Dear, you know you mustn't." Then the heir to the Russian throne would break down and cry, "Why can other boys have everything and I nothing?"[16]

As a child, Alexei was boisterous. He liked to burst into his sisters' classroom, running about the table and singing loudly, only to be carried away, waving his arms and kicking his legs. "He thoroughly enjoyed life—when it let him—and he was a happy, romping boy," wrote one insider.[17] Some of this enjoyment took a less than imperial form. Once, when several years old, Alexei was brought to a state banquet. Walking from place to place, he said a few words of welcome to each guest, then suddenly dashed off under the table. When he reappeared, it was with the shoe of a lady-in-waiting, which Alexei proudly presented to his father. Nicholas ordered him to replace the shoe, and once again, the tsarevich disappeared beneath the table. With a start, the lady in question screamed; before replacing the shoe, Alexei had put a large, ripe strawberry into the toe.[18]

But such happy and carefree times were few. The disease assumed a deadly hold over the tsarina by virtue of its lack of predictability. One minute Alexei could be quite well, happily romping with his sisters. Then the slightest bump or cut and an agonizing, drawn-out nightmare would begin to play itself out. Bumps or bruises which ruptured tiny blood vessels were terrors for the tsarina. While the blood flowed, the pain was not as great, as it seeped into empty spaces between limbs and joints. But when there was no more room, swellings formed, slowly tightening the skin and turning it blue with internal pressure. There was nothing Alexandra could do to help him; only sit beside his bed, holding her son's hand and listening to his mournful screams.

Although Alexandra overprotected her son, others saw that Alexei had to be allowed to lead a semi-normal life. One such man was Pierre Gilliard, the grand duchesses' French tutor. One day, he suggested to the tsarina that the tsarevich was being stifled by his bodyguards. In time, she relented and ordered that Derevenko and Nagorny stay away. Gilliard wrote:

> No doubt they realized how much harm the existing system was doing to all the best in their son, and if they loved him to distraction . . . their love itself gave them the strength to run the risk of an accident . . . rather than see him grow up a man without strength of character. . . . Everything went well at first and I was beginning to be easy in my mind when the accident I had so much feared happened without warning. The Tsarevich was in the classroom standing on a chair, when he slipped and in falling hit his right knee against a corner of some piece of furniture. The next day he could not walk. On the day after the subcutaneous hemorrhage had progressed and the swelling which formed below the knee rapidly spread down the leg. The skin, which was greatly distended, had hardened under the force of the blood and . . . caused pain which worsened every hour. I was thunderstruck. Yet neither the Tsar nor the Tsarina blamed me in the slightest. . . . The Tsarina was at her son's bedside from the first onset of the attack. She watched over him, surrounding him with her tender love and care and trying a thousand attentions to alleviate his sufferings. . . . For a moment the boy would open his great eyes, around which the malady had already painted black circles, and then almost immediately, close them again. One morning I found the mother at her son's bedside. He had had a very bad night. . . . The hemorrhage had not stopped and his temperature was rising. The inflammation had spread and the pain was worse than the day before. The Tsarevich lay groaning in bed piteously. His head rested on his mother's arm and his small, deadly white face was unrecognizable. At times the groans ceased and he murmured the one word, "Mummy." His mother kissed him on the hair, forehead and eyes as if the touch of her lips would relieve him of his pain and restore some of the life which was leaving him. Think of the torture of that mother, an impotent witness of her

son's martyrdom in those hours of anguish—a mother who knew that she herself was the cause of those terrible sufferings, that she had transmitted the terrible disease against which human science was powerless. Now I understood the secret tragedy of her life.[19]

Despite his frequent attacks, Alexei, in time, grew up to be a tall, good-natured boy, with his mother's blue-gray eyes and golden hair. He was unusually thoughtful. When he was ten years old, his sister Olga found him lying on a grassy hill, staring up lazily at the sky. She asked him what he was doing.

"I like to think and wonder," he answered.

"What about?" Olga questioned.

"Oh, so many things. I enjoy the sun and the beauty of summer as long as I can. Who knows whether one of these days I shall not be prevented from doing it?"[20]

It is not known when Rasputin was first approached by the tsar and tsarina to heal their son. At the beginning of the relationship, it seems that many of the peasant's visits were informal ones having nothing to do with the tsarevich's illness. The tsar's sister Olga Alexandrovna later recalled one such evening many years later:

> All the children seemed to like him. They were completely at ease with him. I still remember little Alexei, deciding he was a rabbit, jumped up and down the room. And then, quite suddenly, Rasputin caught the child's hand and led him to his bedroom. . . . There was something like a hush as though we found ourselves in church. In Alexei's bedroom, no lamps were lit; the only light came from the candles burning in front of some beautiful icons. The child stood very still by the side of the giant, whose head was bowed. I knew he was praying. It was all most impressive. I also knew that my little nephew had joined him in prayer. I really cannot describe it—but I was then conscious of the man's sincerity. . . .[21]

The sanctity and mystery surrounding Rasputin were heightened for Olga Alexandrovna by his healing of her nephew, Tsarevich Alexei:

> The poor child lay in pain, dark patches under his eyes and his little body all distorted and the leg terribly swollen. The doctors were just useless . . . more frightened than any of us . . . whispering among themselves. . . . It was getting late and I was persuaded to go to my rooms. Alicky then sent a message to

Rasputin in Petersburg. He reached the palace about midnight or even later. By that time, I had reached my apartments, and early in the morning Alicky called to me to go to Alexei's room. I just could not believe my eyes. The little boy was not just alive—but well. He was sitting up in bed, the fever gone, the eyes clear and bright, not a sign of any swelling in the leg—later I learned from Alicky that Rasputin had not even touched the boy but merely stood at the foot of the bed and prayed.[22]

Although Olga heard the story of the cure secondhand from Alexandra, it stands as a powerful testament to Rasputin's ability to somehow bring relief to the boy's sufferings. The scene would be repeated on many occasions over the course of the next ten years. The most important question, and perhaps the most fascinating element in the entire Rasputin legend, is how?

There is no doubt that Rasputin could undoubtedly bring relief to the suffering child. Too many witnesses have attested to this fact. Even those hostile to the peasant were forced to admit to it. Numerous theories have been advanced over the years to explain this seemingly inexplicable power.

Some have argued that Rasputin's appearances at the patient's side were merely coincidental with the cessation of the boy's attacks. This theory is as simple as it is unlikely. One hour too early or late would have exposed the peasant as a fake. It also fails to take into account those times when Rasputin relieved Alexei of his symptoms at a distance, when such judgments would have been impossible to make. In answer to this, some have suggested that Rasputin had an accomplice within the palace who could inform him of the tsarevich's condition and recommend the most favorable moment to announce a cure. Usually, in these stories, it is the tsarina's friend Anna Vyrubova who is named as the culprit. This, however, is also unlikely. First, it is very clear from all of the evidence that Anna Vyrubova's first allegiance was to Alexandra, not Rasputin. It is difficult, if not impossible, to imagine her acting in such a duplicitous manner. Second, such an accomplice within the palace would have had, under this theory, enough medical knowledge and expertise to gauge the twists and turns of an attack and predict the outcome. As not one of the doctors at court could do this, it stands to reason that neither could Anna Vyrubova. There is absolutely no evidence that she possessed any medical knowledge; indeed, what is known of her intellect is enough to cancel this possibility.

Anna Vyrubova also figures prominently in another, more sinister theory. According to this, she, Rasputin, and a certain Tibetan herbal doctor named Badmayev formed a cabal designed to trick the imperial couple. Anna obtained certain drugs and potions from Badmayev and gave them to the tsarevich, thus inducing a hemophiliac attack. When Rasputin was then summoned, a second potion—one which this time caused a cessation of the symptoms—was administered, and Rasputin arrived just in time to pray over the boy and thus appear as if he were responsible for the recovery. Again, there is absolutely no evidence to suggest such a conspiracy.

Hypnosis has been suggested as a possible explanation for Rasputin's ability to heal the tsarevich. It is known that Rasputin did indeed later study hypnosis; but this was not until 1912 or 1913—at least five years after Rasputin had begun to treat the tsarevich. While it is possible that hypnosis may have played a part in his visits to the sick boy, there is no evidence that Rasputin affected his cures by this means. It fails to take into account those times when Rasputin healed the boy and was not actually present at his side. If anything, the hypnosis may have calmed Alexei, but it alone could not have been responsible for his cures.

In the end, then, there is only one theory that comports with the known facts and accounts for all of Rasputin's cures of the tsarevich, and it is the most important of all, for it is the one that Alexandra believed: that Rasputin could cure her son through the power of prayer. This belief affected the way in which she perceived Rasputin. From her childhood she retained a belief not only in prayer but in miracles as well, and the Orthodox church taught that both were strong forces operating in the twentieth-century world. Alex De Jonge has made this important point: "If Alexandra believed that he was able to arrest the bleeding it is reasonable to conclude that he did so. However gullible and prone to wishful thinking she may have been, credulity has its limits."[23]

Even though she believed in the power Rasputin claimed, Alexandra was at first reluctant to call him to the palace. It took nearly two years before Rasputin visited with any frequency. His visits were rare because Alexandra was tentative in turning to him at the beginning. But after each summons, each cure, it grew more difficult to resist the power which Rasputin's prayers seemed to offer. Even though she came to rely on the peasant with a growing dependency, Alexandra never confused the man with the gift. In later years, when she was forced to confront the unsavory details of Rasputin's life in the capital, the tsarina never once suggested that he was not the man his enemies alleged. But in addition to the more disagreeable realities concerning the peasant, Alexandra also saw and experienced the very real comfort which his prayers seemed to bring to her son. She later defended Rasputin as a "Man of God," since his prayers seemed to save her son's life, not because she believed him to be a pious holy man untouched by sin.

Years later, Basil Shulgin, a monarchist member of the Duma, called Rasputin "a Janus." He wrote:

> To the imperial family he had turned his face as a humble *starets* and, looking at it, the Empress cannot but be convinced that the spirit of God rests upon this man. And to the country he has turned the beastly, drunken, unclean face of a bald satyr from Tobolsk. Here we have the key to it all. The country is indignant that such a man should be received under the Tsar's roof. And under the same roof there is bewilderment and a sense of bitter hurt. Why should they all be enraged? That a saintly man came to pray over the unhappy heir, a desperately sick child whose least imprudent movement may end in death? So the Tsar and the Empress are hurt and indignant. Why should there be such a storm? The man has done nothing but good. Thus, a messenger of death has placed himself between the throne and the nation. . . . And because of the man's fateful duality . . . neither side can understand the other. So the Tsar and his people, however apart, are leading each other to the edge of the abyss.[24]

24

Years of Isolation

IN THE YEARS FOLLOWING Alexei's birth, Alexandra's health rapidly declined. She suffered from shortness of breath and "an enlarged heart."[1] According to her sister-in-law Olga Alexandrovna, she was "indeed a sick woman. Her breath often came in quick, obviously painful gasps. I often saw her lips turn blue."[2] Often when she was suffering and a friend tried to get help, Alexandra would say, "Don't say anything. People do not need to know."[3] When she thought back to the days of her engagement, she would say, "I was so happy then, so well and strong. Now I am a wreck."[4]

Alexandra had never really been completely well. Even as a girl she had suffered from sciatica. Five difficult pregnancies, two miscarriages, and worry over Alexei further damaged her health. When her son was ill, the tsarina rarely left his bedside; when the crisis ended, she had to lie in bed for weeks in order to recover her strength. To her sister Victoria she wrote:

> Don't think my ill health depresses me personally. I don't care except to see my dear ones suffer on my account, and that I cannot fulfill my duties. But once God sends such a cross it must be borne. Darling Mama also lost her health at an early age. I have had so much that, willingly, I give up any pleasures—they mean so little to me, and my family life is such an ideal one, that it is a recompense for everything I cannot take part in.[5]

And to a friend in Germany she wrote:

> What can I say about my health? For the time the doctors are contented with my heart. . . . But have again strong pains in the legs and back . . . —tho gentle massage, more stroking, it has made the pains worse. You see I have many complaints. What is necessary for one thing is harmful for another, it's all

complicated. Am very tired and weary. . . . If people speak to you about my "nerves," please strongly contradict it. They are as strong as ever, it's the "over-tired heart" and nerves of the body and nerves of the heart besides, but the other nerves are very sound. Very bad heartaches, have not what one calls walked for three years, the heart goes wild, fearfully out of breath and such pains.[6]

After the Revolution, the tsarina's former maid, Mlle. Madelaine Zanotti, remembered:

I spent nearly my entire life with the Empress. I knew her well and had much affection for her. It seems to me that the Empress was ill during the last years of her life. It seems to me that she was suffering from hysteria. . . . What was the cause of the Empress's hysterical condition I do not know. Perhaps she was suffering from a woman's disease. . . . Dr. Grotte found symptoms of a nervous ailment for which he prescribed quite a different treatment than the one which she had been following. Later, Dr. Fisher found the same thing. He presented to the Emperor a secret report. . . . Fisher . . . insisted on treating—not her heart, which he found in good condition—but her nervous system. In some way or another the Empress heard about this report by Fisher and he was instantly dismissed and replaced by Botkin who was, on her express desire, appointed her physician. . . . Observing her as I had the daily opportunity of doing, I was always surprised by one thing. When she found herself among congenial people she was always quite well, and never complained about her heart; but the moment anything displeased her . . . she immediately began to complain. Believing that her heart was affected, she used to spend the greater part of each day lying on her sofa.[7]

Like her mother before her, Alexandra suffered from the symptoms of a psychosomatic illness brought about by worry. Her illness was real enough, but its causes were clearly to be found in the terrible uncertainty surrounding the health of her son. The tsarina's illness might have aroused great sympathy for her among St. Petersburg society had they but known. Like the tsarevich's hemophilia, Alexandra's bad health was deliberately kept a secret. Her increasing isolation at Tsarskoe Selo did a great deal to remove her from the thoughts of the public. Alexandra sincerely believed that when she stepped into her own palace she became, quite suddenly, a private individual. But kings and queens, no matter how much they may long for privacy, remain, regardless of whatever doors are closed behind them, public figures. The tsarina's alienation from public affection showed itself clearly in the gossip which was spread about the imperial family. The further they retreated into their own private existence at Tsarskoe Selo, the more desperate the public was to learn anything about its closeted rulers. For most of the public, in the absence of hard fact about the imperial family, rumor would do just as well.

And the more vicious the rumors, the further Alexandra isolated herself. One of the worst scandals concerned the tsarina and General Prince Alexander Orlov. One night, at a ball, Alexandra waltzed with the prince while the ladies of St. Petersburg society looked on in amazement. It was an enormous breach of imperial etiquette. Soon whispers linked the tsarina and prince in a romantic liaison. The alleged affair became the talk of the capital drawing rooms.[8] The fanciful minds began to speak openly of Catherine the Great and her lover Gregory Orlov. To make matters worse, Alexandra continued to see Orlov, as he was the commanding officer in her Uhlan Regiment. That the tsarina continued to display a marked dislike for anyone outside of her own family also fueled the fires of rumor, since, at least in the prince's case, she appeared to have thrown all caution to the wind. Whatever Orlov's intentions may have been, it is certain that if there was the slightest bit of affection on Alexandra's part for the handsome officer, it remained just that. Her deep love for her husband and her religious faith would have prevented an affair of the heart.

The assertions regarding the affair came to be widely believed among St. Petersburg society simply because no one, with any certainty, knew what was truth and what was fiction when it came to the imperial family. A photograph here, a line in the court circular there, a state parade during the visit of a fellow monarch—these were the images of royalty with which the public had to content itself. Alexandra's refusal to participate in St. Petersburg society led directly to public speculation about the imperial family.

Those who did know the truth were a small, select group of family members, a few officials, and some servants. One of the most extraordinary of this group was Anna Vyrubova, who became Alexandra's only true friend during all of her years as tsarina. Alexandra did not make friends easily; she was too shy and too judgmental of others to overlook their faults. Accutely aware of her own position as tsarina, Alexandra found it nearly impossible to forget her royal dignity and speak freely with those ladies she might encounter at receptions or balls. Those ladies who might have made the best friends kept in the background for fear of being accused of trying to score social points.

Once, in a letter to an acquaintance, Alexandra wrote: "I must have a person to myself; if I want to be my real self. I am not made to shine before an assembly—I have not the easy nor the witty talk one needs for that. I like the *internal being*, and that attracts me with great force. As you know, I am of the preacher type. I want to help others in life, to help them fight their battles and bear their crosses."[9]

Anna Vyrubova came closest to this ideal. She was the daughter of Alexander Taneyev, a composer of some repute and the man who had been head of the imperial chancellory before Alexander Mossolov, and her mother was a Tolstoy before marriage. Anna therefore came into frequent contact with the imperial Family. She first met the tsarina at her father's house outside Moscow, quite close to Ilinskoe, Ella's home. In 1901, Anna fell ill with typhoid. Alexandra remembered her from a previous meeting and included the girl in her usual round of hospital visits. To Alexandra there was nothing particularly significant in the visit, but Anna was immediately overcome with an almost cultlike, obsessive worship of the tsarina. When she had recovered, Anna was invited to the Alexander Palace for tea; Alexandra discovered that she could play the piano, and a bond immediately formed. Alexandra was twenty-nine and Anna seventeen, but in their soulful relationship age did not matter. From their first meeting, Witte said, Anna "regarded the Tsarina rapturously, everlastingly sighing, 'Oh, oh.'"[10]

In a disaster which could have destroyed the friendship, Alexandra pushed Anna into a loveless marriage, telling her it was her duty to have a husband. The man, Alexander Vyrubov, was a survivor of the Battle of Tsushima and was mentally disturbed. Rasputin was even called in to advise on the match, and he pronounced Vyrubov a bad choice. But Alexandra would have none of this, and Anna and Vyrubov were duly wed in 1907, with the tsar and tsarina as witnesses.[11]

The marriage soon fell apart. Anna discovered that her husband was disturbed. Not only had Vyrubov been in the Battle of Tsushima; he had been shell-shocked as well, having stood on the deck of his ship as it slipped beneath the waters, carrying many of his fellow sailors with it. He was also impotent and could not consummate the marriage. Anna was quickly able to obtain a decree from the Holy Synod dissolving the marriage.

Feeling certain that she was to blame for Anna's misfortune, Alexandra invited her to accompany the imperial family on their annual summer cruise through the Finnish fjords. Sitting on the deck of the imperial yacht, the pair talked for hours about their lives, hopes, and fears. Alexandra completely opened up to Anna, and her friend reciprocated by listening with rapt attention. Alexandra recognized in Anna someone to whom she could confide, and Anna, in turn, asked for nothing. Anna was interested only in friendship, not money or titles. When the cruise ended, Alexandra exclaimed with delight, "I thank God for at last having sent me a true friend."[12]

Short, dumpy, and round-faced, Anna did not make much of an impression on anyone she met. "I remember Vyrubova when she came to visit my mother," wrote Tatiana Botkin, daughter of the court physician. "She was pink-cheeked, full and all dressed in fluffy fur. It seemed to me that she was too sweet talking to us, and petting us and we didn't like her very much."[13] Maurice Paléologue, the French ambassador during the First World War, was shocked by Vyrubova's appearance. "No royal favourite ever looked more unpretentious. She was rather stout, of coarse and ample build, with thick shining hair, a fat neck, a pretty, innocent face with rosy, shining cheeks, large, striking clear bright eyes and full, fleshy lips. She was always very simply dressed and with her worthless adornments had a provincial appearance."[14]

Appearances aside, Anna was Alexandra's firm favorite. Every day she went to the Alexander Palace; this was such a regular occurrence that if for some reason Alexandra was unable to invite her, Anna would pout. Amused by this, Alexandra called Anna "our Big Baby."[15] So that she would be closer to her imperial friend Anna bought a small house in the village at Tsarskoe Selo. It was a summer house with no foundation and rested on the earth. As a result, it was terribly drafty in the winter. In fact, when Alexandra and Nicholas came to tea at Anna's, they all sat with their legs up on the chairs and sofas so as to avoid contact with the cold floor.[16] A telephone in the drawing room connected directly to the palace switchboard.

There was much criticism concerning Anna's presence at court. Alexandra and Nicholas had virtually isolated themselves from society; they rarely entertained their own family. The knowledge, therefore, that a plain, unimportant, and naive young girl shared intimate evenings with the tsar and tsarina at their palace grated on the nerves of not only the Romanov family but the court and society as well. To the polished, elegant ladies of St. Petersburg, it seemed impossible that their tsarina should prefer to spend her time socializing with this nobody. To the suggestion that she give Anna an official position and silence her detractors, Alexandra said, "She is my friend. I wish to retain her as such. Surely an Empress is allowed the right of a woman to choose her friends."[17] But later, with the criticism mounting, Alexandra relented and made Anna a maid of honor at the court.[18] Anna herself, in her book *Memories of the Russian Court*, makes this quite clear, although her official position at court has, on the whole, been ignored by writers.

Firmly entrenched in the public mind as the tsarina's friend, Anna assumed a peculiar importance. Every gesture she made, every word which she communicated, all of her tastes and opinions, were taken to be those of Alexandra as well. This assumption was damaging to the tsarina's prestige, particularly where Rasputin was concerned. In the years of his greatest power, Alexandra kept the relationship between the imperial family and the peasant a secret, though word soon spread and everyone in St. Petersburg knew of it. But Anna flaunted her association with Rasputin, and newspapers, which had been forbidden to couple the names of the tsarina and Rasputin, freely printed pictures and stories that linked Alexandra's friend and the peasant. This did the same amount of damage to the tsarina, as St. Petersburg took Anna's actions for her imperial friend's. Anna acted as a go-between for the tsarina and Rasputin and anyone else who wished to communicate with either of them. During the war, she was accused of political intrigues, and someone once described her as "a vehicle" and "an ideal gramophone disc."[19]

Most of the public came to hate Anna simply because she was so friendly with the tsarina. In the public mind, she and Rasputin marched hand in hand in bringing about the downfall of the monarchy. Incredible charges were made against her: that she had organized sexual orgies at the Alexander Palace during the war and had slept with court officials, Rasputin, the tsar, and even Alexandra herself.[20] Following the tsar's abdication in 1917, Anna was dragged off to the Fortress of Peter and Paul in the capital and there imprisoned for her "political activities." Knowing the rumors concerning her sexual activities as well, Anna, in desperation, asked for a medical examination to prove her innocence. The exam took place in May 1917, and much to the surprise and bewilderment of the entire country, Anna Vyrubova was publicly certified to be a virgin.[21]

In August 1909, Alexandra visited England for the last time. She and her family sailed from St. Petersburg aboard the imperial yacht *Standart*, the most elegant of all royal vessels. A huge bowsprit, covered in gold leaf, rose from a deep black hull, 420 feet in length, covered by teak decks and capped with two gleaming white funnels and three tall, varnished masts. As she steamed through the waters, the *Standart* carried the imperial family and their suite, the ship's officers, the crew plus a brass band, a balalaika orchestra, and an entire platoon of the Garde Equipage.[22]

The visit took place the week before the annual Cowes Yachting Regatta off the Isle of Wight, when the waters were at their most blue, the sky was cloudless, and the sun was shining brightly. The *Standart* sailed slowly through the English Channel and into the Solent, down a line of twenty-four battleships, sixteen armed cruisers, forty-eight destroyers, and the British royal yacht *Victoria and Albert*. Suddenly, guns boomed out over the waters, flags dipped and waved, sailors cheered, and brass bands, crashing out unmelodically over the Solent, played "God Save the Tsar" and "God Save the King."[23]

Cowes had not changed since Alexandra's happy childhood days there. The narrow, cobbled streets still wound up from the harbor, past parks and estate cottages, to the grandeur of Osborne House. But Osborne was now a training facility for naval cadets and a retirement home for sailors and, aside from a brief visit to its Renaissance halls, Alexandra remained, for the most part, on one or another of the yachts in the Solent. Daily, she and her daughters dressed in white Edwardian gowns and huge picture hats to meet the king and queen, Uncle Bertie and Aunt Alix, who were "most kind and attentive."[24]

While the tsarina exchanged bits of family gossip, the tsar was taken on a tour of the training facility at Osborne by Prince Edward of Wales, later King Edward VIII and duke of Windsor. The security was elaborate, and the police guards who surrounded Queen Victoria's former summer home viewed everyone with suspicion.

The evenings were filled with parties and balls. The royals vied with each other in the splendor of their banquets. Tenders sped over the dark blue waters, from yacht to yacht and dock to dock and back again, transporting guests in uniform and white gowns to the *Standart* and *Victoria and Albert*, which glowed in the summer night, their lights reflecting in the distance. Brass bands played rousing music and orchestras sent waltzes to the guests, who danced across the polished decks. At the end of the evenings, the royal guests crowded against the rails of their yachts, watching fireworks exploding in the night sky.[25]

At the end of the visit, the *Standart* sailed away from Cowes, churning through the waters of the Solent. Alexandra stood on deck in cream silk and lace, waving a handkerchief and watching as the shores of the Isle of Wight and the towers of Osborne House disappeared into the horizon. She was leaving her last childhood memories behind; within a year, Uncle Bertie would be dead, and Cousin Georgie would become King George V. As she left England, Alexandra was a woman isolated by circumstance. Her seclusion at Tsarskoe Selo had alienated her from public affection. And even on the visit to Cowes, where she had spent so much of her childhood, she was isolated from her family and her own past. The golden days of summer at Osborne were now only halcyon memories from another time, so lost in the past that Alexandra could never recapture them.

25

To Fall Asleep Forever in Your Arms

GRAND DUCHESS ELIZABETH FEODOROVNA, her imperial title contrasting sharply with the gray nun's habit she wore, stepped off a train from the capital and walked to a waiting motorcar. A short drive, and her motorcar swung through the gates of the imperial park at Tsarskoe Selo, following the sweeping drive to the white-and-yellow Alexander Palace. She stepped out, walked into the semicircular entrance hall, through the state apartments, family drawing rooms, and to a doorway guarded by two huge Negroes.

Alexandra waited on the other side of the door for the arrival of her sister. She must have dreaded the inevitable subject of the talk: Rasputin. Everyone seemed preoccupied with the peasant. Only weeks before, Alexandra had dismissed her children's governess, a hysterical woman named Sophie Tiutcheva. The governess had discovered Rasputin in the nurseries of the palace, saying prayers with the young grand duchesses. Her demands that the tsarina bar the peasant from the young girls resulted in her discharge. Madame Sophie Tiutcheva went straight to Ella in Moscow, giving her version of how Rasputin had corrupted the imperial family. She persuaded Ella to speak with the tsarina.

They talked in the Mauve Boudoir, surrounded by memories of their childhood together. Ella began by asking Alexandra if she knew how the people perceived Rasputin, if she realized the damage that the peasant was causing the dynasty. Alexandra stiffened at the first mention of Rasputin's name. She sat impassively while her sister spoke. When she had heard enough, Alexandra stood, telling her sister only that she should be less critical of a "Man of God." They parted not as sisters but as sovereign and subject—coldly, stiffly, formally. Ella walked out of the palace, climbed into her waiting motorcar, drove to the Tsarskoe Selo station, and boarded a train for St. Petersburg. The two sisters rarely spoke again.[1]

Rasputin greeted his followers daily, taking meals with the endless parade which streamed through his apartment, praying with them, advising them, and in some cases, when a visitor struck his fancy, sleeping with them. Five years had passed since Rasputin had arrived in the capital, and he was now a changed man. Gone were the peasant trappings; baggy blouses and dirty boots had been replaced by silk shirts and velvet trousers. Ladies clucked over him, waiting to find momentary favor and a place in his bed. To Father Gregory, it appears that sexual relations were as essential as air to breathe and food to eat. Out of lust, out of loneliness, out of curiosity, many of the women of St. Petersburg flocked to his apartment. With discretion thrown to the wind, Rasputin proceeded to bed as many of these ladies as were willing.

And willing they generally were, for most believed in the gospel of Father Gregory without question. Rasputin preached that true sin must first be committed before salvation could be achieved. It was not merely a desire for intercourse which drove Rasputin but also his early contact with the *Khylsty* and *Skopsty*. Prayer followed intercourse with the peasant, penance after sin.

"Would you be ready to accede to him?" one woman asked another at a St. Petersburg party.

"Of course," came the reply. "I have already belonged to him and I am proud and happy to have done so."

"But you are married! What does your husband say to it?"

"He considers it a very great honor. If Rasputin desires a woman we all think it a blessing and distinction, our husbands as well as ourselves."[2]

This behavior would have been impossible had Rasputin belonged to any religious order; the fact that he remained a peasant—not a monk, not a *starets*—allowed for a certain freedom. He did not fit into the strict religious mold and openly chose to follow his own beliefs and desires, as opposed to the church's, when the two conflicted.

The church, knowing that the general public believed that Rasputin was a religious personage, repeatedly tried to distance itself from the peasant. Bishop Theophan, after hearing confessions from women who had slept with Rasputin, went to the tsarina. Alexandra sent for Rasputin; when questioned about the rumors concerning his sexual activities, the peasant seemed genuinely hurt and surprised. His private life did not concern the church or the tsarina. Denying all, Rasputin left the Alexander Palace.

Alexandra was troubled by these allegations and asked that Anna Vyrubova and two ladies from the imperial court visit Rasputin at his home in Pokrovskoe in 1909. This in itself shows that the tsarina was at the very least aware of the rumors about her friend and determined to try to discover the truth behind them. Anna and one of the women returned to St. Petersburg sometime later, saying that they had observed nothing improper. But the third woman claimed that Rasputin had tried to seduce her maid. It was two against one, and Alexandra, influenced as she was by her need for the peasant, chose to ignore the allegations.

Theophan, who still held his position at court as the tsarina's personal confessor, was not content to give up on the struggle against his former protégé. He joined forces with the Montenegrin sisters Anastasia and Militza, who had initially sponsored Rasputin at the Alexander Palace. The trio also asked Sophie Tiutcheva, the children's governess, to testify about the improprieties which she had witnessed in the imperial nurseries.

The basis of Tiutcheva's arguments against the peasant—that he was often present when the young grand duchesses were in their nightgowns—was easily dismissed by the tsarina. The Montenegrin sisters got no further. And Theophan sealed his own fate by pushing the subject. Alexandra spoke with Nicholas about the incident, and the next day, the priest was dismissed. When Rasputin learned of his departure, he exclaimed, "I have shut his trap!"[3]

Metropolitan Anthony became the next clergyman to visit Tsarskoe Selo in protest. Nicholas told him bluntly that the affairs of the church and those of the imperial family were two different things. "No, Sire," Anthony replied, "this is not merely a family affair, but the affair of all Russia. The tsarevich is not only your son but our future sovereign and belongs to all of Russia."[4] The tsar curtly dismissed the priest without offering any hope.

Alexandra believed in Rasputin. Nicholas certainly thought that he could ease Alexei's suffering. With no Rasputin, Alexandra would find no hope, no peace, only an uncertain future for herself and her son. In an unguarded moment Nicholas hinted at her despair, saying, "Better one Rasputin than ten fits of hysterics a day."[5]

A young monk named Serge Iliodor caused Rasputin much harm. When the two first met, Iliodor invited Rasputin to visit a retreat on the banks of the Volga River. When they arrived, according to Iliodor, Rasputin seized the women and began to kiss them on the lips. This shocked Iliodor, but he said nothing.[6] The pair traveled on to Pokrovskoe. On the train journey Rasputin bragged of the power he held, the women who had given themselves freely to him, and worst of all, his relationship with the imperial family. "The tsar thinks I'm Christ incarnate," he began. "The tsar and tsarina bow down to me, kneel to me, kiss my hands. The tsarina has sworn that if all turn their backs on Grishka she will not waver and still always consider him her friend."[7] He added that he frequently kissed the tsarina, often in front of her young daughters.[8] Iliodor saw no reason to disbelieve him, but

Rasputin had clearly embellished his stories to a great extent. His claims that he kissed the tsarina or that the tsar bowed to him are clearly fabrications. Alexandra and Nicholas never acted this way toward anyone, a prince or a peasant. They were still sovereigns regardless of what Rasputin may have done to help their son, and both were too aware of their own dignity to behave as Rasputin claimed.

In Pokrovskoe, Rasputin showed Iliodor a chest filled with letters from the imperial family. He even let the monk have some of them, saying, "Take your choice. Only leave the tsarevich's letter. It's the only one I have."[9] Accordingly, Iliodor took several of the letters.

Rasputin's friendship with Iliodor took many strange turns before it came to an end. Increasingly, the fiery young priest came to regard Rasputin as an enemy of the throne. Iliodor joined forces with Bishop Hermogen of Saratov, an influential member of the Orthodox church, and the two men began to campaign against the peasant.

In an effort to save the situation, Rasputin asked the tsar to send a representative to Tsaritsyn, where the monk was holed up in his monastery. The peasant suggested Capt. Alexander Mandrika, who he believed would calm the situation and carry a favorable report back to the tsar. Nicholas duly dispatched Mandrika to meet with Iliodor.

The captain was gone for a week. When he returned to St. Petersburg, he immediately requested an audience with both the tsar and the tsarina. He shocked both Alexandra and Nicholas by detailing a list of Rasputin's improprieties, including charges that the peasant had seduced several nuns and that he had openly bragged about his relationship with the imperial family. The strain proved too much for Mandrika, who collapsed in tears while Alexandra tried to calm him down.

Both the tsar and tsarina were furious. Alexandra realized that Rasputin had been lying to her to impress his friends. Worse yet, at the same time, a series of photographs surfaced, taken of the peasant while he was drunk, showing Rasputin surrounded by a group of naked women. The man who owned the photographs tried to blackmail Rasputin with them; ever bold, the peasant grabbed the pictures and went straight to the tsar, claiming that he had been drugged and compromised to discredit him in the eyes of the imperial family. The tsar, still angry over the incident with Iliodor, requested that Rasputin leave the capital for a length of time, suggesting that he make a pilgrimage to the Holy Land. Rasputin agreed and set off for Jerusalem in March 1911, leaving behind him a storm of controversy about to erupt.

The church had had enough of the peasant. A group of clergymen, headed by Bishop Hermogen of Saratov and Iliodor, confronted the peasant with evidence of his sexual exploits later that same year. By 1911 friendship with the peasant had become a liability. Only the tsarina's support kept him in St. Petersburg. Rasputin sat quietly, listening to the churchmen denounce him. The evidence piled up quickly, case after case of a woman bedded, then spurned, of lecherous advances, improprieties, boasts of unrestrained power and influence.

"It's true, it's true, it's all true!" Rasputin sobbed.[10] He fell to the floor, crying hysterically. Hermogen grabbed a large wooden cross and began to beat Rasputin over the head with it until the peasant begged for mercy. The men dragged Rasputin into an adjoining chapel, shoved an icon in front of his face, and demanded that he swear he would leave women, and the imperial family, alone. Terrified, Rasputin complied.

Two days later, Rasputin stood in the Alexander Palace, tearfully giving his own account of the beating and confrontation. Alexandra ordered Hermogen banished to a monastery, and Iliodor went into exile. But the monk vowed vengeance and did everything he could to sully Rasputin's name. He began by publishing the letters he had taken from Pokrovskoe.

Grand Duchesses Olga and Tatiana had written:

> My Dearest Friend:
> I often think of you, your visits, and the way you talk about God. It is hard without you here, there is no one to tell my troubles to. . . . We often go to Anna's; every time I hope to meet you, my dear friend. . . . Pray for me and bless me.
> Your loving Olga.

> My Dear and True Friend:
> When will you come? Are you going to be stuck in Pokrovskoe much longer? How are your children? . . . When we go to Anna's we all think of you. We would like so much to go to Pokrovskoe. When shall we go? Please arrange it, you can do anything. God loves you so. And you say God is so good and kind that He will do anything you ask. So visit us soon, it is so dull without you. Mother is ill without you and it is sad to see her ill. But you know because you know everything. I kiss your hand, my dear friend, I kiss your Holy hand. God bless you.
> Tatiana.[11]

But the most damning letter of all came from Alexandra:

> My Beloved, unforgettable teacher, redeemer and mentor:
> How tiresome it is without you. My soul is quiet and I relax only when you, my teacher, are sitting beside me. I kiss your hands and lean my head on your blessed shoulders. Oh, how

light do I feel then! I only wish one thing: to fall asleep, forever on
your shoulders and in your arms. What happiness to feel your
presence near me. Where are you? Where have you gone? Oh, I
am so sad and my heart is longing. . . . Will you soon be again
close to me? Come quickly, I am waiting for you and I am
tormenting myself for you. I am asking for your Holy Blessing
and I am kissing your blessed hands. I love you forever. Yours,
Mama.[12]

The implications were obvious. All St. Petersburg talked of the letters, hinting that the tsarina and Rasputin were lovers. No one knew
that the tsarina wrote in this florid, bold manner to her friends. This fact
would, in any case, most probably not have changed public opinion.
The rumors, resentment, hatred—all grew.

Alexander Guchkov, leader of the Octobrist party in the Duma,
printed up cheap copies of the letters and circulated them around the
capital. The minister of the interior took them to the tsar. Nicholas sat
behind his massive desk. He carefully examined the familiar handwriting. "Yes, this is not a counterfeit letter," he eventually said and threw
the copy into a drawer with an angry gesture.[13]

Alexandra was furious that the privacy of her personal correspondence had been violated. Guchkov became the subject of an intense campaign by the tsarina directed against those responsible, but
surprisingly, she blamed Rasputin more than the Duma member, sending the peasant an angry cable and refusing to meet with him at his request.[14]

While Nicholas may have been content to ignore the letters' existence by locking them away, his prime minister, Peter Stolypin, ordered
a full-scale investigation. The tsar read the reports but did nothing, and
Stolypin, over Alexandra's protests, banished Rasputin from the capital. Furious, Alexandra defended the peasant. "Saints are always calumniated," she told Dr. Eugene Botkin.[15] "He is hated because we love
him," she complained to Anna.[16] "They accuse Rasputin of kissing
women, etc.," she wrote. "Read the Apostles; they kissed everybody as
a form of greeting."[17]

The imperial couple, according to the tsar's sister Olga, were
"fully aware" of Rasputin's improprieties. Neither Nicholas nor
Alexandra "had the least illusion about him."[18] While this view runs
counter to much of what has been written, it is clear from the evidence that even Alexandra, influenced as she was by her need for
Rasputin, never denied that the peasant was capable of sin. The tsar
and tsarina could have admitted to this publicly, but doing so would
have meant disclosing the reasons they kept Rasputin near them. This

would have been impossible. Since both Alexandra and Nicholas believed that Rasputin was genuine enough in his search for salvation, it was easy for them to ignore the more distasteful realities of the peasant's private life.

Stolypin, faced with a tsar who could not say no to his wife, threatened to resign. "I know and believe you are truly loyal to me," the tsar told Stolypin when the prime minister presented his report. "Everything you say may even be true. But I must ask you never to again speak with me about Rasputin. In any event, I am powerless to do anything about it."[19] The dowager empress summoned the minister of finance, Vladimir Kokovstsov, to her residence in the Anichkov Palace. Over tea, she and the minister discussed the situation.

"My son is too kind. . . ." she began. "I am perfectly sure that the tsar cannot part with Stolypin. . . . He has not given his answer because he is trying to find some other way out of the situation. He seeks advice from no one. He has too much pride and, with the empress, goes through such crises without letting anyone see that he is agitated. . . . My poor son has so little luck with people."[20]

Unfortunately, the prime minister also had little luck that fall. In September 1911 he accompanied the tsar, tsarina, and the two eldest grand duchesses to Kiev for the unveiling of a statue of Alexander III. By coincidence Rasputin stood in the streets of Kiev, watching the imperial procession drive by. When Stolypin passed, Rasputin jumped up and down, waving his arms wildly in the air and shouting, "Death is after him! Death is driving behind him!"[21]

The next night, crowds filled the Kiev Opera House for a gala performance of Rimsky-Korsakov's *Tsar Sultan*. Alexandra, Nicholas, and the two girls sat in the imperial loge, high above the seat which Stolypin occupied. During intermission a young man walked down the aisle to where Stolypin sat, looked at the prime minister, pulled a Browning revolver from his coat, and fired two shots into Stolypin's chest. Stolypin stood, turned to the imperial loge, made the sign of the cross, his uniform stained with blood, and then collapsed. The imperial party immediately left the theater.[22]

Stolypin died on 6 September; the execution of his assassin, a revolutionary named Dimitri Bogrov, followed soon after. The loss did not devastate Alexandra; she hated Stolypin because he opposed Rasputin. After the prime minister's death, she told her husband's cousin Grand Duke Dimitri Pavlovich that "those who have offended God in the person of Our Friend may no longer count on divine protection."[23]

The tsar named Vladimir Kokovstsov the new prime minister. Alexandra worried that he would share his predecessor's hatred of her friend. She summoned him to Livadia. Alexandra sat in an armchair on the terrace overlooking the Black Sea while she spoke to the prime minister. "I notice that you keep on making comparisons between yourself and Stolypin," the tsarina began. "You seem to do too much honor to his memory and ascribe too much importance to his activities and his personality. Believe me, one must not feel sorry for those who are no more. I am sure that everybody does only one's duty and fulfills one's destiny and when one dies that means that his role in the world is ended and that he was bound to go since his destiny was fulfilled." Then, speaking in carefully guarded tones of Stolypin's persecution of Rasputin, she continued: "Life continually assumes new forms, and you must not try to follow blindly the work of your predecessor. Remain yourself; do not look for support in political parties; they are of so little consequence in Russia. Find support in the confidence of the tsar—the Lord will help you. I am sure that Stolypin died to make room for you and this is all for the good of Russia."[24]

But Kokovstsov did not leave Rasputin alone. Quite the reverse; he actively promoted the examination into his scandalous life, thus incurring the tsarina's lasting displeasure. "Strange as it may seem," Kokovstsov wrote, "the question of Rasputin became the central question of the immediate future; nor did it disappear during my entire term of office as Chairman of the Ministers' Council."[25]

Accounts of Rasputin's "victims" filled the headlines. The Moscow newspaper *Golos Moskvy* wrote of "that cunning conspirator against our Holy Church, that fornicator of human souls and bodies— Gregory Rasputin."[26] The tsar warned that any newspaper which mentioned the peasant's name would be fined; but Rasputin sold newspapers, and editors paid the fine and printed their stories anyway. The rumors left St. Petersburg in shock: Did the tsar really wash Rasputin's feet? Had Rasputin actually shoved the tsar out of the imperial bedroom while he himself made love to the tsarina? Had he raped all of the young grand duchesses? Schoolchildren sang lewd songs about their tsarina and her friend and chalked obscene pictures of the two of them on building walls.[27]

"The Emperor . . . is so pure of heart that he does not believe in evil," the dowager empress pronounced to Michael Rodzianko, the president of the Duma.[28] Rodzianko hoped to avoid a confrontation in the Duma by speaking frankly with the tsar. At their audience Rodzianko mentioned Stolypin's report and the fates of Theophan and Hermogen when they confronted the peasant. Nicholas saw no alternative but to agree to his demands for a new investigation. All of the evidence which Stolypin had assembled sat in the files of the Holy Synod; Rodzianko collected it, but on the following day an official from the Holy Synod appeared in Rodzianko's office and ordered him to hand back the papers. When Rodzianko refused, the official declared that he had been sent by "a very exalted person."

"Who is it, Sabler?" Rodzianko asked, thinking that it might be the minister of religion.

"No, someone much more highly placed."

"Who is it?" Rodzianko repeated.

"The Empress Alexandra Feodorovna."

"If that is the case will you kindly inform Her Majesty that she is as much a subject of her august consort as I myself, and that it is the duty of both of us to obey his commands. I am, therefore, not in a position to comply with her wishes."[29]

In the end, Nicholas would not read the completed report even though he himself had authorized it. But Alexandra knew of its existence. When Kokovstsov had become prime minister, the tsarina told him, "I wished to see you to tell you that both the Tsar and I beg you always to be quite frank with us and to tell us the truth, not hesitating lest it is unpleasant for us. Believe me, even if it be so at first, we shall be grateful to you for it later."[30] This, of course, did not apply to Rasputin. Anyone bold enough to criticize Rasputin found only condemnation from the tsarina. Kokovstsov recalled:

At first I enjoyed Her Majesty's favour. In fact I was appointed Chairman of the Ministers' Council with her knowledge and consent. Hence, when the Duma and press began a violent campaign against Rasputin . . . she expected me to put a stop to it. Yet it was not my opposition to the Tsar's proposal to take measures against the press that won me Her Majesty's displeasure; it was my report to His Majesty about Rasputin after the *starets* had visited me. From that time on, although the Tsar continued to show me his favour for another two years, my dismissal was assured. This changed attitude of Her Majesty is not hard to understand. . . .In her mind, Rasputin was closely associated with the health of her son, and the welfare of the monarchy. To attack him was to attack the protection of what she held most dear. . . . She was offended to think that the sanctity of her home had been questioned in the press and in the Duma. She thought that I, as head of the government, was responsible for permitting these attacks, and could not understand why I could not stop them by giving orders in the name of the Tsar. She considered me, therefore, not the servant of the Tsar, but a tool of the enemies of the state, and, as such, deserving of dismissal.[31]

After his dismissal Kokovstsov had an audience with the dowager empress. She said:

> I know you are an honourable man and I know that you bear no ill will toward my son. You must also understand my fears for the future. My daughter-in-law does not like me; she thinks that I am jealous of her power. She does not perceive that my one aspiration is to see my son happy. Yet I see that we are nearing some catastrophe and the Tsar listens to no one but flatterers, not perceiving or even suspecting what goes on all around him. Why do you not decide to tell the Tsar frankly all you think and know, now that you are at liberty to do so, warning him, if it is not already too late?

But, according to Kokovstsov he could do nothing. "I told her that no one would listen to me or believe me. The young Empress thought me her enemy."[32]

Kokovstsov's account of his dismissal squarely places the blame on the tsarina's hatred of him. However, aside from the antipathy which Alexandra may have felt toward him, the tsar had several important reasons for letting him go. In the Duma, he alienated the left wing by making pronouncements against reforms; he fared no better with the conservative deputies by forcing financial reforms. Because of this, Kokovstsov found it difficult to effectively preside over the government or form any sort of working coalition. Historian Martin Kilcoyne argues that this, and not the tsarina's dislike, led to Kokovstsov's downfall.[33]

Most of Rasputin's enemies had by now disappeared. Stolypin was dead, Kokovstsov about to fall from power, Theophan exiled, Hermogen banished, and Iliodor in hiding. The latter denounced the Holy Synod in hotly written letters:

> You have bowed down to the devil! My whole being is for the Holy Vengeance against you! You have sold the Glory of God, forgotten the friendship of Christ. . . . Oh, cheats, serpents, murderers of Christ! . . . Traitors and renegades! . . . You are all careerists; you despise the poor servants of the people, you put present day prophets to the stake! . . . Godless anti Christs, I will not be in spiritual communion with you! . . . You are animals fed with the people's blood![34]

Iliodor decided to remove Rasputin. By chance, he met a former prostitute named Khina Gusseva, whom Rasputin had slept with, then spurned. Iliodor gave her a knife hanging on a chain. As he slipped it around her neck, he said, "With this knife, kill Grishka."[35] To many, murder appeared to be the only way out of the situation; Alexandra would not give Rasputin up. Even the dowager empress felt exasperated. To Kokovstsov she complained: "My poor daughter-in-law does not perceive that she is ruining both the Dynasty and herself. She sincerely believes in the holiness of an adventurer and we are powerless to ward off the misfortune which is sure to come."[36]

26

Spala

In September 1912 the imperial family set out for Poland and their hunting lodges, hidden away in the deep forests. They traveled aboard the imperial train, a miniature palace of comfortable blue salon cars with golden double-headed eagles on their sides. A plush drawing room allowed for relaxation, a dining room for elegant gourmet dinners. When Alexandra tired, she could sit in her gray-and-mauve boudoir, watching the countryside pass by. Comfort notwithstanding, trips aboard the imperial train caused much worry. In the back of Alexandra's mind was always the thought that despite the heavy imperial security, the train might be exposed to revolutionaries. To foil this, two identical trains made every trip so that terrorists could never be sure on which train the imperial family traveled. But this cost money: Security, for every trip, cost 100,000 rubles each way ($51,000).[1]

There were, however, lighter moments as well. On the journey to Poland in 1912 the train came to a halt at the railway siding in Smolensk. The imperial family departed to take tea with the local nobility. The afternoon proved memorable, as the tsar wrote to his mother, because "Alexei got hold of a glass of champagne and drank it unnoticed after which he became rather gay and began entertaining the ladies to our great surprise. When he returned to the train, he kept telling us about his conversations at the party and also that he heard his tummy rumbling."[2]

On their autumn visit in 1912 the family went first to Bielovezh, a hunting lodge located in eastern Poland. Thirty-thousand acres of lush forest stocked with big game awaited the tsar. The rarest was the aurochs, or European bison, which was nearly extinct by the turn of the century. These animals only lived in two places—Poland and the Caucasus—and were deliberately maintained and nursed to provide the tsar and his hunting party with this special trophy.

One day at Bielovezh, Alexei had an accident. While playing in his bathroom, he slipped at the edge of a large sunken tub and knocked his leg against the ledge.[3] When Dr. Botkin examined the boy, he discovered a swelling on the left thigh, just below the groin. In much pain, Alexei took to his bed to recover. Within a few days the pain was gone and Alexei pronounced sufficiently well for the family to keep to their schedule and move on to Spala.

Located in a dense forest at the end of a long, sandy road, Spala was a wooden villa of two stories, surrounded on all sides by a thick forest which cut off all sunlight; it was so dark, in fact, that electric lights had to be left burning inside the villa during the day.[4] Magnificent forests were the chief attraction at Spala. There was stalking for elk and stags; hunting for fox, hare, and other small game; and shooting for grouse, snipe, and various fowl. These hunting parties always followed a rigid standard of tradition. The guests were awakened each morning at seven o'clock by a hunting horn. Luncheon in the forest to the music of a military band preceded carnage on a grand scale. Only stags of ten or more points could be shot on these expeditions.[5] Gameskeepers carefully recorded each day's bag in the estate books, and at dusk the slain stags and all other game were laid out on the lawn in front of the villa for the tsarina and her guests to inspect by torchlight. Alexandra did not care for this spectacle of blood sports but by tradition, had to follow it.

This atmosphere of death, the dark forests, and the gloomy house did little to revive the tsarevich's spirits. His mother thought that perhaps study would be in order to take her son's mind off his troubles. She set Pierre Gilliard to the task of beginning French lessons. According to Gilliard, Alexei was "rather tall for his age . . . a long, finely chiseled face, delicate features, auburn hair with a coppery glint, and large grey-blue eyes like his mother."[6] The lessons began, but the tutor found the tsarevich "ill from the outset. Soon he had to take to his bed."[7]

Alexandra thought that a carriage ride in the fresh air would help reinvigorate her ailing son. She and Anna Vyrubova sat Alexei in a carriage between them and set off down the sandy road from the lodge. The ride was rough. After several miles of bumps and holes in the roadway, Alexei began to complain of an uneasy feeling in his leg and lower stomach. He was hemorrhaging internally. In a panic Alexandra ordered the driver to return to Spala as fast as the carriage would go. Anna later recalled: "That return drive stands out in my mind as an experience in horror. Every movement of the carriage, every rough place in the road, caused the child the most exquisite torture and by the time we reached home, the boy was almost unconscious with pain."[8]

The swelling from Bielovezh had dislodged itself and set off a new hemorrhage. When Dr. Botkin examined the tsarevich, he found a large swelling in the upper thigh. Botkin's colleague Serge Fedorov cabled the St. Petersburg specialists, who sped to Spala by train and carriage. But after examining the boy, they decided that there was nothing to be done. There were no medicines. Only blood. It flowed from the torn vessels in the leg into the lower abdomen, forming a swelling the size of a grapefruit. The left leg drew up to allow the blood in the swelling a new space to fill and relieve the pressure. The blood seeped through the little boy's body, attacking the tissues and bones. And although the blood flowed into the abdomen, it soon reached a point where there was no more room. Yet it continued to flow.

Screams pierced the walls of the villa, mournful, agonizing wails of pain and gasps for breath.[9] Servants and members of the suite had to stuff their ears with cotton in order to continue working. From the beginning of the crisis, Alexandra never left her son's bedside. Anna wrote: "During the entire time, the Empress never undressed, never went to bed, rarely even laid down for an hour's rest. Hour after hour she sat beside the bed where the half-conscious child lay huddled on one side, his left leg drawn up. . . . His face was absolutely bloodless, drawn and seamed with suffering, while his almost expressionless eyes rolled back in his head. Once, when the Emperor came into the room, seeing the boy in this agony, and hearing the faint screams of pain, the poor father's courage completely gave way and he rushed, weeping bitterly, to his study."[10]

The tragedy took its toll on the stricken parents. Nicholas wrote to his mother: "The days between the 6th and the 10th were the worst. The poor darling suffered intensely, the pains came in spasms, and recurred every quarter of an hour. His high temperature made him delirious night and day; and he would sit up in bed and every movement brought the pain on again. He hardly slept at all, had not even the strength to cry, and kept repeating, 'Oh, Lord, have mercy upon me.' "[11]

Nicholas told his mother, "I was hardly able to stay in the room, but, of course, had to take turns with Alix, for she was exhausted by spending whole nights by his bed. She bore the ordeal better than I did."[12] For Alexandra, it became a nightmare. She held Alexei's hand, kissed him, brushed hair from his sweat-matted face, all as he moaned over and over again, "Mama, help me!"[13] There was nothing she could do except pray, begging God to save the life of her little boy. During these terrible days at Spala, her golden hair became tinged with gray.[14]

At moments, everyone thought that the end had come. The tsarevich himself hoped that this was so. "When I am dead, it will not hurt anymore, will it, Mama?" he asked one day.[15] In another moment of quiet, the boy plaintively begged his parents to build him a little monument of stones in the forest after his death.[16]

But life continued at Spala. No one mentioned the boy's illness. The veil of secrecy surrounding the tsarevich's hemophilia was not lifted. It was all a horrible charade. The hunts continued, games of tennis were played in the afternoons, Polish nobles still arrived for evening parties.[17] One such evening, the grand duchesses acted out two scenes from Molière's *Bourgeois Gentilhomme* for the guests. As Marie and Anastasia performed the scenes in French, Gilliard prompted from the wings.

The tsarina sat in the front row, smiling and laughing along with her guests. After the play, Gilliard happened to be in the hall leading to the tsarevich's room. The terrible moaning from inside could clearly be heard. A moment later, the tsarina rushed past the tutor, holding the train of her dress in both her hands as she ran along the corridor. If she saw Gilliard, her terror-stricken face did not betray it. She opened the door to her son's room and disappeared inside. A few minutes later, Gilliard was in the dining room when she returned. Once again, she smiled to her guests, and all seemed well. But to the tsar she managed to throw a glance pregnant with worry and he moved closer to the door in case the situation should worsen.[18]

On 6 October, Dr. Fedorov announced to the grief-stricken parents that their son's stomach was hemorrhaging. Alexei, he said, might die at any moment. Facing the inevitable, the tsar and tsarina at last consented to the publication of medical bulletins on the state of the tsarevich's health. The first bulletin was published on 8 October; however, it still did not mention the nature of the boy's disease. All over the empire, millions prayed for the health of the eight-year-old boy. Since there was no church at Spala, a large green canvas tent erected on the lawn housed daily services. Polish peasants knelt beside members of the household and staff to pray for the life of the little boy.[19]

At luncheon the next day, Alexandra dispatched a hastily scrawled note to her husband, saying that the end was near. The boy's moans were shorter now, quieter, as his strength ebbed. Irene, the tsarina's sister, happened to be at Spala. Late that afternoon, she walked into the dining room where the suite were gathered and announced that her nephew would not be able to survive the night. Down the hallway, a priest began the last rites. Light from the flickering votive candles burning before some icons spilled into the dark shadows of the room, the smell of wax and incense in the air. Alexandra and Nicholas knelt together at their son's bedside, praying for his soul.[20] The medical bulletin for the next day was already drawn up and ready for publication: it announced the death of His Imperial Highness the Tsarevich Alexei.

In the darkness of the night, a cable went out from Spala to the Siberian village of Pokrovskoe, to Gregory Rasputin. Alexandra begged the peasant to pray for the life of her son. For the next few hours, she waited for his answer. At last, in the early hours of the morning, it came: "The Little One will not die. Do not allow the doctors to bother him too much."[21]

Clutching the telegram, Alexandra ran to show her husband, who sat with some members of the suite discussing the funeral arrangements. She was calm and smiling. She explained to the puzzled faces: "The doctors notice no improvement yet but I am not a bit anxious myself now. During the night I received a telegram from Father Gregory and he has reassured me completely."[22] The next morning, the swelling on the boy's thigh began to disappear, and the internal hemorrhage stopped. Alexei lay in bed, pale and contorted but alive. The nightmare had ended.

What happened at Spala in the autumn of 1912 changed Alexandra's life. No longer did she fear for the future. As long as Rasputin remained by her side, Alexei would live, and all would be well. The simple facts are beyond dispute. Alexei was dying. The doctors could do nothing. The last rites had been administered. Alexandra cabled Rasputin, asking him to pray. He sent a telegram saying that the boy would recover. The following morning, the tsarevich stopped bleeding.

Coincidence? If so, the laws of probability were stretched to their very limits. Various theories have been put forth to explain this apparent miracle. But the only significant explanation is the one which Alexandra believed. And for her there was no doubt whatsoever as to how Alexei had recovered. She believed that the cure of her son emanated from Rasputin and Rasputin alone. The facts themselves only tend to confirm the tsarina's own conclusion. And this belief, that Rasputin had saved her son and would continue to do so, remained with Alexandra long after the autumn frosts laid waste the hunting grounds of Poland.

It snowed at Spala the day after Rasputin's telegram arrived. Buried under a blanket of fresh white powder, the lodge poked its gables into the air while gusts of snow glistened and churned in the sun and wind and fell from the heavy branches of evergreen trees standing guard in the forest. As if life had been renewed, all seemed fresh and clear. Even the air was crisp and exquisite.

When the snow thawed, the tsar took to the woods to shoot and hunt. The grand duchesses played games of tennis. Even Alexei ventured out, wrapped in blankets for a ride in a pony cart. Alexandra sat with him as he recovered, reading and sewing. Yet even as life returned, the tsarevich remained a sick child. The tsar wrote that "his complexion is quite good now, but at one time he looked like wax." He added, though, that the doctors "are now stuffing him for all they are worth."[23]

After a month the tsarevich could leave Spala. The roads which the imperial family traveled over had been hand-smoothed and sanded at Alexandra's orders to prevent any bumps. The train back to St. Petersburg crawled along at fifteen miles an hour.[24] For nearly a year after Spala, Alexei had to wear a metal brace to help straighten out his left leg and endured hot mud baths as a treatment for the limp which affected him. Official photographs of the tsarevich showed him seated, standing on steps, or from the waist up so that the bent leg appeared normal.[25] A year after Spala, the author of *Behind the Veil at the Russian Court* for the first time revealed that the tsarevich suffered from hemophilia.[26] But there was no comment from the palace. The deception continued.

Twelve days in the autumn of 1912 had profoundly changed Alexandra's life. Rasputin's position as an intermediary had been dramatically validated. He would pray, God would answer. To Alexandra, it was as simple as that. Whereas she might have been reluctant to turn to the peasant before, after Spala he became her first line of defense against her son's hemophilia. Others were left shaken and confused by Spala. Dr. Fedorov later said: "And look, Rasputin would come in, walk up to the patient, look at him, and spit. The bleeding would stop in no time. . . . How could the Empress not trust Rasputin after that?"[27]

27

1913

In 1913 THE WORLD HUMMED with the mechanical wonders of the enlightened age: vacuum cleaners, airplanes, zeppelins, moving pictures. New motorcars sped over the roadways of Europe, carrying their passengers to the fashionable casinos to gamble the night away. The world watched as Isadora Duncan danced across the capitals of Europe, Vernon and Irene Castle tangoed, and in Germany the Krupp family made arms for the kaiser. In New York, Marcel Duchamp's *Nude Descending a Staircase* caused a minor scandal, while in London audiences watched Anna Pavlova dance in *Giselle* at Covent Garden or went to see the new play by George Bernard Shaw, *Androcles and the Lion*. Eton won against Harrow in cricket, and women marched for the vote. Some women took more drastic measures, such as the unfortunate Emily Davison, who threw herself before King George V's horse at the Derby in the name of women's suffrage and died in the process. The everyday dress of the world changed: Women were first seen in trousers, and men's stiff and formal top hats and tailcoats sank into the oblivion of mothballed closets, replaced with pin-striped suits and straw boaters. It was the last year that two men could be found in a lonely, dew-blanketed field at dawn, ready to fight a duel to the death, all in the name of honor. The sports of the day were tennis, racing, and cricket; the craze, "Alexander's Ragtime Band" by Irving Berlin.[1]

As the new age began, another ended. Through this strange new world of ragtime and the tango moved the monarchs of Europe. The end of the great dynasties, of absolutism, was very near. In another year the world would be turned upside down and plunged into a war on a catastrophic scale never seen before. The imperial houses of Hapsburg, Hohenzollern, and Romanov would fall within five years; those monarchs who did survive would have to learn quickly to adjust to the standards of the new world. The end also grew nearer for the 20 million men who would perish in the First World War.

Ruling over this changing Europe was a dying breed of monarchs.

With Queen Victoria's death in 1901 came the passing of the Victorian age. Her son, Edward VII, had dominated Europe for only nine years before he, too, passed into history. The Europe of 1913 belonged to Kaiser Wilhelm II. It was a military world. The center of all speculation was Berlin. Most of Europe waited for the inevitable; war was a fore gone conclusion, a reflection of the cynical atmosphere surrounding 1913.

In Russia, the year 1913 marked the three hundredth anniversary of Romanov rule. The ceremonies began on 6 March, a rainy St. Petersburg morning wrapped in a blanket of mist, shattered by the thunder of cannon fire from the Fortress of Peter and Paul. People waited for a glimpse of the imperial family on their drive from the Winter Palace to the Cathedral of Our Lady of Kazan for a great choral *Te Deum.*

Michael Rodzianko, president of the Duma, had been at the cathedral for several hours that morning. With the greatest difficulty, Rodzianko had obtained seats for his fellow Duma members. He was standing on the portico smoking a cigarette when an aide rushed out and told him that a strange man in peasant clothing had sat down in one of the Duma chairs and refused to move. When Rodzianko approached, he discovered Rasputin.

"What are you doing here?" Rodzianko whispered.

"What's that got to do with you?" Rasputin said with an insolent glare.

"If you address me as 'thou' I will drag you from the cathedral by the beard. Don't you know that I am president of the Duma?"

Rasputin seemed not to care. He stared deeply at Rodzianko in an apparent effort to hypnotize him, but Rodzianko only returned the gaze. Finally, Rasputin gave up and asked, "What do you want of me?"

"Clear out at once, you vile heretic, there is no place for you in this sacred house!" Rodzianko spat out.

"I was invited here at the wishes of persons more highly placed than you," Rasputin answered, at the same time pulling out an invitation card.

"You are a notorious swindler! No one can believe your words. Clear out at once, this is no place for you!"

Rasputin fell to the marble floor, bowed to the ground, and began to pray. Rodzianko kicked him in the stomach, shouting, "Enough of this tomfoolery! If you don't clear out at once I'll order my sergeants-at-arms to carry you out!"

"Oh, Lord, forgive him such sin!" Rasputin exclaimed. He stood up, walked to the west door of the cathedral, put on his sable-lined coat, and escorted by a court cossack, walked down the steps, climbed into a motorcar, and disappeared.[2]

The imperial family arrived at the cathedral a short time later, following a long carriage procession in miserable rain, thunder splitting the sky, past thin crowds and even sparser applause. They might have expected more for their first major public appearance in the capital in ten years. But even as they climbed the cathedral steps, there were no great ovations: not for the tsar or his heir; not for the tsarina or the dowager empress or for the four young grand duchesses—Olga, Tatiana, Marie, and Anastasia—all clad in summer white as they followed their parents through the west door of the great cathedral and out of the angry storm.

There were no imperial balls in celebration of the Romanov tercentenary: Alexandra refused to host them. She appeared once, at a ball given by St. Petersburg's nobility in the Hall of Columns. In a white gown covered in diamonds, Alexandra walked into the room on the arm of her husband to a polonaise by Chopin.[3] She did not dance that evening; the crowds unnerved her. As the evening grew longer, her anxiety overcame her, and she worked herself into a hysterical frenzy. She motioned to Nicholas, who quickly led her out of the room. Once the doors closed behind them, Alexandra fainted into her husband's arms.[4]

Alexandra also accompanied the tsar to the Mariinsky Theatre for a gala performance of Glinka's *A Life for the Tsar*. She entered the imperial loge, pale, her face expressionless, the turquoises in her parure glowing in the dim light. Meriel Buchanan, the daughter of the British ambassador, sat in a box next to the tsar and tsarina.

> We could see that the fan of white eagles' feathers the Empress was holding was trembling convulsively, we could see how a dull, unbecoming flush was stealing over her pallor, could almost hear the laboured breathing which made the diamonds which covered the bodice of her gown rise and fall, flashing and trembling with a thousand uneasy sparks of light. Presently it seemed that this emotion or distress mastered her completely, and with a few whispered words to the Emperor she rose and withdrew to the back of the box, to be seen no more that evening.[5]

To celebrate the tercentenary the entire Romanov family embarked on a pilgrimage in commemoration of the first tsar, Michael. They cruised up the Volga River on a steamer as far as Kostroma, where Michael was living at the time he learned of his election to the throne. "Wherever we went we were met with manifestations of loyalty bordering on wildness," recalled the tsar's sister Olga Alexandrovna. "When our steamer went down the Volga we saw crowds of peasants wading high in the water to catch a glimpse of Nicky. In some of the towns, I would see artisans and workmen falling down to kiss his shadow as we passed. Cheers were deafening . . ."[6]

Like her sister-in-law, Alexandra saw only the cheers, the crowds, the smiling faces, the devotion of the faithful. But the reality was far different. Kokovstsov wrote: "There was nothing in the feeling of the crowd but shallow curiosity. Down the Volga River from Novgorod there was a biting cold wind and the tsar did not once show himself where stopovers had been planned. There were handsomely ornamented descents from the shore to the water where small groups of peasants were gathered apparently waiting to see their tsar; but in vain, for the steamship went rapidly on till it reached Kostroma, where it stopped for the night. . . ."[7]

The tercentenary celebrations left most of the public unmoved. The tsar's deliberate concentration on rural rather than social fetes meant that the capital once again believed that it had been snubbed. The only amnesties given were to common criminals and thieves; political prisoners remained locked away. Writing shortly after the tercentenary, the author of *Behind the Veil at the Russian Court* spoke of the public's hope:

> . . . that some lasting monument would be raised by the initiative of the sovereign, to render it for ever memorable; that mercies should be shown, miseries relieved, tears dried, an impulse given both to public and private charities; something attempted to raise the moral standard of the people by the creation of new schools and educational establishments. In short, they expectantly hoped that the monarch would look from the height of the throne to where so many needs would be satisfied, where so much was expected to be done, and had to be done if Russia was to emerge from her present state of semibarbarism to take her place among the peopled nations. Not only in political and social spheres did dire need exist, but also and especially exigent was the education of the lower classes, which at present constitute in Russia such a dangerous element in her social fabric, and who threaten to overwhelm the present order of things without being able to replace it by anything rational.[8]

But such advice went unheeded. The tercentenary ended, leaving the public curiously unmoved and the gulf between the imperial family and the rest of the country wider than ever.

After the tercentenary the imperial family went on holiday to Livadia. They did not return to the small wooden palace where Alexander III had died but to a new residence which Alexandra herself had helped design. The White Palace at Livadia sat on a sloping lawn high above the Black Sea, overlooking terraces, rose gardens, and the town of Yalta below. Balconies, colonnades, and loggias skirted the walls of the sixty-room palace, reminders of Alexandra's childhood days at Osborne and her visits to Italy.

The tsarina had worked with the architect Krasnov on the design, which centered around several interior courtyards; in the middle of the largest courtyard was an antique Italian well. After receptions and dinners, the imperial family and their guests often withdrew to the loggias overlooking the carefully laid out flower beds to smoke and chat in the warm, open air. On the first floor of the palace were the state apartments: drawing rooms, reception rooms, and a portrait gallery. The principal rooms were all housed on the second floor. The tsarina had a large boudoir in mauve silk and mahogany, once again furnished by Maples in London. This adjoined the imperial bedroom, all in white, with brass beds set at an angle in a corner of the chamber. The private chapel was executed in Romanesque style, the walls hung with numerous valuable icons. The largest room, the White Hall—which served as the ballroom—rose one and a half stories and opened onto balconies overlooking the Black Sea below. The elegant marble rooms were always filled with fresh flowers and potted palm trees, discarded tennis rackets and the children's toys. Yet its comforts failed to impress many. Princess Paley, the morganatic second wife of the tsar's uncle Grand Duke Paul, called it a "bastard moorish" palace.[9]

The tercentenary celebrations had been among the first opportunities the general public had of observing the young grand duchesses. Unlike Alexei, who might appear with his father at a review as the heir, the girls were almost unknown. Alexandra had kept it that way. Sitting in the warm sunshine on her balcony at Livadia, Alexandra could watch her four daughters romp on the beach below the palace or play tennis matches against their father. They were all growing up fast.

Olga, the eldest, most resembled her father, with long chestnut-blond hair and blue eyes. She referred to her somewhat short nose as "my humble stub."[10] She was kind and good-natured, modest, and innocent. More serious than her sisters, Olga spent a good deal of her time reading. Often she would borrow the books set out for her mother in the Mauve Boudoir. When Alexandra caught her, Olga smiled and said, "You must wait, Mama, until I find out whether this book is a proper one for you to read."[11]

Tatiana, eighteen months younger than Olga, was closest to her mother. Tall, slender and well-proportioned, she had fine features, a pale complexion, and both her mother's golden hair and blue-gray eyes. Tatiana was very elegant; an officer of the guard once said, "You felt that she was the daughter of an Emperor."[12] Although she was more reserved than her sisters, Tatiana was a much better artist and played the piano brilliantly.

Marie, the most beautiful of the girls, had a fair complexion, thick brown hair, and eyes so large that within the family they were known as "Marie's saucers."[13] Her strength was enormous, and she often lifted her tutors, fully grown men, up into the air. She was slightly chubby, and her sisters called her "fat little bow wow."[14] She was also a flirt. When her first cousin, Louis, later Earl Mountbatten of Burma, first met her, he fell hopelessly in love. He kept a picture of her beside his bed until his death in 1979.[15]

Anastasia, the youngest of the girls, was also destined to become the most famous. Nicknamed the "imp" because of her boisterous nature, Anastasia was short, rather stout, with blue eyes and golden hair. She was, writes Gilliard, "very roguish and almost a wag. She had a very strong sense of humour and the darts of her wit often found sensitive spots. She was rather an *enfant terrible*."[16] Anastasia was also very independent, did not generally care for her lessons, and preferred to climb trees in the imperial park.

The four girls were unaffected by their position, as Alexandra had wished. Alexandra's ideals were Victorian: God, family, country. They did not extend to parties and society. In her sheltered world at Tsarskoe Selo, there was no room for the hedonistic excesses of St. Petersburg. She did not want her children surrounded by the decadence of the capital. They were kept artificially young, and in doing so, Alexandra prevented them from growing up. The head of the court chancellery, Alexander Mossolov, wrote: "I never heard the slightest word or suggestion of the modern flirtation . . . even when the two eldest had grown into real women one might hear them talking like little girls of ten or twelve."[17]

Such motherly control was not unusual in royal circles. The tsarina's aunt, Queen Alexandra of England, also prevented her daughters from growing up naturally. Two of the girls managed to escape her domination and find marriages, but for Victoria there was no such luck. The queen simply refused to let go of the past. Grand Duchess Olga Alexandrovna recalled, "Poor Toria was just a glorified maid to her mother. Many a time a talk or a game would be broken off by a message from Aunt Alix, and Toria would run like lightning, often to discover that her mother could not remember why she had sent for her, and it puzzled me because Aunt Alix was so good."[18]

By 1913, Olga was eighteen and Tatiana sixteen—ages at which matrimonial prospects first began to be discussed. One current magazine of the day noted, "Of all the marriageable princesses of Europe there are none that command at the present moment a greater share of popular attention than the two eldest daughters of the Tsar of Russia."[19] There was talk of a possible alliance with Crown Prince Carol of Rumania or with Edward, the Prince of Wales. But while promoting the grand duchesses as attractive candidates for marriage, another contemporary magazine sympathized with the cloistered existence they were forced to lead. The author of "Royal Mothers and Their Children" referred to them as "inmates of the imperial nursery," watched over by their "nerve-wracked mother" who suffered from "abnormal fears" for their futures.[20]

In spite of their immaturity, the four girls were all active and healthy. Seeing them, Alexandra often thought of those who were less fortunate. Her own son was a victim. The hillsides surrounding Livadia housed tubercular hospitals, always in need of contributions. Alexandra devised a social event to help them out, a charity bazaar, an exercise in *noblesse oblige*. She made all her family participate, saying, "They should realize the sadness that lies beneath all this beauty."[21] The Charity Bazaar, an invitation-only event, took place four times, the last in 1914. Alexandra manned a booth, selling embroidery, needlework, and watercolors, including those she and her daughters had done. The amount raised was minimal, but the effort eased Alexandra's mind, convincing her that she had done her duty in helping the poor, in much the same manner as any other European queen of the time would have thought. Even Alexei fulfilled his imperial obligations by making an appearance at his mother's table, dressed in a sailor suit. He sat cross-legged at her booth, bowing to the crowds at a whisper from his mother.[22]

Alexandra felt more comfortable at Livadia than in the capital. Free from the constraints of society and the prying eyes of St. Petersburg, she wandered through Yalta on shopping expeditions, accompanied only by Anna Vyrubova. On one particularly rainy afternoon the pair rushed into a small store to escape the downpour. Alexandra lowered her umbrella, leaving a puddle of water on the floor. "Madame, this is for umbrellas!" the manager said testily, at the same time pointing to a rack near the door. Alexandra apologized and deposited her umbrella in the rack. Only when Anna began addressing her as "Alexandra Feodorovna" did the man realize the identity of the exalted customer whom he had just berated.[23]

Despite the absence of the tsar and his immediate family, the winter social season of 1913 blazed with opulence. Princess Obolensky gave a Greek Mythology Ball, with guests wandering through her neoclassic mansion dressed in tunics and sandals and eating grapes and drinking Crimean wines while the snow fell over St. Petersburg. Meriel Buchanan arranged a variety of grisly tableaux for the Embassy Ball, including Bluebeard and Jack the Ripper. And Countess Kleinmichel hosted a splendid black-and-white ball, at which guests seemed to disappear against the checks of the marble floor.[24]

The St. Petersburg of 1913 bristled with gossip. The tsar's brother Michael had married a twice-divorced commoner the year before and been banished from the country as a result. Rumor had it that Grand Duke Andrei, the tsar's cousin, had fallen hopelessly in love with the ballerina Mathilde Kschessinska. Her magnificent jewels set tongues wagging: Who had purchased them for her? How much had they cost? The tsar, so the story went, refused to allow Andrei to marry the woman who had at one time been his own mistress. But the best morsel of gossip concerned Nijinsky. One night at the Mariinsky Theatre he appeared in a very revealing costume, purposely worn skintight. The dowager empress, watching from the imperial loge, put her opera glasses to her eyes, gave a long stare, put them back down, stood up, and with a look of burning condemnation, turned her back on the dancer and exited the theater. Nijinsky was banished from the imperial ballet the following morning.[25]

Regardless of the glitter, the whole of St. Petersburg was filled with decay. The atmosphere reeked of impending doom as the capital plunged headlong into a last round of sensual pleasures—alcohol, drugs, sexual promiscuity—coupled with despair ending in suicide and murder. W. Bruce Lincoln cites the shocking statistics: To one policeman and to every 150 St. Petersburg citizens there were roughly four to five prostitutes.[26]

The literature of the period reflected the hopelessness which most people felt. Valery Briusov, Bely, and Blok filled their writings with a sense of hopelessness and destruction. Summing up the whole atmosphere and the feelings of many toward the imperial family, the poet Dimitri Merezhkovsky wrote, "In the House of the Romanovs . . . a mysterious curse descends from generation to generation. . . . Murders and adultery, blood and mud . . . the block, the rope and poison—these are the true symbols of the Russian autocracy. God's unction on the head of the tsars has become the brand of Cain."[27]

The royal event of 1913—the last great one before the war in Europe—took place in Berlin. In May the only daughter of Kaiser Wilhelm II, twenty-one year-old Princess Victoria Louise, married Prince Ernest August of Hanover, duke of Brunswick. The ceremonies began on 22 May. Berlin had been draped in flags, bunting, and banners. King

George V and Queen Mary arrived to the welcome of a brass band; then the tsar and tsarina pulled into Berlin's Anhalter Station on their armor-plated ten-car train. According to one witness, the station "looked like a constabulary camp, police and detectives were everywhere. On a platform fifty feet from that at which the tsar's train was to come in was a line of infantry-men stretching far beyond the end of the station. They had rifles loaded with ball cartridge."[28]

The state banquet that night at the Berlin Palace was the last formal gathering of the crowned heads of Europe. Two hundred and fifty guests in uniform and sparkling jewels moved through the elegant rooms. Kaiser Wilhelm II, in full dress uniform as an English Royal Dragoon with the Russian Order of St. Andrew across his breast, led Queen Mary of England. King George V followed, wearing the uniform of the Prussian Dragoons and leading the kaiserin, Augusta Victoria. The tsar, also wearing a Prussian Dragoon uniform with the Hohenzollern Order of the Black Eagle, walked with the kaiser's aunt, the dowager grand duchess of Baden, while Alexandra followed on the arm of Crown Prince Wilhelm, known in the family as Little Willy.[29]

These festivities belied the tension which each of these three monarchs felt; war seemed to be inevitable, and Wilhelm, George, and Nicholas each sensed it. But while they made friendly overtures to allied countries and enjoyed their monarchical privileges, their governments maneuvered to establish the lines and treaties for which they would fight just a year later. As the guests danced that night in the Berlin Palace, the flickering candles in the crystal chandeliers caught the silver inlays of the woodwork and the multitude of jewels, causing them to sparkle for a moment in a final instant of illumination. As the sun set over Berlin that warm May evening, so it set over Europe, its brilliant rays of empire never to be seen again.

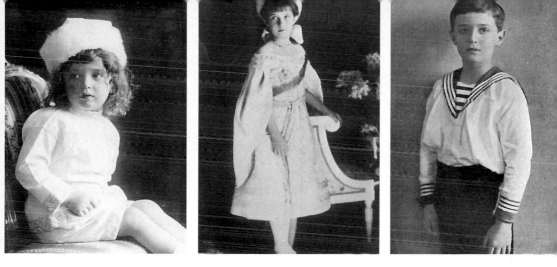

Above left. Tsarevich Alexei, 1906. (*Broadlands Archives*)   *Center.* Grand Duchess Anastasia in Russian court dress, 1910. (*Broadlands Archives*)   *Right.* Tsarevich Alexei, 1910.

Above left. The imperial children in the tsarina's cabin on board the imperial yacht *Standart*, 1906. *Left to right:* Grand Duchesses Marie and Olga, Tsarevich Alexei, and Grand Duchesses Tatiana and Anastasia.
Above right. Grand Duchess Marie Nicholaievich, 1902. (*Broadlands Archives*)

The imperial children, about 1910. *Left to right:* Grand Duchesses Tatiana and Anastasia, Tsarevich Alexei, and Grand Duchesses Marie and Olga. (*Broadlands Archives*)

Above left. The tsar and tsarina with the tsar's brother Grand Duke Michael Alexandrovich, at the hunting lodge of Skernevetski in Poland, circa 1900.   *Above right.* The Tsarevich Alexei laying a foundation stone for a church at the battlefield of Borodino, August 1912. His four sisters and his parents watch.

The tsarevich collecting donations on the Day of White Flowers, one of his mother's charities, in Yalta, the Crimea, 1912. The lady in white to his left is Anna Vyrubova.

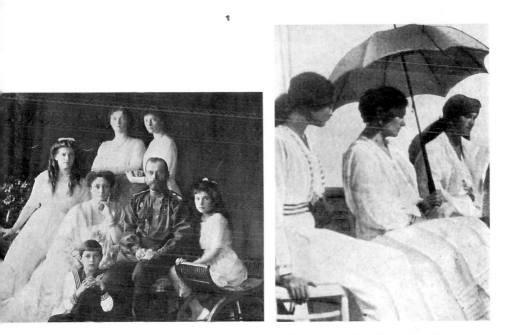

Above left. The Russian imperial family, 1913. *Left to right:* Grand Duchess Marie, Tsarina Alexandra, Grand Duchesses Olga and Tatiana, Tsar Nicholas II, and Grand Duchess Anastasia. Tsarevich Alexei sits in front of his parents. *Above right.* The last photograph ever taken of Empress Alexandra, on the balcony of the Governor's Mansion, Tobolsk, in Siberia, spring 1918. With her are her daughters Olga and Tatiana.

The four grand duchesses in their mother's reception room at the Alexander Palace, Tsarskoe Selo, 1916. *Left to right:* Olga, Tatiana, Marie, and Anastasia.

Above left. Tsarina Alexandra, 1906.   ***Above right.*** Empress Alexandra, followed by the tsar and her daughter Olga, leaving the military reviewing tent at Krasnoe Selo after watching exercises, August 1913.

The Russian imperial family, 1913. *Left to right:* Grand Duchess Olga, Grand Duchess Marie, Tsar Nicholas II, Tsarina Alexandra, Grand Duchess Anastasia, Tsarevich Alexei, and Grand Duchess Tatiana. (*Broadlands Archives*)

The tsar and tsarevich, 1913.

Tsar Nicholas II, 1914 postcard
distributed to the Russian troops.

Empress Alexandra in her Red Cross
nurse's uniform, 1915 postcard
distributed to the Russian troops.

Grand Duchess Olga in hussar
uniform, 1913. (*Broadlands Archives*)

Grand Duchess Tatiana in lancer
uniform, 1913. (*Broadlands Archives*)

Tsarevich Alexei with his tutor, Pierre Gilliard, at the Governor's Mansion, Mogilev, *Stavka*, 1916.

Grand Duke Cyril Vladimirovich.

Gregory Efimovich Rasputin, about 1906.

Prince Felix Youssoupov, while a student at Oxford University, England.

The Youssoupov Palace on the Moika Canal, St. Petersburg, where Prince Felix Youssoupov murdered Rasputin. Contemporary photograph.

The Ipatiev House in Ekaterinburg, Siberia, the last prison of the imperial family. The rounded window in the middle of the basement story to the left is that of the murder cellar.

28

Summer of War

A GLORIOUS SUMMER MORNING greeted Archduke Franz Ferdinand, heir to the thrones of Austria and Hungary, as he arrived with his wife, Countess Sophie Chotek, on a visit to the city of Sarajevo on Sunday, 28 June 1914. The Slavic south, where Sarajevo was situated, had long been a trouble spot in the Hapsburg Empire. Serbia, the principal Slav nation, resented Austrian rule, and the country seethed with revolutionary discord. It was, therefore, akin to political suicide for the next Hapsburg emperor to visit the center of the empire's troubles.

An open black motorcar drove the archduke and his wife through the city streets. Franz Ferdinand wore the light blue tunic of a cavalry general, with a high collar decorated in gold braid, black trousers, and a hat with green feathers; Sophie, seated beside him, had chosen a long white silk dress and a large picture hat ornamented with flowers.

As they drove through the city, a bomb thrown from the crowd exploded off the rear of the archduke's motorcar. Unhurt, Franz Ferdinand made his way to the town hall, where the mayor greeted him with a welcoming address. "To hell with your speech!" the archduke shouted at the mayor. "I have come to visit Sarajevo and am greeted by bombs, it is outrageous!"[1] But the visit continued. Franz Ferdinand and Sophie climbed into their motorcar and set off through the streets of Sarajevo toward the governor's mansion.

On the way the chauffeur forgot a turn, and the archduke's motorcar came to a stop in the middle of the street. Suddenly, a young man rushed forward; with two shots, Serbian student Gavril Princip made history. The first shot struck Sophie in the abdomen; she fell into her husband's lap. The second shot hit Franz Ferdinand; he clutched at his throat, a thin stream of blood spraying across his green tunic. "Sopherl! Sopherl! Don't die! Live for our children!" he screamed, then fell over the body of his wife. Within half an hour, the heir to the Austrian throne and his consort lay dead, Franz Ferdinand muttering to the last, "It is nothing."[2]

The emperor of Austria wrote flatly to his ally the kaiser:

The bloody deed was not the work of a single individual but a
well organized plot whose threads extend to Belgrade. Although
it may be impossible to establish the complicity of the Serbian
government, no one can doubt that its policy of uniting all
Serbian Slavs under the Serbian flag encourages such crimes and
that a continuation of this situation is a chronic peril for my
House and territories. . . .[3] Serbia must be eliminated as a political
force in the Balkans.[4]

The kaiser responded in kind; an imperial archduke had been brutally
killed, the most ghastly of all crimes. Alert, anxious, Europe waited for
an order of general mobilization. However, it would be another five
weeks before the effects of the Sarajevo crime would become apparent
to the world.

Just hours after the assassination of Archduke Franz Ferdinand, in
the Siberian village of Pokrovskoe, Khina Gusseva, Iliodor's demented
disciple, stabbed Rasputin as he walked through the streets. She had
disguised herself as a beggar and asked Rasputin for some change,
pulled out the knife Iliodor had given her, and thrust it violently into
the peasant's stomach. Rasputin warded off another blow before collapsing into the dusty roadway.

A local doctor examined Rasputin on his dining-room table. The
wound stretched from the sternum to the navel, exposing the intestines.
A doctor from Tiumen—a six-hour ride away—hurried to Pokrovskoe;
when he arrived, he found Rasputin in such grave condition that he attempted an emergency operation. Rasputin ordered that no anesthetic
be given, but he soon passed out from the pain. As soon as he could be
moved, Rasputin was put into a wagon and taken to Tiumen over the
rough and dusty roadways.

Rasputin barely survived the journey; he lay in a hospital bed in
Tiumen during the next few months and thus missed being in St. Petersburg during the momentous days of July. The doctor who saved
him, Vladimirsky, soon received a gold watch in gratitude from the tsarina.[6]

On 20 July 1914, Alexandra stood beside her husband on the deck
of the *Standart* , watching as the battleship *France* loomed larger on the
silver horizon, lights glowing bright in the sunset. Silently, the huge
ship churned through the dark blue waters of the Gulf of Finland, carrying the president of France, Raymond Poincaré, on his state visit to

Russia. Suddenly, the sky echoed with cannon fire and military marches blared out by brass bands, followed by the majestic and ironic melodies of "God Save the Tsar" and the "Marseillaise."

A round of parties, banquets, and reviews forced Alexandra into the public eye once again. Alexei had twisted his ankle and could not walk. Rasputin hovered between life and death while all of Europe talked of war. The strain was apparent to the new French ambassador, Maurice Paléologue, who sat next to her at a state banquet at the Peterhof Palace. He wrote:

> During the dinner I kept an eye on the Tsarina Alexandra Feodorovna opposite whom I was sitting. Although long ceremonies are a very great trial to her she was anxious to be present this evening to do honour to the president of the allied republic. She was a beautiful sight with her low brocade gown and a diamond tiara on her head. Her forty-two years have left her face and figure still pleasant to look upon. After the first course she entered into conversation with Poincaré, who was on her right. Before long, however, her smile became set and the veins in her cheeks stood out. She bit her lips every minute. Her laboured breathing made the network of diamonds sparkle on her bosom.[7]

A few days later, the president of France hosted a farewell banquet on board his battleship. Alexandra, according to Paléologue, "seemed worn out." Even so, she forced a smile and said, "I'm glad I came tonight. I was afraid there would be a storm. The decorations on the boat are magnificent. The President will have lovely weather for his voyage." But the exchange was forced. A nearby brass band suddenly began to thunder loudly a few feet away. Alexandra could take no more and put her hands to her ears.

"Couldn't you?" she murmured to Paléologue, pointing toward the group of musicians. The ambassador signaled to the conductor, who cut off the music. Grand Duchess Olga had been watching from a nearby chair; she walked over to her mother and exchanged a few whispered words. Then, turning to Paléologue, Olga said, "The Empress is rather tired but she asks you to stay, *Monsieur l'Ambassadeur*, and go on talking to her."[8]

A few hours later the *France* slipped out of the Gulf of Finland. "It was a splendid night," Paléologue remembered. "The Milky Way stretched, a pure band of silver, into unending space. Not a breath of wind. The *France* and her escorting division sped rapidly away to the west, leaving behind long ribbons of foam which glistened in the moonlight like silvery streams. . . ." As they watched the battleship disappear on the horizon, the tsar and the ambassador spoke of the archduke's murder. "Notwithstanding appearances," the tsar reassured the ambassador, "the Emperor Wilhelm is too cautious to launch his country on some wild adventure and the Emperor Franz Joseph's only wish is to die in peace."[9]

The next morning, Serbia received the Austrian ultimatum. It declared that the archduke's murder had been plotted in Belgrade; that Serbian officials had supplied the pistol; and that border guards had conspired in the assassination as well. The Austrian demands were staggering: Austrian officials were to be allowed to conduct their own investigation in Serbia; all Serb nationalistic groups and anti-Austrian propaganda were to be surpressed; and all anti-Austrian Serbian officials were to be dismissed. Serbia was given forty-eight hours to respond.[10]

"The Austrian demands are such that no state possessing the smallest amount of national pride or dignity could accept them," one Austrian official gleefully announced.[11] It came as such a shock, therefore, when Serbia agreed to all demands that the Austrian official who received the communication hid it for two days. Ultimately, Austria rejected its initial demands and on 28 July declared war on the kingdom of Serbia. The following morning, they began shelling Belgrade from across the Danube.

Traditionally, Russia regarded herself as the protector of all Slavic peoples. Therefore, when Serbia appealed to the tsar for help, Nicholas ordered mobilization of all Russian troops along the Austrian frontier. The kaiser responded to the struggle by coming to the aid of Austria's Emperor Franz Joseph. Wilhelm believed that his cousin Nicky could not possibly participate in a costly European war, and his own ambassador in St. Petersburg, Count Friedrich Pourtales, egged him on by repeating this view. Count Pourtales met the British ambassador, Sir George Buchanan, one day and began to dismiss Russian mobilization. But Sir George was not amused; he grabbed the elderly German ambassador, shook him, and said, "Count Pourtales, Russia means it!"[12]

Willy wrote to his cousin Nicky:

> It is with the gravest concern that I hear of the impression which the action of Austria against Serbia is creating in your country. The unscrupulous agitation that has been going on in Serbia for years has resulted in the outrageous crime to which Archduke Franz Ferdinand fell victim. You will doubtless agree with me that we both, you and I, have a common interest, as well as all

sovereigns, to insist that all persons morally responsible for this dastardly murder should receive their deserved punishment. In this, politics play no part at all. On the other hand, I fully understand how difficult it is for you and your government to face the drift of public opinion. Therefore, with regard to the hearty and tender friendship which binds us both from long ago with firm ties, I am exerting my utmost influence to induce the Austrians to deal straightly to arrive at a satisfactory understanding with you. I confidently hope you will help me in my efforts to smooth over difficulties that still may arise. Your very sincere and devoted friend and cousin,

Willy.[13]

Nevertheless, his general staff pressured Nicholas to order full mobilization against Austria-Hungary. Although Wilhelm warned that "military measures on the part of Russia would be looked upon by Austria as threatening," Nicholas ordered partial mobilization against Austria.[14] When Wilhelm learned of this, he was indignant. "And these measures are for the defense against Austria which is in no way attacking him!!! I cannot agree to any more mediation since the tsar who requested it has at the same time secretly mobilized behind my back."[15]

Two days later, the tsar met with Serge Sazonov, his foreign minister. Russia must mobilize, Sazonov said. Once Austria was established in the Balkans, according to the minister, she would use her influence to remove Russia as a power there. The tsar said nothing. Gently, Sazonov prodded the tsar, saying, "I don't think Your Majesty can postpone the order for general mobilization."[16] Nicholas reluctantly agreed.

That night, when Alexandra learned of the Russian mobilization, she stormed into her husband's study, slamming the door behind her. Anna Vyrubova sat outside, waiting, listening to the angry voices coming from the room which were growing louder by the minute. In the middle of the loud voices, the door opened, and Alexandra ran out, past Anna and into the bedroom. Anna followed her and found the tsarina lying on the bed, crying hysterically. "War!" she choked. "And I knew nothing of it! This is the end of everything!"[17]

The next day, Nicholas received another letter from his Cousin Willy:

I have gone to the utmost limits of the possible in my efforts to save peace. It is not I who will bear the responsibility for the terrible disaster which now threatens the civilized world. You

and you alone can still avert it. My friendship for you and your
Empire which my grandfather bequeathed to me on his deathbed
is still sacred to me and I have been loyal to Russia when she was
in trouble, notably during your last war. Even now, you can still
save the peace of Europe by stopping your military measures.
                                                    Willy.[18]

Apportioning blame for the start of the First World War is impossible; too many circumstances came into play for one individual to avert
the military clash. But in all probability the kaiser was correct. Nicholas
could have prevented the war had he called off his mobilization against
a country which had not taken any aggressive action against the Russian Empire. But a sense of honor and duty, as well as pressure from his
military advisers, acted to force the tsar to come to Serbia's aid, which
in turn forced the inevitable conflict between the powers.

At midnight on 31 July, Count Pourtales went to Sazonov and delivered a message from Berlin: Russia must reverse her decision to mobilize within the following twelve hours. By noon on 1 August, Russia
had not replied, and the kaiser ordered his armies to mobilize.

That evening, Count Pourtales called on Sazonov. With tears in
his eyes, he asked Sazonov if Russia would cancel her mobilization; the
foreign minister replied in the negative. Twice more, pleadingly, Pourtales begged Sazonov to cancel Russian mobilization. Sazonov told him
that it was too late. "In that case, Sir, my government charges me to
hand you this note," Pourtales choked. "His Majesty the Emperor, my
August Sovereign, in the name of the Empire, accepts the challenge and
considers himself in a state of war with Russia."[19] It was 7:10 P.M., 1
August 1914.

When Alexandra first learned of the Russian mobilization, she immediately cabled Rasputin for his advice. He replied with a telegram
dictated from his hospital bed in Tiumen: "Let Papa not plan war, for
with war will come the end of Russia and yourselves and you will lose
to the last man."[20] Alexandra rushed to her husband's study to deliver
the message; Nicholas angrily tore it up before her eyes.[21]

Three more telegrams followed. On 29 July, Rasputin cabled: "Do
not worry too much about war, when the time comes you will have to
declare it but not yet, there will be an end to your troubles."[22] On 1 August, the peasant sent the following telegram: "I believe in, I hope for
peace, they are doing wicked things, we are no part of it, I know how
you suffer, it is very hard to be apart from one another."[23] And again,
on the same day: "My dears, my precious ones, do not despair."[24]

There was also a very disturbing letter. Headed by a crudely scrawled cross, it read:

Dear Friend,

Again, I say a terrible storm cloud hangs over Russias. Disaster, grief, murky darkness and no light. A whole ocean of tears, there is no counting them, and so much blood. What can I say? I can find no words to describe the horror. I know they all want you to go to war, the most loyal, and they do not know that they will destruction. Heavy is God's punishment; when He takes away men's understanding it is the beginning of the end. You are the Tsar, the Father of Your People, don't let the lunatics triumph and destroy you and the people, and if we conquer Germany, what in truth will happen to Russia? When you consider it like that there has never been such a martyrdom. We all drown in blood. The disaster is great, the misery infinite.[25]

On the night of 1 August the imperial family stayed at Peterhof. Alexandra sat down at the dinner table and waited for the tsar to join her. She waited for nearly an hour. At last, Nicholas arrived, pale and shaken. He told her that war had been declared. Her reaction was immediate: She burst into tears and left the room.[26]

On 2 August 1914, the tsar declared war on Germany from the Winter Palace in St. Petersburg. Thousands of people filled the great cobbled square, waiting for a glimpse of the imperial family. The sun was bright and the sky clear as the tsar climbed from a boat onto the palace quay and walked the length of a long red carpet before disappearing into the cool shadows of the palace. Alexandra and her daughters followed, all dressed in white; Alexei remained at Peterhof, unable to walk.

They walked to the Salle de Nicolas , the largest room in the Winter Palace. Eleven enormous windows overlooked the broad length of the Neva River. A thousand people crowded into the hall for a great *Te Deum*. An altar had been erected in the middle of the room, upon which sat the icon of the Virgin of Kazan, the most revered of all Orthodox symbols. "Faces were strained and grave," recalled Grand Duchess Marie Pavlovna. "Hands in long white gloves nervously crumpled handkerchiefs and under the large hats fashionable at the time many eyes were red with crying. The men frowned thoughtfully, shifting from foot to foot, readjusting their swords or running their fingers over the brilliant decorations pinned on their chests."[27] Alexandra stood next to the tsar, her head held high and her face flushed. The ceremony apparently overwhelmed her, and at times she closed her eyes. According to Maurice Paléologue, "her lurid face made one think of a death mask."[28]

At the conclusion of the service, Alexandra and Nicholas began to make their way through the Winter Palace. Princess Julia Cantacuzene has left a memorable glimpse of the scene:

> General [Vladimir] Voikov, commandant of the palace, always quick to be officious, rushed forward to reinforce the Grand Master of Ceremonies and his aides, and he roughly pushed back men and women in their places, saying, "Space must be left clear." It was the Empress who gently stopped him; and it was she who seemed best to understand the movement towards her husband, and to welcome it. Voikov returned to his position in the procession among the Imperial Household, and the Sovereigns continued down the room, the crowd gone wild with love for them. Old men and young, red in the face and hoarse from the effort, kept up the noise. They, and the women too, bowed low, or threw themselves upon their knees, as their Rulers passed. His Majesty, in absolute silence, showed no recognition of any special face. Our beautiful Empress, looking like a Madonna of Sorrows, with tears on her cheeks, stretched her hand in passing to this or that person, now and then bending gracefully to embrace some woman who was kissing her hand. Her Majesty that day seemed to symbolize all the tragedy and suffering that had come upon us; and, feeling it deeply, to give thanks to this group for the devotion their attitude implied. Her expression was of extraordinary sweetness and distress, and possessed beauty of a quality I had never seen before in the proud, classic face. Everyone was moved by Her Majesty's manner in a moment when she must be tortured by thoughts of her old home.[29]

Alexandra and Nicholas went to the balcony overlooking the Palace Square. Below the red-draped balcony, the crowd was enormous; nine years earlier, on this same site, the tsar's soldiers had massacred workers on Bloody Sunday. Now all people were united by faith in the tsar and Russia. Nicholas tried to speak but the roar from below drowned his words. Overwhelmed, Alexandra and Nicholas bowed their heads. Someone in the crowd began to sing the national anthem; soon the human sea joined in and their voices rose to the couple on the balcony:

God Save the Tsar
Mighty and powerful
May He reign for Our Glory
Reign that Our Foes May Quake
O Orthodox Tsar
God Save the Tsar

Standing next to her husband that afternoon, on the balcony against the dark red façade of the Winter Palace, Alexandra gazed down on the surging, patriotic crowd. They cheered the beginning of a war destined to end with the deaths of millions of their countrymen, to destroy the old order of Europe and bring about social and political revolution in Russia. It was the twilight of the only world Alexandra had ever known.

PART FOUR

Sister Alexandra

(1914–17)

29

Russian Slaughter

"No country ever went to war so poorly equipped, so badly led, so foolishly optimistic, as Russia," writes Virginia Cowes.[1] The gigantic army, called "the Russian steamroller" in the British press, stood at 1,400,000;[2] after mobilization, its numbers were increased by 3,100,000 recruits.[3] And there were more waiting to march off and fight for the tsar and Russia: Some 15 million did so in the Great War, and nearly a quarter of them died.

All that the Russians had in their favor was men. To every yard of railway track in Russia, German railways had ten; the kaiser's factories outnumbered the tsar's by the hundreds. Ammunition was in short supply and after the soldiers fired their stocks, they had to wait for re-supply while being bombarded with Germany artillery. Each Russian soldier traveled an average of eight hundred miles to the front, compared to two hundred miles for a German soldier.[4]

Although the situation was grim, the soldiers who marched off that August were optimistic. "For the defense of Holy Russia!" was the battle cry leading the troops to war.[5] And, in a sense, it was a holy war, waged in the name of the tsar as the supreme head of the Russian Orthodox church.

The first major battle of the war occurred in September at Tannenburg. Two hundred thousand Russian troops surged through the bogs and marshes along the Baltic, swinging sabers, only to be met with German artillery; they were mown down in a matter of minutes.[6] The Russians lost half of their men, and the general in command rode off into the woods and shot himself.[7] The Russian soldier was no match for the might of modern artillery; most Russian soldiers had never seen the kinds of weapons that they now faced. Soldiers from Siberia, in particular, knew nothing of the modern world. When they first saw airplanes approaching, they took it as a sign that God was fighting on the side of the enemy.[8]

Unfortunately, the first year was far from successful for the Russian army. Cavalry and infantry, armed with sabers and lances, fell by the thousands as German artillery shells exploded in the forests and swamps of Poland.[9] The officers, while insisting that the troops crawl on the ground, themselves stood erect and walked straight into enemy fire.[10] The rate of officer mortality was staggering: The Preobrajensky Regiment lost forty-eight out of seventy officers,[11] and the Eighteenth Division had only 40 of its original 370.[12] "These people play at war," commented one man.[13] By the end of 1914, some 1 million Russian troops had been lost.[14]

Russia's efforts against Austria-Hungary did not prove more effective. In March 1915 the tsar's soldiers captured Austria-Hungary's strongest fortress, Przemsyl, with nine hundred guns; a month later, the Carpathian mountains were in Russian hands. However, the Germans came to Austria's aid with heavy artillery attacks, in which the Russian forces were reduced from 16 thousand to only five hundred men in four hours.[15] A second line of defense, the Third Caucasian Corps, rushed to the battlefield with forty thousand men; soon they had lost thirty-four thousand. The Germans advanced at a rapid pace. On 2 June, the Russians lost Przemsyl.[16]

On 5 August 1915, Warsaw fell. By the end of the summer, half of the Russian army was gone; 1,400,000 were killed or wounded, and 976,000 were prisoners.[17] General Anton Deniken wrote:

> The spring of 1915 I shall remember all my life. The retreat from Galicia was one vast tragedy for the Russian Army. . . . The German heavy artillery swept away whole lines of trenches, and their defenders with them. We hardly replied—there was nothing with which we could reply. Our regiments, although completely exhausted, were beating off one attack after another by bayonet. . . . Blood flowed unendingly, the ranks became thinner and thinner; the number of graves constantly multiplied. . . .[18]

As the winter drew near, the front was some two hundred miles east of its location in May; it would remain so for the rest of the war.[19]

Berlin, thinking it had crushed the Russian army, moved its main forces to the Western Front; but, in 1916, as soon as the Germans were occupied fighting the allies in the west, Russia attacked from the east. Until the month of October, they kept up the offensive, until they finally retreated after losing 1,200,000 men.[20]

Even with the army cut in half, arms were scarce. "In recent battles a third of the men had no rifles," reported one general. "These poor devils had to wait patiently until their comrades fell before their eyes and they could pick up their weapons. The army is drowning in its own blood."[21] At one time, the minister of war suggested that the soldiers should be armed with axes;[22] at another, he deemed it necessary for the tsar to issue an edict rationing Russian soldiers to only three shots a day [23] Soldiers waiting in the trenches for guns to be brought to them were "churned into gruel" by enemy artillery.[24] They watched their ranks shrink over the days, weeks, and months as the war went on. "You know, Sir, we have no weapons except the soldier's breast," said one private to a visiting general. "This is not war, Sir, this is slaughter."[25]

Russia seethed in anti-German sentiment. The day after war was declared, a violent mob stormed the abandoned German embassy, a huge granite building in St. Petersburg topped with giant bronze equestrian statues. They ripped through the building, destroying tapestries, furniture, paintings, and china, throwing marbles and bronzes through the windows to the street below. The crowd threw ropes around the rooftop statues and pulled the horses down into the canal.[26]

Fear of Germans exploded into violence. The windows of German bakeries were smashed by mobs, schools were threatened, and Bach, Brahms, and Beethoven were banned from orchestral programs.[27] In this narrow-minded and patriotic atmosphere the tsar changed the name of the capital from St. Petersburg to the more Slavic Petrograd. In a final act of intolerance, the Holy Synod banned Christmas trees as a German custom. "I am going to find out about it and then make a row," Alexandra wrote angrily. "It's no concern of theirs nor the church's and why take away a pleasure from the wounded and children because it originally came from Germany—the narrow-mindedness is too colossal."[28]

Hatred directed against Alexandra intensified. Was she not born in Germany? Did her brother not fight for the kaiser? How could she not be a German spy? Or at the very least have German sympathies? However, Alexandra felt quite differently. "Twenty years I have spent in Russia— half my life—and the fullest, happiest part of it," she said to Baroness Buxhoeveden. "It is the country of my husband and son. I have lived the life of a happy wife and mother in Russia. All my heart is bound in this country I love."[29] To Pierre Gilliard, she said, "What has happened to the Germany of my childhood? I have such happy, poetic memories of my early years at Darmstadt. But on my later visits, Germany seemed to me a changed country, a country I did not know and had never known. . . . I had no community of thought or feeling with anyone. . . . I have no news of my brother. I shiver to think that the Emperor Wilhelm may avenge himself against me by sending my brother to the Russian Front. He is quite capable of such monstrous behaviour."[30]

People sneered at Alexandra behind her back, and more wild stories circulated about the imperial family. One told of a general walking through the Winter Palace and finding the tsarevich weeping.

"What is wrong, my little man?" the general asked.

"When the Russians are beaten, Papa cries. When the Germans are beaten, Mama cries. When am I to cry?"[31]

When Alexandra sent prayer books to the wounded Germans, she was accused by the press of treason. "What can we do?" asked one Russian general at the front. "We have Germans everywhere. The Empress is a German."[32] Even Adm. Constantine Nilov, the tsar's flag captain, said, "I cannot believe she is a traitoress, but it is evident she is in sympathy with them."[33] Alexandra could do nothing; the public believed the rumors. After the Revolution, the Alexander Palace was searched for clandestine wireless stations everyone had imagined Alexandra had used to intrigue with her cousin the kaiser in Berlin. But the search was in vain, of course.

One day a huge crowd gathered in Moscow's Red Square. They demanded the tsarina's arrest, the tsar's abdication, Rasputin's execution, and the ascension to the throne of Grand Duke Nicholas Nicholaievich, to be crowned as Tsar Nicholas III. From Red Square, the mob moved to the Convent of St. Mary and St. Martha, where Grand Duchess Ella met them at the gate, wearing the long robes of the order she had founded. The crowd screamed that she was hiding her brother Ernie and that she was a spy. Someone picked up a rock and threw it at Ella, shouting, "Away with the German woman!" Just at that moment a company of soldiers arrived to protect the grand duchess, and the crowd left. But as they walked away, they began to call for the arrest of the tsarina, repeating Alexandra's name over and over again and chanting, *"Niemetzkaia bliad"* —the German whore.[34]

Throughout the early summer months of 1915, Alexandra had but one thought on her mind: the removal of Grand Duke Nicholas Nicholaievich from supreme command of the army. She resented his melodramatic death threat which she felt had convinced her husband to sign the manifesto creating the Duma in 1905.[35] She disliked the way in which the entire army looked up to him, and the Red Square demonstrations added further fuel to her fires of hatred. If all of this were not enough, Nicholas Nicholaievich also hated Rasputin. Rasputin once asked if he could come to headquarters to bless an icon. "Yes, do come," the grand duke replied. "I'll hang you."[36]

Rasputin, in turn, assured Alexandra that her worst fears would come true if the grand duke were not replaced as commander in chief. The tsar spent most of the spring with Nicholas Nicholaievich at headquarters. In a steady stream of letters to her absent husband Alexandra portrayed the grand duke as arrogant, power hungry, and disloyal:

> 12 June, 1915: N. is far from clever, obstinate and led by others— God grant I am mistaken and that this choice may be blessed— but . . . can this man have changed so much? . . . Is he not Our Friend's enemy?[37]

> 24 June, 1915: Please, my angel, make N. see with your eyes. . . .[38]

> 25 June, 1915: Would to God N. were another man and not turned against a Man of God's.[39]

> 29 June, 1915: I have absolutely no faith in N.—know him to be far from clever and having gone against a Man of God, his work can't be blessed or his advice good. . . . Russia will not be blessed if her sovereign lets a Man of God sent to help him be persecuted, I am sure. . . . You know N.'s hatred for Gregory is intense.[40]

> 30 June, 1915: N.'s fault and Witte's that the Duma exists, and it has caused you more worry than joy. Oh, I do not like N. having anything to do with these sittings which concern interior questions, he understands our country so little and imposes upon the ministers with his loud voice and gesticulations. I can go wild sometimes at his fat position. . . . Nobody knows who is Emperor now. . . . It is as though N. settles all, makes the choices and changes. It makes me utterly wretched.[41]

> 8 July, 1915: I loathe your being at headquarters . . . listening to N.'s advice which is not good and cannot be—he has no right to act as he does, mixing in your concerns. All are shocked that the ministers go with reports to him, as though he were now the sovereign. Ah, my Nicky, things are not as they ought to be and therefore N. keeps you near to have a hold over you with his ideas and bad counsels.[42]

It took a long time for the grand duke to fall from power. The tsar liked his cousin in spite of what his wife said and felt proud of the loyalty which he inspired in the army. Nicholas Nicholaievich, in turn, believed that the tsar had been annointed by God and never dreamed of usurping his authority. But on 5 August 1915, Warsaw fell. "The Emperor, white and trembling, brought this news to the Empress as we sat at tea on her balcony in the warm autumn air," wrote Anna. "The Emperor was fairly overcome with grief and humiliation. 'It cannot go on like this,' he exclaimed bitterly."[43]

That night, Alexandra and Nicholas made a private visit to St. Petersburg. First they went to the Cathedral of the Fortress of Peter and Paul. In the darkened marble church they knelt before the tomb of the tsar's father; at the Cathedral of Our Lady of Kazan, they prayed before the famous icon of the Virgin.[44] Nicholas had decided to replace the grand duke with himself as commander in chief of the army. Anna dined with Alexandra and Nicholas that evening. The three dropped to their knees and prayed for courage and strength. While they prayed, Anna pressed a small icon which she wore around her neck into the tsar's hand.[45]

The tsar met with his ministers in the Audience Chamber at the Alexander Palace the following day. After several hours had passed, Alexandra grew worried. She and Anna crept onto the balcony, which wrapped around the corner of the palace to the windows of the Audience Chamber. Looking through the French doors, they clearly saw the tsar pacing back and forth and then sitting rigidly in his chair. He told his ministers that he intended to replace Grand Duke Nicholas Nicholaievich as commander in chief. The ministers argued and argued, but to no avail. Nicholas thanked them and then quietly announced, "Gentlemen, in two days I leave for *Stavka*."[46]

Members of the Romanov family were horrified. Grand Duchess Olga Alexandrovna asked the tsarina how her brother could replace the popular commander in chief. "I'm sick of all this talk about Nikolasha," Alexandra angrily told her. "People talk of nothing else, but Nicky is much more popular."[47]

In spite of the almost universal opposition to the tsar's taking command, there existed real and valid reasons for his doing so. While the command was divided between Nicholas and his cousin, power in the government was destabilized. Grand Duke Nicholas Nicholaievich's chief of staff, Yanushkevich, was responsible for making all war-related decisions at headquarters. Decisions made at headquarters had to be approved back at St. Petersburg, and the other way around. War decisions made at headquarters often affected internal policy, while domestic decisions coming from St. Petersburg often contradicted the plans being made by the commander in chief. Having one man in charge of the situation would consolidate all decision making.

In addition, Nicholas himself keenly felt the need somehow to personally lead his troops, if only symbolically from headquarters. At the beginning of the Russo-Japanese War, he had been talked out of taking over command and had always regretted it. Again, in August 1914, when the Great War began, Nicholas told an assembled group of ministers that he eventually intended to take over command.[48]

Unlike other members of the family, Alexandra was overjoyed.

When Nicholas left for headquarters he had a letter of self-triumph from his wife:

> My Very Own Beloved One:
> I cannot find words to express all I want to. My heart is far too full. I only long to hold you tight in my arms and whisper words of intense love, courage, strength and endless blessing. More than hard to let you go, so completely alone. But God is very near to you, more than ever. You have fought this great fight for your country and throne, alone with bravery and decision. Never have they seen such firmness in you before and it cannot remain without fruit. Do not fear for what remains behind. One must be severe and stop all at once. Lovey, I am here. . . . Whenever I can be of the smallest use, tell me what to do. Use me, at such a time God will give me strength to help you, because our souls are fighting for the right against evil. It is all much deeper than appears to the eye. We, who have been taught to look at all from another side, see what the struggle here really is and means: you showing your mastery, proving yourself the autocrat without whom Russia cannot exist. Had you given in now on these difficult questions, they would have dragged yet more out of you. Being firm is the only salvation. I know what it costs you and have and do suffer hideously for you. Forgive me, my Angel, I beseech you, for having left you no peace and worried you so much, but I know too well your marvelously gentle character and you had to shake it off this time, had to win your fight alone against all. It will be a glorious page in your reign and Russia's history, the story of these weeks and days and God, who is just and near you, will save your country and your throne through your firmness. A harder battle has rarely been fought than yours and it will be crowned with success, only believe this. Your faith has been tried—your trust—and you remained firm as a rock, for that you will be blessed. God annointed you at your coronation, He placed you where you stand and you have done your duty, be sure, quite sure of this and He forsaketh not His Annointed. Our Friend's prayers arise day and night for you to Heaven and God will hear them. Those, who fear and cannot understand your actions, will be brought by events to realize your great wisdom. It is the beginning of the glory of your reign. He [Rasputin] said so and I absolutely believe it. Your sun is rising and today it shines so brightly. And so will you charm all those great blunderers, cowards, led astray, noisy, blind, narrow-minded and false beings this morning. . . . Won't that touch those hearts and make

them realize what you are doing and what they dared to wish to do, to shake your throne, to frighten you with internal black forebodings; only a bit of success out there and they will change. They will go home into clean air and their minds will be purified and they will carry the picture of you and your son in their hearts with them. . . . All is for the good as Our Friend says, the worst is over . . . when you leave, shall wire to Friend through Anna and He will particularly think of you. . . . Tell me the impression if you can. Be firm to the end, let me be sure of that, otherwise shall get quite ill from anxiety. Bitter pain not to be with you. Know what you feel and the meeting with N. won't be agreeable. You did trust him and now you know what months ago Our Friend said that he was wrongly acting towards you and your country and wife. . . . Lovey, if you hear that I am not so well, don't be anxious. I have suffered so terribly and physically overtired myself these two days and morally worried . . . you see, they are afraid of me and so come to you when alone. They know I have a will of my own, when I feel I am in the right, and you are now—we know it—so you will make them tremble before your courage and will. God is with you and Our Friend for you—all is well—and later all will thank you for having saved the country. Don't doubt— believe, and all will be well. . . . The Lefts are furious because all slips through their hands and their cards are clear to us and the game they wished to use Nikolasha for. . . . Sleep long and well, you need a rest after this strain and your heart needs calm hours. God Almighty bless your undertaking, His Holy Angels guard and guide you and bless the work of your hands. . . . You will feel my soul near you. I clasp you tenderly to my heart, kiss and caress you without end, want to show you all the intense love I have for you, warm, cheer, console, strengthen you and make you sure of yourself. Sleep well, my Sunshine, Russia's saviour. Remember last night, how tenderly we clung together. I shall yearn for your caresses. I never can have enough of them. . . . I kiss you without end and bless you. Holy Angels guard your slumber. I am near and with you for ever and none shall separate us.

Your Very Own Wife,

Sunny.[49]

30

Sister Alexandra

"OH, THIS MISERABLE WAR!" Alexandra wrote to her absent husband. "At moments one cannot bear it anymore, the misery and bloodshed break one's heart."[1] She spoke from personal experience, for as soon as the tsar left for army headquarters, she became engrossed in hospital work. During a war, most royal ladies became patrons of hospitals or charitable organizations, but few of them actually took nursing classes, studied anatomy, and assisted in hospital work. Alexandra did all of this, trying to set a national example for others to follow. "To some, it may seem unnecessary, my doing this," she explained, "but . . . help is much needed and every hand is useful."[2]

For many years as tsarina, Alexandra had refused to participate in society or even consent to show herself to the public on certain occasions. The war did not change this, and her desire to engage actively in the war took a peculiar twist. Rather than making public appearances which might have inspired the war-weary of the capital, she chose to isolate herself at Tsarskoe Selo, doing the routine day-to-day hospital work which any number of ordinary nurses were capable of and ignoring the strengths, her power and influence, which, as tsarina, she alone possessed in the fight against the kaiser.[3]

Alexandra established her own hospital for the wounded in one of the wings of the Catherine Palace at Tsarskoe Selo. In late 1914, Alexandra and her two eldest daughters studied first aid in preparation for their war work. The tsarina wrote to her sister Victoria:

> We passed our exams and received the Red Cross on our aprons and got the certificates of sisters of the war time. It was an emotion, putting them on, and appearing with other sisters—40—who had finished their course. . . . Our mornings at the hospital continue and weekly a train arrives with fresh wounded. Three thousand places at Tsarskoe and Pavlovsk. In the big palace we have officers and I go there every afternoon to see one,

who is suffering specially. He is contusioned, and in the last week always unconscious, recognizing nobody. When I come he regularly recognizes me, and then remains with a clear head all day long, suffers hideously—such cramps in the head and whole body—nerves too shattered, poor soul. He is touching with me, I remind him of his mother's kindness and as soon as I come, takes me at first for her (she is dead). When I call him and talk, he stares, then recognizes me, clasps my hands to his breast, says he now feels warm and happy.[4]

The hospital work transformed Alexandra. Before the war, she had slept until noon and rarely left the couch in her boudoir. But during the war, with a purpose which had formerly been lacking in her life, Alexandra attended mass at seven in the morning; by nine, outfitted in a crisp nurse's uniform, she, along with Olga and Tatiana, was at the hospital. "I have seen the Empress of Russia in the operating room," Anna wrote in awe, ". . . holding ether cones, handling sterilized instruments, assisting in the most difficult operations, taking from the hands of busy surgeons amputated legs and arms, removing bloody and even vermin-ridden field dressings, enduring all the sights and smells and agonies of the most dreadful of all places, a military hospital in the midst of war."[5]

The details of her days filled her letters to Nicholas:

Very bad wounds; for the first time I shaved one of the soldiers' legs near and around the wound.[6]

Three fingers were taken off today as blood poisoning had set in and they were quite rotten.[7]

Dear me, what wretched wounds, I fear some are doomed men; but I am glad we have them and can at least do all in our power to help them . . . the poor boy . . . an officer of the 2nd Rifles, whose legs are getting quite dark and one fears an amputation may be necessary. I was with the boy yesterday . . . changed his dressing, awful to see, and he clung to me and kept quiet, poor child.[8]

This morning we were present (I help as always giving the instruments and Olga threaded the needles) at our first big amputation. Whole arm cut off. . . . I had wretched fellows with awful wounds—scarcely a "man" any more, so shot to pieces, perhaps it must be cut off as so black but hope to save it—terrible to look at. I washed and cleaned and painted with iodine and smeared with vaseline and tied them up and bandaged all up. . . .

I did three such—and one had a little tube in it. One's heart bleeds for them—I won't describe any more details as it's so sad but being a wife and mother I feel for them quite particularly. . . . My nose is full of hideous smells from those awful blood poisoning wounds. . . .[9]

During an operation a soldier died. . . . All behaved well, none lost their heads and the girlies were brave—they and Anna had never seen a death. But he died in an instant—it made us all so sad as you can imagine—how near death always is.[10]

I went in to see the wound of our standard bearer . . . awful, bones quite smashed, he suffered hideously during bandaging, but did not say a word, only got pale and perspiration ran down his face and body. . . .[11]

Alexandra experienced the horrific realities of war every day; for her, the battlefield sat across the lake and gardens in the hospital wards of the Catherine Palace. Her presence itself somehow seemed to lift the spirits of the wounded. Walking through a hospital ward, she heard cries of "Tsarina, stand near me! Hold my hand that I may have courage!"[12]

In time, she became attached to a young wounded soldier from the front. Her letters to her husband are filled with details of his last days: "I find the young boy gradually getting worse, the temperature is slowly falling, but the pulse remains far too quick, in the evenings he is off his head and so weak. The wound is much cleaner but the smell they say is quite awful. He will pass away gradually—I only hope not whilst we are away."[13]

Four months later, she wrote:

My poor wounded friend has gone. God has taken him quietly and peacefully to Himself. I was as usual with him in the morning and more than an hour in the afternoon. He talked a lot—in a whisper always—all about his service in the Caucasus—awfully interesting and so bright with his big shiny eyes. . . . Olga and I went to see him. He lay there so peacefully covered under my flowers I daily brought him, with his lovely peaceful smile—the forehead yet quite warm. I came home with tears. The eldest sister cannot yet realize it either—he was quite calm, cheery, said felt a wee bit not comfy and when the sister came ten minutes after she had gone away, came in, found him with staring eyes, quite blue, breathed twice—and all was over—peaceful to the end. Never did he complain, never asked for anything, sweetness itself—all loved him and that shining smile. You, lovy mine, can understand what that is, when daily one has been there, thinking only of giving him pleasure—and suddenly—finished. . . . Forgive my writing so much about him, but going there and all that, had been a help with you away and I felt God let me bring him a little sunshine in his loneliness. Such is life. Another brave soul left this world to be added to the shining stars above. It must not make you sad, what I wrote, only I could not bear it any longer.[14]

In 1915, Alexandra visited a series of military hospitals in Pskov. Grand Duchess Marie Pavlovna accompanied the tsarina as she made her rounds. In apparent contrast, she later wrote: "I was walking behind her and did not so much listen to words, always the same, as watch faces. No matter how sincerely the Empress sympathized with the men's sufferings, no matter how she tried to express it, there was something in her, eluding definition, that prevented her from communicating her own genuine feelings and from comforting the person she addressed."[15]

On that day that the tsarina left Pskov, she had been requested to visit a group of young cadets on their way to the front. But Alexandra said no. Grand Duchess Marie Pavlovna begged her to reconsider, but the tsarina refused to alter her schedule. The grand duchess arranged for the boys to assemble along the route to the train station in the hope that she could somehow persuade the tsarina to stop, if only for a few minutes. They left the hospital and were driving down the roadway toward the station when the grand duchess pointed out the ranks of cadets lined up at the side of their route, waiting to see the tsarina. But Alexandra, according to the grand duchess, refused to stop "just for a second." She sat, her face turning red, silent and immobile for the rest of the trip. At the station she boarded her train, and immediately it left Pskov.[16]

How are we to account for the vast difference between the wife filling her letters to her husband with details of her sympathetic nursing and the cold, unfeeling tsarina presented to us by Marie Pavlovna? Part of the answer undoubtedly lies in the fact that Marie Pavlovna dared to go against Alexandra's wishes—a cardinal sin to the tsarina. But the real answer lies in the tsarina's own perception of her two roles during the war years, as wife of the tsar and as a nursing sister. In the former role, Alexandra stood silent, regal, and proud. She represented the dignity of the House of Romanov. She never let her guard down; neither a smile nor a frown crossed her face. Laughing and crying were private, human emotions, to be kept hidden away from prying eyes.

She insisted on etiquette, on rigid formality, on absolute adherence to the wishes of the imperial family without question. In the wards of the Catherine Palace, she left all of this behind; she was still the tsarina, but also a compassionate, humane woman, with real emotions which no longer had to be suppressed. The apparent contradiction results from the tsarina's perception of her two roles, as tsarina in public and as a nursing sister in private. She could not reconcile the two roles, and by separating them, she further alienated the general public, who no longer saw her as a human being but a Romanov icon without emotion.

Alexandra, of course, was judged by a public aware only of her actions and appearances before their eyes. Her letters to the tsar reveal something more of the tsarina's true character during the war years. During the nearly two years that Nicholas was away at headquarters, Alexandra wrote some four hundred letters to him. Often, she wrote two or three a day. She wrote in English, the everyday language of the imperial family. But it was an English curiously affected by her years in Russia, for the tsarina's letters make it apparent that she had lost much of her ability to spell and punctuate properly. As a result, the letters are long, rambling, and nearly impossible to read.

Her letters reflect the influence of the romantic Victorian writers and poets of whom she was so fond. She filled page after page with expressions of passion and physical love for her husband. When he was gone, Alexandra longed for Nicholas. "Four months we have not slept together," she wrote.[17] When he stayed at headquarters, she faithfully reported her menstrual periods to her husband. "The Engineer Mechanic has come to me."[18] "Becker came to Tatiana and me today, so kind before time, will be all the better for journey."[19] "Shall come to you and leave Becker behind."[20] When, in 1916, a rumor reached her that General Grabbe, the head of the Imperial Cossack Guard, had planned to introduce a certain Madame Soldatenko to Nicholas "so as to get you acquainted with her and that she might become your mistress," Alexandra was enraged.[21] The tsar found out that it had been Anna who had passed on the rumor and wrote back angrily, "You may be quite sure that I shall not make her acquaintance. . . . But you, for your part, must not allow Anna to bother you with stupid tale bearing that will do no good, either to yourself or to others."[22]

Alexandra wrote rapidly. When she had finished, she might scent the paper with a favorite perfume; other times, plucked flowers from the gardens at Tsarskoe Selo were pressed between the pages.

Sleep well, my treasure . . . my bed will be oh, so empty.[23]

Oh, my love. It was hard bidding you goodbye and seeing that lonely, pale face with big sad eyes at the wagon window—my heart cried out, take me with you![24]

I bless you, kiss your precious face, sweet neck and dear loving handies with all the fervour of a great loving heart.[25]

Bless you. Love you. Long for you.[26]

I gave my goodnight kiss to your pillow and longed to have you near me—in thoughts I see you lying in your compartment, bend over you, bless you and gently kiss your sweet face all over—oh, my darling, how intensely dear you are to me; could I but help you carrying your heavy burdens, there are so many that weigh upon you now.[27]

Sweet, brave soul. . . . I long to hold you tightly clasped in my arms, with your sweet head resting upon my shoulder—then I could cover Lovey's face and eyes with kisses and murmur soft words of love. I kiss your cushions at night, that's all I have—and bless it.[28]

I yearn for your kisses, for your arms and shy childy gives them to me in the dark and wify lives by them. . . .[29]

I know I ought not to say this, and for an old married woman it may seem ridiculous, but I cannot help it. With the years, love increases and the time without your sweet presence is hard to bear. . . . Oh, could but our children be equally blessed in their married lives. . . .[30]

She wrote often of the children:

Baby improves playing on the balalaika. Tatiana too. I want them to learn to play together. . . .[31]

Marie stands at the door and, alas, picks her nose![32]

On the train, the girls are sprawling on the floor with the sun shining full upon them to get brown. From where have they got that craze?[33]

Baby was awfully gay and cheery all day . . . in the night he woke up from pain in his left arm and from two on scarcely got a moment's sleep. The girls sat with him a good while. It seems he worked with a dirk and must have done too much—he is so strong that it's difficult for him always to remember and think he must not do strong movements. . . . The pain came with such force. . . . I think it will pass quicker—generally three nights. . . . I cried like a baby in church.[34]

To these letters Nicholas responded in much the same emotional vein:

My beloved wify, the words you write are always so true, and when I read them their meaning goes right to my heart, and my eyes are often moist. It is hard to be apart, even for a few days, but letters like yours are such a joy that it is worth while parting for the sake of them. . . .[35]

I am longing for you so much, so much in need of you. . . .[36]

I . . . kiss often the places which I think were touched by your dear lips.[37]

And so, Nicholas remained at headquarters, sending tender expressions of his love to Alexandra. She rose each morning and worked in the hospital in the Catherine Palace, all the while longing for her absent husband. At Tsarskoe Selo, the sun rose from behind the trees, slanting through the soft haze from the steam rising off the grass while the swans swam in the lakes. The trees changed with the seasons, from green to yellow, red, and copper. The days of the long Russian winter approached. And, in St. Petersburg, Rasputin loomed larger on the darkening horizon.

31

The Shadow of Rasputin

THE BLOCK OF FLATS lining Gorokhovaya Street in St. Petersburg housed, to a large extent, members of the city's middle class. On the third floor of one building, in five rooms, Rasputin lived during the First World War. His flat, furnished with gifts from admirers, had one feature which the peasant found an asset: a back stairway which led to the courtyard. By using this, Rasputin could come and go unobserved. To this simple apartment, the great of St. Petersburg flocked.

Visitors lined up outside the apartment, at all hours of the day and night, waiting for an interview with the peasant. They were well aware of the power and influence rumored to lie behind those doors on the third floor. If Rasputin liked the visitor, he would give him or her a card with a scrawled "My dear and vauled friend: Do this for me. Gregory."[1] Because he did not write well Rasputin usually did not name the favor requested or even the person to whom the card should be delivered. Eventually, he made up a supply of these cards and merely passed them out as people paraded through.

Quite often the recipient of the cards was General Mossolov, head of the court chancellery. "All were drawn up in the same way," he wrote, "a little cross at the top of the page, then one or two lines giving a recommendation from the *starets*. They opened all doors in Petrograd."[2] But on at least one occasion they could not open a door. "A lady in a low cut dress, suitable for a ball . . . handed me an envelope," wrote Mossolov; "inside was Rasputin's calligraphy with his erratic spelling: 'My dear chap, fix it up for her, she is all right. Gregory.' The lady explained that she wanted to become a prima donna in the Imperial Opera. I did my utmost to explain to her clearly and patiently that the post did not depend on me in any way."[3]

A number of police detectives faithfully watched the main entrance to Rasputin's flat. They had a double job: to protect the peasant and to observe his activities. Each kept a small notebook in which he jotted down the comings and goings along Gorokhovaya Street:

Anastasia Shapovalenkova, the wife of a doctor, has given Rasputin a carpet.[4]

An unknown woman visited Rasputin in order to try to prevent her husband, a lieutenant at present in the hospital, from being transferred from St. Petersburg. . . . [She said] "A servant opened the door to me and showed me to a room where Rasputin, whom I had never seen before, appeared immediately. He told me at once to take off my clothes. I complied with his wish and went with him into an adjoining room. He hardly listened to my request; but kept on touching my face and breasts and asking me to kiss him. Then he wrote a note but did not give it to me, saying that he was displeased with me and bidding me to come back next day."[5]

Madame Likhart visited Rasputin . . . to ask him to intervene on her husband's behalf. Rasputin proposed that she should kiss him; she refused, however, and departed. Then the mistress of Senator Mamontov arrived. Rasputin asked her to return at 1 AM.[6]

During the visit of the Pistolkors family Rasputin took the prostitute Gregubova on his knee and murmured something to himself.[7]

As he [Rasputin] went up to his flat he inquired if there were any visitors for him. On hearing that there were two ladies he asked: "Are they pretty? Very pretty? That's good. I need pretty ones."[8]

Rasputin came in an intoxicated state . . . but left again immediately . . . and did not come back till about 2 AM, very drunk.[9]

Rasputin came home at 7:30 AM with two men and a woman; he was dead drunk, and sang songs on the public street. The unknown persons accompanied him up to his flat and then departed.[10]

The wife of Colonel Tatarinov visited Rasputin and . . . the *starets* embraced and kissed a young girl in her presence; she found the incident so painful that she decided never to visit Rasputin again.[11]

Maria Gill, the wife of a Captain in the 145th Regiment, slept at Rasputin's.[12]

Rasputin came back with Varvarova at 9:50 AM; he must have spent the night with her.[13]

Rasputin sent the concierge's wife for the masseuse but she refused to come. He then went himself to Katia, the seamstress who lives in the house, and asked her to "keep him company." The seamstress refused. . . . Rasputin said, "Come next week and I will give you fifty rubles."[14]

Rasputin sent the porter's wife to fetch the masseuse, Utilia, but she was not at home. . . . He then went to the seamstress Katia in her flat. He was apparently refused admittance, for he came down the stairs again and asked the porter's wife to kiss him. She, however, disengaged herself from his embrace and rang his flat bell, whereupon the servant appeared and put Rasputin to bed.[15]

The policemen and their notebooks became the talk of St. Petersburg. It was said that any favor could be obtained through Rasputin: For attractive women, sex became one method of payment. But the wealthy who flocked to call on the peasant brought with them money, jewels, paintings, fine wines, and food. Rasputin himself had little interest in money—he merely threw it into a bureau drawer without counting it. Often, when someone came to call who was needy, Rasputin would pull out a bundle of rubles and hand it over to the visitor.

The guards kept track of all Rasputin's movements, following him about St. Petersburg at all hours of the night and to every spot in the capital. Once the public learned of their existence, there was a black market for all of these notes, and quickly St. Petersburg could be found wallowing in page after page of Rasputin's lustful adventures. "Rasputin's apartments are the scene of the wildest orgies," wrote the American ambassador in St. Petersburg. "They beggar all description and from the current accounts of them which pass freely from mouth to mouth, the storied infamies of the Emperor Tiberius on the Isle of Capri are made to seem moderate and tame."[16]

The question of the notebooks' accuracy has to be addressed. From what we know of Rasputin and his behavior during the last years of his life, it is possible to say that the notebooks could well be true. Rasputin's admirers claimed that the police had simply fabricated their stories, but this seems unlikely, although exactly how the men knew what took place behind the closed doors of Rasputin's flat has never been satisfactorily explained.

Along with the orgies, meals at Rasputin's flat also became legendary. The peasant's aide, Aaron Simanovich, later described Rasputin "plunging his dirty hands into his favourite fish soup."[17] If jam was on the table, it was said that Rasputin would often dip his fingers into the bowl and then turn to his admiring female companions and shout, "Humble yourself, lick it clean, lick it clean!"[18]

Alexandra knew of the notebooks, the rumors of orgies and influence. For years she had listened to reports of Rasputin's misbehavior and dismissed them. But with a report submitted by one of the tsar's aides-de-camp and the deputy minister of the interior, Gen. Vladimir Dzhunkovsky, it seemed that the peasant finally faced ruin. Alexandra would have to accept the overwhelming evidence.

In April 1915, Rasputin traveled to Moscow to pray at the tombs of the saints in the Cathedral of the Assumption in the Kremlin. The British ambassador in Moscow, Robert Bruce Lockhart, later wrote:

> I was at Yar, the most luxurious night haunt of Moscow, with some English visitors. As we watched the music hall performance in the main hall, there was a violent fracas in one of the private rooms. Wild shrieks of a woman, a man's curses, broken glass and the banging of doors. Headwaiters rushed upstairs. The manager sent for the police. . . . But the row and roaring continued. . . . The cause of the disturbance was Rasputin—drunk and lecherous, and neither police nor management dared evict him.[19]

The incident was much worse than Bruce Lockhart let on. Rasputin had smashed most of the elegant trappings of a private dining room and tried to seduce his female companions. When the police finally arrived, Rasputin shocked everyone by undoing his trousers and exposing himself to the diners. On top of this, the peasant began to yell that he acted this way in the presence of the tsar and that he often did what he liked with "the old girl."[20] The police dragged Rasputin away, the peasant unrepentant and "snarling and vowing vengeance."[21]

Dzhunkovsky made out a report on the matter but was reluctant to send it to the tsar. Alexandra's sister Ella, having heard the rumors about the Yar incident, asked Dzhunkovsky's sister to implore the general to intervene at Tsarskoe Selo. From Moscow, Ella let it be known that she was supported by the minister of the interior, Prince Nicholas Scherbatov, and the minister of religion, Alexander Samarin. Whatever vestiges of family loyalty still bound the two sisters, Ella's actions destroyed once and for all any bond between them.

Dzhunkovsky eventually gave the report to the tsar on 4 August. Nicholas angrily summoned Rasputin, demanding an explanation. Rasputin said that he was a simple man and had become drunk due to bad judgment. But he denied that he had ever exposed himself or spoken of the imperial family despite the strong evidence which indicated he had.[22] Nevertheless, the tsar ordered Rasputin to leave St. Petersburg. Before he left the capital, however, Rasputin told one of the policemen outside his flat, "Your Dzhunkovsky's finished."[23]

Nicholas gave his wife the Dzhunkovsky report to read. When she finished it, Alexandra burst into tears and cried uncontrollably.[24] She never once claimed that it was false. But despite what she took to be the truthfulness of the report, Alexandra wanted Dzhunkovsky dismissed. Some of this stemmed from the fact that Rasputin was threatened. She may not have accepted Rasputin the man, but she certainly believed in Rasputin the peasant whose prayers could heal her son. The loss of the drunken, lecherous Rasputin also meant the end of the comfort which he brought to her son. Whatever Rasputin's faults, Alexandra accepted him.

Apart from Rasputin, Alexandra was infuriated by the way in which the report was made public. Dzhunkovsky made no secret of its contents and shared the report with others in the government. Prince Vladimir Orlov, one of the tsar's favorite courtiers, made a public statement on the report, hinting that it would be best for the country if Alexandra were sent away to Livadia for the remainder of the war. Dzhunkovsky was also heard to echo this sentiment, and Sazonov, the foreign minister, joined the pair in speaking out against the tsarina. When she learned that Grand Duke Dimitri Pavlovich had seen the report, she wrote angrily to her husband:

> My enemy Dzhunkovsky . . . has shown that vile, filthy paper to
> Dimitri. . . . If we let Our Friend be persecuted we and our
> country shall suffer for it. . . . I am so weary, such heartaches and
> pain from all this—the idea of dirt being spread about one we
> venerate is more than terrible. Ah, my love, when at *last* will you
> thump with your hand upon the table and scream at
> Dzhunkovsky and others when they act wrongly—one does not
> fear you—and one *must*—they must be frightened of you
> otherwise all sit upon us. . . .[25]

Alexandra's attack on Dzhunkovsky, though under the guise of protecting the peasant, was, in reality, an effort to protect her reputation. Her name had publicly been dragged through the mud, and Alexandra wanted those responsible dismissed. In September 1915, the tsar gave in, and Dzhunkovsky was fired from his post.

In spite of the failure of the Dzhunkovsky report to remove Rasputin as an influence, the peasant's position during the first six months of the war was weak. Alexandra had little time for him, caught up as she was in the hospital work she had undertaken, and Nicholas had too many military concerns to take much notice of the peasant or his advice. Relations were further strained by a feud between Alexandra and Anna, who had acted as chief intermediary for her friends.

Alexandra noticed that Anna seemed to be paying too much attention to the tsar, always trying to be at his side and asking him for advice. Alexandra was not jealous; she trusted her husband and her friend completely. But she was angered by Anna's attempts to insinuate herself into the tsar's confidence and by the letters Anna wrote to her husband. Alexandra herself wrote to Nicholas, denouncing Anna and warning the tsar to burn all of the letters which her friend had sent. Because Anna was chiefly responsible for arranging the meetings between the tsarina and the peasant at her house, Rasputin remained out of contact with the imperial family. It took two miracles to restore both Anna and Rasputin to imperial favor.

On the afternoon of 15 January 1915, a train carrying Anna Vyrubova back to St. Petersburg from Tsarskoe Selo flew off the track and crashed into the deep snow. Anna lay trapped for several hours, her skull shattered and her legs crushed by a radiator; a steel girder had severed her spine. She was taken to the nearest hospital. Alexandra and Nicholas rushed to her bedside, only to be met by a doctor. "Do not disturb her," he said. "She is dying."[26]

Rasputin did not hear of the accident until the following day. He borrowed a motorcar from Countess Witte and hurried to the hospital. Anna lay in bed, delirious, screaming out, "Father Gregory, pray for me!" Alexandra watched as the peasant walked over and took Anna's hand, saying gently, "Annushka, Annushka, Annushka." Finally, the dying woman opened her eyes.

"Now wake up and rise!" Rasputin commanded. Anna tried to get up but fell back, collapsing into unconsciousness. Rasputin stumbled out of the room, saying to Alexandra, "She will recover but will remain a cripple."[27] As Rasputin predicted, Anna lived but had to move about on crutches for the rest of her life. Alexandra had seen the cure with her own eyes: Her faith in Rasputin remained unshakable.

In 1915, headquarters, or *stavka*, was located at the town of Mogilev, on the banks of the Dneiper River. Headquarters was established in the mansion of the provincial governor, a large house on a hill overlooking the river below. In 1915, the tsar decided to bring his son to *stavka* to live.

Alexandra would not hear of it at first, if not because of the boy's age, then because of his hemophilia. But after much discussion with the tsar, she relented, putting Russia's interests before her own. She explained to Pierre Gilliard that the tsar wanted to introduce his ten-year-old son to the concept of leadership. Nicholas, she told him, suffered from crippling shyness which made him agree with all opinions presented to him. He could not take charge in a situation. When Alexander III had died, she said, Nicholas came to the throne totally unprepared for his duties as tsar. He had decided not to make the same mistakes with his own son.[28]

Alexandra wrote daily to the tsar about Alexei, offering all kinds of motherly advice. "See that Tiny doesn't tire himself on the stairs. He cannot take walks."[29] "Take care of Baby's arm, don't let him run about on the train so as not to knock his arms."[30] "Tiny loves digging and working and he is so strong and forgets that he must be careful."[31] Her stifling care of the tsarevich followed him even to *stavka*, and her thoughts were constantly of his safety. Every night, before she went to bed, Alexandra walked up to his darkened, empty room, knelt beside his bed, and prayed for her son's safe return.[32]

But the tsar could not prevent the inevitable. During a visit to the front to review soldiers, the tsarevich caught a cold. On the train back to Mogilev, he began to sneeze. After several hours, his nose bled violently. Professor Fedorov happened to be in attendance; he made the tsarevich rest, but Alexei only grew worse, his temperature higher, the blood flowing unchecked. Worried, Fedorov told the tsar that it might be best to take the boy back to Tsarskoe Selo, where he could be looked after properly. The train ride only made the condition worse; Pierre Gilliard, who sat by the boy's bed, listened to his moans as the train sped across the Russian countryside. Twice, he thought that the end had come.[33]

Nicholas cabled Alexandra at Tsarskoe Selo to inform her that their son might be dying and that he was on his way back to the palace. She waited for her son's return, crying and praying. At last, a motorcar sped up the driveway, and Alexei was carried into the Alexander Palace. Alexei looked at his mother pathetically, his blue eyes circled with black above the red swab of the blood-soaked bandages. He moaned as she held his hand, trying to comfort her apparently dying son. Fedorov and Dr. Derevenko rushed back and forth, changing the bandages, soaking up the blood which poured over the little boy's face each time they unwrapped his nose. Despite their efforts, both said that there was little hope; Alexei could die at any minute.

In despair, Alexandra sent for Rasputin. Perhaps she was reluctant to call the peasant following the Dzhunkovsky report, knowing that Rasputin had incurred her husband's displeasure. When he arrived at the Alexander Palace, Rasputin ran straight to the tsarevich's bedroom. Alexandra sat slumped in a chair beside the bed, now splattered with her son's blood. Rasputin walked to the edge of the bed as Alexandra and Nicholas dropped to their knees to pray. After a while, Rasputin said, "Don't be alarmed. Nothing will happen." He then left the palace. Alexei, who had been crying out in pain, fell asleep. When Alexandra went to his room the next morning, the boy talked with her and sat up in bed: The blood had stopped during the night.[34]

32

"For Baby's Sake"

"WHEN THE EMPEROR WENT TO WAR, of course his wife governed instead of him," explained Grand Duke Alexander Michailovich.[1] From the moment that the Tsar stepped aboard the imperial train and steamed off toward headquarters to take supreme command, Alexandra began to preside over his government. In the two and a half years that followed, it deteriorated with a shocking rapidity that is without parallel in modern history.

It is hard to imagine anything more damaging than the tsar's decision to leave control of the government to his wife, and no one seems to have seriously questioned the role which the tsarina assumed. Although Alexandra may have been involved in certain political decisions in the years before the war, one thing is certain: Her experiences did nothing to sharpen her political sense. At the time of the war, she still believed that the Duma and the ministers were somehow involved in shadowy plotting against her husband, her son, and the throne. Rasputin and a handful of others were the "good men," while the tsarina labeled the Duma and members of the government "bad."

The tsarina's involvement in political matters during the war was her own doing. To the tsar, she wrote: "Let me help you, my treasure. Surely there is some way in which a woman can be of help and use. I do so yearn to make it easier for you. . . ."[2] Again, she wrote: "I long to poke my nose into everything."[3] And in one of her most telling phrases, she says, "Lovey, I am here, don't laugh at silly old wify, but she has 'trousers' on unseen."[4] Over the course of the war, her letters to the tsar were increasingly filled with requests, political judgments, and in many cases, outright orders. Her goal was the preservation of the autocracy, the future inheritance of her son. Nicholas himself valued the role his wife played. "Think, my wify," he wrote, "will you not come to the assistance of your hubby now that he is absent? What a pity that you have not been fulfilling this duty long ago or at least during the war."[5]

One of the most controversial questions of the war years concerns the role which the tsarina played in the political life of Russia through her influence on her husband. Her letters of the war period indicate that the problems of the day concerned her, and at times it is too easy to read political judgments and influence into them. Any word Alexandra spoke or wrote could, by virtue of her position as tsarina, be taken as a political statement. But her influence and power over her husband were real enough and in the end led to ruin.

Alexandra was intoxicated by power. Her marriage to a man regarded as semidivine exposed Alexandra to the ultimately fatal idea that unquestionable, absolute authority was invested in certain persons, endowing them with the ability to make judgments with a certainty provided by God. Over the years, she saw her husband falter in his role. With each perceived mistake Nicholas made, Alexandra drew herself toward the centers of power. If Nicholas could not stand firm, Alexandra would. She clearly felt herself stronger and more capable than her husband. Nicholas might hold the power in the government, but Alexandra claimed and exercised it. For her, there were no moments of self-doubt, no second thoughts. Her convictions were firm, and she would not allow the weak character of her husband to stand in the way of what she saw as his duty.

Of equal question is the influence of Rasputin over the tsarina in the political arena. Given her faith in Rasputin as a "Man of God," it was perhaps natural that Alexandra turned to her friend for guidance on the matters of the day. But the peasant's role in political matters has been greatly distorted. Between 1915 and 1917, Russia had four prime ministers, five ministers of the interior, four ministers of religion, four ministers of justice, three ministers of agriculture, three foreign ministers, and four ministers of war. Twenty-six men held these seven positions over a twenty-month period. Of this number, only four ministerial positions may have changed hands due to Rasputin.

Eight of the twenty-six men either resigned or were relieved of their posts by the tsar over disagreements. Of the remainder, Alexandra campaigned for the removal of only seven men. These seven decisions were made by the tsar and tsarina, without the influence of Rasputin. This is not to suggest that Rasputin had no say in the government through his influence over the tsarina. Indeed, the evidence to support this is overwhelming. It is true that he does appear to have had a certain influence over her, but only on isolated occasions. And although the tsarina consulted Rasputin, she did not follow his advice blindly. He often failed to gain her support for his own candidates, including V. S. Tatishchev as minister of finance in December 1915 and Gen. Nicholas Ivanov as minister of war in January 1916.[6]

The relationship between Alexandra and Rasputin has long been the subject of speculation. But it is important to remember that Alexandra believed that she herself knew what was best for the country. Rasputin was crafty enough to recognize this. Because communication between the tsarina and the peasant took the form of telephone calls or personal talks, we have no record of what one may have said to the other. But it would be incorrect to think that Alexandra sought out Rasputin's advice on ministerial appointments, for the evidence indicates quite the opposite. The tsarina sought out men whom she found agreeable for appointments to the government. These men were inevitably mentioned to Rasputin. He, in turn, knowing that the tsarina's mind was set, almost always reassured her that her choices were correct. By doing so he stayed in favor, at the same time echoing her own thoughts and adding to them his stamp of approval, thereby suggesting that God Himself supported the candidate.

Here is the key to understanding what happened in the Russian government between 1915 and 1917. In saying that Rasputin's influence has been exaggerated, we must necessarily turn to Alexandra, for it was with her that the real power lay. Historian Martin Kilcoyne analyzes the situation this way:

> He used the remarks of the tsarina as testimonials of his power. It was easy for him to create the impression that he was the dominant partner, that he originated ideas and saw to it that they were carried out by Alexandra, who automatically and obediently put her power at his disposal. . . . Despite his position as *starets* he was not free to dispute her. When she was certain of something she was certain beyond her ability to reflect and to question. Her intense assurance was something that even Rasputin dared not go against. In all their dealings she retained the upper hand. In fact, she was the dominant partner and could bend Rasputin to her will. He judiciously acceded to her frenzied importunings and agreed with her judgments of many situations. Without fully realizing what she was doing, Alexandra forced him to agree with her; then she was sure that her recommendations were the same as the will of God. Her faith in her own convictions could not be checked, even by Rasputin. She compelled him to assure her that God had approved her plans. She was not so smug as to think that she could discern His will unaided. She needed Rasputin to interpret it for her, but conviction came first, then endorsement.[7]

Because the tsarina effectively used Rasputin to add weight to her own ideas, his name is often mentioned in connection with this or that particular minister. But it would be wrong to assume that the proposal came from Rasputin. There is little evidence that Alexandra was interested in what Rasputin himself believed. Her interests concerned the preservation of the autocracy. When confronted with opposition from her husband, Alexandra would invoke Rasputin's name, thereby forcing Nicholas to make either a choice based on his own beliefs or a choice blessed by God.

In fairness to the tsarina, the head-turning parade of ministers began before the tsar took command at *stavka*. In the space of ten days in June 1915, Nicholas dismissed his minister of the interior, his minister of war, and his ministers of justice and religion. When the rapid succession continued under the tsarina, one wit dryly observed that there should be a sign hanging outside the cabinet room saying, "Piccadilly—Every Saturday a new program."[8]

Alexandra never understood the political situations of the day; her concerns were restricted to ministers in the government who agitated against Rasputin and the preservation of the autocracy. Such goals seemed only natural to the tsarina; anyone who dared argue against them instantly incurred her wrath. Her prejudices flowed into page after page of her letters. "Russia," she wrote, "thank God, is not a constitutional monarchy."[9] When she met with any opposition, Alexandra perceived the struggle as being directed against her. "It's a hunt against wify," she told her husband. "You must back me up."[10] She was resolute in her determination. It is alleged that when the tsarina met with Sir George Buchanan, the British ambassador, she told him, "I have no patience with the ministers who try to prevent him from doing his duty. The situation requires firmness. The Emperor, unfortunately, is weak; but I am not, and I intend to be firm."[11]

Alexandra faithfully reported Rasputin's latest advice to her absent husband: "No, hearken to Our Friend, believe him. He has your interest and Russia's at heart—it is not for nothing that God sent him to us—only we must pay more attention to what he says. His words are not lightly spoken and the gravity of having not only his prayers but his advice is great."[12]

On the following day, she wrote: "I am haunted by Our Friend's wish and *know* it will prove fatal for us and the country if it is not fulfilled. He means what he says when he speaks so seriously."[13]

Rasputin even sent along rough-draft pronouncements of policy which he thought that the tsar should follow, and Alexandra duly passed them on: "[Rasputin] begs you very much to send a telegram to the King of Serbia, as he is very anxious that the Bulgarians will finish them off. So I enclose the paper for you to use for your telegram—the sense in your words and shorter, of course."[14]

Rasputin even believed that he was mechanically inclined. When he heard that Grand Duke Alexander needed to find engines to support his fledgling aviation corps, the peasant told Alexandra that he had "heaps of things one could perfectly well use for the machinery of the aeroplanes."[15]

During the first weeks of his command at headquarters, Alexandra filled her letters to Nicholas with innocent, if somewhat insulting, advice:

> Forgive me, precious one, but you know you are too kind and gentle—sometimes a good loud voice can do wonders and a severe look—do, my love, be more decided and sure of yourself. You know perfectly well what is right and when you do not agree and are right, bring your opinion to the front and let it weigh against the rest. . . . You think me a meddlesome bore but a woman feels and sees things sometimes clearer than my too humble sweetheart. Humility is God's greatest gift but a sovereign needs to show his will more often.[16]

Following the Russian Orthodox custom of venerating objects belonging to holy men, Alexandra sent her husband a stuffed fish holding a bird impaled on a stick—a gift from Rasputin. "He used it first," she explained, "and now sends it to you as a blessing."[17] She followed this with a photograph of "Our Friend," urging Nicholas to keep it near at all times so that he could have courage.[18] Finally, she forwarded a small comb from Rasputin—"Remember to comb your hair before all difficult talks and decisions, the little comb will bring its help."[19]

The longer the tsar remained at headquarters, the more Alexandra worried:

> Sometimes a word gently spoken carries far—but at a time, such as we are now living through, one needs to hear your voice uplifted in protests and reprimand when they dawdle in carrying them out. They must learn to tremble before you. . . .[20]

> Be more autocratic, my very own sweetheart, show your mind. . . .[21]

> Be firm, I your wall am behind you and won't give way—I know He leads us right. . . . Only out of love which you bear for me and Baby—take no big steps without warning me and speaking over all quietly. . . .[22]

> Russia loves to feel the whip—it's their nature—tender love and

then the iron hand to punish and guide—how I wish I could pour my will into your veins. . . .[23]

Lovy, do you want me to come for a day to give you courage and firmness? Be the master. . . .[24]

For Baby's sake we must be firm otherwise his inheritance will be awful, as with his character he won't bow down to others but be his own master, as one must in Russia whilst people are still so uneducated. . . .[25]

She saw glorious times ahead for Russia if only the tsar would listen to her advice:

I am fully convinced that great and beautiful times are coming for your reign and Russia. . . . We must give a strong country to Baby, and dare not be weak for his sake, else he will have a yet harder reign, setting our faults right and drawing the reins in tightly which you let loose. You have to suffer for faults in the reigns of your predecessors and God knows what hardships are yours. Let our legacy be a lighter one for Alexei. He has a strong will and mind of his own, don't let things slip through your fingers and make him build all over again . . . be Peter the Great, Ivan the Terrible, Emperor Paul—crush them all under you. . . .[26]

Nicholas replied: "Tender thanks for the severe written scolding. I read it with a smile because you speak as if to a child. Your poor little weak-willed hubby."[27]

When the tsar declared his intention of going to headquarters to take command, eight of the thirteen members of the Council of Ministers signed a collective letter of resignation in protest. Nicholas refused to accept it and the ministers stayed on. But Alexandra set herself against those who had signed it and set about removing them from office.

After only eight weeks in office, the new minister of the interior, Prince Shcherbatov, found himself dismissed without explanation. His fall most probably stemmed from his involvement with Dzhunkovsky in denouncing the tsarina. Next, the minister of religion, Samarin, fell due to his role in the Dzhunkovsky affair. Alexandra wrote: "I entreat you, at the first talk with Samarin and when you see him, to speak very firmly—do, my love, for Russia's sake, Russia will not be blessed if her sovereign lets a Man of God sent to help him be persecuted, I am sure. Tell him severely, with a strong and decided voice, that you forbid any intrigues against Our Friend, or talks about him, or the slightest persecution, otherwise you will not be able to help him."[28]

When this plan did not work, Alexandra wrote: "Samarin seems to be continuing to speak against me. We shall hunt for a successor."[29] After three months in his post, Samarin was dismissed.

Two more of the signatories, Minister of Agriculture Alexander Krivoshein, and Minister of Finance A. Kharitanov left soon afterward. Next, Nicholas wanted to replace the elderly, senile prime minister, Ivan Goremykin. Alexandra, who valued Goremykin as the most loyal rubber stamp in the cabinet, wrote: "If in any way you feel he hinders, is an obstacle for you, then you better let him go, but if you keep him he will do all you order and try to do his best." . . .[30]

"To my mind, much better clear out ministers who strike and not change the President. . . . He only lives and serves you and your country. . . ."[31]

Eventually, however, Alexandra was forced to accept her husband's opinion. Goremykin, overcome with senility, could no longer continue to supervise the government. Michael Rodzianko, the president of the Duma, wrote Goremykin a personal letter in which he suggested it would be best for him to leave his post. When the prime minister took the podium in the Duma, he was greeted with shouts of "Resign!"[32] Alexandra wrote, "I fear the old man cannot continue working."[33] In his place, she suggested Boris Stürmer, an obscure, ultraconservative official with one important asset: Rasputin liked him. "Lovy, I don't know but I should still think of Stürmer," Alexandra wrote when Nicholas wavered.[34] Maurice Paléologue, the French ambassador in St. Petersburg, found Stürmer "worse than a mediocrity . . . third rate intellect, a mean spirit, low character, doubtful honesty, no experience and no idea of state business."[35] Nicholas relented, and Stürmer duly became the highest-ranking politician in Russia.

33

The Ruin of the Government

PRINCE SHCHERBATOV'S REPLACEMENT as minister of the interior, Alexei Khvostov, had once described himself as a person lacking "centers of restraint," and his term of office certainly reinforced this.[1] Rasputin liked Khvostov because he could sing well—hardly the qualification for being a minister—yet Alexandra agreeably suggested him to Nicholas. "God grant you will think well of him—therefore I receive him as he begs for it quicker—why he believes in my wisdom & help I don't know, it only shows he wishes to serve you & your dynasty against those brigands and screamers."[2]

Once in office, Khvostov surrounded himself with a disreputable bunch of hangers-on, including the infamous Prince M. M. Andronnikov, a devoutly Orthodox man who called himself the "aide-de-camp to the Lord Almighty" and seduced untold numbers of young military cadets in his icon-hung bedroom.[3] Khvostov and Andronnikov formed an alliance with Stephen Beletsky, the deputy minister of the interior. The trio attempted to take control of the government through Rasputin's influence. They promised the peasant 1,500 rubles a month, skimmed from official police funds, if Rasputin would agree not to accept any other bribes from sources beyond the trio's control.

Eventually, Rasputin's unpredictable behavior convinced the trio that the peasant needed supervision. For this task, they found Michael Komissarov, an Okhrana officer who could be relied on for discretion. But Rasputin, not surprisingly, failed to keep himself confined to the channels the trio had set out for him. Khvostov was in a bad position; if he cut off the police funds the peasant received, there was the very real possibility that Rasputin would reveal the entire episode and disgrace the minister. Gradually, Khvostov felt threatened and decided to kill Rasputin, trying to draw as many people into the plot as he could. He commissioned Komissarov to do the deed, but the Okhrana agent had too many moral scruples to acquiesce. Komissarov contacted Beletsky, and the two men began to plot against Khvostov.

There were several halfhearted attempts made to kill the peasant—all of them unsuccessful. Eventually, Khvostov caught on to his friends' game and exposed their role in attempting to kill the peasant. In turn, Beletsky went to the Tsar and revealed everything. The scandal was enormous: high-ranking officials of the Russian government involved in bribery and murder. "Am so wretched that we, through Gregory, recommended Khvostov to you," Alexandra wrote to Nicholas. "It leaves me no peace—you were against it and I let myself be imposed upon."[4]

Although Alexandra had second thoughts about accepting Rasputin's advice, this did not last for long. She soon set about getting rid of the new minister of war, Alexei Polivanov, a dedicated enemy of Rasputin's. "Forgive me," she wrote, "but I don't like the choice of minister of war—you remember how you were against and surely right and N. too, I fancy."[5] "Quickly clear out Polivanov. Any honest man better than him."[6] "Oh, how I wish you could get rid of Polivanov."[7] Polivanov supported a measure of cooperation between the Duma and the war ministry, a suggestion which angered the tsarina. She wrote:

> Polivanov simply treacherous . . . spoke of responsible
> government which all scream for, even good ones who do not
> realize we are not at all for it.[8]

> Lovy mine, don't dawdle, make up your mind, it's far too serious
> and changing him at once, you cut the wings of that
> revolutionary party; only be quicker about it—you know, you
> yourself long ago wanted to change him—hurry up, sweetheart,
> you need wify to be behind pushing you. . . . Promise me you will
> at once change the minister of war. . . .[9]

When Polivanov fell, she wrote, "Oh, the relief! Now I shall be able to sleep well."[10] An elderly man named Gen. Dimitri Shuvalev replaced Polivanov. One British general said that "he had no knowledge of his work, but his devotion to the Emperor was such that if the door were to open and His Majesty were to come into the room and ask him to throw himself out of the window, he would do it at once."[11]

In July 1916, the minister of agriculture, disgusted with the internal situation in the government, resigned after less than a year in office. That same month, A. A. Khvostov, the minister of justice and uncle to the dismissed minister of the interior, himself fell from power.

Sazonov, the foreign minister, came next on the tsarina's list. Alexandra hated Sazonov because he pushed for autonomous rule of Poland, a clear infringement of the tsarevich's future inheritance, and for his public support of Dzhunkovsky's campaign against her. "Sazonov is such a pancake," she wrote to Nicholas.[12] In the following weeks she denounced "long nosed Sazonov" in a barrage of letters to the tsar.[13] Nicholas gave in, and Sazonov's post was filled by the prime minister, Boris Stürmer, who now held a double office.

Alexandra reserved a particularly vicious campaign for Alexander Guchkov, the leader of the Octobrist party in the Duma and the man who had been the president of the Third Duma. It had been Guchkov who had distributed about the capital the copies of the tsarina's letters to Rasputin. In addition, during the war he led debates in the Duma on the cost to the country and questioned the whole effort. "Guchkov ought to be got rid of," she wrote to the tsar.[14] "Oh, could one not hang Guchkov?"[15] And again, "A strong railway accident in which he alone would suffer would be a real punishment from God and well deserved."[16] But there was nothing the tsar could do, and Guchkov remained in the Duma as a powerful party leader.

The biggest storm broke with the appointment of Alexander Protopopov as minister of the interior in September 1916. Protopopov was the scion of a noble family, trained in running the vast estates which they controlled. He was an ultraconservative, a monarchist who clearly appealed to both Alexandra's and Nicholas's sensibilities. Although he had been a Duma member for some time and found himself well liked, Protopopov had little political aptitude. His main asset came from his position—a monarchist in the Duma. Rasputin liked Protopopov, although he had his doubts about the man's integrity—"his honour stretches like a piece of elastic," he once observed.[17] Yet Alexandra put forth his name: "Gregory earnestly begs you to name Protopopov. You know him and had such a good impression of him—happens to be of the Duma and is not left and so will know how to be with them. . . . I think you could not do better than name him. . . . He likes Our Friend for at least four years and that says much for a man."[18]

The tsar replied:

It seems to me that this Protopopov is a good man, but he has much to do with Factories, etc. Rodzianko has for a long time suggested him as Minister of Trade. . . . I must consider this question as it has taken me completely by surprise. Our Friend's opinions of people are sometimes very strange, as you know yourself—therefore one must be careful, especially with appointments to high office. . . . All these changes make my head go round. In my opnion, they are too frequent. In any case, they are not good for the internal situation of the country, as each new man brings with him alterations in the administration.[19]

St. Petersburg gossips had a field day with Protopopov after his
appointment as minister of the interior. On learning of his new position,
Protopopov ordered the uniform of an imperial gendarmerie, which he
donned for an appearance at the Duma Budget Committee; when he
appeared, the room burst into howls of laughter at the outrageous sight.
It was said that the minister was a necrophiliac.[20] He did consult a
quack Tibetan herbal doctor named Peter Badmayev, who prescribed
all manner of potions from drugs and roots to help the minister in the
execution of his duties. Protopopov himself frequently spoke to an icon
which he kept on his desk; when one man walked in and discovered
this, the minister of the interior hastily explained, "He helps me do
everything, everything I do is by his advice."[21] It is scarcely surprising
that much of St. Petersburg thought he was insane.

With Nicholas away Alexandra found it easier to appoint and dismiss ministers on her own authority. She herself gave Protopopov the
post of minister of agriculture to go along with that of minister of the interior: "Forgive me for what I have done—but I had to—Our Friend
said it was absolutely necessary. Stürmer sends you by this messenger
a new paper to sign giving the whole food supply at once to the Minister of the Interior. . . . I had to take this step upon myself . . . [to] save
Russia. . . . Forgive me, but I had to take this responsibility for sweet
sake."[22]

"The power which the tsarina held angered many. Michael
Rodzianko, the president of the Duma, openly called for the tsarina to
go at once to Livadia and stay there for the rest of the war. "I alone shall
have the power to choose ministers," he declared.[23] Others called for
the joint resignation of the entire cabinet. Often the tsar himself
changed his mind and would appoint one minister, only to turn around
and replace him for no apparent reason. This happened with the prime
minister, Boris Stürmer.

Stürmer's German-sounding name did not sit well with many
Russians, who openly doubted his loyalty. The tsar abruptly fired him
from his post and replaced him with Alexander Trepov. Trepov has
been called "unusually able," the last great politician of imperial Russia.[24]

Alexandra was against Trepov's appointment for one reason: He
was a dedicated enemy of Rasputin's. She wrote: "Trepov I personally
do not like and can never have the same feeling for him as to old Goremykin and Stürmer—they were of the good old sort . . . those two loved
me and came for every question that worried them, so as not to disturb
you—this one, I, alas, doubt caring for me and if he does not trust me
and Our Friend, things will be different. I too told Stürmer to tell him
how to behave about Gregory and to safeguard him always."[25]

As soon as he took office as prime minister, Trepov set about getting rid of Rasputin and all of his appointees. He began with Protopopov. Trepov had, in fact, made it a condition of his accepting the office, and Nicholas had granted him the request. "I am sorry for Protopopov," Nicholas explained to Alexandra. "He is a good, honest man, but he jumps from one idea to another, and cannot make up his mind on anything."[26] Anticipating his wife's next move, he continued, "I beg, do not drag Our Friend into this. The responsibility is with me, and therefore I wish to be free in my choice."[27]

The tsar's strategy did not work. Alexandra wrote: "Forgive me, dear, believe me—I entreat you, don't go and change Protopopov now, he will be all right. . . . Oh, Lovy, you can trust me. I may not be clever enough—but I have a strong feeling and that helps more than the brain often. Don't change anybody until we meet, I entreat you, let's speak it over quietly together. . . ."[28]

The next day she wrote: "Lovy, my angel . . . don't change Protopopov. I had a long talk with him yesterday—the man is as sane as anyone . . . he is quiet and calm and utterly devoted which one can, alas, say of few and he will succeed—already things are going better."[29]

And finally: "Darling, remember that it does not lie in the man Protopopov or X. Y. Z. but it's a question of monarchy and your prestige now, which must not be shattered in the time of the Duma. . . . Remember . . . the Tsar rules and not the Duma. Forgive my writing, but I am fighting for your reign and Baby's future."[30]

Nicholas gave in, and Protopopov stayed on.

When Trepov learned of the tsar's refusal to dismiss Protopopov, he himself threatened to resign. But Nicholas would have none of this: He angrily told Trepov that he would remain in office until his duties were completed. In despair, Trepov tried to bribe Rasputin. He asked his brother-in-law Alexander Mossolov—the head of the imperial court chancellery—to offer Rasputin 200,000 rubles and a house in St. Petersburg if he would refrain from political involvement. Rasputin listened to Mossolov in silence before rejecting his proposal. When Mossolov reported this to Trepov, the prime minister realized that he was "done for."[31] Within three weeks, Trepov was dismissed from his post.

34

Autumn of Delusions

S<small>T</small>. P<small>ETERSBURG</small> in the fall of 1916 showed no sign of the devastating war which raged in the swamps of Poland hundreds of miles away. The streets, filled with gray slush, bustled with elegant ladies and gentlemen taking their daily walks along the palace quay and the Champs de Mars, although their clothing could not now come from Paris and they were often forced to wear Russian fashions. Icy rain deluged the capital, and the spire of the Cathedral of the Fortress of Peter and Paul was wrapped in a veil of mist. Darkness fell by four in the afternoon. With the passing of the weeks, the rain quickly turned to snow, which blanketed the city streets in white.

It was an autumn of delusions. Officers lounged in the smoking rooms of their smart clubs, sipping port and smoking cigars as thousands of their recruits were killed daily in the trenches. The reality of the war hit only those unfortunate enough to serve in the front lines or their families left behind who felt the hunger of the food shortages every night before they went to bed. All else carried on with prewar brilliance. At the theater, Kschessinska enchanted audiences as she danced *The Pharoah's Daughter*; the basso Chaliapin sang *Boris Godunov* and *Don Quixote* at the Narodny Dom; and at the Mariinsky, Tamara Karsavina danced in *Sylvia* and *The Water Lily*. Paléologue remembered:

> From the stalls of the back row of the highest circle I could see
> nothing but a sea of cheery, smiling faces. In the interval the
> boxes came to life with the irresponsible chatter which made the
> bright eyes of the women sparkle with merriment. Irksome
> thoughts of the present, sinister visions of war and the
> melancholy prospects of the future vanished as if by magic the
> moment the orchestra struck up. An air of pleasant unreality was
> in every face.[1]

The war, however, was very much on Alexandra's mind. "Sweet

angel," she wrote to Nicholas, "long to ask you heaps about your plans concerning Rumania. Our Friend is so anxious to know."[2] Indeed, Rasputin dreamed of military strategy for the tsar to follow:

> Now, before I forget, I must give you a message from Our Friend prompted by what he saw in the night. He begs you to order that one should advance near Riga, says it is necessary, otherwise the Germans will settle down so firmly through all the winter that it will cost endless bloodshed and trouble to make them move; now it will take them so aback that we shall succeed in making them retrace their steps. He says this is now the most essential thing and begs you seriously to order ours to advance. He says we can and we must, and I was to write to you at once.[3]

Nicholas received this information coolly. "I told [Michael] Alexeiev [the chief of staff] how interested you were in military affairs and of these details you asked for in your last letter. He smiled and listened silently."[4] And, although he confided military details to his wife, he repeatedly wrote, "I beg you, my love, do not communicate these details to anyone. I have written them only for you."[5] "I beg you, keep it to yourself, not a single soul must know of it."[6] But, inevitably, Alexandra wrote back that she had told Rasputin. "He won't mention it to a soul but I had to ask his blessing for your decision."[7]

Most of Rasputin's advice concerned the Russian advance of 1916. The army moved into Galicia, preparing to march over the Carpathian Mountains and into Austria-Hungary. Casualities were terrible. In the summer of 1916, 1,200,000 had been lost. "Our Friend . . . finds better one should not advance too obstinately as the losses will be too great—one can be patient without forcing things, as ultimately it will be ours; one can go on madly and finish the war in two months but then thousands of lives will be sacrificed—and by patience the end will also be gained and one will spare much blood."[8] "Our Friend hopes we won't climb over the Carpathians and try to take them, as he repeats the losses will be too great."[9] When Nicholas relented and ordered the attack stopped, Alexandra wrote, "Our Friend says about the new orders you gave to Brusilov: 'Very satisfied with Father's orders, all will be well.'"[10]

His generals, however, soon convinced the tsar that he needed to continue the offensive. Having won her first battle, Alexandra despaired to learn of this latest development. "Oh, give your order again to Brusilov—stop this useless slaughter. . . . Why repeat the madness of the Germans at Verdun. Your plan, so wise, approved by Our Friend. . . . Stick to it. . . . Our Generals don't count the lives any—hardened to losses—and that is sin."[11] Nicholas, of course, gave in, and the Carpathian campaign was called off for a second time.

This led to speculation that Alexandra and Rasputin wanted to achieve a separate peace with Germany. Grand Duke Alexander, trying to discover the source of these "incomprehensible libels," spoke with a certain member of the Duma. "If the young tsarina is such a great Russian patriot," the man said, "why does she tolerate the presence of that drunken beast who is openly seen around the capital in the company of German spies and sympathizers?" The grand duke, pledged to secrecy about the role which Rasputin played, said nothing, thus making the situation even worse.[12]

For many years after the Revolution it was often reported that Rasputin acted as a German spy. It is true that the peasant's company frequently included those of doubtful loyalty to Russia. At his parties, attended by various members of society including several later to be accused of treason, Rasputin got quite drunk and spoke freely of all that Alexandra had told him. Prince Felix Youssoupov remembered seeing many "strange" men in Rasputin's apartment who "appeared to be asking questions and taking notes of his replies."[13] After the Revolution, General Alexeiev recalled that "when the Empress's papers were examined, she was found to be in possession of a map indicating in detail the disposition of the troops along the entire front. Only two copies were prepared of this map, one for the Emperor and one for myself. I was very painfully impressed. God knows who may have made use of this map."[14] Because she shared all with Rasputin, it is reasonable to assume that he, as well, knew of this map. Although the evidence that Rasputin actually worked for the Germans is flimsy, one statesman said that "it would have been inexplicable if the German General Staff had not made use of him."[15]

There was perhaps a chance for a separate peace. The tsarina's brother Grand Duke Ernest Ludwig of Hesse is supposed to have made a secret visit to Russia in 1916 to try to arrange a peace treaty. Although the Hesse family still denies that such a visit could ever have taken place, Crown Princess Cecilie recalled that her father-in-law the kaiser mentioned it to her himself. Several persons recorded seeing a man fitting the grand duke's description at Tsarskoe Selo. Prince Dimitri Galitzine, the director of the tsarina's Relief Services, related how he had been at the Alexander Palace when he saw "a gentleman in civilian dress come in rather furtively and disappear through another door." He learned, after much prodding, that the man had in fact been the grand duke of Hesse.[16] Others confirmed this visit: Vladimir von Meck, the head of the Russian Red Cross, knew of it, as did members of the Romanov family. In addition, Alexandra's letters to Nicholas hint at what may have occurred. The tsar left the capital for headquarters and suddenly, two days after arriving there, returned to Tasrskoe Selo for a short time. When he left the second time, Alexandra wrote curiously, "The good will come and you are patient and will be blessed, I feel so sure, only much to be gone through still. When I think of what the 'losses' of lives mean to your heart—and I can imagine Ernie's suffering now.... Excuse bad writing but head and eyes ache and heart feels weak after all this pain."[17] If the offer was made, however, it was rejected.

  Thoughts of a separate peace must have seemed tempting. The war had been going on for nearly two years at the time of the alleged visit, and it had taken its toll on everyone, Alexandra included. Her visits to military hospitals along the front became more and more an ordeal for her to bear. At one, a young officer lay dying of wounds he had received in battle. He heard that the tsarina would be arriving for an inspection shortly and told his nurse that he would live until she came. When Alexandra was told of the young man, she hurried to his bedside, knelt, and held his hand; he died a few minutes later.[18] But such scenes of patriotism were few and far between. The receptions for the tsarina were increasingly cold, although Alexandra seemed not to realize this. During her visit to Novgorod in December 1916, she met an elderly woman, revered in the area as a holy person. When Alexandra approached, the woman said to her, "Here is the Martyr Empress Alexandra." The tsarina did not seem to understand and left the town feeling much happier. Those with the tsarina felt otherwise; they considered the remark an ill omen.[19]

  Certainly the atmosphere in Russia, and St. Petersburg, led to all sorts of rumor and speculation. Many people felt that the imperial family had been corrupted by Rasputin and that they all had to be removed. One group had plans to "bomb the tsar's motorcar from an aeroplane at a particular point along its route."[20] Increasingly, members of the Duma called for the tsarina to go to Livadia and remain there for the rest of the war. Basil Shulgin, a monarchist deputy in the Duma, wrote of the tsarina:

> She is very clever ... she is far above all her surroundings ... she
> has a contempt for—well, just us—in a word, Petersburg.... She
> is sure the simple folk adore her.... She and Rasputin?—no, that
> is impossible ... anything you like, but not that. Her domination
> over her husband is itself an open revolt against the autocracy,
> and is terribly misleading for everyone else. What kind of
> autocracy is that? Even for the most devoted loyal hearts, for
> whom respect for the throne is a sixth sense, it is poison. It
> poisons the very instinct of monarchy.... Just because of the

weakness of one husband to one wife, the sovereign offends his people, and the people offend their sovereign. The scandal is too foul to discuss; he cannot clear it up, and you cannot ask him to. ... How awful to have an autocracy without an autocrat![21]

The rest of the imperial family despaired along with the country. The dowager empress had given her son an ultimatum: Either he send Rasputin away or she would leave the capital. Nicholas, of course, would do no such thing, and his mother duly took up residence in Kiev.[22] There are persistent rumors within the Romanov family and some support in documents that the dowager empress was involved in a conspiracy to overthrow her son in conjunction with this ultimatum. It was well known that both the grand dukes Vladimir and Cyril were campaigning to replace the tsar with the tsarevich under a regency. The dowager empress detested the Vladimirovichs and allegedly sought another solution. There are two versions of what would have taken place. The first is that Grand Duke Paul would seize power in the name of the dowager empress and Marie Fedorovna would then ascend the throne in her own right; the second, that she and Grand Duke Paul would act together to seize the throne and act as coregents for the tsarevich. According to these rumors, Alexandra somehow got wind of this; the dowager empress's ultimatum to her son was supposed to have signaled the beginning of this coup , and she persuaded the tsar to order his mother into exile.[23] With all of the contempt she held for Alexandra unleashed, Marie Feodorovna told one family member, "This is not Nicky, not him. He is gentle and honest and good—it is all her!"[24]

Grand Duke Alexander made five visits to *stavka*, each time trying to persuade the tsar to disregard the advice of Alexandra and Rasputin. "I believe no one but my wife" was the tsar's abrupt reply.[25] After countless appeals, none of which seemed to work, Grand Duke Nicholas Michailovich, the noted historian, wrote his arguments in a letter:

Are you properly informed about the situation with the Empire and particularly Siberia? Do you know the whole truth or do they hide most of it from you? Where does the root of the evil lie? Let me explain in a few words.

So long as your method of choosing your ministers was only known to a small coterie, things could only carry on for better or worse. But as soon as such matters were generally known and discussed in public, it became obvious that Russia could not go on being governed in that way. You often told me that you trusted no one and were constantly being betrayed.

If this is true the remark should apply above all to your wife, who, though she loves you, is constantly leading you in error, surrounded as she is by people in the grip of the spirit of evil. You believe Alexandra Feodorovna. That is natural. But the words she utters are the outcome of clever intrigues, they are not the truth. If you are powerless to rid yourself of such influences, at least be always on your guard against the unceasing and systematic intriguers, who use your wife as a tool.

If you could prevent the persistent intervention of those evil influences, Russia's regeneration would take a great leap forward, and you would regain the confidence you have lost with the immense majority of your subjects. You would find yourself faced with a people who, under a new regime, would be happy to work under your guidance.

I have hesitated for a long time before telling you the truth, but have now decided to do so on the persuasion of your mother and sisters. You are on the eve of new trials, new attempts against your person. Believe me, if I stress my desire that you should cast off the chains that imprison you, it is not for personal motives, as you know, I have none, but only with the hope of saving you and your throne and our dear country from the terrible and irreparable catastrophe that lies ahead.[26]

The tsar sent the letter, unread, to Alexandra. "I . . . am utterly disgusted," she wrote back. "Had you stopped him in the middle of his talk and told him that, if he only once touched upon that subject or me, you will send him to Siberia, as it becomes next to high treason. He has always hated and spoken badly of me since twenty-two years . . . at such a time to crawl behind your Mama and sisters and not stick up bravely . . . for his Emperor's wife is loathsome and treachery."[27]

Grand Duke Nicholas Nicholaievich was the next to arrive at headquarters. Nikolasha met with the tsar for several hours. Although he yelled at his cousin for allowing the ruin of the government, Nikolasha watched as the tsar did nothing but continue to smoke a cigarette. Finally, the grand duke could stand it no more. "I would be more pleased if you swore at me, struck me, kicked me out than your silence!" he bellowed. "Can't you see that you are losing your crown? Collect yourself while it's not too late. Give a responsible ministry. As long ago as June I spoke to you about this. You just procrastinate. For the moment there is still time, but soon it will be too late."[28]

In late December, Alexandra's former sister-in-law Ducky, now married to Grand Duke Cyril Vladimirovich, requested an audience with the tsarina. "It is with grief and horror that I have observed the growth of hostile feeling toward Your Majesty. . . ." the grand duchess began. But Alexandra cut her short, saying, "You are quite wrong, my dear. As a matter of fact, I've been quite wrong myself. Only quite lately I was still thinking that Russia hated me. I know now that it is only Petersburg society which hates me, the corrupt."[29]

Grand Duchess Marie Pavlovna recalled:

> It was about this time that I first heard people speaking of the Emperor and Empress with open animosity and contempt. The word "revolution" was uttered more openly and more often; soon it could be heard everywhere. The war seemed to recede into the background. All attention was riveted on interior events. Rasputin, Rasputin, Rasputin—it was like a refrain: his mistakes, his shocking personal conduct, his mysterious power. This power was tremendous; it was like dust, enveloping all our world, eclipsing the sun. How could so pitiful a wretch throw so vast a shadow? It was inexplicable, baffling, almost incredible.[30]

Grand Duke Paul tried to stay out of the plotting, but he was apparently at least involved with the dowager empress in discussing contingency plans. Even Grand Duke Michael, second in line to the throne, had begun to involve himself in the various conspiracies.

The entire Romanov family felt that the end was near. They had pleaded, argued, and cajoled the tsar to change his policies—to exile Rasputin, to grant a new government with real powers, to prevent Alexandra from meddling in the questions of the day. But the tsar refused to give way. In the fall of 1916, at the urging of Grand Duchess Elizabeth, Princess Zenaide Youssoupov applied for an audience with the tsarina. At the meeting, Alexandra greeted the princess coolly. When Zenaide Youssoupov dared mention Rasputin's name, Alexandra told her to leave at once. The princess, however, refused to be silenced, and the tsarina had to ring for a servant to escort the woman out of the palace. Before she left, Alexandra fixed Princess Youssoupov with an angry glare and declared, "I hope never to see you again!"[31]

The imperial family persuaded Grand Duchess Ella to come once again from her Moscow convent to speak with her sister. Ella arrived at the Alexander Palace dressed in the gray habit of her order. The conversation went badly. Alexandra refused to discuss Rasputin. "Remember the fate of Louis XVI and Marie Antoinette!" Ella told her.[32] At this, the tsarina rose, walked to her desk, picked up the telephone, and ordered a motorcar to take her sister back to the train station at once.

"Perhaps it would have been better if I had not come," Ella offered sadly.

"Yes," Alexandra agreed, and the two sisters parted. They would never meet again.[33]

35

December Nightmare

O~N 2 DECEMBER~ 1916, Vladimir Purishkevich rose to speak in the Duma. It was said that Purishkevich was so right wing that the only further thing right was the wall.[1] A believer in absolute autocracy and a self-described patriot, he possessed great intelligence and a keen, pointed wit. Members of the Duma leaned forward in anticipation as he took the podium.

For two hours, he thundered at the Duma; he spoke of the "dark forces" threatening Russia. "It requires only the recommendation of Rasputin to raise the most abject citizen to high office," he bellowed. He ended with these words: "If you are truly loyal, if the glory of Russia, her mighty future which is closely bound up with the brightness of the name of the Tsar mean anything to you, then on your feet, you ministers! Be off to Headquarters and throw yourselves at the feet of the Tsar! Have the courage to tell him that the multitude is threatening in its wrath! Revolution threatens, and an obscure *moujik* shall govern Russia no longer!"[2]

The members of the Duma leaped to their feet and applauded. In the gallery, another visitor noticed that Prince Felix Youssoupov had not risen; instead, he sat in his chair, pale and trembling.[3]

On 5 December, Prince Felix paid a visit to Purishkevich. "What shall we do?" Purishkevich asked. The prince smiled, looked him in the eye, and said flatly, "Remove Rasputin."

"That's easy to say," Purishkevich replied, "but who will undertake it when there are no resolute people in Russia and the government which might undertake this itself and do it skillfully supports Rasputin and protects him like the apple of its eye?"

"Yes," Youssoupov agreed. "There is no use counting on the government. But, in Russia, such people can be found."

"You think so?" inquired Purishkevich.

"I am confident," finished the prince. "And one of them stands before you."[4] Prince Felix had decided to save Russia: He was going to kill Rasputin.

Prince Felix Felixsovich Youssoupov, Count Sumarakov-Elston, at the age of twenty-nine, expected to inherit perhaps the largest private fortune in Russia. The death of his brother Nicholas in 1908 left Felix sole heir to palaces, jewels, and paintings so fabulous that even the tsar's sister Olga Alexandrovna believed the often repeated legend that the Youssoupov wealth exceeded that of the Romanovs.[5]

The evening before Felix's birth in 1887, his mother attended a ball at the Winter Palace and stayed until dawn, only to rush home in labor. Nearly drowned by the priest at his baptism, Felix disappointed his mother, who had wished for a daughter. To compensate for this she dressed him as a girl until the age of five, with his hair curled and tied in ribbons. Far from objecting to this, Felix became very vain and called out to passersby, "Look, isn't baby pretty?"[6]

The Youssoupovs owned four palaces in St. Petersburg, three in Moscow, and thirty-seven other estates scattered across the country. "One of our estates in the Caucasus," wrote Felix, "stretched for one hundred and twenty-five miles along the Caspian Sea; crude petroleum was so abundant that the soil seemed soaked with it and the peasants used it to grease their cart wheels."[7]

The rooms of the Moscow estate of Arkhangelskoe were filled with fine china and paintings. Another Moscow house had once been the hunting lodge of Ivan the Terrible; during a restoration, rows of skeletons were found chained to the walls of a secret gallery, victims of the wrath of the demented tsar.[8] The Youssoupov Palace on the Fontanka Canal in St. Petersburg had been designed by Quarenghi. Within its walls were three ballrooms, a theater, and an art gallery with the finest private collection in the country, including five Tiepolos, two Rembrandts, a Rubens, and a Velázquez.[9]

The palace at 94 Moika Canal, where Felix was born, stretched for three sides around a large interior courtyard and garden. A private Louis XV theater occupied an entire wing of the house; in another part of the palace, a Moorish room had been copied from an apartment in the Alhambra. "The furniture of the *petit salon* had belonged to Marie Antoinette," Felix wrote. "Paintings by Boucher, Fragonard, Watteau, Hubert Robert and Greuze hung on the walls, the rock crystal chandelier had graced Mme. de Pompadour's Boudoir, the most lovely knick-knacks were scattered on the tables or displayed in cabinets: gold and enameled snuff boxes, ashtrays of amethyst, topaz and jade with gem-incrusted gold settings."[10] Also on display were "crystal bowls filled with uncut sapphires, emeralds and opals," used as table decorations, and the Peregrine, a pearl so round "it always rolled off flat surfaces."[11]

As a youth, Felix had been encouraged by his brother's fiancée to dress in his mother's clothes. The habit became so frequent that much of St. Petersburg knew of the young prince's curious tastes. It began when he and a cousin, at the age of twelve, dressed as women and prowled the streets of the capital. They attracted the amorous attention of some officers and had to duck into a restaurant to escape. Once inside, Felix began to flirt with several of the male diners and became very drunk. He took a string of pearls from around his neck, made a lasso, and aimed it at the heads of several people nearby. The string, of course, broke, and the pearls scattered; Felix tried to leave but had to confess when the manager caught him sneaking out without paying.[12]

His dissolute reputation only increased with age. Tall and handsome, Felix managed to attract the attention of Grand Duke Dimitri Pavlovich, the twenty-six-year-old son of Grand Duke Paul and a cousin of the tsar's. Grand Duke Paul, who had married a commoner as a second wife and lived in exile in Paris, let Alexandra and Nicholas raise his son at the Alexander Palace; consequently, the imperial couple came to consider Dimitri as one of their own children. Felix gushingly remembered Dimitri as "extremely attractive, tall, elegant, well-bred, with deep, thoughtful eyes."[13] Alexandra constantly worried over the relationship, expressing to Dimitri that he should see less of the prince, but to no avail.

A number of writers have implied that Prince Felix and Grand Duke Dimitri were lovers. The two had been friends since childhood; both were cultivated, rich, handsome, with a taste for the pursuit of pleasure. Persistent rumors linked the pair romantically, although any evidence to support the allegation has long since disappeared.

In 1914, Felix married Princess Irina, the daughter of Grand Duke Alexander Michailovich and Grand Duchess Xenia and therefore the only niece of the tsar's. Nicholas himself gave Irina away; she wore a white satin gown and Marie Antoinette's wedding veil. As a wedding present from the tsar and tsarina, Felix and Irina received a bag of twenty-nine diamonds, from three to seven carats each.[14]

The marriage was a curious affair. Felix himself much preferred the company of his friend Dimitri or, when the grand duke was away, the Gypsies on the islands of St. Petersburg. He loved to mingle with Russians of ordinary class, and because of this he came into contact with Rasputin.

A devout monarchist, Felix had, from his childhood days, kept pictures of Louis XVI and Marie Antoinette in his bedroom, with fresh roses before them always.[15] Through some strange twist of misguided loyalty to the throne, Felix believed he had been sent to save the Romanov dynasty from the Siberian peasant. In 1915, he decided to kill Rasputin, later writing that he hoped this action would save the throne from revolution and stop the tsarina from meddling in political affairs. To achieve Rasputin's complete confidence, the prince began to visit him regularly for a supposed "cure."

> The *starets* made me lie down on the sofa. Then, staring intently at me, he gently ran his hands over my chest, neck and head, after which he knelt down, laid both hands on my forehead and murmured a prayer. His face was so close to mine that I could see only his eyes. He remained in this position for some time, then rising brusquely he made mesmeric passes over my body. Rasputin had tremendous hypnotic power. I felt as if some active energy were pouring heat, like a warm current, into my whole being. I fell into a torpor and my body grew numb; I tried to speak, but my tongue no longer obeyed me and I gradually slipped into a drowsy state, as though a powerful narcotic had been administered to me. All I could see was Rasputin's glittering eyes; two phosphorescent beams of light melting into a great luminous ring which at times drew nearer and then moved further away. I heard the voice of the *starets* but could not understand what he said. I remained in this state, without being able to cry out or move. My mind alone was free, and I fully realized that I was gradually falling into the power of this evil man. Then I felt stirring in me the will to fight his hypnosis. Little by little the desire to resist grew stronger and stronger, forming a protective armour around me. I had the feeling that a merciless struggle was being fought out between Rasputin and me, between his personality and mine. I knew I was preventing him from getting complete mastery over me, but still I could not move. I had to wait until he ordered me to get up. Soon I was able to distinguish his silhouette, his face and eyes; the dreadful ring of light had entirely disappeared. "That's enough for the present, my dear boy," said Rasputin.[16]

"I am all powerful," Rasputin once said to Felix. He claimed that the tsar and tsarina "listen to me, so you should listen to me, too."[17] His views on the imperial couple shocked the prince. "The tsarina has a wise, strong mind and I can get anything and everything from her. As for him, he's a simple soul. He was not cut out to be a sovereign ... that's beyond his strength. So, with God's blessing, *we* come to his rescue."[18]

After hearing Purishkevich's speech, Felix decided that he could wait no longer. The prince and the Duma member discussed the plan to murder Rasputin before selecting their fellow conspirators. Felix decided that Dimitri must be among their ranks. A young officer named Ivan Sukhotin—a friend of the prince's from the Preobrajensky Regiment—and a doctor, Stanislav Lazovert, completed the circle. According to Felix, they decided to invite Rasputin to the Youssoupov Palace on the Moika Canal to meet Princess Irina. Once there, they would poison him. His body would be dumped in the Neva River, and Purishkevich would place a call to a local restaurant asking if Rasputin had arrived to divert suspicion from the group at the palace.[19]

Rasputin agreed to come to the Youssoupov Palace on 29 December—the earliest date available to Dimitri, with his heavy social calendar. But as the date approached, Rasputin seemed to sense that his life was in danger. Purishkevich could not keep his mouth shut, and much of St. Petersburg knew the details of the plan itself. Rasputin refused to leave his apartment for a time, afraid of the unknown beyond the doorstep. At their last meeting, Rasputin even refused the customary blessing of the tsar. "This time," he said, "it is for you to bless me, not I you."[20]

Rasputin wrote a strangely prophetic letter before his meeting at the Youssoupov Palace. Headed "The Spirit of Gregory Efimovich Rasputin of the village of Pokrovskoe," it was written for the tsar:

> I write and leave behind me this letter at St. Petersburg. I feel that I shall leave life before 1 January. I wish to make known to the Russian people, to Papa, to the Russian Mother, and to the Children, to the land of Russia, what they must understand. If I am killed by common assassins and especially by my brothers the Russian peasants, you, Tsar of Russia, have nothing to fear, remain on your throne and govern, and you, Tsar of Russia, have nothing to fear for your children, they will reign for hundreds of years in Russia. But if I am murdered by *boyars*, nobles, and if they have shed my blood, their hands will remain solied with my blood, for twenty five years they will not wash their hands from my blood. They will leave Russia. Brothers will kill brothers, and they will kill each other and for twenty-five years there will be no nobles in the country. Tsar of the land of Russia, if you hear the sound of the bell which will tell you that Gregory has been killed, you must know this: if it was your relations who have wrought my death, then no one of your family, that is to say, none of your children or relations will remain alive for more than two years. They will be killed by the Russian people . . . . I shall be killed. I

am no longer among the living. Pray, pray, be strong, think of your blessed family.

Gregory.[21]

On the afternoon of 29 December, Anna Vyrubova visited Rasputin in his flat to give him an icon from the tsarina. Rasputin told her of the proposed midnight visit to the Moika Palace to see Princess Irina. Anna thought the late hour a curious time for a meeting but said nothing. Later that night, however, sitting in the Mauve Boudoir with Alexandra, she mentioned it. "But there must be some mistake," the tsarina replied, "Irina is in the Crimea." She fell silent; then, after a few minutes, again repeated, "There must be some mistake." Nothing else was said of the visit that evening.

"The next morning," wrote Anna, "soon after breakfast, I was called on the telephone by one of the daughters of Rasputin . . . . In some anxiety the young girl told me that her father had gone out the night before in the Youssoupov motorcar and had not returned."[22]

Prince Felix selected a room in the basement of the Moika Palace for the murder. A spiral staircase wound up from one end of the room to an octagonal anteroom on the first floor; halfway up from the landing a door opened onto the courtyard. Felix fussed with the decorations until the room was ready. A small table with several chairs sat in the middle of the room. A little chest of inlaid ebony, with a number of drawers, bronze columns, and secret compartments, sat in one corner; atop it stood a sixteenth-century rock crystal and silver crucifix from Italy. Before the table, covering the stone floor, lay a white bearskin rug. The draperies at the windows were drawn, and a fire had been lit in the red granite fireplace. Felix told his servants to set the table for tea. A number of little cakes and biscuits were sliced open; Dr. Lazovert sprinkled them with a powerful dose of potassium cyanide, sufficient, he said, to kill several men. The wine, also poisoned, came from the Youssoupov vineyards in the Crimea. Lazovert acted as chauffeur to the prince, while Dimitri, Purishkevich, and Sukhotin played the gramophone upstairs, to simulate a midnight party. The plot proceeded. The murder room, Felix later wrote, was "isolated from the rest of the world," and the servants were confined to another wing of the palace. As Felix drove off for the peasant's flat, the strains of "Yankee Doodle" filled the empty palace.[23]

In a heavy overcoat and hat pulled low over his face, Felix crept up the back staircase to Rasputin's apartment. Rasputin had prepared carefully for the evening, for he believed he would meet the beautiful Princess Irina. Felix thought he smelled of cheap soap and noted that his hair and beard had been carefully combed. He wore black velvet trousers, a light yellow silk shirt embroidered with little flowers, and a raspberry-colored cord around his waist, from which hung long tassels.[24] They left the apartment at half-past midnight. The car drove slowly through the dark, snowy streets until it reached the palace at 94 Moika Canal; Lazovert deposited Felix and his guest, then drove off around to the other side of the courtyard.

Once in the basement of the palace, Felix and Rasputin sat down at the table. The prince nervously offered the peasant some tea, which Rasputin accepted. But Felix could not bring himself to offer anything which had been poisoned. After several glasses of unpoisoned wine, Rasputin appeared slightly intoxicated; Felix quickly offered a poisoned cake, which the peasant ate in one bite. Nothing happened. Felix quickly excused himself and disappeared up the spiral staircase.

In the prince's study, next to the octagonal anteroom, he told the other conspirators that the poison had not worked, but they persuaded him to return to the cellar. This time, Felix offered Rasputin poisoned Madeira; two glasses failed to have any effect on the peasant. Instead, Rasputin asked for more and gulped down more of the poisoned cakes.[25]

Felix was hysterical. Rasputin spotted a guitar and asked the prince to play for him; for over an hour, Felix sang and played. When he could continue no longer, he made another excuse and disappeared up the staircase, saying that he wanted to check on whether Irina was ready to meet Rasputin. By Felix's account, it was nearly three o'clock in the morning. From upstairs, the strains of "Yankee Doodle" could still be heard.

The other conspirators huddled around Felix. They could not believe that Rasputin was still alive. Lazovert had already fainted twice due to his nerves. Dimitri suggested that they should give up on the idea but Purishkevich would have none of this; grabbing a pistol, he started off down the staircase. But Felix asked that he might have this honor; clutching Dimitri's Browning revolver behind his back, Felix headed down to the basement once again.

Rasputin, according to Felix, sat at the table, his breathing labored.[26] His head fell and then rose again. Felix gave Rasputin two more glasses of poisoned wine and then walked over to a corner of the room. Rasputin suggested a visit to the Gypsies on the islands; Felix declined due to the lateness of the hour. Rasputin got up and followed Felix across the room to the little ebony cabinet. Felix wrote that

Rasputin "took a childlike pleasure in opening and shutting the drawers, exploring it inside and out."[27]

Felix kept his eyes on the crucifix, as if praying for the strength to act. Rasputin followed his gaze, saying, "For my part, I like the cabinet better."

"Gregory Efimovich, you'd far better look at the crucifix and say a prayer," Felix mumbled. Rasputin looked at him, then turned his attention to the cabinet again. Felix pulled out the revolver, aimed, and fired a shot. With a wild scream, Rasputin fell over backward onto the bearskin rug.[28]

The other conspirators rushed downstairs to find Rasputin lying on his back, Felix standing over him, arm outstretched, gun pointed at the body, smoke rising from the muzzle, a look of grim satisfaction on his face, a wild look in his eyes.

"We must quickly take him off the rug and onto the stone floor so that the blood won't soak up and we can get out of here," Dimitri said.[29] But when they pulled the body off of the white bearskin, there was no blood.

Lazovert pronounced him dead. According to both Felix and Purishkevich, Sukhotin put on Rasputin's heavy cloak and left the Moika Palace with Dimitri and Lazovert in Purishkevich's motorcar. Felix turned off the lights in the cellar, and he and Purishkevich went upstairs. Purishkevich sat down in a comfortable chair and smoked a cigar; Felix wandered off through the palace.

At some point, Felix returned to the darkened room in the basement. Purishkevich later hinted that something strange took place in the cellar while the prince was alone with the body but went no further.[30] According to Felix, he walked up to the corpse, seized it, and began to shake it violently. Suddenly, the left eye opened; then the right eye. "I then saw both eyes—the green eyes of a viper—staring at me with an expression of diabolical hatred. The blood ran cold in my veins. My muscles turned to stone....I realized now who Rasputin really was. It was the reincarnation of Satan himself who held me in his clutches and would never let me go till my dying day."[31] Rasputin grabbed Youssoupov by the shoulder, tearing off an epaulet in the process. Felix fled up the staircase to the dining room and ran off to find Purishkevich.

Still smoking his cigar, Purishkevich heard a "wild, inhuman cry." Felix, screaming, "Purishkevich, fire, fire! He's alive! He's getting away!" ran through the room; according to Purishkevich, the prince's eyes were "bulging out of their sockets." Felix stumbled away into his parents' rooms.[32]

Purishkevich heard Rasputin stumble up the staircase. He withdrew his gun and waited; but the peasant found the secret door to the courtyard and staggered across the snow toward the gate and freedom. As he ran, Rasputin screamed, "Felix! Felix! I will tell everything to the Empress!"[33]

Purishkevich wrote that he stopped, aimed, and fired. The sound of the shot echoed over the courtyard at 94 Moika and on into the dark night. Rasputin staggered on, unhit; a second shot also missed. Purishkevich could not believe his aim had failed. Finally, a third shot hit Rasputin in the shoulder. He stopped running and spun around into the snow, splattering blood over the yard. A fourth shot hit him in the head. Purishkevich ran up to the peasant and kicked him in the head. The body did not move; all Rasputin could do was gnash his teeth.[34]

The night had echoed with the sound of gunfire and screams. Now two soldiers rushed to the Moika Palace. Purishkevich took a gamble and announced that he had just killed Rasputin. The men embraced Purishkevich and helped him drag the body inside.[35]

A policeman had been on patrol along the canal and heard the shots. The officer asked about the disruption; Purishkevich informed him that Rasputin was dead. Purishkevich stated that "if you love the Tsar and the country you must be silent about this and tell no one." The policeman acquiesced and disappeared; he promptly reported the incident to his station.[36]

Felix had disappeared again, and Purishkevich went off to find him; the prince stood in his dressing room, vomiting into a basin. He kept repeating to himself, "Felix! Felix! Felix! Felix!"[37] He managed to pull himself together and followed Purishkevich downstairs; on his way he stopped and picked up a steel-and-leather club.

Rasputin lay in the marble-floored entrance hall, a large pool of blood spreading about him. Youssoupov, in hysterics, began to pound the body with the club. He smashed again and again at the face, crushing it beyond recognition. When he could strike out no longer, Felix began to vomit again and fainted into Purishkevich's arms.[38]

Shortly after five in the morning, Dimitri, Lazovert, and Sukhotin returned to the Moika Palace. They wrapped the body in a blue curtain, bound it with ropes, then pushed it into the back of Purishkevich's car. Across the dark, quiet, snowbound city they flew—to the Petrovsky Bridge across the Neva River. The shots and screams had ceased; the Moika Palace was hushed, bespattered with blood. Now the only noise was the motorcar rumbling to a stop. The men pulled the blue bundle down the embankment and pushed it through the ice into the fast-flowing water below. In their haste the conspirators neglected a boot; a few hours before, it had been on Rasputin's foot. Now it lay beneath the bridge, near a path of blood from the roadway. As the stars began to disappear from the black sky, the three hurriedly made their way back to the Youssoupov Palace on the Moika Canal They had just finished cleaning up the blood and begun to make their ways home as the sun rose over St. Petersburg. The night, and the nightmare, was over.

36

The Palace Revolution Proposal

THE FOLLOWING MORNING, Alexandra awoke to the news that Rasputin had gone off to the Youssoupov Palace the night before and had not returned. She telephoned Protopopov at once, ordering him to investigate. Police who visited the Moika Palace found bloodstains on the spiral staircase and a trail of blood across the snow in the courtyard to a crimson spot near the gate. Felix dismissed their curiosity by saying that a drunken guest the previous evening had shot a dog; he even produced the corpse.[1] But the men left the palace unconvinced and reported that Rasputin's disappearance and the bloodstained rooms at 94 Moika Canal were almost certainly connected.

As soon as she discovered this, Alexandra ordered that both Felix and Dimitri be arrested. But only the tsar could order the arrest of one of his own family; Alexandra demanded that the two suspects be confined to their respective houses. Felix called the Alexander Palace and asked to speak to the tsarina, but she refused.[2] Later, he sent her a letter denying any part in the alleged murder. Grand Duke Paul, who had returned from exile, forced his son Dimitri to swear on an icon and a photograph of his late mother that he had not killed Rasputin. "I swear it," Dimitri answered.[3]

That afternoon, Alexandra lay on the couch in her boudoir, fresh flowers in the Chinese vases and an aromatic fire burning in the stove. The windows were heavily curtained against the cold glass. Had she risen and drawn them back, Alexandra would have seen a white wonderland: broad lawns rolling to the edge of the ice-choked lake, guarded by evergreens heavy with snow—all glowing in the hazy pink of a winter sunset. But her mind saw only bloodstains as she wrote a tormented letter to her husband at *stavka*:

> My Own Beloved Sweetheart:
>   We are sitting together—you can imagine our feelings—thoughts—Our Friend has disappeared.

Yesterday, Anna saw him and he said Felix asked him to
come in the night, a motor would fetch him, to see Irina. A motor
fetched him (a military one) with two civilians and he went away.
This night big scandal at Youssoupov's house—big
meeting, Dimitri, Purishkevich, etc., all drunk; police heard shots,
Purishkevich ran out screaming to the police that Our Friend was
killed. . . . Our Friend was in good spirits but nervous these days.
Felix pretends he never came to the house. . . . I shall still trust in
God's mercy that one has only driven him off somewhere.
Protopopov is doing all he can. . . . I cannot and won't believe that
he has been killed. God have mercy. Such utter anguish (am calm
and can't believe it). . . . Come quickly. . . .
Felix came often to him lately.[4]

The police found Rasputin's body on New Year's Day, 1917. It had
to be thawed out for twenty-four hours before the autopsy took place.
He had been shot three times: once in the head and twice in the back.
The face was crushed, and the eyes and nose were swollen.[5] There is no
evidence that Rasputin swallowed water after being pushed into the
Neva or that he had freed his arm to make the sign of the cross.

Within a matter of hours all of St. Petersburg knew of Rasputin's
death, although newspapers were forbidden to print any details. One
vague report read: "A certain person visited another person with some
other persons. After the first person vanished, one of the other persons
stated that the first person had not been at the house of the second person, although it was known that the second person had visited the first
person late at night."[6]

At the Cathedral of Our Lady of Kazan, a mob surged at the door
to light candles before the icon of St. Dimitri.[7] But the tsar and tsarina
felt quite differently. "I am filled with shame that the hands of my kins-
men are stained with the blood of a simple peasant," Nicholas said.[8] "A
murder is always a murder."[9] As punishment, Felix was banished to an
estate in central Russia and Dimitri sent to Persia on military duty. Purishkevich went free.

Alexandra buried Rasputin on 3 January. His widow and children
joined the imperial family in a corner of the park at Tsarskoe Selo,
where Anna Vyrubova planned to build a small church. Lili Dehn
wrote:

It was a glorious morning. The sky was a deep blue, the sun was
shining and the hard snow sparkled like masses of diamonds. My
carriage stopped on the road . . . and I was directed to walk across

a frozen field towards the unfinished church. Planks had been placed on the snow to serve as a footpath and when I arrived at the church I noticed that a police motor van was drawn up near the open grave. After waiting several moments, I heard the sound of sleigh bells and Anna Vyrubova came slowly across the field. Almost immediately afterwards, a closed automobile stopped and the Imperial Family joined us. They were dressed in mourning and the Empress carried some white flowers; she was very pale but quite composed although I saw her tears fall when the oak coffin was taken out of the police van . . . and the burial service was read by the chaplain and after the Emperor and Empress had thrown earth on the coffin, the Empress distributed her flowers between the Grand Duchesses and ourselves and we scattered them on the coffin.[10]

Before they closed the coffin, Alexandra placed two objects on Rasputin's breast. One was an icon, signed by herself, her husband, and her children.[11] The other was a letter, written out in the tsarina's hand: "My dear Martyr, give me thy blessing that it may follow me always on the sad and dreary path I have yet to follow here below. And remember us from on high in your holy prayers. Alexandra."[12]

In the days and weeks following Rasputin's murder, Alexandra lay collapsed on her couch in the Mauve Boudoir, crying for hours. The murder of Rasputin was a great shock to her, but it did not destroy Alexandra. The conspirators had hoped that by removing Rasputin the tsarina would retreat from political activities. They did not understand that Rasputin's influence over the tsarina in the political arena was greatly overestimated; although the peasant was gone, her desire to preserve the autocracy remained unshaken.

What they did, in fact, was to remove Rasputin the peasant, whose prayers seemed to heal the tsarevich. Rasputin had often told Alexandra, "If I die or you desert me, you will lose your son and your throne within six months."[13] But rather than crumble, Alexandra drew herself together. God had sent Rasputin; God would give Alexandra the power to carry on. Filled with an unwavering faith in the rightness of her own convictions, Alexandra saw her duty clearly: She would carry on as if nothing had happened.

Even though the tsar had returned from headquarters, the ministers continued to make their reports to the tsarina, and the main telephone in the palace sat in her boudoir. If Nicholas did have an appointment, Alexandra eavesdropped on the conversation. "I thought that the door leading from the study to his dressing room was half open, which had never occurred before, and that someone was standing just inside," wrote Kokovstsov. "It may have been just an illusion, but this impression stayed with me throughout my brief audience."[14] For more comfort, Alexandra climbed to the small balcony at the end of the Maple Room, which also opened to the tsar's Audience Chamber on the other side of the former dancing hall. There, on a chaise, she could lie back and listen to the conversation in the tsar's study below.[15]

The ministerial shuffle continued. Trepov, who had replaced Stürmer as prime minister, was himself replaced by Prince Nicholas Galitzine, an elderly man chosen by the tsarina. But Protopopov retained most of the power as well as the confidence of the tsarina. Other ministers despised the man. At the New Year's Day reception, Protopopov walked up to Rodzianko and held out his hand.

"Never and nowhere!" Rodzianko spat angrily.

"My dear friend, surely we can come to an understanding," Protopopov declared agreeably.

"Leave me alone!" Rodzianko answered. "You are repellent to me!"[16]

To hold on to his power, Protopopov brought the specter of Rasputin back into the Alexander Palace. He telephoned each morning, often reporting that he had dreamed of Rasputin in the night and had been given special instructions by his ghost. A popular story circulating in St. Petersburg told of a meeting between the tsarina and the minister. During the middle of an audience, Protopopov reportedly dropped to his knees and shouted fervently, "Oh, Majesty, I can see Christ behind you!"[17]

"Never had the Emperor and Empress of Russia, rulers of nearly two hundred million souls, seemed so lonely or so helpless," wrote Anna. "Deserted and betrayed by their relatives, calumniated by men, who, in the eyes of the outside world seemed to represent the Russian people, they had no one left except a few faithful friends. . . ."[18] Anna was one of them; soon after Rasputin's murder, she began to receive threatening telephone calls. Alexandra feared that her friend would be the next to die and ordered her to move into the Alexander Palace.

Although Alexandra continued to dominate her husband, she felt increasingly unsure and troubled. Lili Dehn thought that she looked particularly sad one evening and whispered, "Oh, Madame, why are you so sad tonight?"

"Why am I sad, Lili?" Alexandra said slowly. "I can't say, really, but . . . I think my heart is broken."[19]

Alexandra and Nicholas once again opened the rooms of the palace and entertained. In the midst of the war and hatred of the aristocracy, the court came to life. There were concerts in the drawing rooms and plays for the children. At a diplomatic state banquet for the

British High Commission, Alexandra appeared in a cream silk gown embroidered with silver and blue. The group dined off cream of barley soup, trout in aspic, roast veal, chicken with cucumber salad, and tangerine ice cream.[20] The dinner was elegant, but there was no gaiety or laughter. Following Rasputin's death, they desperately tried to maintain the image that all was well; but it was a horrible charade.

In the early weeks of 1917, before the tsar returned to headquarters, the general staff would send newsreels of the front to Tsarskoe Selo so that Nicholas might view them. The entire family gathered in one of the drawing rooms to watch, and they would be followed by movies. One night, Alexandra and Nicholas watched a film called *Madame Du Barry*, filled with scenes of an angry mob putting members of the French aristocracy to death.[21] With her world collapsing around her, Alexandra failed to sense the approaching storm.

The imperial family waited with hope for Alexandra to retreat from politics. If the dynasty was to continue, the tsar must turn his government around. In a final effort to save the situation, Grand Duke Alexander Michailovich went to Tsarskoe Selo to speak with the tsarina. Although he had requested a private audience, when he arrived, he found Nicholas sitting beside her, smoking a cigarette.

Alexandra lay in bed, dressed in a white negligee embroidered with lace. Despite the tsar's presence, Sandro began bluntly: "Nobody knows better than I your love and devotion for Nicky, and yet I must confess that your interference with affairs of state is causing harm both to Nicky's prestige and to the popular conception of a sovereign." He stated that although for "twenty-four years" he had been "your faithful friend," he had to "point out to you that all classes of the population are opposed to your policies." He asked, "Why can you not concentrate on matters promising peace and harmony? Please, Alix, leave the affairs of state to your husband."

According to the grand duke, Alexandra blushed and looked at Nicholas, who said nothing. Sandro explained that "the granting of a government acceptable to the Duma and coming at this dangerous moment would lift the responsibilities from Nicky's shoulders and would make his task easier." He ended with a plea for cooperation. "Please, Alix, do not let your thirst for revenge dominate your better judgment."

"All of this talk is ridiculous!" Alexandra shouted. "Nicky is an autocrat. How could he share his divine rights with a parliament?"

"You are very much mistaken, Alix!" Sandro bellowed back, referring to the creation of the Duma. "Your husband ceased to be an autocrat on 17 October, 1905!"

In desperation, the grand duke continued: "Remember, Alix, I remained silent for thirty months! For thirty months, I never said as much as a word about the disgraceful goings-on in our government, better to say, your government!" Screaming that although Alexandra might be "willing to perish," she had no right to ask them all to "suffer for your blind stubbornness! No, Alix, you have no right to drag your relations with you down a precipice! You are incredibly selfish!"

"I refuse to continue this dispute!" Alexandra announced. "You are exaggerating the danger. Someday, when you are less excited, you will admit that I know better." The grand duke stormed out of the palace, never to return again.[22] Later, he sent a letter to Nicholas in a last bid for reason:

> Strange as it may sound, Nicky, we are witnessing the unbelievable spectacle of a revolution being promoted by the government. Nobody else wants a revolution. . . . I do not know whether you will take my advice or not, but I do want you to understand that the coming Russian Revolution of 1917 is a pure product of the efforts of your government. For the first time in modern history, a revolution is being engineered not from below but from above, not by the people against the government, but by the government against the welfare of the people.[23]

What Sandro did not know was that there already existed a plan to begin a revolution. That plan, however, did not come from the government but from the imperial family itself.

The idea of a palace revolution to sweep Nicholas off the throne grew gradually. Unlike a popular revolt—initiated and carried out by the people—this idea of a palace revolution came from within the ranks of the imperial family.

Marie Pavlovna, widow of the tsar's uncle Vladimir, aggressively anti-English, and one of Alexandra's worst enemies, actively plotted a way to remove her nephew from the throne. Grand Duke Vladimir had barely tolerated the ascension of Nicholas to the throne; he had always been jealous of his older brother Alexander III, and his ambitions led to many family quarrels. When he died, he passed on his ambitions and hatred to his wife. After Marie Feodorovna and Alexandra, Marie Pavlovna ranked as third lady in the land. Socially prominent, intelligent, graceful, and very, very rich, the widowed grand duchess had set up a rival court to that at Tsarskoe Selo, slowly building her own strength among the powerful of the capital. She hated the tsarina. Once, when one guest complimented her after a particularly brilliant party, the grand duchess icily replied, "One ought to know one's job. You may pass that on to the Great Court."[24]

Marie Pavlovna had three sons, all touched by scandal. Cyril, the eldest, had wed Alexandra's former sister-in-law Ducky in an illegal marriage, for which he was stripped of his offices and honors and banished from the country; although the tsar eventually restored the lost honors and allowed his cousin to return to Russia, he did not grant retroactive permission for the marriage, and this placed a cloud over Cyril's claim to the imperial throne. Nevertheless, his mother plotted to place him on the throne as regent for Tsarevich Alexei—at least at the beginning.

Another brother, Andrei, openly lived with the tsar's former mistress Mathilde Kschessinska and had fathered a bastard child by her. The youngest, Boris, had proposed to the young Grand Duchess Olga, Alexandra's daughter. The tsarina, terrified at the thought, wrote, "What an awful set his wife would be dragged into . . . intrigues without end, fast manners and conversations . . . a half worn, blasé . . . man of thirty-eight to a pure, fresh girl of eighteen years his junior and live in a house in which many a woman has 'shared' his life."[25] Marie Pavlovna never forgave Alexandra for this seething denial.

Cyril, a commanding officer in the Garde Equipage, drew soldiers from this regiment, many of whom had served aboard the imperial yacht, into the plot. It was chillingly simple: One night, four guards regiments would seize the Alexander Palace, force the tsar to abdicate in favor of Alexei, and install Cyril as regent. In this manner, Marie Pavlovna and her family would gain the power they so desperately wanted.

Maurice Paléologue recalled one night particularly well:

> Yesterday evening, Prince Gabriel Constantinovich gave a supper
> for his mistress, formerly an actress. The guests included the
> Grand Duke Boris . . . a few officers and a squad of elegant
> courtesans. During the evening the only topic was the
> conspiracy—the regiments of the Guards which can be relied on,
> the most favourable moment for the outbreak, etc. And all of this
> with the servants moving about, harlots looking on and listening,
> Gypsies singing and the whole company bathed in the aroma of
> Moët and Chandon *brut imperial* which flowed in streams.[26]

Nevertheless, no one actually took the plotters seriously; no one, that is, until Rodzianko attended a luncheon at the Vladimir Palace in January 1917. Marie Pavlovna, talking of Alexandra, became "more and more excited, dwelling on her nefarious influence and interference in everything, and said that she was driving the country to destruction; that she was the cause of the danger which threatened the Emperor and the rest of the Imperial Family; that such conditions could no longer be tolerated; that things must be changed, something done, removed, destroyed. . . ."

"What do you mean by 'removed'?" asked Rodzianko.

"The Duma must do something," Marie Pavlovna announced. "She must be annihilated."

"Who?"

"The Empress."

"Your Highness, allow me to treat this conversation as if it had never taken place, because if you address me as the President of the Duma, my oath of allegiance compels me to wait at once on His Imperial Majesty and report to him that the Grand Duchess Marie Pavlovna has declared to me that the Empress must be annihilated."[27]

Rodzianko took the train from the capital to Tsarskoe Selo for his weekly audience with the tsar. Although he did not mention Marie Pavlovna, clearly the situation was fast becoming critical. Rodzianko had no choice but to be blunt. "It is an open secret that the Empress issues orders without your knowledge, that ministers report to her on matters of state. . . . Indignation against and hatred of the Empress are growing throughout the country. She is looked upon as Germany's champion. Even the common people are speaking of it."

"Give me the facts," Nicholas demanded. "There are no facts to confirm your statements."

"There are no facts," Rodzianko admitted, "but the whole trend of policy directed by Her Majesty gives grounds for such ideas. To save your family, Your Majesty ought to find some way of preventing the Empress from exercising any influence on politics. . . . Your Majesty, do not compel the people to choose between you and the good of the country."

"Is it possible that for twenty-two years I tried to act for the best and for the twenty-two years it was all a mistake?" Nicholas asked quietly.

"Yes, Your Majesty, for twenty-two years you followed a wrong course," Rodzianko answered.[28]

Rodzianko left the palace convinced that "the Empress must renounce all interference in affairs of state and remain at Livadia until the end of the war."[29] He believed that "Alexandra Feodorovna is fiercely and universally hated, and all circles are clamouring for her removal."[30] This talk apparently convinced the tsar to grant new reforms and powers to the Duma. He planned to deliver a speech to the delegates in person, but at the last minute changed his mind and left the capital for headquarters.

Marie Pavlovna's idea of a palace revolution had grown into an uncontrollable tide of dissent. The aristocracy, the government, the military, even the imperial family—all plotted to remove the tsar from the throne. General Krymov stood in the Duma and said, "A *coup d'état* would be welcomed with joy, because the Emperor attaches more weight to his wife's pernicious influence than to all the honest words of warning."[31] St. Petersburg braced itself for revolution as the snows of winter fell upon the capital and the angry shouts grew louder in the marble halls of the palaces lining the frozen Neva.

37

Revolution

WHILE THOUGHTS OF A palace coup drifted in and out of the minds of the Romanov family like the snowflakes falling across the frozen capital, Nicholas headed south on his train toward Mogilev. His own ministers seethed with anger. On 23 February 1917, two weeks earlier, Rodzianko had had his last audience with the tsar. The president of the Duma threatened Nicholas, saying, "I warn you, that before three weeks are out, a revolution will flare up, which will sweep you off your throne—so that you will no longer reign."

"Where do you get all this information?" Nicholas asked.

"From the general trend of events," Rodzianko replied. He left Tsarskoe Selo "in the firm conviction that this is my last report."[1]

Rodzianko had good reason to be convinced.

On 18 January the Okhrana—the tsar's secret police—filed away a report on the state of the government. It read: "The wildest rumours circulate in society about the intention of the government to take various reactionary steps as well as predictions that hostile elements and groups are preparing for possible revolutionary acts and excesses." Two weeks later, the Okhrana security chief, Constantine Globachev, reported a disturbing trend among the high officers of the government. Many members of the Duma openly talked of supporting a palace coup.[2]

Alexander Kerensky, a liberal member of the Duma, took the podium of the legislature one day in the last week of February. His speech bordered on treason. "The Ministers are but fleeting shadows!" he bellowed. "To prevent a catastrophe the Tsar himself must be removed, by terrorist methods if there is no other way. If you will not listen to the voice of warning, you will find yourselves face to face with facts, not warnings. Look up at the distant flashes that are lighting the skies of Russia!"[3]

Members of the imperial family, cabinet ministers, government officials—even the president of the Duma—wished to remove the tsar in a coup. Even as the conspirators talked and plotted, peasants and factory workers huddled in the chill St. Petersburg dawn, waiting for food stores to open. By March 1917, the locomotives which normally transported supplies to the capital lay frozen and abandoned in the snow. By 1917, food prices had soared to over 400 percent higher than at the beginning of the war.[4] The majority of the people who crowded the streets of St. Petersburg during the momentous weeks of March did not want a revolution; they only wanted food.

International Women's Day fell on Thursday, 8 March 1917. The morning began at nearly forty below zero, but by the afternoon the snow had melted from the streets of the capital.[5] Early that morning, before the sun rose, crowds of peasant women waited in line for the shops to open; war rationing and price increases made daily market visits a necessity for many. They waited and waited for the stores to open; but on this morning the supply of black bread—the staple of most Russian diets—ran out. Even if the people could find the food supplies, most people could not afford to buy them. Hungry, tired, frustrated, they turned from the stores and began to walk home once again.

As they walked through the streets, they came upon factory workers—thousands of them—disillusioned, on strike. Two days before, the Putilov Ironworks laid off twenty-eight thousand workers; they were joined by nearly sixty thousand of their comrades. The socialists were also in the streets, celebrating International Women's Day. The strikers and socialists mingled with the poor. Small groups began shouting, "Down with the autocracy!" and singing the "Marseillaise."[6] They came together out of hunger, discontent, and circumstance.

Violence erupted on Friday. Thousands crowded into the streets of the capital, smashing shop windows and stealing what little food remained. Students joined the protests and spent most of the afternoon throwing snowballs at the police who patrolled the city streets.[7] Cossacks wandered up and down the avenues; at first, the crowds feared the sullen men. But after a while the cossacks began to fraternize with the strikers and told them, "Don't worry. We won't shoot."[8] The Revolution had begun.

At Tsarskoe Selo, Alexandra heard that there were some minor bread riots in the capital. She decided to issue a decree that the food must be fairly distributed and also that the workers "should be told they must not picket!"[9] She did not understand that there was no food; all incoming shipments had been stopped.

In Znamenskaia Square stood a large equestrian statue of Tsar Alexander III. Like a magnet, it drew thousands, chanting antiwar slogans and demanding food. At three in the afternoon, someone from the crowd shot a policeman; rumor had it that the assassin was a member of the Cossack Guard.[10]

That night, the imperial cabinet met. The situation had become critical. The schools were closed, the students locked out. Taxicabs and streetcars had ceased to run. The ministers were careful; most favored Grand Duchess Marie Pavlovna's idea of a palace revolution, and, indeed, there is some evidence that the plan had actually begun to unfold when the problems in St. Petersburg erupted. They could not have dreamed of a scenario more favorable to their plans. The capital was in revolt; something had to change. They cabled the tsar an urgent request that he return at once to St. Petersburg and create a responsible government. Nicholas knew only that there were street disorders in the capital. He telegraphed Gen. Serge Khabalov, the military governor of St. Petersburg: "I order that these disorders in the capital, intolerable during these difficult times of war with Germany and Austria, be ended tomorrow. Nicholas."[11]

General Khabalov refused to admit that a potential crisis was occurring. He wrote to General Alexeiev, the tsar's chief of staff at *stavka*, that although the strikes and demonstrations were spreading, there was no cause for alarm. When the tsar's telegram arrived, Khabalov reluctantly ordered his troops into the streets. They were among the worst soldiers in the country—men who had been rejected for duty at the front. Those who had been in proper military service had been wounded and sent back to the capital; most were factory workers who had been drafted but held back. Untrained and undisciplined, these soldiers walked the streets of the capital as St. Petersburg continued to riot.

Sunday began with a promise of peace. The sun was warm, the air crisp and clear. The sound of church bells echoed throughout the capital. When General Khabalov looked out over this scene, he felt reassured. He telegraphed the tsar that "the city is quiet."[12]

During the night Khabalov had ordered posters put up around the capital saying that all assemblies and public meetings were forbidden and that all strikers who did not report to work the following morning would be fired and shipped to the front.

Violence erupted Sunday afternoon. In Znamenskaia Square some forty people were shot by the soldiers of the St. Petersburg Garrison. Peasants, factory workers, and the curious, parading through the streets, some sporting red armbands and shouting antimonarchist slogans, met lines of soldiers stretching across the bridges and avenues of the capital. Rifles lowered from the sky shot forth their ammunition into the screaming groups, leaving bodies littered on the slushy pavement. By the end of the day, over two hundred people had been killed.

At the Cathedral of Our Lady of Kazan, soldiers of the Pavlovsky Regiment fired on a group of demonstrators. A second battalion rushed to the cathedral, hoping to convince their comrades to return to the barracks. The two groups clashed, shots were exchanged, and the commanding officer of the Pavlovsky Regiment lay dead in the street, killed by his own men.[13]

For Rodzianko, it was the point of no return. Personally supportive of the idea of a palace revolution, Rodzianko had also involved himself in its unfolding. The conspirators had wanted a responsible government; now public pressure gave them every reason to push their plans for a coup forward. The revolt in the capital made the removal of the tsar inevitable either through a full coup or by the granting of an independent ministry. The cable Rodzianko sent the tsar read more like an ultimatum: "Situation serious. Anarchy in the capital. Government paralyzed. Transport of food and fuel in full disorder. Popular discontent growing. Disorderly firing in the streets. Some military units fire on one another. Essential immediately to order persons having the confidence of the country to form a new government. Delay impossible. And delay deadly. I pray to God that in this hour the blame does not fall on the crown."[14]

When he received this cable, Nicholas angrily told General Alexeiev, "That fat Rodzianko has sent me some nonsense which I shall not even bother to answer."[15]

As night fell, the capital lay silent. The British ambassador, Sir George Buchanan, drove through St. Petersburg Sunday evening after a holiday in Finland. He wrote that "the part of the city through which we passed on our short drive to see the Embassy was perfectly quiet and, except for a few patrols of soldiers on the quays and the absence of trams and cabs, there was nothing unusual."[16] Paléologue, driving through the streets at eleven that night, noted that the Radziwill Palace on the Fontanka Canal blazed with light; inside, a magnificent party was taking place.[17]

On Monday morning, Meriel Buchanan looked out over the city from a window in the embassy. The streets were empty—no trams, no food lines, no carriages, no people. Through the pearl haze of dawn, she noted that the imperial standard fluttered over the Fortress of Peter and Paul.[18]

Early that morning the Volinsky Regiment mutinied. They spent Sunday night arguing among themselves about whether to join with the people or obey General Khabalov's orders to fire on them. When their commander tried to read them the tsar's orders, he was shot. The Volinsky Regiment left their barracks and joined the mob in the streets. The flood began. The Preobrajensky Regiment followed the Volinsky, then the Litovsky; the Semanovsky; the Ismailovsky; the Oranienbaum Machine Gun Regiment—one by one, company after company of the tsar's elite soldiers deserted him and joined the Revolution.

A young policeman happened to be on patrol along the Fontanka Canal when he suddenly came face-to-face with a violent mob. They fell upon the young man and beat him until his face was covered with blood. Someone screamed that they should throw him in the canal. The terrified policeman pleaded with them, saying, "Brothers! Brothers! Don't drown me! I swear by God! I did nothing wrong! I didn't hurt anyone! Brothers!" Ignoring his cries for help, the crowd seized the man and threw him over the canal railing and into the icy water. When he tried to swim away, the mob grabbed up stones and hurled them at the splashing figure. They kept throwing stones until the water turned crimson and the policeman disappeared below the surface.[19]

The imperial cabinet met for the last time at the Mariinsky Palace. They decided to divide up their power with the Duma in the hope that the Revolution would end. The prime minister turned to Protopopov, the minister of the interior, and asked for his resignation. As he had been in charge of food distribution in the capital, the request did not surprise Protopopov. He resigned his post, saying, "Now there is nothing left to do but shoot myself."[20]

On Monday night Nicholas cabled that he was returning to the capital. Even as he prepared to leave *stavka*, a new government formed in St. Petersburg. The Tauride Palace—home of the Duma—became the center of all attention. The imperial ministers wandered up and down the marble halls, trying to decide what to do next. Rodzianko, although he wanted the tsar off the throne, faced a situation which could mean total chaos. "I don't want a revolution," he said to himself. "I've not made one and I won't make one."[21] But Rodzianko refused to obey the tsar's order to close the Duma. The decision had to be made. Basil Shulgin, a monarchist member of the Duma, reached the conclusion that "perhaps in order to save the monarchy we must sacrifice the monarch."[22] Overnight, the imperial government of Russia gave way to a provisional government.

Amid the turbulence and confusion of the new government, Alexander Kerensky rose to prominence. Shulgin wrote that Kerensky's " words and gestures were sharp and clear-cut and his eyes shone.

He seemed to grow with every minute."[23] Quickly, Kerensky became vice-chairman of the Soviet, which he housed under the Duma's roof, and the minister of justice.

On Tuesday 13 March, Nicholas decided to send reinforcements to the capital. He chose Gen. Nicholas Ivanov. Ivanov took with him the St. George Battalion, every member of which had been decorated with the Order of St. George. Four more regiments were to be culled along the way before the unit marched on St. Petersburg. But the march never happened. The soldiers reached Tsarskoe Selo, where they were surrounded by revolutionaries. Ivanov was determined to reach St. Petersburg until General Alexeiev cabled him that the capital was in order and that Ivanov and his men should withdraw.[24] Ivanov saw no reason to disbelieve the tsar's chief of staff, and he discharged his men as the capital continued to riot.

On Tuesday morning, with his fifteen hundred loyal troops, Khabalov took refuge in the Winter Palace. The loyalists were given twenty minutes to clear out; across the Neva, the guns of the fortress were trained on the three blocks of the palace. Khabalov had no choice. When the Winter Palace fell, the resistance also died away.

Crowds surged through the darkened streets of the capital, waving red flags, breaking into shops, burning official buildings. Wild butchery took place among the mutinous troops. In Kronstadt, sailors murdered all of their officers, shooting one and throwing a second into the grave alongside the corpse, to be buried alive.[25] The elegant mansions of St. Petersburg fell victim to the Revolution. Mathilde Kschessinska escaped from her house just in time; a violent mob broke into the mansion, smashing furniture, breaking windows, smearing carpets and walls with ink, and filling the bathtubs with cigarette butts.[26]

On Wednesday the Imperial Guards deserted. Sporting red ribbons and flags, they marched through the streets of the capital to the Duma. That same day, Grand Duke Cyril broke his oath of allegiance to the tsar and led the Garde Equipage to the Duma. At the Tauride Palace, Cyril pledged his men and himself to the provisional government. When he returned home to his palace on Glinka Street, Cyril ordered that a red flag be flown from the top of his roof.[27]

Cyril had sealed his own fate by cooperating with the revolutionaries. He gave a seething interview to a St. Petersburg newspaper a week after the Revolution. "I have asked myself several times if the ex-Empress were an accomplice of Wilhelm but each time forced myself to recoil from the horror of such a thought," Cyril said dramatically.[28]

The Revolution had triumphed. A day after the Imperial Guard deserted, Nicholas II fell from power. Gen. Alfred Knox heard a man talking of the future and sensed that this was only the beginning. "We have only one wish: to beat the Germans," the man said. "We will begin with the Germans here, and with a family that you know called Romanov."[29] On 16 March 1917 the Romanov dynasty was swept away in the flood of revolution.

38

Abdication

A SNOWSTORM LATE SUNDAY NIGHT dropped a fresh blanket of white across the capital. At Tsarskoe Selo the park melted into the white horizon of the winter sky. Behind the thick stone walls of the Alexander Palace, Alexandra stepped from her private elevator onto the second floor and walked through the darkened hallways to her children's bedrooms. Olga, Tatiana, and Alexei had the measles—severe cases with high temperatures. Anna Vyrubova lay in another wing of the palace, also having caught the disease. Nicholas remained at Mogilev with his generals. As she read *Aunt Helen's Children* to the invalids, her mind wandered to the troubles in the capital.[1] People marched, rioted, demonstrated, and died. Darkness crept over the palace as, one by one, lights were extinguished in the drawing rooms. Alexandra was alone.

At ten the next morning, the telephone rang in Lili Dehn's apartment in St. Petersburg. "I want you to come to Tsarskoe Selo by the ten-forty-five train," Alexandra told her. "It's a lovely morning. We'll go for a run in the car. You can see the girls and Anna and return . . . at four PM. . . . I'll be at the station."[2] When Lili stepped from the train at the Tsarskoe Selo station, Alexandra asked her, "How is it in Petersburg? I hear things are serious." Lili tried to reassure the tsarina, but on their way back to the palace, Alexandra had her car stopped so that she might question a captain in the Garde Equipage; to her query, the man answered, "There is no danger, Your Majesty."[3]

But that afternoon the news from the capital began to drift in. Alexandra told her friend in a hushed voice: "Lili, it is *very* bad. . . . The Litovsky Regiment has mutinied, murdering the officers, and left the barracks; the Volinsky Regiment has followed suit. I can't understand it. I'll never believe in the possibility of revolution."[4] A few hours later, Alexander Taneyev, Anna Vyrubova's father, arrived at the palace, out of breath and hysterical. "Petersburg is in the hands of the mob!" he shouted. "They are stopping all cars. They commandeered mine and

I've had to walk every step of the way."[5] Alexandra picked up the gilded telephone in the Mauve Boudoir and dialed the number at the governor's mansion in Mogilev; suddenly, the line went dead. To her desperate cable, Nicholas replied that he would be home on Wednesday the fourteenth. Lili camped out that night on a sofa in the Red Drawing Room; Count Paul Benckendorff, grand marshal of the imperial court, happened to pass by the open door and saw Lili and Anastasia sitting on the floor before the fireplace, doing jigsaw puzzles.

Before she went to bed, Alexandra visited Lili. "I don't want the girls to know anything until it is impossible to keep the truth from them but people are drinking to excess and there is indiscriminate shooting in the streets. Oh, Lili, what a blessing that we have here the most devoted troops. There is the Garde Equipage; they are all our personal friends."[6]

Rodzianko called Tsarskoe Selo, urging Count Benckendorff to tell the tsarina that she and her children were in danger and should leave immediately. Benckendorff cabled Nicholas for instructions, and the tsar replied that his family should wait for his return. The delay proved fatal. The next morning, Alexandra sent a message to Rodzianko that she would not leave by herself and "that owing to the state of her children's health, especially that of the Heir Apparent, departure with them was completely out of the question."[7] Rodzianko replied that "when a house is burning the invalids are the first to be taken out."[8] Benckendorff did not bother to pass this message along to the tsarina. Two hours later, all railway lines leading in and out of Tsarskoe Selo were severed.[9] "We could not leave," wrote Gilliard, "and it was highly improbable that the tsar would be able to reach us."[10]

The tsar, clad in an officer's greatcoat, walked the length of the platform at the Mogilev train station. He took the salute and climbed aboard the imperial train. The stationmaster signaled with his lamp, and the lights on the locomotive blazed out into the dark night. With a puff of smoke the train lurched forward. At five o'clock on the morning of Tuesday 13 March 1917, the tsar left *stavka* for St. Petersburg.

The riots in the capital greatly disturbed Nicholas. He believed that Khabalov would be able to shoot the crowds and force them into submission. Then, on Monday night, he received a desperate cable from his wife: "Concessions inevitable. Street fighting continues. Many units gone over to the enemy. Alix."[11]

At two on Wednesday morning, the tsar's train came to an abrupt halt at Malaya Vishera, one hundred miles south of the capital. A soldier boarded the imperial train and told Gen. Vladimir Voikov, a member of the tsar's suite, that the track ahead was blocked. Revolutionary soldiers had somehow got hold of a machine gun and sat waiting for the tsar's train.[12] Voikov woke the tsar. They could not proceed to the capital; instead, Voikov recommended the nearest military headquarters at Pskov, where Gen. Nicholas Ruzsky commanded loyal troops and the tsar could contact his wife. After a short talk with his suite, Nicholas agreed and said sleepily, "Well, then, to Pskov."[13]

Late Tuesday afternoon a group of mutinous soldiers decided that they would drive out to Tsarskoe Selo from the capital, storm the Alexander Palace, and take the tsarina and tsarevich back to the Fortress of Peter and Paul. When the men arrived in the village, they set off for the imperial park. On their way, however, they broke into a store and stole several bottles of vodka and wine. By the time night fell, the soldiers were too drunk to reach the entrance to the park.

The sound of gunfire echoed across the imperial park. Alexandra heard the shots from her children's bedrooms. "Lili, they say that a hostile crowd of 300,000 is marching on the palace," she whispered to her friend. "We shall not, must not be afraid. Everything is in the hands of God. Tomorrow the Emperor is sure to come. I know that when he does, all will be well."[14]

The Alexander Palace prepared for an attack. The day before, Count Benckendorff had ordered up a battalion of the Garde Equipage; two battalions of the Composite Regiment of the Imperial Guard; two regiments of Cossack Guards; a squadron of the Railway Regiment; and a company of field artillerymen; in total, there were some fifteen men to guard the palace.[15] They stationed themselves in the courtyard between the main block of the palace and the Corinthian colonnade; additional soldiers were on guard at the main entrance and around the front lake nearest to the Catherine Palace. Fires blazed in the snowy courtyard to keep the soldiers warm, and in the center sat a huge field gun. Looking at this scene from an upstairs window, Anastasia remarked, "How astonished Papa will be."[16]

A telephone call at nine that night warned the tsarina that the mob had begun marching toward the imperial park. Just minutes later, a shot rang out; they had killed a sentry less than five hundred yards from the palace.[17] The night echoed with gunfire. Alexandra ran to the windows several times to reassure herself and the children, who also heard the shots. To their questions, Alexandra explained that special maneuvers were being held. Countess Benckendorff and Baroness Buxhoeveden lay on couches in the Green Drawing Room.[18] Several times Alexandra wandered in and out, bringing extra blankets and, one time in her stocking feet, offering them some fruit and biscuits from her bedside table.[19]

At midnight, Alexandra threw a black fur cloak over her nurse's uniform, and she and her daughter Marie and Count Benckendorff walked out into the palace courtyard to speak with the soldiers. Baroness Buxhoeveden watched from the windows of the Green Drawing Room. "The scene was unforgettable," she wrote. "It was dark. . . . The troops were lined up in battle order . . . the first line kneeling in the snow, the others standing behind, their rifles in readiness for a sudden attack. The figures of the Empress and her daughter passed from line to line, the white palace looming a ghostly mass in the background."[20] Alexandra moved from man to man, telling each one that she trusted him completely and saying that the tsarevich's life lay in their hands. Back inside the palace, she kept repeating to Lili, "They are all our friends. They are so devoted to us."[21]

During the night, Alexandra did not undress; she lay down for a few hours on the sofa in her boudoir, but the gunfire kept her awake. By morning, the seige had ended; the mutineers had swaggered as far as the Chinese Village before they passed out or gave up and went home.

Alexandra expected Nicholas to arrive at Tsarskoe Selo at six on Wednesday morning. She paced her boudoir, waiting for the appointed hour. At seven, she said, "Perhaps the blizzard detains him." She lay down on her sofa to rest. But Anastasia sensed that something was wrong, saying, "Lili, the train is *never* late. Oh, if only Papa would come quickly."[22] By eight in the morning, Alexandra began sending off telegrams to her husband; a few hours later, she learned that he had been stopped at Malaya Vishera. That afternoon, and over the next few days, all of Alexandra's cables to the tsar were returned to the Alexander Palace. Scrawled across the top of each in blue pencil someone had written, "Address of person mentioned unknown."[23]

By Wednesday the loyal troops defending the Alexander Palace had begun to desert. When she happened to look from a window, Alexandra saw that many of the men had white handkerchiefs tied about their wrists—a symbol worked out by the Duma so that the troops would not fire on looters in the village.[24] Seeing this, Alexandra remarked grimly, "Well, so everything is in the hands of the Duma."[25]

When she learned that her husband's train had been detained, Alexandra sent one of her last letters, imploring the tsar not to act in haste:

Clearly they do not want to let you see me unless you sign some paper, a constitution or some other horror like that. And you, all alone, without the backing of the army, caught like a mouse in a trap, what can you do? This is the greatest infamy and a low down trick, unheard of in history: to arrest the sovereign. . . . If

you are forced to make concessions, you are in no case obliged to
carry them out, because they have been obtained from you in a
shameful fashion. . . . The two movements—the Duma and the
revolutionaries—are two snakes and I hope they bite each other's
heads off, which would save the situation. . . . I can advise you
nothing, only be yourself, my precious one. Should you have to
submit to circumstances, God will help you free yourself from
them.[26]

Early Thursday morning, Lili Dehn walked into the Mauve
Boudoir to find Alexandra standing at the window, her face pale, her
eyes red. Seeing her friend, Alexandra turned to her and said, "Lili, the
troops have deserted!"

"Why, Madame? In the name of God, why?"

"Their commander—the Grand Duke Cyril—has sent for them."

Alexandra was silent for a moment, then cried, "My sailors! My
own sailors! I can't believe it!"[27]

By Thursday afternoon Anastasia had taken to her bed with a high
fever, and Marie confessed to Baroness Buxhoeveden that she felt "in
for it." She caught cold, then double pneumonia; Marie had terrible
nightmares about soldiers coming to murder her mother.[28] "I must not
give way," Alexandra kept repeating over and over to Lili. "I keep on
saying, 'I must not'—it helps me."[29] The situation grew worse with each
passing hour. On Wednesday afternoon the water supply to the palace
had been cut off. Fresh water could only be obtained by breaking the ice
on the lake. That same night, the palace lay in darkness—soldiers had
cut the electricity that afternoon.[30] Earlier that day, Alexandra had visited Rasputin's grave. "The sun shines so brightly and I feel such peace
and calm when I visit his dear grave," she wrote. "He died to save us."[31]

General Ruzsky met the tsar's train at the Pskov station on
Wednesday night. When he learned of the mutinies, Nicholas ordered
Ruzsky to cable Rodzianko with permission to grant a responsible gov-
ernment, hoping that this would prevent the disturbances. But
Rodzianko angrily cabled back:

His Majesty and yourself apparently are unable to realize what is
happening in the capital. A terrible revolution has broken out. . . .
Hatred of the Empress has reached a fever pitch. To prevent
bloodshed, I have been forced to arrest all ministers. . . . Don't
send any more troops. . . . I am hanging by a thread myself, power
is slipping out of my hands. . . . The measures you propose are too
late. The time for them is gone. There is no return.[32]

The new government decided that Nicholas must abdicate in favor of his son, with Grand Duke Michael installed as regent. "It is of vital importance that Nicholas II should not be overthrown by violence," argued one member of the Duma, Alexander Guchkov. "The only thing which can secure the permanent establishment of a new order, without too great a shock, is his voluntary abdication."[33]

General Alexeiev had requested the opinions of the tsar's generals as to the abdication. These cables arrived on the morning of 15 March—Thursday. Nicholas looked them over thoughtfully; all were unanimous in calling for his abdication. Even Grand Duke Nicholas Nicholaievich had begged—"on my knees"—for his cousin's abdication.[34]

Nicholas stood at the window in his train compartment, looking out blankly. Suddenly, he turned and told Ruzsky, "I have decided that I shall give up my throne in favour of my son Alexei." He made the sign of the cross, and the other men present also crossed themselves. "I thank you, gentlemen, for your distinguished and faithful service," the tsar said. "I hope it will continue under my son."[35] Nicholas walked over to his desk, took the Instrument of Abdication which Ruzsky had already written, and signed it in his own hand, adding the date: 15 March 1917, 3:00 P.M. A manifesto to be released in the capital announced the ascension of His Imperial Majesty Tsar Alexei II, emperor and autocrat of all the Russias.

At Tsarskoe Selo a fresh storm swept through the park on Thursday night. Early Friday morning a few servants returning from the capital brought printed leaflets announcing the tsar's abdication. Alexandra refused to believe them. That afternoon, the tsar's uncle Paul arrived at the Alexander Palace. He went straight to Alexandra's boudoir. She stood gazing out of a window, dressed in her nurse's uniform.

"Dear Alix," Paul said to her, "I wanted to be with you at this painful moment."

"Nicky?" the tsarina quickly asked, fearing the worst.

"Nicky is safe and well," the grand duke answered, "but be brave, as brave as he has been." Calmly, he told Alexandra that her husband had abdicated.

"I don't believe it!" Alexandra screamed. "It's all lies! The newspaper invented it! I believe in God and the Army. They haven't deserted us yet." To which the grand duke bluntly replied that both God and the army were now on the side of the Revolution.[36]

Alexandra said nothing. Suddenly the realization of the abdication hit her. She burst into tears, her face twisted with grief. Lili and

Grand Duchess Marie waited in an adjoining room. Suddenly, the door opened, and Alexandra entered. She stumbled so badly that Lili rushed forward to help her to a writing table. Alexandra leaned against it, her head bowed, took Lili's hands into hers, and said in a broken voice, "*Abdiqué.*" Then, through her tears: "Poor darling—alone there and suffering—my God! What he must have suffered. . . . And I was not there to console him."[37]

That evening, Alexandra received her personal staff and broke the news to them. Baroness Buxhoeveden collapsed in her arms, crying uncontrollably as Count Benckendorff held the tsarina's hands. "It's for the best," she said, "it is the will of God. God gives this to save Russia. That is the only thing that matters." As they left the room, Alexandra fell into a chair, covering her face with her hands and crying bitterly.[38]

That same evening, Gilliard remembered, "I saw her in Alexei Nicholaievich's room. . . . Her face was terrible to see, but with a strength of will which was almost superhuman, she had forced herself to come to the children's rooms as usual so that the young invalids . . . should suspect nothing."[39] Only Marie knew, as she had been present. "Mama cried terribly," she told Anna. "I cried too, but not more than I could help, for poor Mama's sake."[40]

The next morning, a servant burst into Alexandra's bedroom without knocking and announced in an excited voice, "The Emperor is on the phone!" Alexandra gave him a cold stare, then realized what he had said and rushed to the telephone.[41] "You know?" Nicholas asked quietly. Alexandra whispered, "Yes."[42]

Guchkov and Shulgin arrived at Pskov late Thursday evening. The Duma had sent them to witness the abdication's signing and bring it back with them to the capital. It took them nearly six hours to reach Pskov from St. Petersburg.

During those six hours, Nicholas reconsidered his decision to abdicate in favor of his son. The tsar assumed that Michael would shoulder most of the responsibilities and that Alexei would be free to remain with his family. But Dr. Fedorov pointed out that the new government, already hostile to the tsar and tsarina, would hardly allow them to continue to raise the boy and influence him. If the imperial family went abroad to live—to England, for instance—Alexei would have to remain behind in Russia.

When Guchkov and Shulgin arrived at nine that evening, Nicholas received them in the train's drawing room. Guchkov started to explain why the tsar must abdicate, but Nicholas interrupted him by saying, "This long speech is unnecessary. I have decided to renounce my throne. Until three o'clock today I thought I would abdicate in favour of my son Alexei. But now I have changed my decision in favour of my brother Michael. I trust you will understand the feelings of a father."[43]

The tsar got up, took a draft of the abdication into another room, and amended it to his satisfaction. It removed both him and his son from power—technically an illegal move, as power had already passed to Alexei. He kept the date and time the same as on the original. He signed it once again; Guchkov and Shulgin countersigned as witnesses and then placed a coat of varnish over the tsar's signature.[44]

Nicholas stood by a window, staring vacantly. He looked at Shulgin, tears clouding his eyes. "Oh! Your Majesty, if only you had done all this earlier, even as late as the last summoning of the Duma, perhaps all that–" Shulgin began then broke off. Nicholas looked at him strangely, and then, in a hushed voice, said with resignation, "Do you think it might have been avoided?"[45]

At ten in the evening of 18 March, Count Benckendorff knocked on the door to the tsarina's boudoir. He told Alexandra that a group of revolutionaries were on their way to the Alexander Palace, most likely to arrest her. Quickly, she dressed and waited for their arrival.

The revolutionaries turned out to be Guchkov and Gen. Lavr Kornilov, along with a handful of members of the Revolutionary Council at Tsarskoe Selo. They inquired after the tsarina's health and asked if she needed anything special. The thought that a group of men might burst into the palace at any time and confiscate her personal things preyed on Alexandra's mind. On Nicholas's advice, she began the monumental task of destroying her private papers and correspondence.

On a cold late-winter day, with snow still fresh on the ground, Alexandra stood in the Red Drawing Room before a raging fire burning in the fireplace. On a table next to her stood stacks of papers—letters from her father, brother, sisters, friends, cousins. One by one, she set each on the glowing coals—memories of her first two visits to Russia, holidays with Queen Victoria at Osborne, Balmoral, and Windsor, summer-engagement days with Nicholas, her hopes and fears as a wife and mother—all devoured by the orange flames. Into the fire went all of the letters from Queen Victoria. The carefully tied bundles disappeared into the leaping flames. Alexandra stood by the fireplace, clutching the last boxes, the letters from her husband. The only letters she did not destroy were those written during the period of the First World War, fearing that they might be necessary should she or the tsar be accused of treason. She opened the boxes and began to reread the letters, sobbing now and then, tossing page after page into the roaring inferno, watching the paper glow red for a moment before disappearing into white ash.[46]

General Kornilov returned to the Alexander Palace on 21 March, this time to arrest the tsarina. Alexandra received him in the Green Drawing Room. She wore her nurse's uniform and stood silent, not offering her hand in greeting when Kornilov entered the room.[47] Kornilov explained that the arrest protected the tsarina from the angry mobs in St. Petersburg and that the tsar had also been arrested. He would return the following morning. From Kornilov, Alexandra learned that her brother-in-law Michael had rejected the throne, ending the Romanov dynasty. As soon as the plans could be finalized, Kornilov said, the imperial family would be exiled to England. When Kornilov stood to leave, Alexandra took both his hands in hers. The general left the Alexander Palace with tears in his eyes.[48]

"The Tsar is coming back tomorrow," Alexandra said to Pierre Gilliard. "Alexei must be told everything. Will you do it? I am going to tell the girls myself."[49] Dutifully, Gilliard went to the tsarevich's room. Quietly, he began to explain to the little boy that his father would return from headquarters the next morning and that he would not be going back.

"Why?" Alexei said.

"Your father does not want to be commander-in-chief anymore," Gilliard explained.

Alexei said nothing for a few minutes. He looked at Gilliard curiously, waiting for some explanation.

"You know your father does not want to be tsar anymore, Alexei Nicholaievich."

"What! Why?"

"He is very tired and has had a lot of trouble lately," Gilliard said.

"Oh, yes. Mother told me that they had stopped his train when he wanted to come here. But won't Papa be the tsar again afterwards?"

Gilliard then told the tsarevich that his father had abdicated for him in favor of his Uncle Michael. It seemed that Uncle Misha did not want to be the tsar either.

"But who's going to be tsar, then?" Alexei asked.

"I don't know," Gilliard told him. "Perhaps nobody now. . . ."[50]

Alexandra told her daughters that their father had abdicated and that they were now prisoners of a new government. Marie, who already knew, had to fill in the gaps in her mother's story when Alexandra broke down, unable to continue. To make things worse, Tatiana was temporarily deaf as a result of her illness, and the tsarina had to write down the details so that she would understand.

The night sky over Tsarskoe Selo was clear, a full moon shining over the white landscape. The doors to the Alexander Palace had been sealed off and revolutionary guards posted to prevent the prisoners from escaping. Lili Dehn slept in the Mauve Boudoir that night, to be closer to the tsarina. A fire burned in the grate as Lili piled sheets and blankets onto the tsarina's chaise longue. Alexandra stood by watching, her long golden hair unbound and brushed out, wrapped in a loose silk dressing gown. She smiled at her friend's feeble efforts.

"Oh, Lili, you Russian ladies don't know how to be useful," Alexandra said. "When I was a girl my grandmother, Queen Victoria, showed me how to make a bed. I'll teach you." After the lights had been extinguished, the boudoir was flooded with moonlight. Lili lay on the couch, tossing and turning, listening to the tsarina coughing in the bedroom next door.[51] Outside, the wind whistled on mournfully, broken only by the sound of shots ringing out in the park as the new soldiers killed the tame deer the children had kept as pets.

PART FIVE

Alexandra Romanova

(1917–18)

39

Prisoners

NEARLY A QUARTER OF A CENTURY earlier Alexandra had become tsarina of Russia, much against the wishes of her grandmother, Queen Victoria, who feared that the throne of the Romanovs was too unstable for her granddaughter to marry its handsome young heir. The Revolution proved the aged queen correct. Alexandra lost all of the power and prestige she had ever known, abruptly swept away in the bitter cold of the Russian spring.

Deprived of her titles, Alexandra became a woman without a sense of identity. She had always taken from her surroundings her strength and sense of purpose, whether at Darmstadt, London, or St. Petersburg. The associations became less clear; the German titles meant nothing during the war, and now her only other name, that of empress of Russia, had vanished. She was simply Alexandra Feodorovna Romanova, the wife of an ex-tsar.

The change in position was hard for Alexandra to accept. Nicholas was so overwhelmed with humiliation on returning home after the abdication that he broke down, falling into Alexandra's arms and crying like a child.[1] Following their arrest, they were confined to a wing of the Alexander Palace, guarded by revolutionary soldiers, who were filled with contempt for the imperial family.

Public hatred of the Romanovs, and particularly of the tsarina, reached a fever pitch following the Revolution. St. Petersburg devoured stories of "Alexandra the German" and her "lover" Rasputin. The dirty pictures of the tsarina and her friend which had formerly been chalked upon the walls of the city's buildings now found a home in the pages of the capital's newspapers. One cartoon showed the tsarina bathing in a tub filled with blood and saying, "If Nicky killed a few more of these revolutionaries I could have such a bath more often."[2]

On a warm spring day in April 1917, Alexandra stood in the Red Drawing Room, tense, proud, and anxious, waiting, listening, for the click of heels against the marble of the hallway floor beyond the polished doors. Alexander Kerensky, the new minister of justice in the provisional government, had declared his intention of questioning the tsarina about her "treasonous activities" during the war.

Alexandra could only speculate on what might happen to her. Although she had destroyed most of her private papers and correspondence to preserve the sanctity of her private life, Kerensky might well accuse her of trying to hide evidence of her treason. The minister of justice also wanted to question the tsar, who sat beside his wife, waiting and smoking.

Suddenly, the doors opened. Count Benckendorff stepped into the room and announced, "His Majesty bids you welcome." Kerensky, dressed in a blue shirt with no collar or cuffs and worn buttoned up to the neck, stumbled forward, his big workman's boots pounding on the floor.[3] The minister, beside himself with "feverish agitation," strode up to the tsar, put forth his hand, and said, "Kerensky."[4] Nicholas greeted the man like an old school chum, but Alexandra was less certain. Slowly and deliberately, she put out her hand to receive Kerensky, but their fingers parted at the slightest touch.[5]

Kerensky ran about the palace, opening doors and looking into rooms, searching through desk drawers, crawling on his knees to check underneath the furniture, grabbing objects from the tables and playing with them.[6] He declared that Nicholas would have to live apart from his wife while the investigation proceeded. The tsar, confined to a separate wing of the palace, could only see his wife at mealtimes, and then only if an officer of the guard was present and all conversation took place in Russian.

The investigation took eighteen days. When questioning the tsar about the government, Kerensky mentioned that the tsarina might have to be put on public trial. Nicholas's only reply was "Oh, well, I don't think Alix is really involved. . . . Have you any proof?"

"I don't know," Kerensky said. "Not yet."[7] Nor would he find any. Kerensky questioned Alexandra about her life in Russia as tsarina, her dealings in politics, and Rasputin's role in the government. Alexandra replied honestly to his inquiries, saying that she and Nicholas were very open in their marriage and that because of this they had no secrets from each other. Politics played such an enormous role in her life because she and her husband often discussed situations when they arose and Alexandra wished to be of help to the tsar, who had so many problems to worry himself over. As for Rasputin, the tsarina answered that she had listened to his advice because he had been a man of God, humble and innocent, who had only tried to help preserve her husband's rights. Kerensky accepted these answers; he did not argue with the tsarina over Rasputin, realizing that this was her own perception of the man. When he had finished his investigation, he declared the tsarina innocent of the allegations of treason and told the tsar, "Your wife does not lie."[8]

Before he left the Alexander Palace, Kerensky wandered to the sickroom where Anna Vyrubova and Lili Dehn were resting. When Anna heard the sound of a strange voice in the hallway, she whispered, "They are coming!" to Lili, at the same time pulling the sheet from the bed over her head. Suddenly, the door "flew open" and soon "the room seemed to fill up with men." Kerensky—"a small, clean-shaven, theatrical person"—walked up to Anna, who peeked nervously over the top of her sheet. "I am the Minister of Justice," Kerensky announced to her. "You are to dress and go at once to Petrograd." Anna continued to lie on the bed, terrified; Kerensky commanded one of his men to go and fetch Dr. Botkin. When the doctor arrived, Kerensky asked him if Anna could leave in her condition. Botkin said yes, suffering, according to Anna, from "craven fear."[9]

Baroness Buxhoeveden believed that Anna had to be removed, as "her presence in the palace had been a source of constant anxiety to the Household, on the Empress's account; for the soldiers not only openly attacked her but coupled the Empress's name with hers, and were continually threatening to murder first Madame Vyrubova and then the Empress."[10] Alexandra did not share her lady-in-waiting's view. When she learned what had happened, she called Botkin to the boudoir.

"How can you?" she cried out, pacing back and forth. "How can you? You—who have children of your own!" But Kerensky's decision stood, and Anna had only enough time to pack a few belongings before she had to leave.

Alexandra waited in the portrait gallery to say good-bye to her friend. Anna hobbled into the room on her crutches, crying. Alexandra rushed forward and held her. Tatiana, also in tears, asked Anna if she could have a small gift to remember her by. Anna gave her the only thing that she had—her wedding ring. As Anna left the palace, she saw Alexandra standing in the doorway, pointing upward and saying, "There we are always together."[11]

Kerensky had also told Lili Dehn to leave the palace that same day. Alexandra forced herself to smile, then told her friend, "Lili, by suffering we are purified for heaven. This goodbye means little. We shall meet again in another world."[12] Lili climbed into the same motorcar with Anna, and they sped away over the drive. Alexandra ran back through the palace to the nursery on the second floor and pressed her face against the glass of the panes, watching the motorcar follow the curve of the drive. Lili and Anna gazed out from the rear window, waving good-bye to the tsarina until the car disappeared into the darkness of the storm raging outside.

Life as a prisoner of the provisional government bore no relation to the daily existence Alexandra had grown to know. Confined to the Alexander Palace, Alexandra spent most of each day lying on a chaise in her boudoir, her mind lost in the past, turning over, endlessly, the decisions she had made and encouraged her husband to make. Had everything been a mistake? As the days became weeks and the weeks months, Alexandra began to understand that her role in Russian politics had helped to bring her husband down. The weight of this agonizing knowledge crushed her spirit. For a quarter of a century she had fought against those who opposed her—the dowager empress, the Duma, Stolypin, Nikolasha, Rasputin's enemies, even her own husband. Now she could fight no longer; there was nothing left to fight for. Deprived of her political role and her nursing work, Alexandra gave herself over to a dangerous fatalistic belief. Although she retained the belief that the majority of Russians remained faithful to the imperial family, Alexandra felt certain that she and her husband were bound to pay for the previous sins of the Romanov dynasty. As such, her thoughts turned toward what she believed to be their impending martyrdom.

Her daily life reminded Alexandra of her new position in the most unsavory ways. The provisional government declared fruit a "luxury that prisoners could not be allowed." The tsarina could no longer fill her rooms with fresh bunches of roses and lilacs, since the hothouses at Tsarskoe Selo had been abandoned. When a maid brought her a branch of lilac from the garden, Alexandra was so overwhelmed that she wept with happiness.[13]

Security surrounding the imperial family ensured that they had no contact with the outside. They were more closely guarded as prisoners than they had been as a ruling family. Only members of the household and suite could make telephone calls, and they had to use a central telephone in the guardroom. Everything entering or leaving the Alexander Palace went through a thorough examination. Tubes of toothpaste were ripped apart, chocolates bitten into pieces, and containers of yogurt prodded with soiled fingers.[14]

Alexandra rarely heard news of her friends. Lili had been released when she arrived in the capital, but Anna sat in prison at the Fortress of Peter and Paul. Most of the suite had left the palace. Those who remained looked like "the survivors of a shipwreck." There were two ladies-in-waiting, Baroness Buxhoeveden and Countess Anastasia Hendrikov; Count Benckendorff and his wife; Count Fredericks; Prince Vassili Dolgoruky; two aides-de-camp; three tutors, Mademoiselle Schneider, Pierre Gilliard, and Charles Gibbes; two doctors, Botkin and Fedorov; and, from the household, two valets; ten footmen; a dozen chambermaids; several nurses; secretaries; cooks, and houseboys.[15] When the children were well enough, their school lessons began again. Gilliard taught French; Mr. Gibbes, English; Mademoiselle Schneider, arithmetic; Countess Hendrikov, art; Baroness Buxhoeveden, music; Nicholas, history and geography; and Alexandra, religion.

The men who guarded the imperial family bordered on the absurd. Once, Baroness Buxhoeveden and Grand Duchess Tatiana happened upon one of the guards on duty in front of the palace. He had evidently tired of standing, for he sat in a gilt armchair from the palace, a footstool beneath his feet, propped up by sofa cushions and reading the newspaper, his rifle lying discarded at his feet.[16] On another occasion, Nicholas greeted his wife one morning with an amusing story. "When I got up," he explained, "I put my dressing gown on and looked through the window. . . . The sentinel who was usually stationed there was now sitting on the steps—his rifle had slipped out of his hand—he was asleep! I called my valet and showed him the unusual sight, as I couldn't help laughing—it was really absurd. At the sound of my laughter the soldier awoke . . . he scowled at us and we withdrew."[17]

The guards were also a nuisance. They shot and killed not only the tame deer but also the swans from the lakes. One guard deliberately stationed himself directly in front of Alexandra's dressing-room window. When she went to dress, Alexandra did so behind a Chinese screen as the guard would not allow her to close the curtains at the window.[18]

Although Alexandra suffered from depression, those around her did all they could to cheer her up. Once, Baroness Buxhoeveden showed her a letter she had received—addressed to "the Ex-Baroness Buxhoeveden, the Ex-Lady-in-Waiting to the Ex-Empress."[19] Alexandra laughed, and Nicholas picked up on the idea. It became a private joke within the household. "Don't call me an Empress anymore," Alexandra would say. "I'm only an ex."[20]

But the situation was far too serious for anyone to pretend that the imperial family was free to joke about their captivity. The St. Petersburg Soviet repeatedly insisted on their imprisonment in the Fortress of Peter and Paul. Kerensky, although not hostile to the Romanovs, had to fight for the very survival of his own government. As a prisoner of the provisional government, Alexandra could not even leave her own palace. Her friends had been taken away. She could not even turn to Rasputin. The night the tsar returned to Tsarskoe Selo from headquarters, a group of soldiers had found Rasputin's grave. Shortly after midnight, they dug up the coffin. By torchlight the men pried the lid up from the coffin. Rasputin's face had turned black, and he smelled horribly.[21] The soldiers loaded the corpse onto a truck and drove it to the Pargolovo Forest. They drenched the rotting body with gasoline, then set it on fire.

For six hours the corpse burned; by twilight a wind swept up the ashes and carried them away. Rasputin had predicted that after his death his body would not be left in peace but destroyed and his ashes cast to the wind.[22] The breeze wailing mournfully through the Pargolovo Forest in the pale March light proved him correct.

In May 1917, Col. Eugene Kobylinsky became the new commander of the Revolutionary Guard at Tsarskoe Selo. Kobylinsky bore no grudges toward the tsar or his family and allowed them access to the garden of the Alexander Palace for two days a week.

This minor coup represented a considerable triumph. The imperial family had begged to be allowed out into their garden for any length of time. Kobylinsky had even secured permission for the family to begin a garden in a corner of the park. There were, however, still difficulties. Alexandra followed her family out into the garden in her wheelchair; the soldiers complained about this, often insisting that she walk along with her husband and children. Even though permission had been granted, there were long delays in unlocking the main door to the Alexander Palace.[23] Crowds, hearing that the imperial family was exercising, lined the railings of the iron fence surrounding the imperial park. They waved and shouted at the children, hissed and spat when they saw the tsarina or her husband.

The harassment continued on through the two-hour exercise session. Once, Nicholas strolled about the park, only to be stopped by a group of six soldiers armed with rifles. "You can't go there, Mr. Colonel," one of the men said. The tsar began to turn, only to be pushed by another guard. "We don't permit you to walk in that direction, Mr. Colonel," the guard told the tsar. Forced into a confrontation, the tsar stood silent, only to be pushed back with rifle butts. "Stand back when you are commanded, Mr. Colonel," a third guard spat out. Nicholas looked from one guard to another, then slowly walked away.[24] Even so, he remained friendly to all. "Good morning," he said to one soldier, holding out his hand.

"Not for anything in the world," the soldier replied.

"But, my dear fellow, why?" the tsar asked. "What have you got against me?"[25] The animosity often took a physical form. As the tsar rode a bicycle along a path one day, a group of soldiers lunged forth and one of them thrust a bayonet between the spokes. Nicholas fell over into the mud, and the soldiers laughed; but the tsar merely got up and walked away.[26]

The children found this treatment hard to accept. The girls tried to stay occupied, carrying away mounds of earth from the garden and planting rows of vegetables under the inquisitive eyes of their jailors.

But Alexei took the humiliation personally. His father had gone from great respect to shame and degradation. Even the tsarevich could not escape the mistrust and resentment surrounding his parents. Once, he was playing with a toy rifle when a guard spotted it and shouted, "They are armed!" Alexei ran to his mother, but soon several men arrived and demanded "the weapon." Gilliard tried to explain its true nature, but the men would have none of this. They seized the rifle and walked away. When Kobylinsky learned of the incident, he took the gun apart and smuggled it, piece by piece, back to the boy.[27] His sailor Derevenko had deserted to the Revolution. One day, he simply decided he would serve no more. He sprawled in a chair and barked out orders to his charge, telling the tsarevich to bring him trivial objects. Confused by this, the tsarevich wandered around the room, trying to please the man until someone came to his rescue.[28]

Curiosity about the tsarina caused soldiers to follow her about the garden, mocking her and calling out names. Alexandra usually sat on a rug beneath a tree, away from the prying eyes. Once, when Baroness Buxhoeveden walked away temporarily, one of the guards ran up to the rug and sat down next to the tsarina. Baroness Buxhoeveden protested, but the man replied that "*now* it was turn about." The baroness looked to the tsarina, but Alexandra, fearful that if she protested the entire family would be forced back inside the Alexander Palace, gestured to her lady-in-waiting to remain silent. Alexandra edged away from the soldier, but he moved closer. He accused the tsarina of "despising" the people, saying that she did not care to meet ordinary Russians and that she hated her adopted country. Alexandra gently explained that in the first ten years of her marriage she had given birth to five children and that this had prevented her from traveling about. The soldier seemed to accept this and began to grow less hostile. He asked the tsarina about her life in Germany as a girl, hinting that she might have sympathies with the kaiser's army. Alexandra replied that she had been a German in her youth but had married a Russian. Her children were Russians, and she herself felt wholeheartedly Russian. An officer of the guard had been fetched by Baroness Buxhoeveden. He arrived just as the soldier rose from the rug. The man took hold of the tsarina's hand and said, "Do you know, Alexandra Feodorovna, I had quite a different idea of you? I was mistaken about you." Later, Alexandra learned that the soldier had been a Soviet deputy.[29]

Despite the sometimes pleasant surprises, Alexandra waited anxiously for news of her family's fate. As Kerensky had found her and her husband innocent of all charges of treason, Alexandra did not fear a trial. But the St. Petersburg Soviet openly called for their imprisonment in the Fortress of Peter and Paul, and Alexandra never knew from one day to the next where she might end up. Her hopes and thoughts centered on England. She heard rumors of an English exile, and this fueled her spirits. But day after day slipped into the tedium of prison life, and the imperial family had no word. They did not know that in London King George V had washed his hands of his Romanov cousins.

40

Royal Betrayal

KING GEORGE V OF GREAT BRITAIN had been born a member of the royal House of Saxe-Coburg-Gotha, the minor German state Prince Albert had called home. Queen Victoria's son and King George V's father, Edward VII, married the Danish princess Alexandra, whose father had, in fact, been a German prince before his ascension to the throne of Denmark. George V's own wife, Queen Mary, had a German father, a prince of the House of Teck. Of George V's twenty-six cousins on his father's side, half were German. Much as Alexandra found herself the victim of rumor concerning her loyalty during the war, so her Cousin Georgie had to grapple with appeasement of public hostility. Pressure from the cabinet and the general public had caused him to accept the resignation of his cousin Prince Louis of Battenberg as first sea lord of the British admiralty merely because the poor man had a German name. In the summer of 1917, King George V bowed to the hysteria and with a flourish swept away the German trappings from the British royal family: the duke of Teck became the marquess of Cambridge, the Battenbergs called themselves the Mountbattens, and the House of Saxe-Coburg-Gotha was rechristened the House of Windsor.

As a constitutional monarch, King George V had but three real powers: "the right to be consulted, the right to encourage and the right to warn," in the words of the nineteenth-century writer Walter Bagehot. Real power lay in the hands of his prime minister, David Lloyd George, the militant Welshman whose liberal views often clashed with those of the king. When Tsar Nicholas II abdicated on 15 March 1917, Lloyd George excitedly cabled the new provisional government:

> It is with sentiments of the profoundest satisfaction that the
> people of Great Britain . . . have learned that their great ally
> Russia now stands with the nations which base their institutions
> upon responsible government. . . . We believe that the Revolution

is the greatest service which they have yet made to the cause for
which the Allied peoples have been fighting since August 1914. It
reveals the fundamental truth that this war is at bottom a struggle
for popular government as well as for liberty.[1]

Lloyd George touched a raw nerve. The Russian Revolution captured
the imagination of the British public, and the idea of a similiar happening on their own shores prompted speculation as to the future of the
royal family. In a letter to *The (London) Times*, H. G. Wells wrote that
"the time has come to rid ourselves of the ancient trappings of throne
and sceptre."[2] Against this volatile background King George V pondered the fate of his Russian cousins.

When he first learned of the tsar's abdication, George dispatched
a telegram to Nicholas: "Events of last week have deeply distressed me.
My thoughts are constantly with you and I shall always remain your
true and devoted friend, as you know I always have been in the past."[3]
The provisional government believed the message too politically sensitive, but the British embassy actually ordered that it not be delivered.
King George, in consultation with Lloyd George, had decided that the
cable might be too easily misunderstood as an invitation of asylum.
This the king wished to avoid.[4]

The War Office in London sought the advice of a General Waters,
who had been a British military attaché in St. Petersburg. Waters declared that "if a fast torpedo boat and a few bags of British sovereigns
should be promptly dispatched to the Gulf of Finland," the rescue
should be easy to accomplish.[5]

Sir George Buchanan, the British ambassador in St. Petersburg,
wrote, on 19 March, to the Foreign Office in London, informing them of
a talk he had with Paul Miliukov, the new foreign minister in the provisional government: ". . . the Emperor . . . had requested the government to allow him to go to Tsarskoe Selo and to remain there till his children had recovered from measles and subsequently to proceed to Port
Romanov. His excellency gave me to understand that this permission
would be granted and asked me whether I knew if arrangements were
being made for H. M. to go to England."[6]

The following day, Miliukov again saw Buchanan and pressed for
the imminent removal of the imperial family. "It's the last chance of securing these poor unfortunates' freedom and perhaps of saving their
lives," Miliukov declared.[7]

This report worried the Foreign Office. They wrote back to
Buchanan asking if Switzerland or Denmark might be suggested rather
than England. Miliukov would have none of this; according to
Buchanan, he became "most anxious" and asked if ". . . the King and

His Majesty's government would not at once offer the Emperor asylum in England."[8]

The British government now had to decide what to do. Lloyd George summoned the chancellor of the exchequer, Andrew Bonar Law; the King's private secretary, Lord Stamfordham; and the undersecretary at the Foreign Office, Lord Hardinge, to a late-night meeting at No. 10 Downing Street. These men, and not the king, made the decision to offer formal asylum to the imperial family.

The next day, Sir George Buchanan received the cable announcing the news: "In order to meet the request made by the Russian Government the King and His Majesty's Government readily offer asylum to the Emperor and Empress in England which it is hoped they will take advantage of during the war."[9]

They also sent Buchanan a personal telegram: "In order to avoid any possible doubt in the future as to the reason for asylum being given . . . you should emphasize the fact that the offer made has been entirely due to the initiative of the Russian Government."[10]

Buchanan told Miliukov of the British government's decision. He also relayed a message that once the imperial family took up residence in England, their royal cousin would not be willing to support them. Miliukov replied that the tsar would be able to support his family with his own funds and that the provisional government would supplement this.

Kerensky and Miliukov had been working on the removal of the imperial family when the offer of asylum arrived. By this time they knew that the kaiser had ordered that any British warship coming through the Baltic to take his cousins away should under no circumstance be attacked or hindered.[11]

In London, however, King George reconsidered his government's offer. With the last of his three powers—the right to warn—the king began to exert all of his weight to change the prime minister's mind. Beginning on 30 March, he corresponded regularly over the matter by way of his private secretary, Lord Stamfordham:

> The King has been thinking much about the Government's proposal that the Emperor Nicholas and his family should come to England. As you are doubtless aware, the King has a strong personal friendship for the Emperor, and therefore would be glad to do anything to help him in this case. But His Majesty cannot help doubting, not only on account of the dangers of the voyage, but on general grounds of expediency, whether it is advisable that the Imperial Family should take up residence in this country. The King would be glad if you could consult the Prime Minister,

as His Majesty understands no definite decision has yet been come to on the subject by the Russian Government.[12]

The letter went to Arthur Balfour, the foreign secretary. He quickly replied: "His Majesty's ministers quite realize the difficulties to which you refer in your letter, but they do not think, unless the position changes, that it is now possible to withdraw the invitation which has been sent, and they therefore trust that the King will consent to adhere to the original invitation which was sent on the advice of His Majesty's ministers."[13]

Several days later, the king received two letters from members of the House of Lords, each expressing doubts about allowing the imperial family to come to England. On 6 April, Stamfordham again wrote to Balfour:

> Each day the King is becoming more concerned about the question of the Emperor and Empress coming to this country. His Majesty receives letters from people in all classes of life, known or unknown to him, saying how much the matter is being discussed, not only in clubs, but by working men, and the Labour Members in the House of Commons are expressing adverse opinions to the proposal. As you know, from the first, the King has thought the presence of the Imperial Family (especially of the Empress) in this country would raise all sorts of difficulties, and I feel sure that you appreciate how awkward it will be for our Royal Family who are closely connected both with the Emperor and the Empress. You probably also are aware that the subject has become more or less public property, and that people are either assuming that it was initiated by the King, or depreciating the very unfair position in which His Majesty will be placed if the arrangement is carried out. The King desires me to ask you whether after consulting the Prime minister, Sir George Buchanan should not be communicated with, with a view to approaching the Russian Government to make some other plan for the future residence of Their Imperial Majesties.
>
> Yours very truly,
Stamfordham.
>
> P.S. Most people appear to think the invitation was initiated by the King whereas it was his government who did so.[14]

The thought that his cousins might be granted British asylum weighed so heavily on the king's mind that he ordered Stamfordham to dispatch a second letter that very same day:

The King wishes me to write again on the subject of my letter this morning. He must beg you to represent to the Prime Minister that from all he hears and reads in the press, the residence in this country of the ex-Emperor and Empress would be strongly resented by the people, and would certainly compromise the position of the King and Queen. . . . Buchanan ought to be instructed to tell Miliukov that the opposition to the Emperor and Empress coming here is so strong that we must be allowed to withdraw from the consent which was previously given to the Russian Government's proposal.[15]

Of course, the only real opposition to the Romanovs' coming to England came from King George V himself. Fear over his own position had pushed the king into this callous stance. In his mind Alexandra and Nicholas posed a threat to the stability of his own throne. But the threat existed only in the king's mind. Balfour sent the two letters to the secretary of the cabinet and added, "Perhaps we may have to suggest Spain or the South of France as a more suitable residence than England for the Tsar."[16] King George asked Balfour to have the cabinet avoid all references to himself if possible, as he did not wish to have his royal name dragged through the political mud of the asylum question. Lloyd George briefed the cabinet and told Buchanan not to mention the subject of the imperial family or their asylum. The Foreign Office also sent along a new message to the provisional government: "His Majesty's Government does not insist on its former offer of hospitality to the Imperial Family."[17]

Buchanan suggested France might be the wiser choice. At the same time, Lord Hardinge wrote to Lord Frances Bertie, the British ambassador in Paris, suggesting the idea of a French exile. Bertie replied:

My dear Charlie:
I do not think that the ex-Emperor and his family would be welcome in France. The Empress is not only a Boche by birth but in sentiment. She did all she could to bring about an understanding with Germany. She is regarded as a criminal or a criminal lunatic, and the Emperor as a criminal from his weakness and submission to her promptings.
Yours ever,
Bertie.[18]

This letter, filled with vicious lies against Alexandra, sealed official British involvement in the Romanov asylum. King George had done all he could to see to it that Alexandra and Nicholas never set foot in his country.

In May, Buchanan told Miliukov that "... we should probably refuse permission to any member of the imperial family to reside in England during the war."[19] The provisional government, however, still had hopes of sending the imperial family to England.

> [We] inquired of Sir George Buchanan as to when a cruiser could be sent to take on board the deposed ruler and his family [wrote Kerensky]. ... I do not remember exactly whether it was late in June or early July when the British ambassador called, greatly distressed. ... With tears in his eyes, scarcely able to control his emotions, Sir George informed the Russian minister of Foreign Affairs of the British Government's final refusal to give refuge to the former Emperor of Russia. I cannot quote the exact text of the letter which Sir George read out ... but I can say quite definitely that this refusal was due exclusively to consideration of internal British politics.[20]

When Kerensky published his account, both Lloyd George and Sir George Buchanan quickly denounced it as a lie. They insisted that the offer of British asylum had never been withdrawn but that the imperial family had not left Russia due to the provisional government's inability to control its internal situation. In 1932, Meriel Buchanan, the ambassador's daughter, cleared up the situation: She admitted that her father had lied and falsified his memoirs to protect the British government. He had no choice, because the Foreign Office threatened to cut off his pension.[21]

The role of the king faded into bureaucratic oblivion, filed away with papers, dispatches, and cables into the records of the Foreign Office. But those closest to the king knew the truth. In April 1917, Sir Clive Wigram, assistant secretary to the king, wrote to Sir William Lambton:

> You have probably heard rumours of the Emperor and Empress of Russia, together with many Grand Dukes, coming to England to find asylum here. Of course the King has been accused of trying to work this for his royal friends. As a matter of fact His Majesty has been opposed to this proposal from the start, and has begged his ministers to knock it on the head. I do not expect that these Russian royalties will come, but if they do their presence here will be due to the War Cabinet and not to His Majesty.[22]

In the end no one wanted to place the blame for the refusal on the king, even though it clearly originated with him. After the imperial family was murdered, when it became obvious that the king's decision had paved the way for his cousins' deaths, George V's role in the affair was hotly denied by everyone involved. "I understand . . . that Mr. Lloyd George was not responsible for the decision, but that it is not expedient to say who was. . . ." wrote one insider.[23] Speaking in 1971, the late Lord Mountbatten, son of Alexandra's sister Victoria, commented on the king's actions, saying, "He discussed it with my mother, he was very anxious to offer them asylum over here, but the Government, the Prime Minister, Lloyd George, was understandably opposed on political grounds at that time of the war, and I think it would have been very difficult therefore to go against him. . . ."[24]

The king's role in the refusal of his government to grant asylum to his cousins remains a taint on the royal family that time will not erase. Perhaps the king learned his lesson in the spring of 1917, for he showed no hesitation in sending off a ship to rescue the Greek royal family in 1922. This action most probably saved the Greek royal family from a fate similiar to that of the Romanovs. Because of this royal action, six-month-old Prince Philip escaped to live in England. In 1947 he married the future Queen Elizabeth II.

41

Exile

"THE BOLSHEVIKS ARE AFTER ME," Kerensky told the tsar, "and then will be after you."[1] Fifteen miles north of Tsarskoe Selo, in the marble halls of the Tauride Palace, the Soviets argued among themselves. They wanted to storm the Alexander Palace and execute the imperial family. Kerensky had to fight them off, at the same time preventing members of his own provisional government from putting the tsar and tsarina on public trial. After months of negotiations with the British government, King George V had refused to allow his relatives asylum in his country. With each day the threat to the imperial family's safety grew.

Alexandra hoped for an exile to Livadia. But the move presented too many problems for Kerensky. The train journey would take the imperial family through rural central Russia, where nearly the entire peasant population was in revolt, burning country houses and villages. After some deliberation, Kerensky later wrote, he chose Tobolsk, a small river town on the Tobol and Irtysh river junctions in Siberia.

> Certain royalists [wrote Kerensky] have asserted . . . that the only reason for this choice was our wish to "pay the Tsar in his own coin"—to send him to Siberia, where he used to send the revolutionaries in days gone by. But Tobolsk could be reached by the northern route, without crossing any thickly populated districts. And as for vengeance—why, there was no need to make complicated arrangements for a journey to Tobolsk: we had the Fortress of Peter and Paul within easy reach; or better still, Kronstadt. The reason why I chose Tobolsk was because it was an out and backwater . . . had a very small garrison, no individual proletariat, and a population which was prosperous and contented, not to say old fashioned. In addition, I happened to know that the climate in Tobolsk was excellent in winter, and that the town could boast a very passable Governor's Residence . . .

where the Imperial Family could live with some measure of comfort.[2]

This may not be true. Kerensky's decision to send the imperial family to Siberia does not make sense. If he wanted to move the Romanovs out of the country, as he wrote, why would he move them only as far as Tobolsk? Clearly he had no interest in keeping them in internal exile. The continued presence of the imperial family in Russia could only cause his government further problems. He undertook intense negotiations with the British government to try to obtain permission for a foreign exile. If they were going on a "safe" railway line to Tobolsk, then why not go any farther? The risks of moving the imperial family out of the country would be small compared with those of keeping them in a safe internal exile.

There are indications that this is exactly what Kerensky intended. When the imperial family left Tsarskoe Selo for Siberia, their train carried a placard reading "Japanese Red Cross Mission" and bore two Japanese flags. Such a train could pass through Siberia and on into Manchuria without any great risk. It is entirely possible that Kerensky intended to move the family out of the country on this train and that the Bolsheviks discovered this while the train was en route, forcing it to stop at Tiumen. In view of Kerensky's attitude and the fact that when the imperial family arrived in Tobolsk they had to wait a week while the governor's mansion was fitted up, this explanation is entirely possible.

On 11 August, Nicholas told Alexandra that they would be leaving Tsarskoe Selo for an unknown destination within a few days. That same day, Kerensky had told the tsar that the women should take with them warm clothing and their furs. Alexandra quickly guessed that their new residence would not be Livadia.

The following day, Alexei turned thirteen. He spent his birthday packing up his belongings for the journey. Alexandra wandered through the deserted rooms of the Alexander Palace; curtains had been drawn across the tall windows and the furniture covered with dust sheets. The tsarina emptied the contents of her wardrobes onto her dressing-room floor. She made two piles of dresses, a small one for herself to take into exile and a larger one to be given to help centers for refugees and war victims.[3] Her steamer trunks filled the Portrait Gallery, holding photographs and paintings, rugs, furniture, and linens for their new home.

Few of the household and staff accompanied the imperial family into exile: Countess Hendrikov and Prince Dolgoruky as lady- and gentleman-in-waiting; Gen. Ilya Tatishchev as marshal of the imperial court, replacing Benckendorff, who remained behind due to his wife's ill health; Dr. Botkin and his two children, Gleb and Tatiana; Dr. Derevenko; Pierre Gilliard, and Mademoiselle Schneider as tutors; and, from the staff, two valets, ten footmen, six chambermaids, three cooks, a butler, a wine steward, four kitchen assistants, a clerk, a nurse, a barber, a secretary, and 330 soldiers of the guard.[4] Baroness Buxhoeveden and the tutor Gibbes later joined the imperial family in Tobolsk.

The departure had been set for 1:30 A.M. on the morning of 14 August 1917. Kerensky spoke to the soldiers a few hours before the train arrived. "Remember, no hitting a man when he is down," Kerensky told them. "Behave like gentlemen, not like cads. Remember that he is a former Emperor and that neither he nor his family must suffer any hardships."[5] Kerensky placed Colonel Kobylinsky in charge of the operation and left him with a document stating, "Colonel Kobylinsky's orders are to be obeyed as if they were my own. Alexander Kerensky."[6]

Alexandra dressed in a traveling suit and went to the Portrait Gallery to wait for their departure. Alexei wandered about in excitement, but the stress was too much for the tsarina; Kerensky found her sitting in a corner, weeping.[7] But Kerensky had his own worries: by 1:30 A.M., the Tsarskoe Selo railway station still stood empty. The train for the imperial family had not yet been dispatched. Two o'clock passed, then three, and four and five. Suddenly, Kerensky rushed into the Portrait Gallery and announced that the train was waiting at the station.

At five-thirty, a group of motorcars pulled into the driveway and up to the front of the Alexander Palace and sounded their horns. The French doors opened, and the luggage was loaded. Alexandra walked through the doors, down the stairs, and climbed into one of the vehicles. Her husband sat next to her; the children, the household, and staff followed. Above, the sky had turned a brilliant pink, and the first rays of the morning sun were already slanting through the tops of the pine trees. Alexandra pressed her face to the motorcar's window and watched as the Alexander Palace shrunk away in the distance of the pearl-colored morning light.

The journey to Siberia took a week. The imperial family traveled on a train of comfortable wagon-lits cars; the dining car had been well stocked with wines from the imperial cellars. The days passed endlessly. They ate breakfast at eight, coffee at ten, luncheon at one, tea at five, and dinner at eight. Each night, the train came to a stop beside a stretch of water or a grove of trees so that the tsar and his children could walk the two dogs they had brought with them—Alexei's King Charles spaniel, Joy, and Tatiana's little spaniel, Jimmy. Alexandra sat by the windows, watching her husband and children; she never left the train.

On the third day of the trip the train crossed the Urals into Siberia, and the air grew cooler. The next morning, it came to a stop at Tiumen, at the junction of the Tura and Tobol rivers. The imperial family boarded the steamer *Russ*, which sat at dock, and they slowly steamed up the river to Tobolsk. On the way, the *Russ* sailed past Pokrovskoe, Rasputin's village. Alexandra stood on deck watching; Rasputin's two-story house towered over the simple peasant huts in the rest of the town. Rasputin had told Alexandra that one day she would gaze upon his humble village with her own eyes.[8]

Finally, the *Russ* sailed around a bend in the river and came into view of Tobolsk just as the sun set. A fortress high on a crag dominated the town of twenty thousand, spreading out along dusty, unpaved streets lined with log houses, stone buildings, and a few ornate villas.

The governor's mansion, where the imperial family was to live, sat on the newly renamed Liberty Street, a dusty avenue in the middle of town. A large, two-story white building, the mansion sported balconies at either end of the second floor. A large compound surrounded the mansion, and there were several smaller outbuildings—woodsheds, carriage house, barn, and greenhouse—but no garden of any kind. The mansion itself, although fairly large, could not house the imperial family and all of those who had accompanied them. Most of the servants were housed directly across the street in a mansion belonging to a merchant named Kornilov.

When Kobylinsky examined the governor's mansion, he found it in terrible shape. The wallpaper peeled from the walls, and the rooms were scarcely furnished, if at all. Kobylinsky ordered new wallpaper put up and hired painters to redecorate the rooms. He bought some new furniture from a shop in the town and brought rugs and paintings from the *Russ* to the house. While waiting for these improvements to be completed, the imperial family sailed up and down the Tobol River on the *Russ*, going ashore to picnic and exercise the dogs.

At eight in the morning on 26 August, the *Russ* docked at the wharf of the West Siberian Steamship and Fur Trading Company. Kobylinsky could only secure one carriage, and Alexandra and Tatiana rode in this. The rest of the imperial family had to walk the mile through the town streets to the governor's mansion.

The imperial family took over the entire second floor of the mansion. The four grand duchesses shared a corner bedroom. Alexei had another; Alexandra and Nicholas, a third. Kobylinsky had furnished a large drawing room for the tsarina and a study for the tsar. Nagorny—Alexei's male nurse—had a room close by his imperial charge, and the rest of the household and staff were dispersed between the governor's mansion and the Kornilov mansion across the street.[9]

For the first few days in Tobolsk the imperial family enjoyed relative freedom. They strolled about the streets of the town, visiting members of the household and staff at the Kornilov mansion. When the garrison objected to this, Kobylinsky reluctantly agreed and had a high wooden fence erected around the residence, enclosing a small section of the roadway. The idea of actual imprisonment for the entire family raised an interesting point because technically only the tsar, tsarina, and those servants who had accompanied them were under arrest. Alexei and the four girls were not prisoners and had accompanied their parents voluntarily. Kobylinsky suggested that the children be given some measure of freedom in Tobolsk, but once again the soldiers objected.[10]

For Alexandra, life in Tobolsk was not unpleasant, at least at the beginning. Although her rooms were cold—with temperatures averaging only fifty degrees for most of that winter—they held family photographs, familiar rugs, and personal items from Tsarskoe Selo. Surrounded by these objects, with her family close by, Alexandra felt strangely at peace. She no longer had to fight against politicians, society, or public opinion. Life in Tobolsk reinforced her belief that the simple Russian people were loyal to the tsar. When she sat near a window or out on the balcony, Alexandra noticed that a group of curious people began to assemble in the street and cross themselves. The four girls used to gather at their bedroom windows and wave to the people until the guards told them that they would be shot if it happened again.[11]

In time, however, the soldiers guarding the imperial family became friendly. They stopped the grand duchesses on their walks to chat with them, and the girls enjoyed these innocent flirtations. But Kobylinsky's open sympathy toward the family he guarded irritated the hardcore revolutionaries among the garrison. When they complained to Kerensky, the provisional government reluctantly dispatched two new commissars to report on the situation and monitor Kobylinsky's behavior.

Vassili Pankratov and Alexander Nikolsky, Kerensky's two observers, had both been imprisoned in Siberia under the tsarist regime. Pankratov bore no grudges, but Nikolsky hated the tsar and everything he stood for. When Pankratov arrived, he went to see the tsar. "Not wishing to infringe upon the rules of politeness . . ." Pankratov began, then asked the tsar's valet to inform Nicholas that he wished to speak with him.

"Good morning," the tsar said, entering the room. "Did you have a good journey?"

"Thank you, yes," Pankratov replied, shaking the tsar's outstretched hand.

"How is Alexander Feodorovich Kerensky?" asked the tsar, and the conversation carried on in polite terms, following the strict rules of imperial etiquette.[12]

Nikolsky clearly felt otherwise. When the tsar offered his hand, the commissar grabbed it and squeezed until the tsar cringed.[13] He walked into the imperial family's private rooms without knocking and insisted that all of the prisoners be photographed for identification purposes. When a case of wine from the imperial cellars arrived at Kerensky's orders for the family, Nikolsky had the wine thrown into the Tobol River, the case unopened.[14]

Winter descended upon Tobolsk with a vengeance. Rivers froze solid, temperatures dropped to 68 degrees below zero, and the governor's mansion lost what little warmth it had. Fires burned in the stoves all day long, but the temperature in the drawing room, the warmest place in the house, rarely rose above 44 degrees.[15] Alexandra shivered through the days, trying to avoid the drafts which blew in through the cracks around the windows of the cold house.[16] She tried to knit or write, but her fingers were so stiff from the cold that she could scarcely move them. For the first time in her married life, she had to remove her pink pearl engagement ring and gold wedding band, as they had begun to cut off her circulation.[17]

With the winter came the harsher realities of imprisonment. Alexandra found life "desperately dull."[18] She read the Bible and taught the girls' German lessons; her eyes were so weak that in order to see clearly she now always had to wear her spectacles. When she could, Alexandra tried to knit stockings for her family or repair their clothing, as most of it was filled with holes. The tsar wore patched trousers, and the four girls had to make do with their own ragged underlinens.[19]

Shortly before Christmas Alexandra received permission to write to Anna Vyrubova, who had recently been released after five months in the Fortress of Peter and Paul.

> My Darling,
> I was inexpressibly glad to get news of you and I kiss you fondly for all your loving thoughts of me. . . . The more we suffer here the fairer it will be on that other shore where so many dear ones await us. . . . My heart is full, but words are feeble things. . . .[20] I read much, and live in the past, which is so full of rich memories. . . .[21] God is very near us, we feel His support and are often amazed that we can endure events and separations which once might have killed us. Although we suffer horribly, still there is peace in our souls. . . . I don't understand anything any longer. Everyone seems to have gone mad. . . . My love, burn my letters.

It is better. I have kept nothing of the dear past. . . .[22] One keeps only tears and grateful memories. One by one all earthly things slip away, houses and possessions ruined, friends vanished. One lives from day to day.[23]

Alexandra grew more fatalistic as Christmas approached, her mind turning over mistakes of the past and coming to believe that she should prepare for her own death. Because the imperial family could not attend church, Alexandra had no one to counsel her. Evening prayer services in the downstairs drawing room were not a substitute for the real thing, and because the governor's mansion lacked a consecrated altar the priest could not say mass. Kobylinsky eventually arranged for the imperial family to attend services at a church just down the road, but these were infrequent and held early in the morning, before the public masses.

Christmas in exile compared sadly with the previous celebrations. The imperial family had little or no money with which to purchase gifts, and, in any case, they could not leave the governor's mansion to go shopping. Alexandra had to make do with giving some ribbons which she had painted as bookmarks, a few watercolors, and knitted socks or scarves. On Christmas morning the imperial family bundled up in scarves and coats and walked down the street, surrounded by two lines of soldiers, to attend a special mass at the nearby church. After the service the priest prayed for the imperial family but used their titles, which had been struck from the Orthodox liturgy, rather than their Christian names. For this, the imperial family was forbidden to attend church any further.[24]

With the humiliation of a Christmas spent imprisoned came vague rumors of another revolution in St. Petersburg. Lenin had wandered in and out of the country since returning in April, planning the courses that the Bolsheviks should take and then running to Finland when the situation became desperate. But finally, in November, luck caught up with Lenin, and by an extraordinary set of coincidences the Bolsheviks seized power.

They had no plans, no organized set of rules to follow in order to guarantee their success. Kerensky realized that a conflict between his provisional government and the Bolsheviks would require reinforcements, and so, on 7 November 1917, he left the Winter Palace—the ironic seat of his power—to head to the front for troops. His remaining ministers huddled together in the Malachite Drawing Room, protected by a troop of army cadets and a battalion of women soldiers. Across the Neva, the cruiser *Aurora* sported red flags and trained her guns on the bulk of the Winter Palace lining the quay. The Bolsheviks, fighting with each other, following their own individual plans, managed to capture and secure—many times accidentally—the railway stations, the state banks, the post office, all connecting bridges, and the telephone exchange. At nine on the evening of 7 November, the *Aurora* fired a blank shell at the Winter Palace, and the women's battalion surrendered. An hour later, two shells from the cruiser struck the palace; two hours later, on the morning of 8 November, the remaining ministers gave up, and Kerensky's provisional government fell. Most of St. Petersburg had no idea that there had even been a Revolution.

Nevertheless, Lenin now controlled the government, not Kerensky. The change certainly spelled disaster for the imperial family. A revolutionary provisional government had tolerated the imperial family, and Kerensky had tried to maintain some degree of comfort in their lives as prisoners. But Lenin, whose elder brother Alexander had been executed at the orders of Nicholas's father, felt differently. With the Bolsheviks in power, the fate of the Romanovs was sealed.

42

Siberian Winter

THE WINTER DAYS at Tobolsk passed slowly. Alexandra rarely left her rooms in the governor's mansion, but her husband and children took daily exercise in the small, enclosed compound. The girls still wore fashionable clothes from Paris—gray wool capes and red-and-black angora caps—but their underclothes were in rags. They took turns pulling their brother through the snow on his sled. The tsar himself liked nothing better than sawing wood, with Pierre Gilliard often called upon to do duty at the other end of the double-handled blade.

At night the children acted out plays. Pierre Gilliard and Charles Gibbes, the English tutor, produced the children in selections ranging from Russian classics to light Edwardian comedies. When the group did *The Bear* by Anton Chekhov, Nicholas acted as a greedy landlord trying to extract rent from a poor peasant. Another play had a part for an old country doctor; when Botkin heard of this, he absolutely refused to accept the role. But Alexei took his arm one day, saying, "I want to talk to you about something, Eugene Sergeievich." The tsarevich argued that only Botkin could provide the necessary realism, successfully, it appears, as the doctor duly performed his small role.[1]

One play proved particularly memorable. Gibbes had a play called *Packing Up*, an Edwardian farce by Henry Grattan in which Anastasia, then sixteen, took the principal male role. At the end of the play, she had to turn her back to the audience, open her dressing gown, and say, "But I've packed my trousers; I can't go." Anastasia turned her back to the audience and began to say her lines when her hand caught the side of the dressing gown. Without realizing it, she pulled it up her back, exposing her chubby legs and bottom packed into her father's Jaeger underwear. The audience said nothing for a moment, then collapsed in laughter, Alexandra, Nicholas, servants, and suite. "I shall always remember that night," wrote Gibbes; "it was the last hearty unrestrained laughter the Empress ever enjoyed."[2]

Certainly the bright spots of life at Tobolsk were few. As the realities of the Bolshevik Revolution settled in, the situation grew hostile. In February the new government demobilized all of the old soldiers from the imperial army—those friendliest to the Romanovs. They were replaced with young, brutal revolutionaries. These new soldiers carved obscene words on a pair of swings used by the children; Alexei spotted them, but before he could investigate further, the tsar removed the seats. Not to be thwarted, the soldiers thereafter wrote or scrawled their doggerel on the high fence, where it could not be removed.[3]

On 3 March 1918, at the border town of Brest-Litovsk, Germany and Russia signed a peace treaty giving the kaiser territories that included Poland, Finland, the Baltic States, the Ukraine, and the Crimea. Both the tsar and tsarina were shocked. "What a nightmare it is that it is Germans who are saving Russia. . . ." Alexandra wrote to Anna. "What could be more humiliating for us? With one hand the Germans give, and with the other they take away."[4]

The changes were immediate. Money had been the biggest problem for the imperial family for some time. Kobylinsky had been given a large sum of money to pay for the household expenses; the soldiers were to be paid by the provisional government. But when the provisional government fell to the Bolsheviks, the money stopped coming. Kobylinsky had to use the household money to pay the soldiers. Eventually the money ran out, and Kobylinsky and General Tatishchev had to visit the local district commissar, each time borrowing 15,000 rubles.[5] In St. Petersburg, Count Benckendorff frantically collected money for the imperial family; eventually he managed to gather 200,000 rubles. He sent it off to Tobolsk but somehow the money disappeared along the way and never reached the prisoners.

The imperial family's financial woes were solved by the Bolshevik government on 1 March 1918. According to an announcement, the family would henceforth be put on soldier's rations—600 rubles per person per month, or 4,200 rubles total for the family. For a family of seven the sum would have been more than adequate, but out of the 4,200 rubles, the entire household had to be taken care of—cooks, doctors, tutors, ladies- and gentlemen-in-waiting, valets, and maids. Nicholas drew up a budget and had to dismiss ten servants, some whose families had accompanied them to Tobolsk. When Anna Vyrubova sent some money to the imperial family, Alexandra wrote, "I was keenly touched by the money you sent, but do not send any more as for the present we have all we need. There have been days when we did not know what to do. . . . We hear that the soldiers in Smolny have seized all available food and are quite indifferent to the prospects of people starving. Why was money sent to us rather than having been given to the poor?"[6]

Even with the ration cards, meals at Tobolsk remained, for the

most part, decidedly unimperial. Butter and coffee were considered "lux-
uries" that the imperial family could do without. Luncheon, the chief
meal of the day, consisted of soup, meat or fish, and some wine. For
their evening meal, the imperial family dined on meat, vegetables, and
on more fortunate occasions, macaroni. When the people of Tobolsk
heard of the situation, they sent caviar, sweetmeats, eggs, and fresh fish;
Alexandra called them "gifts from Heaven."[7]

With the situation worsening around her, Alexandra turned in-
ward, to her faith in Orthodoxy. Although her views were often fatalistic, her deep trust in God gave her the strength to continue. She wrote
to Anna:

> Life here is nothing—eternity is everything and what we are
> doing is preparing our souls for the Kingdom of Heaven. Thus
> nothing, after all, is terrible, and if they do take everything from
> us they cannot take our souls. . . . Have patience, and these days
> of suffering will end, we shall forget all the anguish and thank
> God. . . . I cannot write all that fills my soul. . . . We live here on
> earth but we are already half gone to the next world.[8]

Among the papers found after the imperial family's disappearance was a poem, copied by Grand Duchess Olga. The authorship is
doubtful. It has been suggested that Countess Hendrikov wrote the
verse, but it is more reminiscent in style of Alexandra. It expresses, in
any case, the sentiments which she often wrote to Anna during that last
winter at Tobolsk:

> A Prayer
>
> Give Patience, Lord, to us, Thy Children,
> In these dark stormy days to bear
> The persecution of our people,
> The tortures falling to our shores.
>
> Give strength, Just God, to us who need it,
> The persecutors to forgive,
> Our heavy, painful cross to carry
> And Thy great meekness to achieve.
> When we are plundered and insulted,
> In days of mutinous unrest
> We turn for help to Thee, Christ Saviour,
> That we may stand the bitter test.
>
> Lord of the world, God of Creation,

Give us Thy blessing through our prayer
Give peace of heart to us, O Master,
This hour of utmost dread to bear.
And on the threshold of the grave,
Breathe power divine into our clay
That we, Thy children, may find strength
In meekness for our foes to pray.[9]

The Siberian winter ended, with the situation in Tobolsk uncertain and Alexandra growing more apprehensive about the future. What she did not know was that serious efforts were under way to spirit her and her family out of Russia and to freedom in England.

The Brotherhood of St. John of Tobolsk, a monarchist organization bent on rescuing the imperial family, sported, as its leader, one Boris Soloviev. His father had been the treasurer of the Holy Synod, and Boris maintained contact with both Rasputin and Anna Vyrubova during the First World War. As such, Alexandra knew him personally. Following Rasputin's death, Soloviev led a group of believers who tried in vain to contact the peasant's soul. Aside from his family connection with the government and his friendship with Anna Vyrubova and Rasputin, Boris seemed an unlikely center for monarchist hopes. In Alexandra's eyes, however, he possessed the most important credential of all: Not only had he been friendly with Rasputin before his death, but in October 1917 he married the peasant's eldest daughter, Maria.[10]

Soloviev quickly established himself as the authority for all rescue attempts. Monarchists bearing gifts of money for the imperial family willingly gave their rubles to Soloviev in the hope that he would succeed in setting them free. Through the maid Romanova, Soloviev began to pass notes to the tsarina, promising her that "Gregory's family and his friends are active."[11] The imperial family managed, through the same source, to smuggle out several pieces of the jewelry which they had brought with them into exile, intending that it help pay for the cost of the rescue. Alexandra absolutely believed Soloviev when he said that three hundred officers were ready to act on his word, storm the governor's mansion, and set the imperial family free.[12] After all, how could "Our Friend's" son-in-law possibly deceive her?

Soloviev's detractors eventually wanted to see the rescue plans. This he refused to do; however, Soloviev arranged for skeptics to watch the Tiumen Garrison drill. According to Soloviev, he had converted the regiment to his plot; at a selected time, one of the officers of the garrison even made a prearranged signal to Soloviev. He even worked out a plan for a member of the imperial family to come out on the balcony of the governor's mansion and signal to a skeptic in the street below. Seeing the imperial family's cooperation, all doubts about Soloviev vanished.

Nothing ever came from Soloviev's elaborate rescue plans, for none existed. When the imperial family left Tobolsk for Ekaterinburg, Soloviev found himself conveniently arrested, thus providing himself with the perfect alibi for not executing his grandiose plans. Although later branded as a Bolshevik bent on destroying monarchist plans, Soloviev's real motive seems to have been money. A banker in St. Petersburg raised some 175,000 rubles which he sent to Soloviev at Tiumen for the imperial family. Of this sum, only 35,000 rubles were delivered to the prisoners; the rest simply disappeared.[13] Whatever Soloviev's intentions, the Brotherhood of St. John of Tobolsk evaporated into the slush of the Siberian spring.

While monarchist efforts to save the imperial family came to nothing, definite plans existed for a rescue of the Romanovs. Speaking in 1974 with British writers Anthony Summers and Tom Mangold, Prince Vladimir of Russia said, "There were plans, distinct from monarchist plots, while the imperial family were at Tobolsk, and they involved George V and others. . . ."[14] Vladimir did not elaborate, but at least two serious efforts involving the British royal family are known.

On 15 December 1917, Alexandra asked her children's English tutor Charles Gibbes to draft a letter to her former tutor Margaret Hardcastle Jackson. Miss Jackson had long before retired from teaching and lived in a home for former governesses in Regent's Park, London. Superficially, it was a harmlessly descriptive letter.

> Dear Miss Jackson,
> You will have read in the newspapers of the many different changes which have taken place. In August the Provisional Government decided to change the residence from Tsarskoe to Tobolsk, a small town far away in Siberia. . . . Our House . . . is entirely isolated and possesses a small garden besides a piece of the roadway which has been railed in to make a recreation ground. . . . As in almost all Russian houses, on mounting the principal staircase you enter the salon on one side of which is the study and on the other the drawing room. After these come the principal bedroom and a room which the four daughters use as a dormitory. . . . The youngest has a room to himself on the other side of the corridor. . . .
> The days do not vary much. . . . On Sunday we are generally permitted to go to the Parish Church to the communion service. . . . The younger members of the family have lessons in the morning before lunch, after which we all take exercise and

recreation in our small railed-in plot.

It is ages since you wrote, or maybe your letters have not arrived.... I hear David is back from France, how are his father and mother? And the cousins, are they also at the Front?[15]

The actual letter is much longer and contains a detailed account of the church services the family attended, the times they went, and the number of guards that accompanied them on their journey.

Why would Gibbes, who did not know Miss Jackson at all, bother to write such a long, detailed account? He himself reported later that Alexandra had asked him to do so and that its intended destination was Buckingham Palace. If so, the letter apparently never reached King George V and Queen Mary, for there is no record of it at all in the royal archives at Windsor. The most telling line in the whole letter is the last— "I hear that David is back from France, how are his father and mother?" Within the royal family, George V's son Edward, the Prince of Wales, was known as David. This concealed cry for help remains an enigma.

The same cannot be said of the plans involving Jonas Lied. Lied, a Norwegian businessman, had worked in Siberia in the years before the war. In 1913 he personally planned a new trade route in Siberia, from Tobolsk upriver and into the Kara Sea. He had formed the Siberian Steamship and Manufacturing Company with a British partner, and Nicholas himself had personally granted Lied honorary citizenship.[16]

In the spring of 1918, while the imperial family remained at Tobolsk, Lied found himself summoned to London. He met with Frederick Browning, a senior British intelligence officer working for the Secret Service; Arthur Balfour, the minister for foreign affairs; Lord Robert Cecil, the diplomat handling the question of the imperial family; and Sir Reginald Hall, the director of British naval intelligence.[17] Clearly, these important men had something in mind for Lied, and after several days in London, he found out what they intended: rescuing the imperial family from Tobolsk.

Lied discussed the possibility of sending a boat to fetch the family from the Bolsheviks at Tobolsk and then spirit them away to the Kara Sea, where a torpedo boat supplied by the British Navy would pick them up. "King George backed the plan," recalled one diplomat and friend of Lied. "But the Prime Minister, Lloyd George, had no use for the Tsar. Whatever the reason for the change of plan, Lloyd George virtually murdered the Tsar. Lied had it on his conscience for the rest of his life that the plan failed to materialize."[18]

George V's son, the late Duke of Windsor, recalled:

It has long been my impression that, just before the Bolsheviks seized the Tsar, my father had personally planned to rescue him with a British cruiser, but in some way the plan was blocked. In any case it hurt my father that Britain had not raised a hand to save his cousin Nicky. "Those politicians," he used to say. "If it had been one of their own kind, they would have acted fast enough. But merely because the poor man was an Emperor. . . ."[19]

A year earlier, King George V had plotted to keep his imperial cousins from coming to England. Only when he realized the seriousness of the situation did the king make an effort to help the family. But it came too late for the Romanovs. The Lied affair ended British involvement with the imperial family once and for all. And, in place of George V and England, the Romanovs found a most unlikely ally: Cousin Willy, the kaiser of imperial Germany.

43

"God's Will"

On a bitterly cold day in January 1918 a group of concerned monarchists walked into the office of Count Mirbach, the German ambassador in Moscow. This curious group appealed to Russia's enemy of the past four years to ensure the safety of the imperial family in Tobolsk. But Mirbach seems to have been expecting such an inquiry. To their pleas, the ambassador said, "Be calm. We Germans have the situation well in hand, and the Imperial Family is under our protection. We know what we are doing and when the time comes, the German Imperial Government will take the necessary measures."[1]

Within several months, on 3 March, the Treaty of Brest-Litovsk virtually guaranteed German control of much of Russia. A British Foreign Office memorandum definitely refers to "overtures made on their [the imperial family's] behalf by the Germans at Brest-Litovsk."[2] The kaiser himself allowed Alexandra's brother Ernie to write a letter to her, offering help in rescuing the imperial family. Grand Duke Ernest Ludwig of Hesse gave the letter to a certain Serge Vladimirovich Markov, a former officer in the tsarina's Crimean Cavalry Regiment. Apparently Markov delivered the letter through secret channels, because Nicholas answered the proposal with a definite no. Alexandra, however, felt compelled to answer and explained to Ernie why the offer could not be accepted. Markov took the letter back to Germany. A general later wrote that "the letter which Markov brought actually existed. It was seen by others. It was seen by people who could know the Empress's handwriting."[3]

The tsar's refusal to cooperate angered the Germans. When Count Benckendorff wrote a long plea to Count Wilhelm Mirbach asking after the imperial family, he received a disturbing reply: "The fate of the tsar is a matter for the Russian people. We now have to concern ourselves with the safety of the German princesses on Russian territory."[4] Instead, Mirbach reported to Berlin: "I have . . . delivered to the People's Commissars a statement regarding our expectations that the German princesses will be treated with all possible consideration, and specifically that unnecessary petty annoyances, as well as threats against their lives, will not be permitted."[5] All of this occurred on the kaiser's orders. Cousin Willy, despite his bombastic nature, genuinely worried about his Russian relatives. According to Queen Olga of Greece, after speaking to the kaiser's daughter-in-law Crown Princess Cecilie, "the German Emperor . . . spends sleepless nights in mourning over the Romanovs' fate."[6]

On the afternoon of 22 April 1918 a mounted detachment of 150 soldiers rode into Tobolsk. At their head was Vassili Vassilievich Yakovlev. A man in his middle thirties, Yakovlev commanded this squadron of Bolsheviks on the orders of Moscow. His instructions were direct: to bring the tsar and his family to the capital.

Yakovlev impressed the imperial family with his politeness and manner. When he took tea with Alexandra and Nicholas on the evening of his arrival, he addressed the tsar as "Your Majesty" and spoke to Gilliard in French. Yakovlev showed Kobylinsky two letters signed by Jacob Sverdlov, the president of the Central Committee in Moscow; both threatened death if Yakovlev's orders were not instantly obeyed.[7]

Moscow's decision to move the Romanovs from Tobolsk was a direct result of the interest expressed in their fate by the nearby Omsk and Ekaterinburg Soviets. In February, Ekaterinburg hosted the Third Regional Congress of Soviets, at which important Bolsheviks from the Urals were elected to key positions. One of those voted into power, Isaac Goloshchekin, the new military commissar of the Ural Soviet, was an intimate friend of Sverdlov's in Moscow. Goloshchekin's personal views on the Romanovs are not known, but the Ural Regional Soviet feared that with the coming of spring the former tsar and his family would attempt to escape from Tobolsk. Many of these Ural Bolsheviks were personally hostile to the imperial family and wished to deal out their own brand of justice to the former sovereign; but there was also the fear that one of the monarchist groups might eventually succeed in rescuing the Romanovs. At a meeting of the Ural Regional Soviet in March, the five-man Presidium voted to request a transfer of the Romanovs from Tobolsk to Ekaterinburg. A formal declaration was made to Sverdlov in Moscow. At the same time, Ekaterinburg dispatched its own group of Bolsheviks to investigate the situation in Tobolsk. In Tobolsk itself, Ekaterinburg representatives found a similiar group of Bolsheviks from rival Omsk, which also campaigned for the transfer of the imperial family to its town. The Ekaterinburg delegation retreated—temporarily—to gather reinforcements.

In light of the political conflict over transfer of the prisoners, the

Ural Regional Soviet sent Goloshchekin on a mission to Moscow at the end of March to determine jurisdiction. There is some disagreement as to the outcome of these meetings. Peter Bykov, a member of the Ural Regional Soviet who produced the closest thing to an official Soviet version of events surrounding the fate of the Romanovs, claimed that Sverdlov decided to authorize transfer of the imperial family to Ekaterinburg on the condition that Goloshchekin take full personal responsibility for their safety.[8] But the official minutes of the Central Executive Committee show that on 1 April 1918 the Presidium voted to bring the Romanovs to Moscow. To this end, a special commissar, Vassili Yakovlev, was dispatched to Tobolsk.

Without waiting for word of Moscow's decision, Ekaterinburg sent a second expedition to Tobolsk. On 13 April it arrived in the city. The commissar in charge, S. S. Zaslavsky, requested permission to move the imperial family to Ekaterinburg; Kobylinsky refused this request. Zaslavsky next suggested that they be transferred to the local prison; again, Kobylinsky rejected the proposal. After this, Zaslavsky openly campaigned against Kobylinsky's authority in an effort to inspire his soldiers to revolt. It was at this highly dangerous moment that Yakovlev arrived from Moscow.

For many years Yakovlev's true identity remained a mystery. Recent Russian journals have identified him as Constantine Miachin, a thirty-two-year-old Bolshevik born near Orenburg. Although it has been reported that Yakovlev was a British agent, it is now quite clear that he was a trusted member of the Soviet hierarchy. He served as a delegate to the Second Congress of Soviets and was a member of the ruling body of the Cheka, the successor of the tsar's secret police force, the Okhrana.

It is also quite clear, despite later speculation surrounding his mission, that Yakovlev was charged with bringing the Romanovs to Moscow. This he made quite clear to Kobylinsky and to the tsar. He carried with him a special order signed by Sverdlov authorizing the move to Moscow; and, in addition, a second order to this effect signed by Lenin himself.[9] Yakovlev also met, en route to Tobolsk, with Isaac Goloshchekin and informed him of the decision to bring the imperial family to Moscow. This must have come as something of a surprise to Goloshchekin, who, recently returned from Moscow, had received assurances that Ekaterinburg could transfer the imperial family to its own prison.

Goloshchekin returned to Ekaterinburg and informed the Ural Regional Soviet of Yakovlev's mission. Quickly, they voted to send their own detachment to Tobolsk to intercept the transfer of the Romanovs and bring them back to Ekaterinburg. There is no evidence that

Ekaterinburg acted in defiance of Moscow, for they had also received permission to imprison the imperial family.

At first, Alexandra did not realize that all of these men were Bolsheviks. When the first detachment from Ekaterinburg arrived in Tobolsk, she took them for Soloviev's group of loyal monarchists and pointed them out to her daughters from the windows of the governor's mansion as their rescuers, "good Russian men."[10] To Anna, she wrote with hope of the English gardens she remembered from her childhood, daring to think that she might see them again.[11]

Alexandra also faced a potential crisis with Alexei. A week earlier, the tsarevich had used a sled on the interior stairway of the house and fell; a severe hemorrhage in the groin began immediately.[12] The pain was unbearable. "Mama, I would like to die," the boy cried out. "I am not afraid of death, but I am so afraid of what they will do to us here."[13] Alexandra could not turn to Rasputin; desperate, she prayed day and night for a miracle not only to save her son but her family as well. To Anna, she wrote:

> Sunbeam has been ill in bed for the past week. . . . He is better now, but sleeps badly and the pains, though less severe, have not entirely ceased. . . . But yesterday, he began to eat a little and Dr. Derevenko is satisfied with his progress. The child has to lie on his back without moving, and he gets so tired. I sit all day beside him, holding his aching legs, and I have grown almost as thin as he is. . . . The blood recedes quickly—that is why today he again had very severe pains. Yesterday for the first time he smiled and talked with us, even played cards, and slept two hours during the day. He is frightfully thin, with enormous eyes, just as at Spala. He likes to be read to, eats little—no appetite at all, in fact.[14]

Yakovlev asked to see the tsarevich to check on his condition. When he found the boy was too ill for travel, he cabled Moscow for instructions. He received his reply on 25 April and informed Kobylinsky that he had been sent to remove the entire imperial family from Tobolsk and the hostile Urals. The tsarevich's illness made this impossible and now he had been told to take the tsar to Moscow at once and leave the rest of the family behind.

When Yakovlev related this to the tsar, Nicholas said flatly, "I refuse to go."[15] Yakovlev pointed out that if the tsar refused to comply, Moscow might force the issue with a less scrupulous man. "Be calm," Yakovlev said. "I am responsible with my life for your safety. If you do not want to go alone, you can take with you any people you wish. Be ready, we are leaving tomorrow at four o'clock."[16]

"I can't let the Tsar go alone," Alexandra cried to Pierre Gilliard. "They want to separate him from his family as they did before. . . . I ought to be at his side in the time of trial. But the boy is still so ill. . . . Oh, God! What ghastly torture! For the first time in my life I don't know what to do. I've always felt inspired whenever I had to take a decision and now I can't think."[17]

The tsarina sat with Tatiana, trying to decide what she should do. "It is the hardest moment of my life," she said.[18]

"But Mother, if Father has to go, whatever we say, something must be decided," Tatiana said.[19] "You cannot go on tormenting yourself like this."[20] Alexandra paced up and down the room, talking to herself. Suddenly, she said, "Yes, that will be best; I'll go with the Tsar."[21]

Although Yakovlev explained that Moscow was the destination, everyone assumed that they would go on to England. Kobylinsky himself said that from Moscow they were "to be taken to Petrograd, then to Finland, Sweden and Norway."[22] Dr. Botkin told his children that "Yakovlev has finally announced that he has come to take us all to Moscow. . . . It is actually true that the Soviets have promised Germany to release the Imperial Family. But the Germans have had the decency not to demand that the Imperial Family go to Germany. Accordingly, it has been decided that we shall be sent to England."[23]

Alexei had no idea of what was occurring. When his mother did not show up after luncheon as usual, he began to cry out, "Mama! Mama!"[24] The sound echoed throughout the house. When she did appear, her eyes were red. She quietly explained to her son that the following morning she and the tsar were leaving for Moscow. But she continued to pray that they would not be forced to leave. "I know, I am convinced, that the river will overflow tonight, and then our departure must be postponed. This will give us time to get out of this terrible position. If a miracle is necessary, I am sure a miracle will take place."[25]

But there was no miracle for Alexandra that night. Just before dawn a group of carriages drew up before the governor's mansion; all night long the house blazed with light. Snow continued to flurry in the long hours leading up to the departure until, at half-past three in the morning, Alexandra and Nicholas walked down the main staircase to climb into the waiting carriages. The vehicles selected for the trip were peasant carts similar to a sledge, having neither springs nor seats. In these, they were to travel some two hundred miles.

Alexandra asked her daughter Marie to come with them as a companion. Both ladies were wrapped in heavy furs, but Yakovlev insisted that the tsarina take Dr. Botkin's overcoat as well. The tsar came out, wearing his usual military officer's greatcoat.

"What!" Yakovlev exclaimed. "You're only wearing an overcoat!"

"That's all I ever wear," said Nicholas.

"But that's out of the question," Yakovlev replied, and sent for several heavy coats and furs.[26] He also gathered some straw from the pigsty and placed it in the bottom of Alexandra's cart, along with an old, rotting mattress.

Alexandra climbed into her cart slowly. Nicholas began to follow her, but Yakovlev stopped him, saying that the tsar must ride with him in a second carriage. Marie then climbed in beside her mother. Botkin, Prince Dolgoruky, the valet Terenty Chemodurov, the maid Anna Demidova, and the footman Alexei Trupp all followed in other carts. The gates of the compound swung open, and escorted by a cavalry regiment, the group of carts sped down the street and out into the Siberian night.

The journey over the melting snow and frozen rivers took a little over two days. They changed horses at different stations along the way. Alexandra described the journey in her diary:

> Marie in a tarantass [a Russian sledge]. Nicholas with Commissar Yakovlev. Cold, grey and windy, crossed the Irtusk after changing horses at 8, and at 12 stopped in village and took tea with our cold provisions. Road perfectly atrocious, frozen ground, mud, water up to the horses' stomachs, fearfully shaken, pains all over. After fourth change, the poles on which the body of the tarantass rests, slipped, and we had to climb over into another carriage box. Changed horses five times. . . . At 8 got to Yevlevo, where we spent the night in house where was the village shop before. We slept three in one room, we on our beds, Marie on the floor on her mattress. . . . One does not tell us where we are going from Tiumen. Some imagine Moscow, the little ones are to follow us soon as river free and Baby well.[27]

One of these changes took place at Pokrovskoe, where the carts pulled up directly beneath Rasputin's house. His widow, Praskovie, stood in one of the windows, looking down. Staring at Alexandra, she carefully made the sign of the cross, then disappeared behind the curtain.[28]

A regiment of Bolshevik cavalry joined up with the group fourteen miles out of Tiumen.[29] At the train station Yakovlev sent his prisoners to a first-class carriage, then disappeared into the telegraph office to communicate with Moscow.

There were only two railway lines to Moscow: One passed directly from Tiumen through Ekaterinburg and then to Moscow; the other, more southern route ran from Omsk to the Soviet capital, bypassing Ekaterinburg altogether. The distance from Tiumen to Ekaterinburg was some two hundred miles; a journey by way of Omsk involved several extra days of travel. Yakovlev grew concerned about his prisoners' safety if he took them by the direct route through Ekaterinburg. He asked Moscow for permission to remove the prisoners by way of Omsk in an effort to avoid the Ekaterinburg line; Sverdlov agreed to this. As a result, Yakovlev instructed the stationmaster to send the train west, toward Ekaterinburg; at the next station, he intended to switch engines and double back, heading east through Tiumen to Omsk, and from there to take the southern route by way of Cheliabinsk to Moscow. The train bearing the imperial prisoners steamed out of Tiumen in the early morning hours of 28 April, heading toward Ekaterinburg, then abruptly switched direction and doubled back along the same spur of track toward Omsk.

Ekaterinburg had nervously followed Yakovlev's movements since leaving Tobolsk through a series of guards posted along the route. As soon as the train failed to appear as expected, Ekaterinburg was immediately suspicious. Through cable communications, they learned of the train's reversal of direction. The Presidium of the Ural Regional Soviet branded Yakovlev "a traitor to the revolution" and suspecting that he intended to spirit the Romanovs out of the country, dispatched cables to the Omsk Soviet demanding that it stop the train and send the prisoners to Ekaterinburg.[30]

It was a race against time for Yakovlev. The Omsk Soviet hastily dispatched a detachment of soldiers to Kulominzo, where the railway line connected to the southern spur to Cheliabinsk. Somehow Yakovlev learned of this move; he unhitched the train's engine and left the carriages with the Romanovs standing at the railway station in Liubinskaia and himself proceeded to Omsk to speak directly with Moscow for instructions.

We have only Bykov's word for what now transpired. In his book he relates that Sverdlov proposed taking the prisoners directly to Ekaterinburg and turning them over to the authority of the Ural Regional Soviet. This seems unlikely. As Yakovlev was acting on the direct orders of Moscow, there is no reason to believe that either Sverdlov or Lenin suddenly changed his mind because of Ekaterinburg's demands. It has been argued that Sverdlov, rather than force a clash between his representative and the more powerful detachment from Ekaterinburg, simply gave up on his plans to bring the Romanovs to Moscow and instead gave permission to turn them over to the Ural Bolsheviks. Again, this does not satisfy. Why would Moscow suddenly drop its plans and bow to local pressure? Isaac Goloshchekin, Sverdlov's friend in Ekaterinburg, would scarcely dare affront the Presidium of the Central Executive Committee by such action. Richard Pipes speculates that Sverdlov actually ordered Yakovlev to proceed to Moscow as planned, but to do so by way of Ekaterinburg to relieve suspicions that he was trying to spirit the Romanovs away. In any case, Yakovlev received his orders: Reverse direction and proceed to Ekaterinburg. "Omsk Soviet would not let us pass Omsk, and feared one wished to take us to Japan," Alexandra noted in her diary.[31]

Yakovlev's train arrived in the capital of the Urals on the morning of 30 April 1918. The train pulled into the main station, where a large, hostile crowd waited. Their cries of "Show us the Romanovs!" could clearly be heard by the prisoners inside.[32] Yakovlev's route toward Moscow was blocked; he disembarked the train and rushed to the local telegraph office. When informed of the situation, Moscow refused to continue with the mission; there existed the very real possibility that if Yakovlev attempted to proceed, the train would be ambushed and the prisoners injured. Ekaterinburg won out; shortly before noon, the train bearing the imperial prisoners steamed into a second Ekaterinburg depot, this one cleared of demonstrators. "Yakovlev had to give us over to the Ural Regional Soviet," the tsarina commented bitterly in her diary.[33] And the tsar was heard to remark, "I would have gone anywhere but to the Urals."[34] The chairman of the Ural Regional Soviet, Alexander Beloborodov, boarded the train and issued to Yakovlev a formal receipt for the prisoners:

1. The former Tsar, Nicholas Alexandrovich Romanov
2. The former Tsarina, Alexandra Feodorovna Romanova
3. The former Grand Duchess Marie Nicholaievna Romanova.
All of them to be kept under guard in the town of Ekaterinburg.[35]

Nicholas stepped out first, followed by Alexandra, leaning heavily on her cane and carrying her own luggage. When Marie and her servants were unloaded, the small group climbed into several waiting motorcars and left the station. Prince Dolgoruky did not accompany the imperial family; the Bolsheviks took him to the town jail and executed him.

The group drove through the back streets of Ekaterinburg until they arrived at their destination, a mansion belonging to a merchant named Ipatiev. They carried their luggage to the doorstep. Waiting at the door was a triumphant Isaac Goloshchekin, who greeted the tsar with the words "Citizen Romanov, you may enter."[36]

Before she left Tobolsk, Alexandra, in her last letter to Anna, wrote of what the future held. "The atmosphere around us is fairly electrified. We feel that a storm is approaching, but we know that God is merciful and will care for us. . . . Though we know that the storm is coming nearer and nearer, our souls are at peace. Whatever happens will be through God's will."[37]

44

The House of Special Purpose

STRETCHED ON THE EASTERN SLOPE of the Ural Mountains, the city of Ekaterinburg rose and fell across a series of low hills, ending in the dark forests of pine and birch surrounding the town. If Tobolsk was provincial, Ekaterinburg was a thriving industrial center, the capital of the Urals, home to some seventy five thousand residents. Many were workers either in the city's factories or in the mines on the outskirts of the town. It was an important Bolshevik center, and the long, dusty, unpaved streets were generally crowded with officers attached to the Academy of the General Staff.

The hills on which the town sprawled boasted vast amounts of iron, copper, marble, gold, and malachite. Once these resources were discovered, money flowed into the town. A number of wealthy merchants sponsored improvements of their town: elegant avenues, shaded with lime and linden trees, were laid out; a large Municipal Gardens skirted the lake lying in the foothills; and two grand hotels, the America and the Palais, fronted the wide Voznesensky Avenue, which cleaved through Ekaterinburg.

On Voznesensky Avenue stood the home of Nicholas Ipatiev. On 27 April, a delegation from the Ural Regional Soviet called on Ipatiev and gave him twenty-four hours to pack up his household. When Ipatiev protested, he was informed that the Soviet needed the premises for "reasons of state." Ipatiev did as instructed; he and his family spent the entire day packing their things: Carpets, curtains, linens, paintings, silver, and kitchen accessories were all stored in a low shed at the rear of the property. On 28 April, the Bolsheviks took possession of the villa. They whitewashed all of the windows on the main floor, preventing anyone from either looking in or seeing out, and erected a tall wooden stockade around the property. Ominously, the Ural Regional Soviet rechristened the mansion "The House of Special Purpose."

Ipatiev had no idea why the Soviet wanted his house. On the afternoon of 30 April, a long line of automobiles pulled up before the main entrance, and a group of people were hurried inside. Only a week later did the newspaper *Ural Worker* make the formal announcement: "Conforming to a decision of the Soviet Commissar of the People, the ex-Tsar Nicholas Romanov and his family have been lodged in the local, heavily guarded home after having been moved from Tobolsk to Ekaterinburg."[1] Soon crowds of curious people gathered on the streets to gaze at the mansion where their former tsar and his family were being held prisoners.

The Ipatiev house stood at the edge of a hill. From its front it faced Voznesensky Avenue and Ascension Square, where a large white-washed cathedral stood. Viewed from the square, the house was only one story, with basement windows just peeking out above the ground. But at the sides, where the hill fell away from the square, the basement became fully exposed, so that from the rear the house was two stories. It was an ornate house in the late Empire style, with stucco ornaments, iron railings, and curved attic dormers sunk deep into the green iron roof. The main entrance, facing Voznesensky Avenue, was next to a large arched gateway giving access to the inner courtyard. A second entrance stood at the side of the house, opening onto Voznesensky Street, which sloped down to the Municipal Gardens. At the rear of the property, overlooking a small garden, was a double balcony attached to both floors of the mansion.

The imperial family was confined to the main floor of the house. Here they had use of several rooms. From the main entrance of the house, a large, carved wooden staircase led to the first floor. Two doorways communicated with the apartments. First came a room occupied by the commandant of the house. Down a hallway was a large double drawing room divided by an arch, filled with massive furniture, a piano, and decorated with potted palms and floral wallpaper. Another door led to the dining room. There were three bedrooms on this floor, all of which were given to the imperial family and their suite. Alexandra and Nicholas took the largest room, set at the corner of the house overlooking Voznesensky Avenue and Voznesensky Alley. The walls were hung with a flowered yellow paper. Two beds were eventually set up here—one for the tsar and tsarina, the other for the tsarevich. Next door was a large room, its single arched window looking out onto the alley. This room, with a large pier glass, stove, and blown-glass chandelier, would be used by the four grand duchesses. Anna Demidova took the last room, at the rear of the house. When they first arrived, the house was empty of any ornaments; soon cases of linens, rugs, and photographs which the imperial family had brought with them to Tobolsk arrived, and the tsarina spent several days decorating their new prison.

On the window frame of what was to become her last bedroom, Alexandra scrawled a swastika, her favorite good luck symbol, and penciled the date: 17/30 April 1918.

There were ten guard posts at the Ipatiev house. The first guard was stationed in the entrance hallway on the main floor; a second stood duty in the rear hallway leading to the bathroom and lavatory; the third, just outside the main entrance on Voznesensky Avenue; the fourth on the exterior side of the wooden stockade by the gateway to the courtyard; the fifth in a sentry box surveying the length of Voznesensky Avenue; the sixth at the corner of Voznesensky Avenue and Street; the seventh between the walls of the house and the stockade at the side of Voznesensky Street; the eighth at the rear of the property, in the garden; the ninth on the rear balcony; and the tenth in a hallway on the lower floor of the house. Two machine guns were mounted on the balcony and in one of the attic dormer windows. The Ipatiev house had become an impregnable fortress from which the imperial family could not escape.

The Romanovs arrived at the Ipatiev house on 30 April. On entering their new prison, they were ordered to open all their luggage. Alexandra immediately objected. The tsar tried to come to her defense, saying, "So far we have had polite treatment and men who were gentlemen, but now—" He was quickly cut off. The guards informed him that he was no longer at Tsarskoe Selo and that refusal to comply with their request would result in his removal from the rest of his family; a second offense would be rewarded with hard labor. Fearing for her husband's safety, Alexandra quickly gave in and allowed the search.[2]

After a week in Ekaterinburg, Alexandra was allowed to write to her four other children, still in Tobolsk. The letter, written by her maid Anna Demidova but dictated by the tsarina, urged the girls to "dispose of the medicines as had been agreed."[3] Before leaving Tobolsk, the tsarina informed her daughters that if they received this message, they should begin concealing the jewelry which the imperial family had brought with them into exile. For several days the three remaining grand duchesses worked at sewing diamonds, rubies, emeralds, and pearls into the linings of corsets and bodices.

The children joined their parents in Ekaterinburg on 23 May. Following a nervous journey escorted by Bolshevik officials, the grand duchesses and the tsarevich arrived in the city during a rainstorm. The Ekaterinburg Soviet had sent several carriages to collect them. The tsarevich's sailor Clementy Nagorny carried the sick boy in his arms; the three girls, loaded down with suitcases, followed. Pierre Gilliard, watching from a window aboard the train, saw Tatiana sink deeper and deeper into the mud, struggling to keep hold of her suitcase and her little dog, Jimmy. When Nagorny tried to come to her aid, soldiers roughly pushed him away. "A few minutes later the carriages drove off with the children," Gilliard recalled. ". . . How little I suspected that I was never to see them again."[4]

The Soviet divided the accompanying entourage into three groups. The first, consisting of General Tatishchev, an aide-de-camp; Countess Hendrikov, a lady-in-waiting; Alexei Volkov, the tsarina's groom of chamber; and Mademoiselle Schneider, the tsarina's reader— was sent to prison, where most of them were later shot. The second— Baroness Buxhoeveden, Dr. Derevenko, Gilliard, and Gibbes—were all set free. The cook, Ivan Kharitonov, and the fourteen-year-old kitchen boy Leonid Sedinev, were sent to the Ipatiev house to join the prisoners.

The arrival of the children was a relief to their worried parents. Accommodations were cramped. Nicholas, Alexandra, their children, and the maid Demidova had taken the bedrooms. The remainder of the servants slept on couches in the drawing room or in the hallways. The Soviet allowed the imperial family to keep eight servants: Dr. Eugene Botkin; Anna Demidova; Alexei Trupp; Ivan Kharitonov; the manservant Ivan Sedinev and his nephew Leonid; the sailor Nagorny; and the valet Chemodurov. Fifteen people in all shared the six rooms on the upper floor. In the first few weeks there was no running water and the house lacked any kind of proper ventilation. The windows were closed and whitewashed and barred so that they could not be opened in the sweltering, incessant heat of an Ekaterinburg summer.

Seventy-five men did guard duty at the Ipatiev house, nearly all of them Russians. They were divided into two categories—interior and exterior guards. The smaller, interior detachment lived in the basement rooms of the Ipatiev house, while the exterior guard was billeted in the Popov house just across Voznesensky Street. Many of these men were factory workers selected from the local Zlokazovsky Factory and the Verkh-Isetsk Factory. The commissar of the Ipatiev house, Alexander Avadeyev, was thirty-five, tall, and with a thin mustache. Friends described him as "a real Bolshevik."[5] There is some conflicting evidence as to Avadeyev's behavior toward the imperial family. Some accounts speak of his deferential treatment, citing the fact that he referred to Nicholas as "the Emperor." But the majority of the witnesses recall him as coarse, brutish, and a heavy drinker. If a request for a favor on behalf of the family reached Avadeyev, he always gave the same response: "Let them go to hell!"[6] The guards in the house often heard him refer to the tsar as "Nicholas the Blood-Drinker" and Alexandra as "The German Bitch."[7]

The realities of imprisonment showed themselves clearly at the Ipatiev house. Ekaterinburg was another world. The disintegration of manners, respect, and even creature comforts, which had begun at Tobolsk, came full circle. The guards entered their rooms at all hours of the day and night, and the family had been forbidden to lock their doors. They were forced to listen to the Bolsheviks' lewd jokes and taunts, and at night the grand duchesses had to play for them on the piano in the drawing room. Their demands ranged from "You Fell as a Victim in the Struggle" and "Let's Forget the Old Regime" to "Get Cheerfully in Step, Comrades" and "You Don't Need a Golden Idol." [8]

A visit to the bathroom was an ordeal. The prisoners had to leave their quarters and walk through a hallway which connected to the guardroom below, through the kitchen and a second hallway before reaching the lavatory. Soldiers lounged about the outside hallway, waiting for someone to pass by. They had scrawled obscene verse on the walls, where the family could not avoid seeing it. When the girls went to the bathroom, the soldiers accompanied them, using the pretense that they had to ensure there would be no escape attempts. A guard stationed himself just outside the door. The linoleum inside was warped and cracked, and the water pipes were exposed. In a desperate attempt to maintain a degree of dignity, someone, probably Alexandra, had written out a sign and hung it above the toilet: "Please be so kind as to leave the seat as clean as you found it."[9] Opposite this, someone had scrawled pornographic drawings of the tsarina with Rasputin. When one of the young girls went to the lavatory, the soldier on duty outside told them to be sure to notice the "art" inside. In this volatile and sexually charged atmosphere, it is not surprising that the tsarina insisted that all of her daughters wear corsets.

For the Romanovs, life at the Ipatiev house was a nightmare of uncertainty and fear. The imperial family never knew if they would still be in the Ipatiev house from one day to the next or if they might be separated or killed. The privileges allowed them were few. For an hour each afternoon they could exercise in the rear garden under the watchful eye of the guards. Alexei could still not walk, and his sailor Nagorny had to carry him. Alexandra rarely joined her family in these daily activities. Instead, she spent most of her time sitting in a wheelchair, reading the Bible or the works of St. Seraphim. At night, the Romanovs played cards or read; they received little mail from the outside world, and the only newspapers they were allowed were outdated editions.

Meals at the Ipatiev house were brought in from the local Soviet soup kitchen; the imperial family ate whatever had been left over by the Bolsheviks from the previous day. Breakfast usually consisted of black bread and weak tea. The prisoners ate luncheon, the main meal, at two in the afternoon. Ivan Kharitonov, the cook, carefully rewarmed the cutlets and soup which arrived daily from the public kitchen. Dinner was usually the same as luncheon. On some days, the food did not arrive at all, and the imperial family had to make do with bread and tea. Avadeyev ordered the family and their servants to dine together, a breach of etiquette which caused great embarrassment to both groups. They ate at a table devoid of linen or silverware, although later, after much pleading, they were given five forks to use among the fifteen people who ate together. Avadeyev often brought his friends in to watch as the Romanovs ate and purposely humiliated the prisoners to impress his fellow Bolsheviks. Once, Avadeyev reached past the tsar to fetch himself a piece of food, at the same time jabbing Nicholas in the face with his elbow.[10] On another occasion, he grabbed some food from the tsar's hands, saying, "Enough for you! I will take some myself."[11]

Occasionally, there were visits from outside. Avadeyev sometimes allowed Dr. Derevenko, who remained in Ekaterinburg, to come and look after the tsarevich. A barber came several times to cut the hair of both the tsar and his son. And local priests came on at least three occasions to conduct religious services. At the end of June, when news of the imperial family's poor diet began to circulate, nuns from the Novotikhvinsky Monastery received permission to bring eggs, milk, butter, meats, cheese, and pastries for the Romanovs, but it is not known how much of this made it past Avadeyev and his soldiers.

Security, at first stringent, became relaxed. Most of the Romanovs' belongings had been stored in the low shed behind the house. Guards freely went through these items, selecting what they wanted; there was nothing the imperial family could do. They received permission to open several of their windows, but this nearly resulted in disaster. One day, when Anastasia stuck her head out the window to look around, the sentry on duty fired his rifle at her. The bullet just missed her, instead smashing into the window frame.[12] Both the sailor Nagorny and the manservant Sedinev protested the thievery and mistreatment of the prisoners; as a result, on 24 May, they were taken from the Ipatiev house and placed under arrest at the local prison. Four days later, both were executed by the Cheka.

Gradually, however, the guards' attitudes toward their prisoners began to change. They saw before them not a group of bloodthirsty tyrants but a simple, devoted, and scared family. One of these soldiers, Anatoly Yakimov, recalled:

> Though I did not speak to them when I met them I still got an impression, that entered my soul, of them. The Tsar was not young any more; he had grey hair in his beard. . . . His eyes were

kind and he had altogether a kind expression. I got the impression that he was a kind, modest, frank and talkative person. Sometimes I felt that he would speak to me right away. He looked as if he would like to talk with any one of us.

The Tsarina was not a bit like him. Her look was severe. She had the appearance and manner of a haughty and grave woman. Sometimes we used to speak about them amongst ourselves and we all thought that Nicholas Alexandrovich was a modest man but that she was very different and looked exactly like a Tsarina. She seemed older than the Tsar. There was grey hair on her temples and her face was not the face of a young woman. . . .

After I personally saw them several times I began to feel entirely different towards them. I began to pity them. I pitied them as human beings. . . . I had the idea in my mind to let them escape, or to do something to allow them to escape.[13]

One Sunday in June, a priest came to the Ipatiev house to say mass. The priest, Storozhev, entered the drawing room of the house to find the imperial family waiting for him. Alexei lay, pale and thin, on a cot at the side of the room. Alexandra sat near him in a chair, wearing a loosely flowing dark blue dress. Storozhev noticed that the tsarina wore no jewelry. He noted her bearing, which he described as "stately." But, he recalled, she seemed to be ill and looked as if she could barely control her emotions during the service.[14]

The idea of escape from the Ipatiev house seemed to occupy the thoughts of many monarchists in Ekaterinburg. The British consul in the town, Thomas Preston, later recalled: "With 10,000 Red Soldiers in the town and with Red spies at every corner and in every house, to have attempted anything in the nature of an escape would have been madness and fraught with the greatest danger to the royal family themselves. . . . There was never any organized attempt at Ekaterinburg to do so."[15]

For many years, the official Soviet version given by Peter Bykov disputed this. "From the very first days of the Romanovs' transfer to Ekaterinburg," he wrote, "there began to flock in monarchists and baronesses of every caliber and ending with nuns, clergy and representatives of foreign powers."[16] Bykov claimed that letters alerting the imperial family to escape attempts were smuggled in by Dr. Derevenko and by the nuns from the Novotikhvinsky Monastery.

Certainly four letters are known to have reached the imperial family. The first, which probably arrived early in June, read:

The friends sleep no longer and hope the hour so long awaited has arrived. The revolt of the Czechoslovaks menaces the Bolsheviks more and more seriously. Samara, Cheliabinsk and the whole of Siberia, eastern and western, are under the control of the provincial national government. The army of the Slavic friends is eighty kilometers from Ekaterinburg. The soldiers of the Red Army do not effectively resist.

Be watchful of every movement from without, wait and hope. But at the same time, I beseech you, be prudent, because the Bolsheviki before being defeated are a real and serious danger to you. Be ready all the time, day and night. Make a sketch of your two rooms, the places of the furniture, of the beds. Write exactly when you all go to bed. One of you should not sleep between two and three o'clock all the following nights. Reply in a few words, but give, I beg you, all useful information to your friends outside. It is to the same soldier who gives you this note that you must give your written answer, but do not speak a single word.

One who is ready to die for you—
An Officer of the Russian Army.[17]

The answer to this, written most probably by the tsar, follows: "From the corner of the balcony five windows face the street, two the square. All the windows are closed, glued and painted shut. The Little One [the tsarevich] is still sick in bed and cannot walk at all. Every disturbance causes him pain. . . . It is important not to risk anything without being absolutely sure of the result. We are almost all the time under watchful observation."[18]

It is likely that along with this letter came a rough floor plan of the Ipatiev house, which is known to exist in the papers of the children's English tutor Charles Gibbes. This plan, reproduced in both *The File on the Tsar* and *The House of Special Purpose*, is mistakenly identified as the governor's mansion in Tobolsk. But a comparison of the sketch with the floor plans of the Ipatiev house reproduced in Nicholas Sokolov's book shows that the two plans are the same.

The second letter that arrived at the Ipatiev house again spoke at length of a rescue attempt:

With the help of God and your sangfroid we hope to succeed without any risk. It is absolutely necessary that one of your windows be unglued so that you may be able to open it at the given moment. Please indicate this window accurately.

The fact that the little tsarevich is not able to walk complicates matters, but we have foreseen this and I do not believe it will be too great an inconvenience. Please write if two persons are necessary to carry him or if one of you may be able to take care of that. Is it possible to make the Little One sleep for one or two hours in case you should know in advance the exact hour?

It is the doctor who must give his opinion, but in case it is necessary we may furnish something or other for that purpose.

Do not be uneasy. No attempt will be made without being absolutely sure of the result.

Before God, before history and our conscience, we give you solemnly this promise.

An Officer.[19]

To this, the tsarina replied:

The second window from the corner, facing the square, has been open for two days—day and night—the seventh and eighth windows facing the square at the side of the main entrance are always open. The room is occupied by the commandant and his assistants, who are also the interior guard, about thirteen people at least, all armed with rifles, revolvers and bombs. None of the doors have keys (except ours).

The commandant and his assistants enter our rooms when they please. The one on duty makes the outside round twice each hour of the night, and we hear him talk to the sentinel beneath our windows. There is a machine gun on the balcony, another one below for a possible alarm. If there are more, we do not know.

Don't forget that we have the doctor, a chambermaid, two men, and a little boy cook with us. It would be ignoble of us, even if they didn't want to burden us, to leave them behind after their following us into exile voluntarily. The doctor has been in bed for two days after an attack in the kidneys but he is recovering. We want all the time the return of two of our men who are young and strong, and who have been locked up for a month without our knowing why [Nagorny and Sedinev, who were, in fact, already executed by the Cheka]. In their absence the Little One is being carried around by his father through the rooms and gardens.[20]

In the midst of these covert preparations, the Bolsheviks suddenly became apprehensive. On 13 June, Ascension Thursday in the Orthodox calendar, the imperial family was up early, expecting a priest to come and say mass. They waited in vain. At four o'clock that afternoon, when the Romanovs went to take their daily walk in the garden, Avadeyev abruptly informed them that this day they could not do so.

He told the prisoners that the Ural Regional Soviet feared an attack of a group of anarchists and that, as a result, the family would be transferred to Moscow immediately. They quickly packed their belongings. At eleven that night, Avadeyev told them that their departure had been delayed for a few days. The following afternoon, a drunken Avadeyev entered their rooms and told the family that the threat had passed and that therefore the journey would not take place.

A few days after this, on 21 June, a delegation from Moscow arrived to invesigate conditions in the Ipatiev house. The commander of the Northern Urals, Ian Berzin, conducted a room-by-room search, checking windows and questioning guards. He reported back to Moscow that everything was in order. The day following his departure, Alexandra noted in her diary, "Two of the soldiers came and took out one window in our room, such joy, delicious air at last and one window no longer whitewashed."[21]

At some point during these tense days, a third letter arrived at the Ipatiev house:

> Do not be uneasy about the fifty men who are in the small house opposite your windows; they will not be dangerous when it is necessary to act.
>
> Tell us something more precise about your commandant in order to make the beginning easier. One cannot say at this moment whether it will be possible to take all your people. We hope yes, but, in any event they will not be with you after leaving the house, except the doctor. . . .
>
> We much hope to indicate to you before Sunday the detailed plan of the operation. For the present it is arranged in this way. Upon the expected signal you close and barricade with furniture the door separating you from your guards who will be blockaded and terrorized in the interior of the house. By a rope made specially for this purpose you descend through the window. You are expected below. The rest is not difficult. The means for getting away are not lacking and the escape (its success) is surer than ever. The main question is taking the Little One down. Is this possible? Answer this question after considering it carefully. In any case it is the father, the mother and the son who must go first. Then the daughters and the doctor follow. Answer if this is possible in your opinion and if you can make a suitable rope, since it is a difficult matter at present to get a rope for you.
>
> An Officer [22]

Between the receipt of this letter and the Romanovs' answer, security at the Ipatiev house was suddenly tightened. On 28 June, Alexandra wrote in her diary: "We heard in the night sentries under our rooms, being told quite particularly to watch every movement at our windows—so they have become again most suspicious since our window is opened. . . ."[23] Whether this trumped-up security or perhaps a feeling of uneasiness was responsible, the Romanovs suddenly refused to cooperate with their alleged rescuers. In answer to the third letter, the tsar responded:

> We do not want to and cannot flee. We may be rescued only by force as it was by force that we were taken from Tobolsk. Therefore do not count on any active aid on our part. The commandant has many assistants. They change often and have grown weary. They conscientiously guard our prison as well as our lives and are good to us. We do not want them to suffer for our sake, nor you for us. Above all, in the name of God, avoid bloodshed. Get information yourselves about them. It is utterly impossible to descend from the window without a ladder. Even if one has descended, one is in great danger on account of the open window in the room of the commandant and from machine guns on the lower floor, which one enters from the inside court.
>
> Give up the idea of carrying us off. If you are guarding over us, you may always come and save us in the case of imminent and real danger. We are fully ignorant of what is going on outside, receiving neither papers nor letters. Since it has been permitted to open the windows, the guard has been increased, and one is forbidden to put one's head out of the window, at the risk of receiving a bullet in the face.[24]

Security was indeed being strengthened. A second, higher palisade, completely enclosing the walls of the first stockade, was erected at the beginning of June. The stark reassurances of safety which the letter writer gives to the imperial family seem most suspect; storming a heavily guarded house equipped with machine guns certainly entailed a tremendous risk not only to the would-be rescuers but to the prisoners as well.

The imperial family may have been suspicious of this proposal; judging by the tone of the answer to the third letter, it seems likely that they were actively trying to distance themselves from the rescue attempt and wrote as if they expected their answer to be seen by their guards. Even so, apparently the agreed-upon signal was given to the prisoners, for on the night of 27 June, the imperial family sat up all night dressed in their clothing, awaiting a rescue. Nothing happened, however, and the tsar noted in his diary that "the waiting and the uncertainty were very upsetting."[25]

What are we to make of these letters? For many years, the Soviets used them as evidence of the Romanovs' intentions to flee and the danger which they faced due to outside influences acting to storm the Ipatiev house. The American journalist Isaac Don Levine, who obtained the first copies of the letters from the Soviets in 1919, believed that they indicated the existence of a very real plot to spirit the family out of Ekaterinburg. Michael Pokrovsky, the deputy commissar of education, told Levine: "Ekaterinburg was surrounded on three sides when four letters in French and signed 'Officer' were found in possession of the Romanovs. These letters proved the existence of an organized plot to kidnap the tsar and his family. The local Soviet then hurriedly evacuating the city took the matter up and decided to execute the tsar, the tsarina and all the children."[26]

Clearly, the Soviets used the discovery of the letters as an excuse for assassinating the imperial family. But the Russian press has recently reported that the letters were the result of a Cheka plot to discredit the Romanovs and provide evidence of their intention to escape—all in an effort to justify the murders of the prisoners.[27] The imperial family may have sensed this—hence, their lukewarm response to the third letter they received.

The fate of the imperial family was fast becoming a thorn in the side of the Bolsheviks. The Cheka involvement in discrediting them shows how concerned they were over the situation at the Ipatiev house. By the beginning of July, time—for both the Romanovs and the Bolsheviks—was quickly running out.

45

The Last Days of the Romanovs

BY THE BEGINNING OF THE SUMMER OF 1918, Russia was in turmoil. The civil war between the Bolshevik Red Army and the monarchist Whites spread over the country. The stability of Lenin's regime had been further weakened in March when he signed the Treaty of Brest-Litovsk, ending the war with Germany. In return for cessation of hostilities, the Bolsheviks were forced to give over large tracts of the country to the kaiser: the Crimea, the Ukraine, and most of White Russia. The treaty humiliated Lenin's government and left Germany as Russia's master.

At the same time as the German occupation, the Czechoslovak revolt broke out in Siberia. At the beginning of the summer, there were between forty thousand and fifty thousand Czechoslovak prisoners of war in Russia. The Red Army tried to commandeer their services, but with little result. Most of the prisoners were actually leaving Russia when, on 14 May 1918, a conflict between Czech and Hungarian soldiers erupted in Cheliabinsk. The Bolsheviks responded by arresting the Czechs; three days later, the Czech army marched through the town, freeing the prisoners and overwhelming the local Red soldiers. Suddenly, the Czechs became a powerful force to be reckoned with. Out of sympathy with the Bolsheviks, the Czech forces joined with the White Army and began a heated offensive in Siberia. Within two weeks, the Czech troops had captured several important Bolshevik centers, including Omsk on 7 June and Samara in the central Volga on the following day.

The Czech offensive threatened the Bolshevik hold in the Urals, traditionally a Red center. Quickly, the Bolsheviks lost control of the Trans-Siberian Railway, the Volga River, and all train lines to the east of the Urals. Ekaterinburg, the capital of the Urals, was soon cut off from direct communication with Moscow except by telegraph. Against this background, the fate of the imperial family was decided in Moscow.

The question of what to do with the Romanovs had received little attention from the Bolsheviks prior to the signing of the Treaty of Brest-Litovsk. Lenin was too consumed with the survival of his own regime to worry over the former rulers. One of the earliest references to Soviet consideration of the Romanovs' fate came in February 1918. At a session of the Council of People's Commissars, the idea of holding a public trial of the former tsar was discussed. The Soviet commissar of justice, Isaac Steinberg, argued against such a course of action, and Lenin himself seemed to have doubts about such a show trial. Nevertheless, Lenin ordered Steinberg to begin preparing a file to be used in prosecuting Nicholas if the time came for a trial.

In March, when Isaac Goloshchekin went to Moscow to meet with Sverdlov, the question of what to do with the imperial family was again raised. During this meeting in Moscow, at which Goloshchekin asked for the transfer of the Romanovs from Tobolsk to Ekaterinburg, Sverdlov apparently agreed in principle that such action was acceptable until such time as a trial could be arranged in Moscow.

The next definite discussion of the imperial family's fate occurred on 23 May during a night session of the Central Executive Committee, headed by Sverdlov. Again, the question of a public trial was raised, and it seems to have been voted down. Even so, some—like Leon Trotsky—continued to push for a show trial. Trotsky, who himself hoped to act as the Soviet prosecutor, later wrote:

> During one of my brief visits to Moscow—I think it was several weeks before the execution of the Romanovs—I remarked in passing to the Politburo that, considering the bad situation in the Urals, one should speed up the tsar's trial. I proposed an open court that would unfold a portrait of the entire reign (peasant policy, labour, nationalities, culture, the two wars, etc.). The proceedings of the trial would be broadcast nationwide by radio; in the journals, accounts of the proceedings would be read and commented upon every day. Lenin replied to the effect that this would be very good if at all possible. But that there might not be enough time for such a course of action. No debate took place, as I did not insist on my proposal, being too absorbed in different work. And in the Politburo there were only three or four of us: Lenin, myself, Sverdlov. . . .[1]

But the idea of a public trial fell victim to the political situation. On 29 May, Lenin declared martial law in effect in Moscow. A number of plots and strikes against the government threatened Lenin's hold on the reins of power. It is doubtful that the Romanovs presented any threat to the survival of the Bolshevik government. Nevertheless, the possibility that the prisoners might fall into White hands preyed on Lenin's mind.

Personally, Lenin was hostile to the Romanovs. From 1887, when his elder brother Alexander was executed for trying to assassinate Tsar Alexander III, Lenin seems to have determined that it was politically necessary to exterminate the imperial family if given the opportunity. In 1911 he wrote that "it was necessary to behead at least one hundred Romanovs."[2] On another occasion, Lenin quoted the views of fellow Bolshevik Serge Nechayev. When asked which of all of the Romanovs gathered together should be assassinated, Nechayev answered, "The whole House of Romanov." Lenin cited this example, saying, "This is simplicity to the point of genius."[3]

When Lenin embarked his country on the Red Terror, he certainly intended to rid himself of any opposition. The aide to Felix Dzerzhinsky, the founder of the Cheka, later said: "We are not carrying out war against individuals. We are exterminating the bourgeoisie as a class. We aren't looking for evidence or witnesses to reveal deeds or words against the Soviet power. The first question which we ask is—to what class does he belong, what are his origins, upbringing, education or profession. These questions define the fate of the accused. This is the essence of Red Terror."[4]

The first decisive action toward exterminating the Romanovs came on the night of 12 June, when a group of Bolsheviks abducted and killed the tsar's brother Grand Duke Michael in Perm. The grand duke, who had been living under house arrest at a local hotel, was taken—along with his English secretary Nicholas Johnson—to a deserted forest on the outskirts of the city, and there both men were shot, their bodies subsequently destroyed in a factory smelter.

The Soviets announced that the grand duke had disappeared, that a group of White Guards had kidnapped him, that Michael had escaped, that his whereabouts were unknown—all in an effort to confuse the circumstances and hide the truth of their crime. Similiar tactics of deception would later be used by the Bolsheviks following the disappearance of the imperial family from Ekaterinburg.

At the same time as Michael's assassination, Moscow allowed rumors to be spread to the effect that the tsar and his family had been killed. Richard Pipes believes this occurred "to test the public reaction of the proposed murder of the ex-Tsar."[5] If this was the case, the near silence which greeted the news must have proved a deciding factor in the later action they took against the Romanovs. On 3 July *The Times* of London reported: "Every time this kind of public prominence is given to the Romanov Family people think that something serious is on foot. Bolsheviks are getting impatient of these frequent surprises about the deposed dynasty, and the question is again raised as to the advisability of settling the fate of the Romanovs, so as to be done with them once and for all."[6]

There appears to have been no protest at this hint of what the Bolsheviks might do with the imperial family—not from any of the tsar's former allies or even from his numerous royal relatives in Europe.

By the first week of July 1918, the Czechoslovak forces were within a few hundred miles of Ekaterinburg. The city was in chaos, and it was only a matter of weeks before the Bolsheviks would be forced to evacuate the Urals. Faced with this imminent disaster, Moscow now decided to deal with the question of the Romanovs once and for all. Ominously, the Ekaterinburg newspaper the *Ural Worker* warned: "Romanov and his relatives will not escape the Court of the People when the hour sounds."[7]

In the first week of July, Isaac Goloshchekin was in Moscow, a guest of his friend Sverdlov. Bykov relates that Goloshchekin had been dispatched to Moscow to discuss the fate of the imperial family. The Ural Regional Soviet wanted their immediate execution; there was still talk in Moscow of a show trial, although the rapidly worsening situation in the Urals soon put an end to it.

The decision to execute the imperial family was made during this week in Moscow. On 4 July, the Fifth All-Russian Soviet Congress convened at the Bolshoi Theatre. During this time, Lenin and Sverdlov were, of necessity, working in close contact. Certainly Lenin must also have been in close contact with Goloshchekin at this time, for on 7 July he ordered that Alexander Beloborodov, the chairman of the Ural Regional Soviet, be connected directly by telegraph with the Kremlin.

It seems likely that the decision was made prior to 4 July. On this day, Alexander Beloborodov dispatched the following cable to Moscow: "Chairman Central Execeutive Committee Sverdlov for Goloshchekin: Syromolotov has just gone to organize matters in accordance with instructions of center. No cause for alarm. Avadeyev replaced. His assistant Moshkin arrested. In place of Avadeyev, Yurovsky. Internal guard entirely changed, replaced by others."[8]

This cable informed Goloshchekin and Moscow of events at the Ipatiev house. It seems to indicate that Moscow had expressed concerns as to the situation in the House of Special Purpose, and asked for a change of guard and commandant. The responsibility for looking after the prisoners now switched from the local Ekaterinburg Soviet to the Cheka.

We now know that Lenin personally ordered the execution of the imperial family. Although official Soviet accounts place the responsibility for the decision with the Ural Regional Soviet, Trotsky, in his diary, makes it quite clear that the assassination took place on the authority of Lenin. Trotsky wrote:

> My next visit to Moscow took place after the fall of Ekaterinburg. Talking to Sverdlov, I asked in passing, "Oh, yes, and where is the tsar?" "It's all over," he answered. "He has been shot." "And where is his family?" "And the family with him." "All of them?" I asked, apparently with a touch of surprise. "All of them," replied Sverdlov. "What about it?" He was waiting to see my reaction, I made no reply. "And who made the decision?" I asked. "We decided it here. Ilyich [Lenin] believed that we shouldn't leave the Whites a live banner to rally round, especially under the present difficult circumstances.[9]

Goloshchekin returned to Ekaterinburg on 12 July. An emergency meeting of the Ural Regional Soviet was held that evening, at which Goloshchekin presumably communicated to his comrades Moscow's permission to execute the Romanovs.

On 14 July the Ekaterinburg newspaper *Izvestiya* reported: "Last night the Chairman of the Soviet had a long conversation by direct wire with Moscow with the Chairman of the Sovnarkom Lenin. The conversation concerned a military review and the security of the former Tsar Nicholas Romanov."[10] That evening, a second meeting of the Ural Regional Soviet took place. At this meeting, the members discussed the proposed execution of the tsar and his family. It was now a question of details.

There appears to be some confusion as to when the final orders came from Moscow. Peter Voikov, the regional commissar of supplies, later recalled:

> We then submitted for ratification to the Central Committee of the Bolshevik Party and the Soviet of the Ural Region. It was ratified immediately. That same evening Goloshchekin, the Kremlin's special envoy, telegraphed to Moscow. Moscow approved our decision and stressed that the whole family must disappear at the same time as the tsar. In Moscow, as with us in the Ural region, they were afraid of a plot to rescue the Tsarevich, the Tsarina and the Grand Duchesses after Nicholas's death and then to make the Tsarina regent. . . .[11]

Of course, Voikov's story was meant to present Moscow in the best possible light and places the responsibility for the initial decision to execute with the Ural Regional Soviet. This we know to be untrue, since Goloshchekin carried back to Ekaterinburg Moscow's death warrant. The meetings of the Ural Regional Soviet on 12, 14, and 15 July were apparently held not to determine the fate of the Romanovs—which had already been decided—but the manner and time of their execution.

In 1989 the memoirs of Jacob Yurovsky, the last commandant of the Ipatiev house, were published in the Soviet press. Yurovsky's account relates that the final order for execution came only on 16 July 1918. It was an order which had come from Lenin in answer to a telegram sent from Ekaterinburg. At six o'clock that evening, Goloshchekin signed the order.[12] The fate of the Romanovs was now decided.

On 4 July 1918, Jacob Yurovsky, the chief of the Ekaterinburg Cheka, was appointed commandant of the Ipatiev House. Little is known of his early life. His first job was as a watchmaker in Tomsk. He became a Bolshevik in 1905. Although a party member, Yurovsky converted to the Lutheran faith following a brief stay in Berlin. Up until the outbreak of the First World War he owned and operated a photographic studio. During the war, he served as a medic on the front lines. Following the Revolution, he joined the Cheka and served as the Ural regional commissar of justice.

Yurovsky was a loyal Bolshevik, a man Moscow could rely on to carry out its orders regarding the imperial family. On taking up his appointment as commandant of the Ipatiev house, Yurovsky quickly tightened security. He put a stop to the petty thievery of the Romanovs' possessions by the guards. He forbade the exterior guards from entering the rooms where the family lived. From the imperial family he collected all of their jewelry and valuables; these he placed in a box which he sealed and left with the prisoners. Alexandra kept only two bracelets which her uncle Leopold, the duke of Albany, had given her as a child and which she could not take off. He did not know, however, that underneath their clothing the tsarina and her daughters had concealed diamonds, emeralds, rubies, and ropes of pearls.

The interior guard of the Ipatiev house was also changed. With Yurovsky came ten new men, variously identified as Lettish soldiers or Magyar prisoners of war. The old exterior guards resented the new soldiers, who were allowed on the main floor of the Ipatiev house and dined personally with Yurovsky and his assistant Gregory Nikulin.

Soon after Avadeyev was replaced, the imperial family received a fourth letter promising rescue:

> The change of the bodyguard and the commandant has hindered our writing you. Do you know the cause of this? We answer your

questions. We are a group of officers in the Russian Army who have not lost the conscience of duty to the Tsar and the country. We don't inform you in detail about ourselves, which you understand well, but your friends D. and T. [presumably Dolgoruky and Tatischev, who had been executed], who are already saved, know us. The hour of deliverance is approaching and the days of the usurpers are numbered. In any case, the Slavic armies are advancing more and more toward Ekaterinburg. . . . The moment is becoming critical and now one need not fear bloodshed. Don't forget, the Bolsheviki at the last moment will be capable of any crime. This moment has arrived. One must act. Be sure that the machine gun on the lower floor will not be dangerous. As to the commandant, we will have to carry him off. Wait for the whistle about midnight. That will be the signal.

> An Officer.[13]

On Sunday, 14 July, two priests came to the Ipatiev house to say mass. One of the priests, Father Storozhev, later recalled:

I went into the living room first, then the deacon and Yurovsky. At the same time Nicholas Alexandrovich entered through the doors leading into the inner room. Two of his daughters were with him, I did not have a chance to see exactly which ones. I believe Yurovsky asked Nicholas Alexandrovich, "Well, are you all here?" Nicholas Alexandrovich answered firmly, "Yes, all of us."

Ahead, beyond the archway, Alexandra Feodorovna was already in place with two daughters and Alexei Nicholaievich. He was sitting in a wheelchair and wore a jacket, as it seemed to me, with a sailor's collar. He was pale, but not so much as at the time of my first service. In general he looked more healthy. Alexandra Feodorovna also had a healthier appearance. She wore the same dress as on 2 June. As for Nicholas Alexandrovich, he was wearing the same clothes as the first time. Only I cannot, somehow, picture to myself clearly whether he was on this occasion wearing the St. George Cross on his breast. Tatiana Nicholaievna, Olga Nicholaievna, Anastasia Nicholaievna and Marie Nicholaievna were wearing black skirts and white blouses. Their hair . . . had grown and now came to the level of their shoulders at the back.

It seemed to me that on this occasion Nicholas Alexandrovich and all of his daughters were—I won't say in depressed spirits but they gave the impression, just the same, of being exhausted. . . .

According to the liturgy of the service it is customary at a certain point to read the prayer, "Who Resteth with the Saints." On this occasion for some reason the deacon, instead of reading the prayer, began to sing it, and I as well, somewhat embarrassed by this departure from the ritual. But we had scarcely begun to sing when I heard the members of the Romanov family, standing behind me, fall on their knees. . . .

After the service everyone kissed the Holy Cross. Father Deacon and I gave the Host to Nicholas Alexandrovich and Alexandra Feodorovna. . . . As I went out I passed very close to the former Grand Duchesses and heard the scarcely audible word "Thank you"—I don't think I just imagined this. . . .

Father Deacon and I walked in silence to the Art School Building, where he suddenly said to me, "Do you know, Father Archpresbyter, something has happened to them there." Since Father Deacon's words somewhat confirmed my own impression, I stopped and asked him why he thought so. "Yes, precisely," the deacon said, "they are all some other people, truly. Why, no one even sang." And it must be said that actually, for the first time, no one of the Romanov family sang with us during the service of 14 July.[14]

On the following day, when the nuns from the Novotikhvinsky Monastery arrived at the Ipatiev house, Yurovsky asked them to bring fifty eggs and some milk with them when they came again on Tuesday. He also passed along a note from one of the grand duchesses asking for some thread.

That afternoon, a group of women from a local labor union came to wash the floors of the Ipatiev house. No talking was permitted, but the four grand duchesses helped the women move the furniture and seemed cheerful enough. One of the women later recalled seeing Yurovsky sitting with the tsarevich, asking about his health. That evening, Alexandra noted in her diary, "Heard a report of an artillery shot in the night and several revolver shots."[15]

Tuesday, 16 July 1918, dawned hot and dusty in Ekaterinburg. The Ipatiev house, with its closed, whitewashed, and barred windows, baked in the summer heat. The day passed normally for the imperial family. At four o'clock in the afternoon, the tsar and his daughters took their usual walk in the small garden. Early in the evening, Yurovsky sent away the fifteen-year-old kitchen boy Leonid Sedinev, saying that his uncle wished to see him. Nicholas and Alexandra passed the evening playing bezique; at ten thirty, they went to bed.

As night fell over Ekaterinburg, the sound of nearby artillery fire shattered the sky. The White Army and Czechoslovak forces were only a matter of days from capturing the city. There was an early curfew in effect for the time, and at midnight all traffic on Voznesensky Avenue was stopped. When Arthur Thomas, an aide to the British consul Thomas Preston, walked along the street before the Ipatiev house late that evening, the guards at the House of Special Purpose quickly ordered him to the other side of the avenue.[16]

Early on the morning of 17 July, a peasant named Buivid, who lived in rooms on the lower floor of the Popov house just across Voznesensky Street from the Ipatiev house, went into the garden and was sick. As he stood watching the Ipatiev house, he suddenly heard muffled shots which came from within the basement. Fearing for his life, Buivid quickly returned to his room.

"Did you hear?" his roommate asked.

"I heard shots," Buivid answered.

"Did you understand?"

"I understand," Buivid answered, and the two men fell silent. Twenty minutes later, the gates at the Ipatiev house opened, and the two men heard an automobile drive out of the courtyard and disappear into the Siberian night.[17]

46

The End of the Romanovs

THERE WAS NO HINT that anything was out of the ordinary when Alexandra, Nicholas, and their children went to bed at half-past ten on the night of 16 July 1918. It was simply the end to another dreary, uncertain, sweltering, summer day in the Ipatiev house.

Earlier in the evening, Yurovsky had summoned thirty-one-year-old Paul Medvedev, the captain of the guards, to his office on the upper floor. "Tonight, Medvedev," Yurovsky said, "we will have to shoot them all. Notify the guardsmen not to be alarmed if they hear shots." Yurovsky also asked Medvedev to collect the revolvers from the guards on duty; Medvedev brought back to Yurovsky twelve revolvers—Brownings, Mausers, and Nagants.[1]

Three hours later, Yurovsky woke Dr. Botkin and asked him to tell the imperial family that the uncertain situation in the city posed a danger to their safety; they were to dress at once and spend the night in the basement where they could be more easily protected.

It took the prisoners thirty minutes to wash and dress. While they were preparing to go below, Yurovsky waited impatiently in the drawing room. Below, in the guardroom, the execution squad waited.

Just past two in the morning, the imperial family came out of their rooms. No one seemed alarmed. Nicholas came first, carrying Alexei in his arms, followed by Alexandra, limping on her cane. The four girls, dressed in black skirts and white blouses, came next, Tatiana carrying her pet King Charles spaniel, Jimmy. The maid, Anna Demidova, held two pillows; sewn deep inside were small metal boxes containing many pieces of valuable jewelry belonging to the tsarina and her daughters. Dr. Botkin, the valet Alexei Trupp, and the cook Ivan Kharitonov followed.

Yurovsky led the prisoners through the empty first-floor rooms of the Ipatiev house, down a secondary staircase, and out a doorway into the courtyard at the side of the mansion. He then opened a set of double doors into the basement, and the Romanovs and their servants followed him through a series of hallways and guardrooms to the opposite side of the house. He stopped in a hallway directly beneath the bedroom used by the grand duchesses and gestured them into a small semi–basement room with a vaulted ceiling. One arched window sat high in the wall. Opposite the doors to the hallway, a second set of double doors led to a small storage room. There was no escape. "The Romanovs," recalled Yurovsky, "had no idea what was taking place."

The basement room was empty. On entering, Alexandra asked, "Why is there no chair here? Is it forbidden to sit down?" Yurovsky ordered two chairs brought in. Alexandra sat in one, Nicholas—still holding his son—in the other. The four girls and the servants stood to the side and behind the imperial couple. Yurovsky asked them to wait until the danger had passed and disappeared, closing the doors to the hallway behind him.

In the courtyard of the house, a Fiat truck stood waiting. Yurovsky asked the driver to gun his engine to muffle the sound of the shots from the murders inside the basement. He then went to collect his men. There were ten members of the execution squad, six Hungarians and four Russians. When all was ready, Yurovsky reentered the room where the imperial family waited.

The family watched anxiously as Yurovsky stood before them. The commandant told the family that "in view of the fact that your relatives are continuing their offensive against Soviet Russia, the Ural Executive Committee has decided to execute you."

The tsar turned from the execution squad and faced his family. He then turned back to Yurovsky and asked, "What? What?" Yurovsky repeated what he had said and then gave the order to begin firing. The men in the execution squad had each been assigned a particular victim and told to aim at the heart to avoid excessive bloodshed. They crowded in the doorway in rows to avoid hitting each other.

Yurovsky personally fired the first shot; his bullet struck Nicholas in the head, and the tsar fell forward onto the floor, falling over the body of his son. Alexandra quickly crossed herself; just as she finished, a bullet ripped through her skull, knocking her backward off of her chair and killing her instantly. The four girls, screaming and crying, huddled together as the shooting continued. It went on for two or three minutes, the bullets ricocheting around the small room "like hailstones."

When the first volley ended, the room was filled with an acrid smoke. Alexandra lay next to Nicholas, both in a spreading pool of blood. Low moans filled the silence of the murder room. Alexei had not died, shielded from the bullets when his father fell over him. He was trying to crawl across the bloodstained floor, his arms raised to his face in a final effort to ward off the attackers. Nikulin, Yurovsky's assistant, was paralyzed with fear, firing round after round at the struggling boy before Yurovsky ran to his side and fired several shots into the thirteen-year-old. Only one of the four girls had fallen in the first volley; the others huddled together in a corner of the room screaming, splattered with their parents' blood. The guards turned on them, shooting and stabbing them with bayonets. To the horror of the assassins, their bayonets met with firm resistance as they plunged them repeatedly into the girls' upper bodies. After several minutes, the three grand duchesses, covered in blood and stabbed repeatedly, fell silent. Kharitonov was shot so hard that he "sat down and died." Botkin and Trupp were still alive, and the soldiers quickly finished them off. Demidova, hiding behind the pillows she had brought from the rooms above, was chased back and forth across the rear wall, stumbling over the dying bodies of the imperial family; in a feeble effort to save herself, she clutched at the soldiers' bayonets as they stabbed at her again and again, slicing her hands to ribbons until she, too, fell dead.[2]

The entire execution took some twenty minutes. Yurovsky and his men wandered around the room, checking pulses. The scene was one of confusion. They could barely see through the thick smoke. No one knew what to do. Several of the soldiers began to strip the bodies of their jewelry and watches, but Yurovsky put a quick stop to this. He ordered his men to fetch sheets and blankets from the bedrooms upstairs. These were used to wrap the corpses. The heavy bundles were carried through the basement rooms to the courtyard where the Fiat truck waited and were loaded inside.

As the bodies were being loaded, several of the guards noticed moaning coming from within the bloody sheets. One of the four grand duchesses suddenly sat up and began screaming, quickly followed by two of her sisters. The men were horrified. The nerves of several of the guards gave way completely, and they ran back inside the Ipatiev house to fetch Yurovsky. They could not shoot them in the open courtyard for fear the sound of gunfire would attract attention. On Yurovsky's orders they grabbed bayonets and stabbed at the girls as they lay struggling in the truck, covering their faces with their arms and hands. Yurovsky watched in disbelief as the bayonets would not penetrate the bodies. Finally, the crying from within the vehicle stopped.[3]

At three in the morning, the truck left the Ipatiev house and made its way into the forests on the outskirts of Ekaterinburg.

The execution having been ordered by Moscow, the details of the destruction of the bodies were left to the Ural Regional Soviet. Yurovsky had suggested an abandoned mine shaft thirteen miles from Ekaterinburg. Known as the Four Brothers, it sat in the middle of the

Koptyaki Forest, in an area surrounded by swamps and pits. The truck, with its grisly cargo, was to meet up with a second group of Bolsheviks near the roadway leading back into the forest, and there the bodies were to be transferred to horse-drawn carts. The journey was fraught with difficulties: The driver of the truck lost his way and took a wrong turn, sinking the vehicle deep in the muddy roadway. Yurovsky got out and wandered off into the forest along with most of the execution squad, searching for the road leading to the mine shaft. Finally, the truck was extricated and continued on its way into the dark forest. Halfway along the road, the second party waited for Yurovsky and his cargo. Yurovsky recalled:

> There were workers (members of the Soviet, its executive committee and so on) assembled by Yermakov [Peter Yermakov, a member of the Cheka]. They shouted: "Why did you bring them dead?" They thought they were to be entrusted with the execution of the Romanovs. They started to transfer the bodies to carts. . . . Right away they began to clean out their pockets. Here to I had to threaten death by shooting and to post guards. It turned out that Tatiana, Olga and Anastasia wore some kind of special corsets. It was decided to strip the bodies naked—but not here, but rather where they were to be buried.[4]

The party continued along the road into the pine forest. By this time, it was nearly seven in the morning. Once the carts were unloaded, Yurovsky ordered that the bodies be stripped and burned. "When the men undressed one of the girls [writes Yurovsky], they saw that her corset had been ripped in places by the bullets. And through the lining they could see diamonds. The men could not keep their eyes off the diamonds so . . . [I] decided to send them away except for a few guards and five members of the firing squad."[5]

The others were dismissed, leaving Yurovsky and his most trusted men alone with the corpses. Yurovsky's sudden need for secrecy may have arisen from fear of petty thievery. But there may have been another, more pressing reason for this intense privacy, a dark secret which sent Yurovsky into a panic and which lay hidden in the Koptyaki Forest for nearly seventy-five years.

As they undressed the bodies, Yurosvky began to take note of the jewels. Inside the corsets were sewn belts stuffed with diamonds. Alexandra wore a long belt made of pearls, sewn into the lining of her corset. Alexei as well, Yurovsky recalled, had such jewels under his clothes.

Once all of the jewels had been collected, the naked bodies were thrown into the open mine shaft. Grenades were then tossed down the shaft to blow it up. But the mine would not collapse. The men dumped some tree branches down the shaft to disguise the contents below. Yurovsky ordered a cleanup of the area surrounding the shaft. Cloth- ing, shoes, and personal items belonging to the family were placed in a large bonfire and burned. Finally, after nearly a full day at the mine shaft, Yurovsky returned to the Ipatiev house.

Yurovsky later wrote that the pit was "only to be a temporary grave." There was no chance of concealing the bodies where they lay. Along the Koptyaki Road, there were a number of other, deeper mine shafts hidden in the marshes and swamps of the forests. Yurovsky de- cided to remove the bodies from the Four Brothers mine shaft and hide them elsewhere. On the night of 18 July, he and his men returned to the abandoned mine shaft. One of the men was lowered down the shaft and attached ropes to the bodies. One by one, they were raised to the surface and laid out on the clay slope of the pit. When all of the corpses had been exhumed, they were loaded into the back of the Fiat truck. Yurovsky and his men drove back along the forest road. Along the way, the truck got stuck in the mud. After trying to extricate it, Yurovsky finally decided to bury the bodies nearby. The commandant and his men wanted to burn the bodies of the tsarina and the tsarevich, but mistook one of the other women for Alexandra and threw the wrong body onto the funeral pyre. These two bodies, Yurovsky wrote, were buried at the place where they were burned. A shallow pit just off the side of the road became the Ro- manovs' final grave. The naked bodies were thrown into the hole, some still bound with the ropes used to haul them to the surface of the Four Brothers mine shaft. Sulphuric acid was poured over the bodies and their faces were smashed in with gun butts to prevent identification. The makeshift grave was covered with dirt and brush and the truck driven over it several times to compact the ground.[6] Finally, on the morning of 19 July, Yurovsky and his men returned to Ekaterinburg.

On the morning of 17 July, the two nuns from the Novotikhvinsky Monastery returned to the Ipatiev house with the supplies Yurovsky had requested the day before. They waited to see the commandant him- self, but one of the guards told them that he was out. Confused, the two nuns waited until one of the sentries roughly informed them, "Go away! Don't bring things any more!"[7]

The Ipatiev house was still heavily guarded; but the soldiers had all been told that the imperial family had been shot the night before. One of the guards, Anatoly Yakimov, later recalled:

On the table in the commandant's office lay many different kinds of valuables. They were stones, earrings, pins with stones, and beads. Many were ornamented. Some were in cases. The cases were all open.

The door leading from the ante-room into the rooms which had been occupied by the imperial family was closed as before, but there was no one in the rooms. This was obvious. No sound came from there. Before, when the imperial family lived there, there were always sounds of life in their rooms: voices, steps. At this time there was no life there. Only their little dog stood in the ante-room, at the door to the rooms where the imperial family had lived, waiting to be let in. I well remember thinking at the time: you are waiting in vain.[8]

On 20 July, the first official announcement on the imperial family came from the Ural Soviet:

DECISION
of the Presidium of the Divisional Council of Deputies of Workmen, Peasants and Red Guards of the Urals:

In view of the fact that Czechoslovakian bands are threatening the Red Capital of the Urals, Ekaterinburg; that the crowned executioner may escape from the tribunal of the people (a White Guard plot to carry off the whole Imperial Family has just been discovered) the Presidium of the Divisional Committee in pursuance of the will of the people, has decided that the ex-Tsar, Nicholas Romanov, guilty before the people of innumerable crimes, shall be shot.

The decision of the Presidium of the Divisional Council was carried out on the night of 16-17 July. Romanov's family has been transferred from Ekaterinburg to a place of greater safety.[9]

At the same time, Moscow issued its official statement:

At the first session of the Central Executive Committee elected by the Fifth Congress of the Councils a message was made public, received by direct wire from the Ural Regional Council, concerning the shooting of the ex-Tsar, Nicholas Romanov.

Recently Ekaterinburg, the capital of the Red Urals, was seriously threatened by the approach of the Czechoslovak bands. At the same time a counter-revolutionary conspiracy was discovered, having for its object the wresting of the tyrant from the hands of the Council's authority by armed force. In view of this fact, the Presidium of the Ural Regional Council decided to shoot the ex-Tsar, Nicholas Romanov. This decision was carried out on 16 July.

The wife and son of Romanov have been sent to a place of security. Documents concerning the conspiracy which were discovered have been forwarded to Moscow by a special messenger.

It had been recently decided to bring the ex-Tsar before a tribunal, to be tried for his crimes against the people, and only later occurrences led to delay in adopting this course. The Presidency of the Central Executive Committee, after having discussed the circumstances which compelled the Ural Regional Soviet to take the decision to shoot Nicholas Romanov, decided as follows: "The Russian Central Executive Committee, in the persons of the Presidium, accepts the decision of the Ural Regional Council as being regular.[10]

Both official announcements made reference only to the tsar as having been killed; Alexandra and Alexei, they said, had been sent to a safe place. No mention was made of the four grand duchesses. There were political reasons for this deception. At the time of the announcements, the kaiser's government had issued repeated warnings to Moscow that no harm must come to "the German Princesses"—presumably Alexandra and her daughters. While the Soviets later admitted that the entire family had perished, they intentionally withheld this information at the time. The announcements also squarely placed the decision to execute the imperial family with Ekaterinburg and not Moscow, which is known to be untrue.

Before the announcements were made public, the members of the government were informed of the execution. On the evening of 18 July, as the commissar of health was reading a draft of a new public health proposal to the Council of Peoples' Commissars, Sverdlov entered the room and whispered a few words to Lenin.

"Comrade Sverdlov wants to make a statement," Lenin said.

"I have to say," Sverdlov announced, "that we have had a communication that in Ekaterinburg, by a decision of the Regional Soviet, Nicholas has been shot. The Presidium has resolved to approve." Silence fell over the room. Then Lenin said slowly, "Let us now go on to read the draft clause by clause."[11]

On 25 July, Ekaterinburg fell to the advancing White and Czechoslovak forces. The Ipatiev house was empty, the basement room stained with blood. Although both Moscow and Ekaterinburg had announced the execution of the tsar, there remained the very real possibility that the rest of the family might still be alive.

Over the course of the following year, no less than five separate investigations were undertaken. Three of these were judicial in nature; the other two—the Officers' Commission Inquiry and the Military-Criminal Investigatory Divisonal Report—were sponsored by the White Army.[12] Of these five investigations, the last was conducted by Nicholas Sokolov, a highly trained jurist. Sokolov took on the case five months after the imperial family's disappearance. From the beginning, his inquiry was beset with difficulties, both practical and political. He had only five months in Ekaterinburg before the city fell back into Red hands. He carried the investigation into European exile with him. The results of his inquiry—published in 1924 as *The Murder of the Imperial Family* —have stood as the official version of events at Ekaterinburg.

Sokolov's inquiry produced a wealth of circumstantial evidence. The basement room of the Ipatiev house was stained with human blood and filled with bullet holes. He discovered a coded Bolshevik telegram sent to Moscow by Alexander Beloborodov within hours of the murders which informed Jacob Sverdlov that the entire family had perished. Four former guards at the Ipatiev house—Paul Medvedev, Anatoly Yakimov, Michael Letemin, and Philip Proskuriakov—all gave statements to the Whites that the imperial family had been shot, although all but Medvedev heard their information second- or third hand. Finally, at the Four Brothers mine shaft, the investigators found charred remains of clothing, shoes, handbags, splinters of jewels, and other objects all identified as having belonged to the imperial family.

But Sokolov never found the bodies. The piles of ashes at the mine shaft seemed to point toward a grim conclusion, and Sokolov was further convinced when he found that an order for many gallons of sulphuric acid had been placed the day after the imperial family disappeared. Here Sokolov found his answer. His investigation concluded that the Romanovs and their servants had been burned at the mine shaft, their remains then dissolved in sulphuric acid.

Throughout the early years of the investigation, the Bolsheviks kept strangely silent. Finally, when the first accounts were published, Soviet versions began to appear closely following the White theory. It was clearly in the Soviet interest to conceal the truth behind the crimes. No purpose would be served if the actual disposal of the bodies was revealed, and the Soviets themselves did not want to provide the Whites with any tsarist relics.

Over the years, the Sokolov report has been the subject of an immense body of criticism. Nevertheless, it is now apparent that the majority of his report came close to the truth. The final mystery—the burial place of the Romanovs—was revealed in 1989, seventy-one years after the murders.

47

The Secret of Koptyaki Forest

O<small>N</small> 12 A<small>PRIL</small> 1989, the Soviet journal *Moscow News* printed a startling article. In "The Earth Yields Up Its Secrets," writer Geli Ryabov claimed to have discovered the bodies of the imperial family buried in a mass grave on the outskirts of the Koptyaki Forest.

The manner of the story's appearance itself was something of a mystery. A week before the story appeared, President Mikhail Gorbachev had called on Queen Elizabeth II. There was considerable speculation in the press that he would invite the queen to make a state visit to the Soviet Union. If the queen accepted, she would be the first British monarch to visit Russia since the Revolution, and the British press openly debated the propriety of the queen's accepting such an invitation when the questions surrounding the murder of her cousins still remained unresolved.

The queen did accept Gorbachev's invitation. Rumor had it that one of the conditions of any state visit to Russia was a clarification of the fate of the imperial family. Neither the queen nor Gorbachev have ever acknowledged that any conditions were made, nor was there an official Soviet answer to the question of the Romanov mystery.

A week after Gorbachev returned to the Soviet Union, the Ryabov story appeared. Speculation had it that the story was Moscow's answer to the queen's concerns. This has never been acknowledged, either, but the timing certainly lends itself to this theory.

Ryabov began to research the fate of the imperial family in the mid-1970s. In 1976 he managed to locate the son and daughter of Jacob Yurovsky in Leningrad. According to his children, Yurovsky suffered from guilt over his role in the imperial family's murder for the rest of his life. He told his son that an effort had been made to destroy the bodies of the imperial family at the Four Brothers mine shaft but that they were later reburied and a simulated destruction then took place, to conceal the actual grave. He explained that although the entire family had been executed, Moscow deemed it necessary to hide the fact of the deaths of the Tsarina and her five children for political reasons.

On learning of this version of the end of the Romanovs, Ryabov set out on a quest to discover the truth. Yurovsky's son Alexander, a retired admiral, gave Ryabov his father's notes on the imperial family's murder. Ryabov spent several years searching through Kremlin archives with the permission of the Interior Ministry, for which he worked as an assistant. His quest led him to the forests around the Four Brothers area. After three years, he and a number of assistants, including Alexander Avdonin, found the burial pit on 30 May 1979. It was a shallow grave—approximately six by ten feet and only three feet deep. "We took a water pipe several inches in diameter [said Ryabov], sharpened it and began to insert it over the approximate grave site, using a heavy mallet. At first we hit virgin topsoil, undisturbed by human hands, but further down we hit soil which showed evidence of human action. . . . Soon we made the first find—the very first one was black-green. . . . It was the pelvic bone of Nicholas II."

Ryabov and his assistants "reached into the grave" and "touched at least eight or nine skeletons. . . ." Although they did not fully excavate the site, Ryabov claimed that there were in fact eleven sets of remains. "I would stake my life on that fact," he later explained.

In all, Ryabov exhumed three skulls, which he declared to be Nicholas, Alexandra, and "either Alexei or Anastasia—we aren't sure which yet." In the skull of Alexandra there was a large gunshot wound to the face.[1] "Even for me," Ryabov explained, "it was not difficult to identify them, the number of bodies, the character of the wounds, false teeth which had frequently been described in foreign publications, and the remnants of smashed ceramic pots of acid around the bodies."[2]

The grave itself was located in a clearing at the edge of the forest, just off the small side road leading toward the abandoned mine shaft and some six hundred feet from the Moscow Road and the railway track. Ironically, Sokolov had examined the area and concluded that this was where the truck carrying the bodies had broken down; he even reproduced a photograph of the site in his book, never knowing that it was the actual burial place. The bodies had been thrown into the grave hastily, one on top of the other. Some of them were still bound with the ropes which had been used to pull them up from the Four Brothers mine shaft after the first burial. The remains were only skeletal, although a few bones still bore traces of fatty tissue and clumps of hair that had somehow survived the passage of time.

Ryabov made photographs of the remains, including the three skulls and a few other bones. No attempt was made to excavate the entire grave. Later the skulls were reburied in the grave.

Ryabov kept the discovery a secret until 1989. "Ten years ago, when we opened up the grave where the naked bodies were thrown and even later, I just could not publish the results of my investigation," he said.[3] This apparently changed under the Gorbachev administration, with its policy of glasnost.

Ryabov's claims made headlines around the world, hailed as the final solution to the decades-old mystery of the fate of the Romanovs. However, he produced no evidence to support his claims, and much of what he had declared was clearly—to be generous—hopeful fabrication. He had no dental records with which to compare the teeth in the skulls, no identifying features, save for a scar on the skull believed to be that of Nicholas, a legacy from the attack on his life in Japan in 1892. His identification of "the pelvic bone of Nicholas II" was equally absurd. Yet Ryabov repeatedly expressed that he was "a trained investigator, a police specialist . . . and I can analyze. I was taught that."[4]

Ryabov refused to reveal the location of the burial pit to the authorities, saying that he would do so only when he obtained assurances from the authorities that the remains would be given a Christian burial. But because he had worked from Yurovsky's notes in the Kremlin archives, it was a simple matter for the Soviets to undertake their own investigation.

On 13 July 1991, the grave in the Koptyaki Forest was opened. In the dead of night, a group of Soviet officials—police, archaeologists, forensics experts, cameramen—began the exhumation. The grave had been considerably disturbed not only by Ryabov's dig twelve years earlier but also by the laying of a power cable a few feet away. The bones were barely distinguishable from the surrounding mud, so badly had the site disintegrated. One by one, the skeletons were exhumed. But of the eleven bodies which should have been in the grave—Nicholas, Alexandra, Alexei, the four grand duchesses, and the four servants—only nine were found. The remains were taken to the Department of Criminal Pathology in Sverdlovsk, formerly Ekaterinburg. Here the remains were simply dumped in a massive heap on the floor of the firing range, a pile of some seven hundred bones, the apparent physical remains of the imperial family.[5]

Authorities in Sverdlovsk announced that they hoped to undertake an identification of the bodies. Concurrent with this, the Sverdlovsk Komsomol, the youth branch of the Communist party, agreed to host a forum on the fate of the Romanovs which they hoped would address all outstanding questions. The congress, to which pathologists, historians, and Romanov experts would be invited, was to take place in August 1991.[6]

That August, however, events in Moscow overtook concerns in Sverdlovsk. The attempted hard-line coup against President Gorbachev and the subsequent foundering of the Soviet government diverted attention from the mystery of the imperial family. The meetings never took place. The Soviet Union ceased to exist, Boris Yelstin took office from Mikhail Gorbachev, and the town of Sverdlovsk was renamed Ekaterinburg. The bodies were left in the Department of Criminal Pathology to await identification.

Vadim Viner, curator of the Komsomol Museum in Ekaterinburg, was appointed to head the civilian investigation into the identification of the remains. He suggested that the skeletons might be those of an Ekaterinburg merchant and his family who had disappeared at the same time as had the Romanovs, or, alternately, victims of either the Red or White army.[7] Throughout the autumn of 1991, a team of Russian forensics experts, headed by Dr. Vladislav Plaksin, chief medical examiner in the Ministry of Health, worked toward identification.

The first step was to return to the gravesite and undertake a more meticulous search. This second sweep of the area recovered another 250 bone fragments, lost or trampled into the mud by the earlier team. Slowly, the bones were matched, pieced together until skeletons were completed with reasonable certainty, a thankless task conducted by Plaksin's assistant Serge Abramov and Ludmilla Koryakova, an archaeologist at Ural State University.[8]

Gradually, the team began to draw conclusions. The skeletons represented four men and five women; of the nine, five were almost certainly from the same family. From all accounts, they appeared to closely fit the Romanovs and their servants. The skull presumed to be that of Alexandra bore the most horrible wound: a gunshot to the face that destroyed the bridge of the nose, cheekbone, jawbone, and upper forehead. In the portion of the lower jawbone which remained, the teeth had been capped with platinum. The skull assumed to be that of the tsar bore a deep scar across the upper left forehead, the possible "Otsu" mark, as well as a jawbone with six 18-karat-gold crowns. The two missing skeletons were presumed to be of the tsarevich and one of the grand duchesses. Plaksin was loath to name names, but speculation centered almost immediately on Anastasia as being the missing daughter.

During a visit to the city by Secretary of State James Baker in February 1992, officials asked for independent assistance in identifying the remains. Baker was taken to see the bodies. The remains were laid out on several mortuary tables, having been kept frozen since their exhumation the previous July. Baker agreed to send American forensics experts to consult with the Russian team when the identification process began.

The summer of 1992 brought with it a number of startling announcements from Ekaterinburg concerning the skeletons in the morgue. On 22 June 1992, Serge Abramov announced that they had positively identified the bodies of Alexandra, Nicholas, and Dr. Botkin after several months of intensive study. The identification was effected by means of a computer-enhanced photographic analysis which matched cardinal points on the skulls to existing pictures of the family. The rest of the skeletons remained unidentified.

On 19 July 1992—two days past the seventy-fourth anniversary of the murders—a group of respected American forensics experts arrived in Ekaterinburg at the invitation of the authorities there to undertake an examination of the remains. They had been sent as a response to Secretary of State Baker's pledge the previous February to help in the investigation. Their arrival caused a great deal of animosity in Plaksin's offices in Moscow, where, not without reason, they felt they were being ignored in favor of Western experts.

The American team was headed by Dr. William Maples, director of the C. A. Pound Human Identification Laboratory at the University of Florida, Gainesville. Maples had previously assisted in the identification of the remains of Spanish explorer Francisco Pizarro and worked on the forensic team which examined the remains of American president Zachary Taylor for suspected poisoning. With Maples were Dr. Michael Baden, former chief medical examiner for the city of New York and a member of the House of Representatives' Assassinations Committee, which reinvestigated the murder of President John F. Kennedy; Dr. Lowell J. Levine, a dental expert with the New York State Police Forensics Department, who had worked on the identification of the infamous Dr. Josef Mengele in Brazil; Catherine Oakes, a hair and fiber expert from Levine's Forensics Department; and William Goza, a historian.

After two weeks of intensive study, the American team announced that the remains appeared to be those of the missing Romanovs. All of the bodies found in the pit now seemed to have been positively identified. In addition to Alexandra, Nicholas, and Dr. Botkin, the experts confirmed that Olga, Tatiana, and Marie were also in the same grave, along with the maid Demidova and the servants Trupp and Kharitonov. Missing were Anastasia and Alexei.

Again, the identification was achieved by using computer-enhanced photographic analysis and anthropological data. "All of the skeletons appear to be too tall to be Anastasia and there is nothing in the skeletal material we have looked at that could represent Alexei," Maples said. He believed that somewhere in the Koptyaki Forest was the grave with the two missing corpses. But the Russians had gone over the surrounding area with a fine-tooth comb, and expected to find nothing further."We're still left with a mystery," Maples declared, "and in some ways it's going to be interesting for some time to come."[9]

The announcement on 28 July 1992 immediately put an end to years of speculation about the fate of the Russian imperial family. It is now clear that the family was shot to death in the basement room of the Ipatiev house on the night of 16 July 1918. Stories that the tsarina and her daughters may have been taken away to Perm by the Bolsheviks may have been a clumsy attempt at disinformation aimed at the German government in an effort to keep the names of the Romanovs as negotiating tools.

If, in fact, the imperial women had been taken away, there is little chance that the Bolsheviks, in the middle of the civil war, would have killed them and then transported their bodies back to Ekaterinburg, some two hundred miles, simply to bury them alongside the tsar and the servants. The identification, therefore, of Alexandra and three of her daughters means that they all died at the same time and in the same place as the tsar.

The bulk of the report by Nicholas Sokolov must now be accepted as fact. The identification of the bodies solves most of the mystery surrounding his case. Sokolov was wrong only in describing the destruction of the bodies at the Four Brothers mine shaft. He could not have known that the secret of the Romanovs lay beneath his feet as he wandered through the Koptyaki Forest that hot summer seventy-three years ago.

The announcement of 28 July, 1992, while resolving many of the questions about the fate of the imperial family, also raised the possibility that Anastasia and Alexei may have survived the Ekaterinburg massacre. Speculation that one or more of the Romanovs may have escaped is not new. But for the first time in seventy-four years, the speculation has now been supported by scientific evidence.

Critics have argued that it was impossible for anyone to have survived the massacre in the basement, saying that there were too many soldiers present, too many people in too small a room for anyone to have survived. Yet if there was a chance for survival, it was precisely because of such conditions. We know from Yurovsky's account that the scene was chaotic, filled with misdirection. Some members of the execution squad were drunk. Three of the grand duchesses survived the first volley, as did Alexei. In the accounts left by the participants in the murders, we are told that several of the victims were still alive as they were being loaded on the Fiat truck in the courtyard of the Ipatiev house and that they had to be bayoneted. The bayonets would not go through the bodices.

Was it possible for someone to have survived? We know that the corsets filled with diamonds and other jewels helped deflect the bullets and bayonet blows. It is likely, therefore, that even on the drive to the mine shaft, some of the members of the imperial family were still alive.

But even if we accept that someone may have been alive, how could he or she have escaped? The truck was filled with members of the execution squad. Members of the Ural Soviet and the local Cheka waited along the road and joined the group on its journey to the Four Brothers. But hidden in the memoirs of those participants to the shooting at the Ipatiev house are clues to what may have happened.

On the way to the mine shaft the truck broke down. Yurovsky and his men rode off into the woods, accompanied by members of the Cheka escort, leaving a few drunken soldiers with the Fiat and its grisly cargo. Perhaps we will never know with any certainty what transpired in those few minutes along the side of the roadway. If one of the girls, Anastasia, was still alive, her moans may have attracted the attention of those few men gathered in the twilight. The soldiers were already confused, half-drunk, perhaps filled with guilt over the shooting. The fall of Ekaterinburg was expected; the Bolsheviks were losing ground. If one of the girls was alive, here was a chance to save her, and perhaps themselves.

Although Yurovsky's memoirs speak specifically of the fact that all members of the imperial family were killed, hidden clues point to the inevitable conclusion that two of the family were missing from the truck by the time it reached the mine shaft. He later wrote that two of the bodies were burned away from the rest. He named specifically Alexei and Anastasia. But why burn two of the bodies? If the Bolsheviks went to the trouble of burning two bodies, why not burn all of them? It certainly stands out as strange, given that the objective of the mission was to quickly get rid of any evidence. What now seems likely is that when Yurovsky got to the mine shaft and saw the bodies being unloaded, he realized that two were missing. Very quickly, he sent most of the men from the Cheka away, using the jewels sewn into the bodices of the girls as an excuse. There, in the twilight, he, Peter Yrmakov, and perhaps several others counted and recounted the bodies. We do not know if soldiers were questioned or if a decision was made at the mine shaft to simply ignore the missing corpses. But certainly none of these men could ever reveal this secret to their superiors. Thus, when Yurovsky wrote his account, he mentioned burning two of the bodies, in the unlikely event that the others were ever found, to explain their disappearance. Ermakov did the same thing in his account. They were careful to keep their secret for fear of retribution from Moscow.

One might ask if Yurovsky's story of burning the two missing bodies should not be accepted as fact. After all, the other aspects of his account have been demonstrated as correct. Yet the absurd notion that the Bolsheviks would have burned two of the bodies and not the rest speaks very much in favor of a cover-up. Time was minimal. Yurovsky failed to give any good reason for the alleged burning of the two corpses. The only assumption that can be made is that the story was invented as a deception, to hide the truth.

Russian writer Edvard Radzhinskii discovered this evidence while researching his biography of Nicholas II.[10] He was visited by a man who gave the bare details of the story told above, saying that the men had made up the story of the two bodies being burned to protect themselves. What makes this story so compelling is the likelihood that this anonymous visitor was in fact one of the members of the Cheka squad which accompanied the truck to the Four Brothers mine shaft. If he himself were an eyewitness to the events of that morning at the Koptyaki Forest, then his story suddenly would make sense, and his knowledge of the rescue of two of the victims from the truck would be our only real clue as to what happened.[11]

And what of the other missing body? Yurovsky himself relates that Alexei did not die in the first volley and that his assistant, Nikulin, had to pump an entire cartridge of bullets into the boy before he stopped crawling across the floor. If we assume for a moment that the tsarevich, like the grand duchesses, was wearing some sort of inner wrap containing jewels, this would account for the bullets' failure to end his life. If Alexei did somehow survive the murder at the Ipatiev house, he must have been badly wounded. How long could he have survived before his hemophilia set in and carried him away?[12] Whatever the answers, the fact remains that both he and Anastasia were missing from the mass grave where their parents and sisters were found.

On 11 December 1992 the remains of Alexandra were positively identified by a team of forensics experts at the Home Office Science Laboratory at Aldermaston, England. For the first time, there was definite scientific proof that the skeletons found in the shallow pit in the Koptyaki Forest were those of the imperial family and their servants.

Earlier, in the fall, the Russians in Ekaterinburg had sent nine left femur bones to England for identification. They were subjected to a new, state-of-the-art DNA test developed by Dr. Peter Gill at Aldermaston. Fragments of DNA were extracted from the femurs in order to begin the sequencing process. Gill compared the mitochondrial DNA rather than chromosomal DNA; mitochondrial DNA is passed down matrilineally, so that it remains virtually unchanged from generation to generation. The DNA extracted from the bones was tested against that taken from known Romanovs and other close blood relatives.[13]

DNA testing is still a rather controversial science, although accepted widely in English courts of law as proof of identification. To make the comparisons, samples were obtained from several close relatives of the Romanov family, including the husband of Queen Elizabeth II, the Duke of Edinburgh (a direct matrilineal descendant of Alexandra's mother Princess Alice), and extant hair clippings from within the family.

DNA taken from the skull presumed to be Alexandra's was matched against a blood sample donated by Prince Philip. The processing was identical: The remains were Alexandra's. Further tests established that the remains of three of the grand duchesses were also present among the others. Difficulties arose in the sequencing process for the remains presumed to be those of Nicholas II, and it was only after the remains of his brother Grand Duke George, who had died of tuberculosis in 1899, were exhumed from his tomb in the Fortress of Peter and Paul that a positive match could be made. In September 1995, British, American, and Russian forensic and DNA experts all agreed: They had the skull and remains of Russia's last tsar and his family. It has taken seventy-five years; but the events of that hot summer night in July 1918 no longer remain hidden among the dark trees of the Koptyaki Forest outside Ekaterinburg.

Epilogue

Tʜᴇ ᴇɴᴅ ᴏғ ᴛʜᴇ Rᴜssɪᴀɴ ɪᴍᴘᴇʀɪᴀʟ ғᴀᴍɪʟʏ, characterized by violence, political corruption, and deceit, somehow seems an appropriate end for the Romanov dynasty. The tragic, pathetic end of the imperial family seems today to have been foreshadowed by their extravagant and careless manner of life. Desperately out of touch with the modern world, the Romanovs continued, against all warnings, to exist as a seventeenth-century dynasty in the industrial and enlightened twentieth-century world. The end of this one family marked the end of an era. Although the death knell of Europe's great royal families first sounded in Russia, the Bolshevik Revolution quickly exported not only insurrection but regicide.

The murder of the imperial family was only one in a series of numberless crimes carried out in Russia, begun before the Bolshevik Revolution and carried on through the terrible reigns of Lenin and Stalin. But somehow these seven victims stand out—innocents in a list of atrocities demanded by the state. Unlike King Charles I or King Louis XVI, Nicholas II was given no trial; his sentence was carried out in secret, above and beyond the existing laws, and his wife and children were gunned down with him. Historian Richard Pipes has called it "a prelude to twentieth-century mass murder."

> When a government arrogates to itself the power to kill people, not because of what they had done or even might do, but because their death is "needed," we are entering an entirely new moral realm. Here lies the symbolic significance of the events that occurred in Ekaterinburg on the night of July 16–17. The massacre . . . carried mankind for the first time across the threshold of deliberate genocide. The same reasoning that had led the Bolsheviks to condemn them to death would later be applied in Russia and elsewhere to millions of nameless beings who happened to stand in the way of one or another design for a new world order.[1]

381

This same determination to eliminate the Romanovs from the public mind led to the execution of many other members of the imperial family. In April 1918, a group of Bolsheviks seized Alexandra's sister Ella at her Moscow convent. Told that the tsar wished to see her, Ella quickly packed a few things and, with an assistant named Sister Barbara, set off for the Moscow train station.[2] The Bolsheviks sent her to Perm, where she and Sister Barbara were imprisoned with Grand Duke Serge Michailovich; Igor, Ivan, Constantine Constantinovich, and Grand Duke Paul's son from his second, morganatic marriage, Prince Vladimir Paley.

After a few days at Perm, the Bolsheviks transferred the prisoners to Alapayevsk, a small town a hundred miles from Ekaterinburg. On the night of 18 July 1918 a truck pulled up to the abandoned schoolhouse where the prisoners lived and took them away. Escorted by an armed division of Bolshevik soldiers, the truck drove to a secluded mine shaft in the forest. After all of the prisoners had climbed off the vehicle, the guards told them that they were going to be thrown into the shaft—alive. Ella asked that she be allowed to cover her head with her scarf and then began to sing her favorite hymn, "The Cherubim." Slowly, she stepped over the edge of the pit and disappeared into the blackness of the shaft. The others fought or pleaded or prayed, but all followed Ella into the abandoned mine shaft. At the last moment, Grand Duke Serge Michailovich reached out to the soldiers; they shot him, then kicked his body over the edge of the pit. Once all of the prisoners had disappeared, the Bolsheviks threw two grenades down the shaft and then drove away.[3]

Over the next few days, peasants who crept to the edge of the pit heard the sound of singing coming up from the bottom. But they dared not try to rescue the prisoners for fear the Bolsheviks would come back and kill them as well. It was not until the White Army took Alapayevsk that the bodies were raised from the shaft. During the autopsies, they discovered that not all of the prisoners had died before reaching the bottom of the shaft. Ella, for instance, had used a piece of her head scarf to bandage a wound on Ivan Constantinovich. And an autopsy revealed that Constantine Constantinovich had become so hungry that he had eaten some of the dirt from the shaft. Eventually, after hours, days, the prisoners died from their head injuries, exposure, and starvation.[4]

The White Army took the bodies to Perm for burial in the cathedral there. But the advance of the Red Army back across the Urals forced the removal of the coffins, the Whites fearing that the Bolsheviks would not allow them to rest in peace. After a long journey across Siberia and into Manchuria, Ella's coffin finally arrived in Jerusalem.

There, on the Mount of Olives, in the Russian Orthodox church, Ella was finally laid to rest.

Prior to the Alapayevsk murders, the Bolsheviks shot the tsar's brother Grand Duke Michael in Perm. In January 1919, four grand dukes—the tsar's uncle Paul; Dimitri Constantinovich; and Nicholas and George Michailovich—who were imprisoned in the Fortress of Peter and Paul, were removed from their cells and shot to death.

Many of the Romanovs did, however, survive the Revolution. Marie Feodorovna, the dowager empress, managed to escape to the Crimea, and in April 1919, King George V sent a British warship to fetch her and other members of her family. Marie Feodorovna settled in Denmark, her homeland, living in a wing of the palace of her nephew, King Christian X. There were constant arguments over money. Once, one of the king's footmen knocked on the dowager empress's door and announced, "His Majesty has sent me over to ask you to switch off all these lights. His Majesty said to mention to you that the electricity bill he had to pay recently was excessive."[5] Imperious as ever, the dowager empress immediately ordered her servants to turn on all of the electric lights in her wing. Stubborn to the end, Marie Feodorovna refused to believe that any of her family had been killed at Ekaterinburg. She often stated that she knew for a fact that Nicholas and his family were alive somewhere but refused to discuss her information with anyone. She died on 13 October 1928 after slipping into a coma. She was eighty-one.

Marie Feodorovna's daughters, Xenia and Olga, also lived in exile for many years. Xenia settled in England. She and her husband Grand Duke Alexander Michailovich lived separate lives. In 1933, Sandro died. King George V offered Xenia the use of a grace-and-favor mansion, Wilderness House. She lived there until her death in 1960. Olga lived a quiet life with her second husband and two children in Canada for many years. Her last days were spent living with a Russian couple above a barbershop in Toronto. On 24 November 1960 the grand duchess died.

In 1912, the tsar's brother Michael had married a twice-divorced commoner, Nathalia Cheremetevskaya. Two years before, Nathalia had given birth to the grand duke's bastard son, George. After the Revolution, both Nathalia, who had been reluctantly granted the courtesy title of Countess Brassova, and her son George, Count Brassov, managed to escape Russia. In exile, no Romanov would receive her. In July 1931, George, Count Brassov, died in a motorcar accident in Cannes. With the last of her money, Nathalia purchased a funeral plot at Passy Cemetery in Paris for her and her son. Her last years were lived in near poverty in a small bedroom–sitting room in a shabby hotel in Paris. Her clothing was in rags, and she never quite had enough money for food. None of the Romanovs in exile would help her. On 23 January 1952 she died. She was buried beside her son at Passy.[6]

Other Romanovs who died in exile included Grand Duke Nicholas Nicholaievich, the object of Alexandra's wartime hatred, who passed away in France in 1929. Alexandra's other vehement enemy, Grand Duchess Marie Pavlovna, fled the country clutching a box of jewels. For seven weeks, she survived on black bread and soup before reaching the West. She died in Switzerland in 1920.[7]

Grand Duke Cyril and his wife, Ducky, also managed to escape. At the time of the Revolution, Ducky was pregnant with their third child, having given birth previously to two girls. They left St. Petersburg on a special train arranged for them by the Bolsheviks and went to Finland, where Ducky gave birth to a son, Vladimir. In 1924, Cyril proclaimed himself tsar of all the Russias—a move which alienated him from the rest of the Romanov family. When Cyril died in 1938, his son Vladimir proclaimed that he was the heir to the throne.

The claims of the Vladimiroviches to the throne caused a division in the Romanov family which remains to this day. Although Vladimir's parents married without the tsar's permission, Nicholas II did grant recognition and full status in the Imperial House to Ducky and her children, making the issue eligible to succeed to the throne. In 1948, Vladimir married the daughter of a Georgian prince. They had one daughter, Maria, who herself has one son, Grand Duke George. Before his death in April 1992, Vladimir declared that his daughter Maria would be styled curatrix of the House of Romanov for her son, George.[8] Their claims, though supported by the Fundamental State Laws of Russian Empire and recognized by the Russian Orthodox Church, are not accepted by the remaining members of the Romanov family, who look on Prince Nicholas Romanov in Switzerland as the rightful heir and head of the House. Although Nicholas is himself the product of a morganatic marriage and thus ineligible to succeed, the rift between the two branches of the family continues to divide family members and Russian exiles alike.

In exile, Grand Duke Dimitri Pavlovich, alone of all the assassins of Rasputin, remained silent about the events of that December night. He died in 1942. His friend Prince Felix Youssoupov escaped to France with his wife, Irina, and their daughter, also named Irina. Little remained of the great Youssoupov wealth, but Felix always helped out the Russian exiles as best as he could. He alone helped support the destitute Countess Brassova in the years before her death. Felix and Irina quickly became the toast of French society and after the Second World War moved in a glamorous circle which included the duke and duchess of Windsor.[9] On 27 September 1967 the man who killed Rasputin died at the age of eighty in Paris. His wife followed him to the grave a few years later, and their only daughter, Irina, died in 1983.

Of Alexandra and Nicholas's crowned cousins, the kaiser abdicated from the German throne in 1918 after his navy mutinied at Kiel. He died in 1941. King George V and Queen Mary, alone among the cousins, emerged from the First World War with their prestige intact. In 1930, the king had to receive the first Soviet ambassador, a Mr. Sokolnikov, at Windsor Castle. "What do you think it means to me to be forced to shake hands with a man of the party that murdered my cousins?" he exclaimed.[10] George V died in 1936; Queen Mary, in 1953.

Many of Alexandra's friends survived the Revolution. Chief among them was Anna Vyrubova. After her release from the Fortress of Peter and Paul, Anna made her way to Finland, where she had enjoyed so many happy days picnicking with the tsarina and her children on day trips from the *Standart*. She died in 1964 at the age of eighty. Count Benckendorff died in 1921, Count Fredericks, a year later. Gilliard lived in Switzerland until his death in 1962, while Gibbes died in England in 1963. Baroness Buxhoeveden continued to work for members of the Romanov family in exile and spent much time as lady-in-waiting to Alexandra's sister Victoria. Lili Dehn went to live in Argentina. Alexei's King Charles spaniel, Joy, caught the attention of a British officer who found the dog running about in the streets before the Ipatiev house nearly a year after the imperial family's execution. He carried the dog back to England with him, and Joy lived on for several years in the peaceful countryside near Windsor Castle before he died.[11]

Alexandra's brother Ernie lost his position with the kaiser's abdication in November 1918 but kept the title of grand duke of Hesse and was prepared to pass it on to his first son, George. Ernie's health gradually declined, and on 9 October 1937 he died. He was buried in the Hessian royal crypt at Rosenhohe. In February 1931, Prince George of Hesse had married the daughter of Prince Andrew of Greece, the pretty Cecilla, whose mother was Alexandra's sister Victoria's eldest daughter, Alice; Cecilla's brother Philip later married Queen Elizabeth II.

Ernie's widow Eleonore did not survive him long. A month after the grand duke's death, Eleonore, along with her son George, his wife Cecilla, who was expecting a fourth child at this time, and their two sons, Ludwig and Alexander, left Frankfurt to attend the wedding of Ernie's second son, Louis, to the Honorable Margaret Geddes in November 1937. Their Junkers trimotor encountered heavy fog and on the approach crashed into a brick smokestack, killing all on board. Also on the plane, and destroyed in the crash, were the famous Hessian pearls and the veil of Honiton lace worn by Princess Alice at her fateful marriage so many years before.[12]

Prince Louis and Margaret Geddes were married privately the next morning, with Lord Louis Mountbatten standing as best man. Two hours later, the wedding party departed England, following the five coffins back to Darmstadt and Rosenhohe, to join Ernie, Grand Duke Ludwig, and Princess Alice.

Alexandra's sister Irene also lived on for many years in her native Germany. She died in 1953. Victoria died in September 1950. Her youngest son, Lord Mountbatten, served with distinction in the British navy during World War II and later became the last viceroy of India in 1947. He always remembered the long summers he had spent with his Russian relatives, when he had fallen in love with Alexandra's third daughter, Marie. In 1979, he died, the victim of an IRA bomb at his castle in Ireland. His grandson Lord Romsey, Norton Knatchbull, is the present heir to the Mountbatten title. In 1979, Lord Romsey married the former Penelope Eastwood. The couple have two children, a boy named Nicholas and a girl named Alexandra.

Today, in the wooded hills outside Frankfurt, Princess Margaret—the last surviving member of the Hesse family—continues to live in Wolfsgarten. It has remained a family home, visited frequently by members of the British royal family on holiday. The old lodge is at its best in the summer, when the roses in the garden come into bloom, overwhelming the pergolas and scenting the air with their fragrance. In the courtyard where Alexandra played as a child, Nicholas visited, Kaiser Wilhelm tried in vain to charm his cousins, and the young grand duchesses romped with their German relatives, a small fountain splashes, a peaceful reminder of the golden days of a century before.

In the seventy-five years since the Bolshevik Revolution, the Soviet Union made a determined effort to eliminate the Romanovs from the minds of its citizens. They vanished from the pages of history books and became nonentities, reviled when discussed and condemned by the state. Ekaterinburg was renamed Sverdlovsk, in honor of Jacob Sverdlov, the man who, along with Lenin, decided the fate of the imperial family. It remains a coal center of some repute and the town over which the American U-2 spy plane was shot down in 1960. For many years, the Ipatiev house stood as a Bolshevik museum, and tour groups were led downstairs to the sinister basement room where the family had been shot.

In 1977, it was razed to the ground in the dead of night. The man who carried out the order was the then first secretary of the Sverdlovsk Provincial Committee, Boris Yeltsin. He later wrote:

A return to the sources of our distorted and falsified history is a natural process. The country wants to know the truth about its past, including the terrible and unpalatable truths. The tragedy of the Romanov Family is precisely such an episode. . . . People have always come to look at the Ipatiev House. . . . The terrible tragedy that occurred there in 1918 drew people to that place—they would peer through the windows or simply stand in silence and stare at the old house. . . . Information about the large number of pilgrims visiting the Ipatiev House, however, found its way through certain channels to Moscow. . . . I soon received a letter from Moscow . . . a decree from the Politburo, adopted in closed session, ordering the demolition of the Ipatiev House. . . . The necessary machinery was driven up to the Ipatiev House in the middle of the night—and by next morning nothing was left of the building. Then the site was covered with asphalt. That was yet another sad episode of Brezhnev's "era of stagnation." I can well imagine that sooner or later we will be ashamed of this piece of barbarism. Ashamed we may be; but we can never rectify it.[13]

The tenure of Mikhail Gorbachev as leader of the Soviet Union witnessed a number of dramatic revelations concerning the Romanovs. In addition to the findings of Geli Ryabov, Soviet researcher Edvard Radzhinskii discovered documents which clearly indicated that Lenin himself ordered the imperial family shot.

Since the publication of Ryabov's story in 1989, interest in the Romanovs has been growing. On 17 July of that same year, a group of monarchists held a memorial service for the Romanovs in the cemetery of the Donskoy Monastery outside Moscow. It was the first of many such demonstrations. At the traditional May Day Parade in 1990, members of the Soviet leadership watched as groups carried the old Russian Tricolor and banners bearing portraits of Nicholas through Red Square. A Monarchist party today openly campaigns for the restoration of the former imperial house. The collapse of the Soviet Union in 1991 has only served to further increase interest in the dynasty which formerly ruled for over three hundred years.

The introduction of Gorbachev's policy of *glasnost* allowed for the first time in seventy years a dialogue about the Romanovs to take place. Thousands of Muscovites stood in line to view an exhibition of photographs of Alexandra and Nicholas, and a play based on the murder of the imperial family was sold out for months in advance. Street vendors for the first time have begun selling Romanov memorabilia, and popular magazines feature stories on the last tsar and his family.

Changing public opinion, along with a growing distaste for communism and its symbols, led to perhaps the most dramatic signal: the citizens of both Leningrad and Sverdlovsk—cities closely associated with the Romanovs and bearing the names of the two men responsible for the murder of the imperial family—voted to change the names of their towns back to St. Petersburg and Ekaterinburg. On 1 October 1991 this change became official. Once more, Peter the Great's Venice of the North bore the name of its creator.

In Ekaterinburg itself, at the site of the former Ipatiev house, monarchists have erected a memorial chapel dedicated to the last tsar and his family. They have also declared their intention to build a museum on the square to house exhibitions concerning the murder of the Romanovs and the life of the last Russian imperial family as well as a new church, the Church of the Blood. An iron cross marks the site where the house once stood, and it has become fashionable for couples on their wedding days to visit and leave flowers as a sign of respect for the murdered family. Just down the street, at the Komsomol Youth Museum, an exhibition details the life of the town's children. The first room is a recreation of the murder room in the Ipatiev house, where pictures of the five children of Alexandra and Nicholas have been hung on a wall ripped apart with bullet holes and splattered with stage blood.[14]

The rechristened city of St. Petersburg also witnessed the autumn 1991 visit of the late self-styled grand duke Vladimir, the claimant to the Romanov throne. Vladimir, accompanied by his wife, visited the former palaces where his family once resided and laid flowers at the tombs of his ancestors in the Fortress of Peter and Paul. Many Russians seem to have seized on the presence of the grand duke as a symbol of national unity, and calls for a restoration of the monarchy have become more prevalant. Ironically, within six months, Vladimir would return to St. Petersburg, this time for his funeral. A few years earlier, the scene would have been unthinkable: a claimant to the Romanov throne lying in state amid the splendors of St. Isaac's Cathedral, surrounded by throngs of mourners and the hierarchy of the Orthodox church, returned once again to their greatest church.

The present-day monarchist movement in Russia owes much to dissatisfaction with the current government and curiosity about the Romanovs. Because of the volatile situation in Russian politics, it is impossible to say what influence such groups may have on the shape of future governments. But renewed interest in the Romanovs has certainly united many disgruntled citizens hungry for a change.

In the face of all of these developments, perhaps the most dramatic are still to come. The bodies of Nicholas, Alexandra, and three of their daughters have been positively identified. It now remains to settle the last questions: what became of Anastasia and Alexei? The same members of the team of forensics experts in Ekaterinburg have declared that they believe the bodies of the two missing children are still to be found in the Koptyaki Forest. The logic of such a search, however, runs counter to what we now know. The White Army carried out extensive exhumations in the entire area during the investigations surrounding the fate of the Romanovs in 1918 and 1919. It is unlikely that any present-day search will uncover the corpses of the two children.

In October 1994, Dr. Peter Gill announced the DNA test results on hair and tissue samples from Anna Anderson, who for many years claimed to have been Anastasia. Gill concluded that she was not Anastasia, nor did her DNA profile match those of Alexandra or the other remains. He also concluded, on the basis of a similar DNA test whose results remain controversial, that Mrs. Anderson was, in fact, a Polish factory worker named Franziska Schankowska. Thus, it seemed, one of the twentieth century's most enduring mysteries was finally resolved.

The question of what to do with the remains of the Russian imperial family continues to haunt Russia. Both Ekaterinburg and St. Petersburg have waged an impassioned battle over who should be awarded permission to bury them. Ekaterinburg proposed building a church on the site of Ipatiev house as a memorial, while St. Petersburg wants the bones for burial in the Cathedral of the Fortress of Peter and Paul, the traditional resting place of the Romanovs. The issue appeared to be settled when the Russian government announced formal plans for a state funeral in St. Petersburg. The recent burials of the remains of Grand Duke Cyril and his wife in the Fortress, and of Grand Duke Serge in Moscow, may serve as a preview of the larger ceremony still to come.

Despite the DNA evidence, certain groups have questioned the identity of the remains and expressed concerns that the bones of the servants may be buried with those of the Romanovs. Then, too, the Orthodox Church seems torn between a funeral and a canonization ceremony, making the imperial family saints. Three dates for the funeral have been canceled; the ceremony is now tentatively set for sometime in 1996, though, given the turmoil over the affair and the numerous cancellations of previous dates, it may be years before the issue is resolved. While the arguments continue, the pathetic last remains—chopped and burned bones, battered skeletons, and smashed skulls—rest in the morgue at the Department of Criminal Pathology in Ekaterinburg, apparently forgotten by those who had argued so passionately for a decent burial.

An icy wind howled through the streets of New York City on 1 November 1981. Outside the Russian Orthodox Cathedral of Our Lady of the Sign, crowds waited patiently, some for more than six hours. They watched as the church filled with clergy, princes, and members of international society. In the raw wind, the old imperial standard fluttered against the gray sky, the proud Romanov double-headed eagle gazing out across the bleak length of Park Avenue. On this cold autumn day, the Russian imperial family was canonized.

The faithful had for many years regarded the Romanovs as un-canonized saints. But their apparent martyrdom in the Urals required sixty-three years to be rewarded. Unlike the Roman Catholic church, which requires evidence of miracles as a sign of sainthood, the Russian Orthodox church bases its canonizations on signs of faith. Death for the cause of Russian Orthodoxy constitutes ample evidence for sainthood in the laws of the Holy Synod. Speaking before the service began, the church's prelate, Bishop Gregory, said, "The last Tsar was murdered with his family precisely because he was a crowned ruler, the upholder of the splendid concept of the Orthodox state."[15] As the spiritual leader of the Russian Orthodox church, Nicholas represented the leadership of God on earth to the faithful. His death, therefore, had not only political but spiritual repercussions.

Inside the red-brick cathedral a thousand votive candles cast their eerie glow on the frescoes and icons. Carnations in white, blue, and red—the shades of the old Russian Tricolor—decorated the altar where a new icon stood for veneration by the faithful. It showed Christ descending from heaven, surrounded by a host of angels, to greet the imperial family. They stood together on a dais: Nicholas, Alexei, the four girls, Ella, Michael, and all of those shot to death by the Bolsheviks. Alexandra was there as well, cloaked in a mantle of ermine, a golden halo shining around her head, gazing serenely toward the blue sky of heaven.

As the candles burned down, the choir burst into a new hymn written specially for the ceremony, "We Glorify You, O Martyred Tsar."[16] There, in the twinkling iridescent light, Queen Victoria's shy granddaughter became the Holy Royal Martyr St. Alexandra Feodorovna. With her love of pomp and glitter, Alexandra would most certainly have been impressed.

Outside St. Petersburg, on the edge of the Russian plain, the town of Tsarskoe Selo, now called Pushkin, still celebrates its former imperial glory. At an edge of the otherwise exquisitely manicured park, the Alexander Palace, where Alexandra and Nicholas lived, lies hidden in a grove of wild trees and overgrown lawns. For many years after the Revolution, the palace was kept exactly as it had been on that August day in 1917 when Alexandra, Nicholas, and their children left their home for Siberia. In the elegant drawing rooms and reception halls, Nicholas's military uniforms, Alexandra's court gowns, the childrens' toys, were all displayed, visible memories of a vanished world. In the private apartments, nothing had changed: In the tsar's study, his pens lay on his desk, the calendar still read 30 July; books and writing paper stood ready for the tsarina in the Mauve Boudoir. The imperial bedroom still smelled of roses from the fragrant oil Alexandra had used in her icon lamps.[17] It was as if the occupants had stepped out into the park for an afternoon stroll and would return at any minute. In 1942, the invading Nazi forces captured the town and looted the palace, ripping paintings from the walls, smashing furniture and hurling it through the windows before setting fires in the empty rooms. The sheet of flames roared through the palace, destroying the Mauve Boudoir, the tsar's study, and the imperial bedroom. In the aftermath of the war, portions of the palace were restored, including the Portrait Gallery, a tapestry room, and the tsar's vaulted Audience Chamber. The remainder of the space was divided up into offices. It is now occupied by the St. Petersburg Naval Academy, surrounded by high stockade fences and guard posts. Several years ago, a petition was circulated in the city asking that the navy be removed and that the palace be used either for an extension of the Pushkin museum or that an imperial museum be created within its walls. The navy is currently trying to dislodge itself from the palace but is responsible for finding a new tenant. Plans are currently under way, headed by an American, Robert Achinson, to restore the palace to its former glory. Today the Alexander Palace looks abandoned, the yellow and white paint flaking from its walls, the lake in front of the park dry and choked with weeds, the lawns overgrown, the stonework crumbling. It seems a fitting memorial to its former occupants. The former curator of the palace, Anatoly Kuchumov, told author Suzanne Massie that on several occasions he felt an uneasy presence in the rooms, a hint that he was not alone. One night, while working in the empty palace, he caught a glimpse of a shadowy figure, a tall, middle-aged woman dressed all in black who quickly disappeared as he turned his head.[18] He is convinced that late at night, when the officials of the navy have abandoned the palace and returned to St. Petersburg, Alexandra's restless ghost wanders the darkened rooms of her former home, searching for the peaceful end she was denied in life.

Acknowledgments

THIS BOOK WAS WRITTEN over the course of twelve years and revised and rewritten over another three; many people have contributed to the result. To them all, named and unnamed, I am deeply grateful.

I am honored to be able to thank Prince Nicholas Romanoff for his assistance throughout my researches and for his valuable and enlightening foreword to this book. His words on Alexandra serve as a concise, effective introduction to my own views and add greatly to its content.

Acknowledgment must be made to the trustees of the Broadlands Archives, University of Southampton, for permission to reproduce many of the photographs contained herein and also for permission to quote from unpublished letters and memoirs, notably that of Empress Alexandra's sister Victoria. Likewise, Wartski in London has graciously provided several useful photographs.

In England, Lord Brabourne has proved particularly agreeable over the years in allowing access and permission to family documents. The assistance and cooperation of Lord Romsey in this effort was invaluable, and he opened many doors to me, for which I am truly grateful. Dr. C. M. Woolgar, archivist at the Broadlands archives, Hartley Library, University of Southampton, graciously spent much time working on my behalf, answering requests and obtaining permissions, as did the staff at the Public Records Office in Kew. The friendly, patient staff at the archives were always willing to humor my wishes, and their assistance is most appreciated. Mr. Robert Parsons provided me with valuable information regarding the imperial family's transactions with Fabergé and Alexandra's jewelry, as did Ms. Suzy Menkes. Mr. George Gibbes, the son of the imperial children's former English tutor, Charles Sydney Gibbes, spent an afternoon with me, allowing me to view his father's collection of imperial papers and photographs. Mrs. Pauline Hol-

393

drup, granddaughter of Nathalia Cheremetevskaia, morganatic wife of Nicholas II's brother Grand Duke Michael, likewise shared her memories and personal collection with me. Finally, Her Majesty the Queen allowed me access to the royal archives at Windsor Castle, an experience made all the more valuable and pleasant through the friendly and knowledgeable presence of Ms. Frances Dimond.

In Germany, Her Royal Highness Princess Margaret of Hesse graciously allowed me to visit Wolfsgarten, Alexandra's former childhood summer residence outside of Darmstadt. Mrs. Gudrun Illgen, the photo archivist at the Hessian royal archives, facilitated my examination of many of Alexandra's family photographs.

In Russia, my researches were greatly aided through the work of Ms. Irene Fochkina in Moscow and Mr. Roman Vartanov in St. Petersburg. In Moscow, Mr. Mikhail Kupriyanov and his charming wife, Milan, generously escorted me around the city, from palace to palace, often opening, through their persuasive talk, doors which would otherwise have been closed to me. In St. Petersburg, Ivan Scubichev and Tamara Dubko worked wonders, patiently indulging my somewhat odd requests and wishes. I thank both of them for having made the entire experience such a worthwhile and rewarding one. Finally, Mr. Edvard Radzhinskii, author of *The Life and Death of Nicholas II*, generously shared his information and ideas relating to the murder of the imperial family with me.

A great many people here in America have kindly read through portions of this book at different stages of its development. Terry Della Penna, Mary Hendricks, Charles and Eileen Knaus, Matt Kumma, Desiree Michael, Elizabeth Roraback, and Margaret Scarborough each contributed to the end result through their comments and suggestions. Likewise, Robert Achinson, Leslie Field, Linda Greenwald, James Blair Lovell, Alexandra Pat Ormsby, Greg Rittenhouse, G. Nicholas Tantzos, and Father Konstantin Tivetsky provided information and answered questions regarding various elements in the book.

I had the good fortune of having a tremendous group of writers help with the initial manuscript. Their contribution has shaped the way in which I tackled the writing of this book, and many will see their thoughts and ideas incorporated here—the highest degree of thanks which I can offer. Stephen Bird, Ellie Brauer, Lillian Canzler, Shirley Cooper, Phyllis Damish, Ed Dorian, Ron Fleshman, Mary Jane Hayfield, Marilyn Kapp, Elaine Leslie, Linda McMichael, and Kay Nelson all have my deepest gratitude and respect.

Researching and writing this book has sometimes proved an emotionally tiring experience; luckily, for me, I have been surrounded with a number of sympathetic and helpful co-workers and associates whose own sacrifices and indulgences have allowed my progress. Michelle Fischer, Dan Kaufmann, Julie Miller, Jason Pickering, Amy Torgerson, Edd Vick, and, especially, Ryan Sharp and Courtni White, often allowed me time away from work, ran errands, and assisted me in innumerable ways. I thank all of them.

This has been a solitary project, made even more difficult over the years by the sheer length of time it has taken to reach this final point. My friends have demonstrated support and understanding beyond my expectations. Now that it's here, Wendy Collins, Andrea Cuddy, Angela Manning, Mark Manning, Murika Matz, and Seth Van Dyke all share my deepest thanks. And a special thank you to three of the best friends anyone could ask for—Sharlene Aadland, Cecelia Manning, and Russell Minugh—for not only believing in me but for making me believe as well.

Marlene Eilers has proved herself an invaluable friend and colleague. Her energy, enthusiasm, and support have been a constant source of inspiration to me. Marlene never failed to keep me up to date on the latest information or share her own immense resources with me. The results lie scattered throughout this book.

Laura Enstone has gone beyond the bounds of friendship, sacrificing her own vacations, not to mention her finances, to allow me to visit another palace, to sit in another library somewhere in England, and always with a smile and an indefatigable sense of humor, which kept both of us going through some incredible adventures. This book would have been something far less than it is now without her valued presence and understanding.

Susanne and Denis Meslans have undertaken a great amount of work on my behalf. Whether reading the manuscript, offering advice, helping with odd bits of research, or simply supporting me, they have repeatedly sacrificed many hours of their time to enrich this story. I owe them both an enormous debt.

I must also acknowledge the interest and support of all those at Carol Publishing Group. From his first reading of the manuscript, my editor, Allan J. Wilson, has shown a remarkable attention to the project, providing continued enthusiasm not only in the book but also in the subject itself. And Frank Lavena and Donald Davidson have patiently dealt with my sometimes curious and unconventional explanations and requests. Every writer inevitably fears that tense moment when his or her edited manuscript first arrives back from the publisher for approval. My utmost thanks, and deep gratitude, to everyone involved in the process at Carol, in making that moment, for me, a true pleasure.

Finally, I must say a word about the support which my parents have given to me over the years. Whether emotional or financial, their assistance has proved incalculable and kept me on track when things looked bleak. For over a decade, they waited as I wrote and rewrote. Now that it is finished, I hope it pleases them.

GREG KING
October 1993

Source Notes

ALONG WITH THE WORKS CITED in the bibliography, I have drawn on some unpublished archival material. In my source notes, these are quoted as follows:

BA Broadlands Archives, the family papers of the Mountbattens, currently housed at Southampton University in Southampton, England

VMH The unpublished reminiscences, in two volumes, of Alexandra's sister Victoria Milford-Haven, also housed at Broadlands Archives

PRO/FO Public Records Office/Foreign Office Files, housed at the Public Records Office in Kew, England

N's Diary The unpublished diary of Tsar Nicholas II, cited by date, in TsGAOR—the State Central Archives of the October Revolution, Moscow

The following works are cited in abbreviated form:

AF to N Alexandra Feodorovna, *The Letters of the Tsarina to the Tsar, 1914–1916*

N to AF Nicholas II, *The Letters of the Tsar to the Tsarina, 1914–1917*

N to MF and MF to N *The Secret Letters of the Last Tsar*, edited by Edward J. Bing

N's Diary The published version of Nicholas II's diary

FOT Anthony Summers and Tom Mangold, *The File on the Tsar*.

In some cases, where additional information is to be found in different translations, both works may be cited, for example, Serge Witte's *Memoirs of Count Witte* and Witte's fuller memoirs in Russian, *Vospominaiia*.

Preface

1. Crankshaw, 307–9.

Chapter 1

1. Benson, 76.
2. Cited, Longford, 309.
3. Epton, 5.
4. Balfour, 60.
5. Duff, *Hessian Tapastry*, 20.
6. Ibid, 21.
7. Jagow, 233.
8. Longford, 370.
9. Quoted in Epton, 84.
10. Hough, *Louis and Victoria*, 1.
11. Ibid, 21.
12. Epton, 88.
13. Martin, 5:253; see also Victoria, *Letters*, 1 December 1869.
14. Duff, *Hessian Tapestry*, 67.
15. Ibid, 71.
16. Corti, 77.
17. Longford, 307.
18. Duff, *Hessian Tapestry*, 112.
19. Benson, 119–21.
20. Ibid, 119.
21. Lee, 382.
22. Alice, 130.
23. Epton, 152.
24. Ibid, 124.
25. Cited, Duff, *Hessian Tapestry*, 102.
26. Noel, 113.
27. Ibid, 223–25.
28. Ibid, 166.
29. Cited, Hough, *Louis and Victoria*, 20–21.
30. Noel, 136.
31. Ibid, 175.

Chapter 2

1. Alice, 289.
2. Buxhoeveden, 1–2. The New Palace was destroyed during an RAF bombing raid on Darmstadt in 1942. Today the site is once again a park.
3. Ibid, 4.
4. Ibid, 5.
5. Quoted, Dimond and Taylor, 92.
6. Oustimenko, *Royalty*, 64.
7. Mouchanow, 46.
8. Hough, *Louis and Victoria*, 38.
9. Duff, *Hessian Tapestry*, 168.
10. Noel, 177.
11. Alice, 327.

12. Cited, Epton, 122–23.
13. Donaldson, 9.
14. VMH, 26.
15. Hough, *Louis and Victoria*, 43.
16. Ibid, 45.
17. Noel, 167.
18. Cited, Epton, 154.
19. VMH, 41.
20. Alice, 373–74.
21. Duff, *Hessian Tapestry*, 179.
22. Longford, 424.
23. Ibid, 425.
24. Hough, *Louis and Victoria*, 48.
25. Longford, 425.
26. Epton, 155.
27. Ibid.
28. Duff, *Hessian Tapestry*, 181.
29. Victoria, *Advice*, 9.

Chapter 3

1. Buxhoeveden, 7.
2. Ibid, 12.
3. Ibid.
4. Hough, *Louis and Victoria*, 54.
5. Victoria, *Advice*, 61.
6. Hough, *Louis and Victoria*, 202.
7. Ponsonby, 41.
8. VMH, 39.
9. Ibid.
10. Ibid, 26.
11. Ponsonby, 35.
12. Pope-Hennessy, 140.
13. Buxhoeveden, 7.
14. Ibid, 14.
15. Ibid, 15.
16. Ponsonby, 180.
17. Marie Louise, 50.
18. Buchanan, *Queen Victoria's Relations*, 94.
19. Cowles, *Kaiser*, 47–48.
20. Longford, 477.
21. VMH, 78.
22. Quoted, Hough, *Louis and Victoria*, 117.
23. Victoria, *Advice*, 62.
24. Hough, *Louis and Victoria*, 116.
25. Ibid, 117.
26. Cited, Hough, *Louis and Victoria*, 120.
27. Hough, *Louis and Victoria*, 120.
28. Ibid, 121.

Chapter 4

1. Hough, *Louis and Victoria*, 125.

2. Bergamini, 95.
3. Alexander, 66–67.
4. Massie, *Nicholas and Alexandra*, 11.
5. N's Diary, TsGAOR, 27 May 1884.
6. Buxhoeveden, 18.
7. Oustimenko, *Royalty*, 66.
8. N's Diary, TsGAOR, 31 May 1884.
9. Vyrubova, 19.
10. Kochan, 48.
11. Buchanan, *Dissolution*, 24.
12. Mossolov, 191.
13. Salisbury, 237.
14. Buxhoeveden, 23.
15. Marie Pavlovna, 38.
16. Buxhoeveden, 24.
17. Marie Pavlovna, 63.
18. Quoted in Kochan, 82–83.

Chapter 5

1. Hough, *Louis and Victoria*, 159.
2. Duff, *Hessian Tapestry*, 213–14.
3. Victoria, *Advice*, 89.
4. Airlie, 89.
5. Buxhoeveden, 22.
6. Ibid, 25.
7. Hough, *Louis and Victoria*, 166.
8. Buxhoeveden, 31.
9. Ibid, 29.
10. Victoria, *Advice*, 116.
11. Buxhoeveden, 30.
12. Vyrubova, 7.
13. Almedingen, *Empress Alexandra*, 8.
14. Ponsonby, 84.
15. Buchanan, *Dissolution*, 12.
16. Victoria, *Advice*, 96.

Chapter 6

1. Harrison, 30.
2. Ibid, 32.
3. Nicolson, 17.
4. Pope-Hennessy, 178.
5. For more information, consult Knight, *Jack the Ripper*.
6. Victoria, *Advice*, 89.
7. Epton, 196.
8. Pope-Hennessy, 178.
9. Quoted in Hough, *Louis and Victoria*, 149.
10. Victoria, *Advice*, 104.
11. Ibid, 100.
12. Ibid, 104.
13. Pope-Hennessy, 183.
14. Cited, Edwards, 41.
15. Pope-Hennessy, 211–12.

16. Ibid, 187.

Chapter 7

1. Victoria, *Advice*, 111. Princess Maud later married Prince Charles of Denmark, and later the pair became king and queen of Norway.
2. Sazonov, 110.
3. Victoria, *Advice*, 113.
4. Pope-Hennessy, 242.
5. Buxhoeveden, 37.
6. Longford, 522.
7. Victoria, *Advice*, 42.
8. Ibid, 106.
9. Ibid, 108.
10. Ibid, 110.
11. Almedingen, *Unbroken Unity*, 35.
12. N's Diary, 31.
13. Harrison, 218.
14. N to MF, 61.
15. N's Diary, TsGAOR, 21 December 1891.
16. N's Diary, 32.
17. Victoria, *Advice*, 122.
18. Vassilli, 189; see also Witte, 45.
19. Duff, *Hessian Tapestry*, 233.
20. N to MF, 63.
21. VMH 154.
22. Almedingen, *Empress Alexandra*, 20.
23. Tyler-Whittle, 155.
24. AF to N, 321.
25. Cited, Duff, *Victoria Travels*, 320.
26. Marie Louise, 56.

Chapter 8

1. Witte, *Memoirs*, 39.
2. Vorres, 21–22.
3. Essed-Bey, 20.
4. Pobedonostsev, 34–35.
5. N to MF, 35.
6. MF to N, 33.
7. N's Diary, 34.
8. Ibid, 35.
9. Ibid, 37–38.
10. Witte, *Memoirs*, 189.
11. Alexander, 46.
12. Pares, *History*, 403.
13. Lincoln, *In War's Dark Shadow*, 167.
14. Alexander, 59–60.
15. Vorres, 13.
16. Hamilton, 163–64.
17. Essed-Bey, 24.
18. Lincoln, *In War's Dark Shadow*, 28.

19. N's Diary, quoted in Radziwill, *Nicholas II*, 33.
20. N's Diary, quoted in Essed-Bey, 27.
21. N's Diary, 21.
22. Ibid, 46.
23. Florinsky, *Russia,* 2:1141–42.
24. Charques, 49.
25. Witte, *Vospominaiia*, 1:435.
26. Cited, Bergamini, 386.

Chapter 9

1. Victoria, *Advice*, 124–27.
2. Vassilli, 225.
3. Witte, *Memoirs*, 197.
4. Buxhoeveden, 36.
5. Hough, *Louis and Victoria*, 152.
6. Buxhoeveden, 36.
7. Victoria, *Advice*, 123–24.
8. Massie, *Nicholas and Alexandra*, 37.
9. Victoria, *Advice*, 124.
10. Buxhoeveden, 38.
11. Bainbridge, 56.
12. Buxhoeveden, 38.
13. *The Lady*, 5 July 1894.
14. Hough, *Louis and Victoria*, 53.
15. Ibid, 153.
16. N to MF, 73.
17. N's Diary, 75.
18. Ibid, 75–76.
19. Ibid, 77–78.
20. Ibid, 62.
21. Ibid, 78.
22. Ibid, 83.
23. Ibid, 85.
24. Hough, *Louis and Victoria*, 154.
25. Victoria, *Advice*, 127.

Chapter 10

1. Buchanan, *Dissolution*, 1–2.
2. Vorres, 63.
3. N's Diary, 103–4.
4. Alexander, 168.
5. Ibid, 168–69.
6. N's Diary, 110.
7. Buxhoeveden, 41.
8. Cited, Battiscombe, 205.
9. Cited, Magnus, 248.
10. Gilliard, *Thirteen Years*, 48.

Chapter 11

1. Buxhoeveden, 44.
2. Kennett, 36.
3. Ibid, 41.
4. Buxhoeveden, 43.

5. Poliakoff, *Empress Marie*, 234–35.
6. Buxhoeveden, 43.
7. Information from Mr. Robert Parsons of Wartski to author.
8. Hough, *Louis and Victoria*, 126.
9. Poliakoff, 76.
10. Mouchanow, 17–18.
11. Vassilli, 206.
12. Cited, Pope-Hennessy, 300.
13. Mouchanow, 25.
14. Quoted, Oldenburg, 1:46.
15. N's Diary, 125.
16. Buxhoeveden, 50.
17. N's Diary, 125.

Chapter 12

1. Richards. Chapter 4 gives extensive financial information from which these figures are drawn.
2. Quoted, Massie, *Nicholas and Alexandra*, 55.
3. Ross, 197.
4. Buxhoeveden, 44.
5. Cited, Magnus, 249.
6. A to Prince Louis, 22 December 1894, BA.
7. Vorres, 52.
8. Vassilli, *Confessions*, 20–21.
9. Almedingen, *Empress Alexandra*, 43.
10. Mouchanow, 50–51.
11. Essed-Bey, 80.
12. Vorres, 62–63.
13. Hamilton, 126.
14. Mouchanow, 46.
15. *Cosmopolitan*, 487.
16. Vyrubova, 4.
17. Ibid, 4–5.
18. *Century*, 847.
19. Cited, De Jonge, 96.
20. Bogdanovich, 82.
21. Radziwill, *Intimate Life*, 75–76.
22. Botkin, 26.
23. Cited, Cowles, *Last Tsar*, 52.
24. Cowles, *Edward VII*, 324.
25. Mossolov, 36.

Chapter 13

1. Mossolov, 10–11.
2. Radziwill, *Nicholas II*, 253.
3. Florinsky, *End*, 2:1147.
4. Radziwill, *Nicholas II*, 102–3.
5. Witte, *Memoirs*, 190.
6. Cited in Salisbury, 7.
7. Cited, Kochan, 67.

8. Salisbury, 101–2; Lincoln, *In War's Dark Shadow*, 123–28.
9. Lincoln, *In War's Dark Shadow*, 213.
10. Payne, 62.
11. Ibid, 127–28.
12. Fischer, 32–33.
13. Payne, 174.

Chapter 14

1. Bovey, 10, 32.
2. Salisbury, 53.
3. Harcave, *Years of the Golden Cockerel*, 292.
4. Vassilli, 144.
5. Bovey, 15–17.
6. *Strand*, 487.
7. Vorres, 72.
8. Alexandra's coronation gown is preserved in the Kremlin armory, where it is currently on display.
9. Buxhoeveden, 64.
10. Narishkyn-Kurakin, 148.
11. *Illustrated London News*, 30 May 1896, 679.
12. Buxhoeveden, 63.
13. Oldenburg, 1:59–60.
14. Buxhoeveden, 65.
15. Ibid, 64.
16. Alexander, 157.
17. Essed-Bey, 65.
18. Ibid, 63.
19. *Harper's*, 349.
20. Buxhoeveden, 66.
21. Bovey, 26.
22. Buxhoeveden, 66.
23. Kschessinska, 59.
24. Harcave, *Years of the Golden Cockerel*, 293.
25. Salisbury, 52.
26. Harcave, *Years*, 293.
27. Salisbury, 57; see also Alexander, 171–72.
28. Salisbury, 56.
29. Harcave, *Years*, 294.
30. Vorres, 79.
31. Izvolsky, 259.
32. Salisbury, 58.
33. Ibid, 58.
34. Alexander, 172.
35. Mouchanow, 54.

Chapter 15

1. Buxhoeveden, 71.
2. Haslip, 271.

3. Quoted, Sulzberger, 153.
4. Quoted, Cowles, *Kaiser*, 150–51.
5. Lee, 411.
6. N to MF, 110.
7. Cited, Longford, 545.
8. Duff, *Victoria in the Highland*, 222.
9. Buxhoeveden, 73.
10. Quoted, Poliakoff, *Tragic Bride*, 125.
11. Oldenburg, 1:69–73.
12. Buxhoeveden, 75.

Chapter 16

1. Vyrubova, 9.
2. Youssoupov, *Lost Splendour*, 86.
3. Vyrubova, 54–55; also, Buxhoeveden, 51–52, Dehn, 70.
4. Grey, Marina, 28.
5. Mouchanow, 25.
6. Ibid, 113.
7. Dehn, 68.
8. Vorres, 93.
9. Mouchanow, 28.
10. Ibid, 67.
11. Ibid, 143.
12. Vyrubova, 84.
13. Mouchanow, 37.
14. Marie Pavlovna, 47.
15. Grabbe, 136.
16. Botkina, 8.
17. Vyrubova, 159.
18. Botkin, 43–44.
19. Vyrubova, 93.
20. Mossolov, 20.
21. Mouchanow, 40.
22. Dehn, 68.
23. Mouchanow, 40.
24. Vorres, 128.
25. Marie Pavlovna, 34.
26. N to MF, 96.
27. MF to N, 100.
28. Buxhoeveden, 56.
29. Victoria, *Advice*, 136.
30. Mouchanow, 68.
31. Buxhoeveden, 77.
32. MF to N, 128.
33. Mouchanow, 91.
34. N to MF, 130.
35. Ibid, 132.
36. Buxhoeveden, 89.
37. Witte, *Vospominaiia*, 1:172.

Chapter 17

1. Ponsonby, 128.
2. Buxhoeveden, 90.

3. Ibid, 90.
4. Ibid.
5. Judd, 42.
6. Ibid.
7. Hough, *Louis and Victoria*, 208.
8. Duff, *Hessian Tapestry*, 276.
9. Judd, 42.
10. Buxhoeveden, 98–99.
11. Michael of Greece, 140.

Chapter 18

1. Lincoln, *In War's Dark Shadow*, 239.
2. Quoted, Massie, *Nicholas and Alexandra*, 90.
3. Mansergh, 52.
4. Witte, *Memoirs*, 250.
5. Harcave, *Years of the Golden Cockerel*, 333.
6. Cited, Salisbury, 93.
7. Dillon, 133.
8. Cited, Cowles, *Last Tsar*, 65.
9. Witte, *Memoirs*, 117.
10. Pares, *History*, 440.
11. Kleinmichel, 220–21.
12. Lincoln, *In War's Dark Shadow*, 260.
13. Rollins, in Oldenburg, editor's note, 2:273–74.
14. Ibid, 2:274.
15. Lincoln, *In War's Dark Shadow*, 262–63.
16. Oldenburg, 2:96.
17. Massie, *Nicholas and Alexandra*, 95.
18. Harcave, *Years*, 333.
19. Rollins, in Oldenburg, editor's note, 2:284; also, see Lincoln, *In War's Dark Shadow*, 266.
20. Harcave, *Years*, 356.
21. Vorres, 113.

Chapter 19

1. Vorres, 114.
2. Cowles, *Last Tsar*, 73–74.
3. Harcave, *Years*, 345–46.
4. Massie, *Nicholas and Alexandra*, 102.
5. Oldenburg, 2:110.
6. Harcave, *Years*, 342–43.
7. Harcave, *1905*, 88–89.
8. Cited, Lincoln, *In War's Dark Shadow*, 289.
9. Pares, *Fall*, 79; see also Salisbury, 129.
10. Mazour, *Rise and Fall*, 356.
11. *Times (London)*, 25 January 1905.
12. Buxhoeveden, 108–10.

13. Buxhoeveden, 61; see also Mouchanow, chapter 6.
14. Mouchanow, 64.
15. Victoria, *Advice*, 67.
16. Almedingen, *Empress Alexandra*, 171.
17. Bergamini, 395.

Chapter 20

1. Salisbury, 135–36.
2. Lincoln, *In War's Dark Shadow*, 217.
3. Charques, 44.
4. Ular, 79.
5. Vassilli, 127.
6. Youssoupov, *Lost Splendour*, 90.
7. Ular, 76–77.
8. Mossolov, 80.
9. Paléologue, 1:152.
10. Almedingen, *Empress Alexandra*, 18.
11. Alexander, 139–40.
12. Vyrubova, 13.
13. Almedingen, *Unbroken Unity*, 52.
14. VMH, 235.
15. Youssoupov, *Lost Splendour*, 118.
16. Essed-Bey, 132.
17. Youssoupov, *Lost Splendour*, 118.
18. VMH, 2:237.
19. Paléologue, 1:160.
20. Buchanan, *Victorian Gallery*, 148.
21. Lincoln, *In War's Dark Shadow*, 310.
22. Mossolov, 90.
23. Pipes, 20.
24. Ibid, 27.
25. Salisbury, 162.
26. Harcave, *Years of the Golden Cockerel*, 375.
27. Kokovstsov, 129–30.
28. Vassilli, 345.
29. Mossolov, 139.

Chapter 21

1. Buxhoeveden, 83.
2. Fullop-Miller, 120–24.
3. Witte, *Memoirs*, 194.
4. Youssoupov, *Lost Splendour*, 62.
5. Paléologue, 1:206.
6. Fullop-Miller, 118.
7. Cowles, *Last Tsar*, 90.
8. De Jonge, 113.
9. Dillon, 155–56.
10. Vorres, 119.
11. Mouchanow, 155.
12. Buxhoeveden, 104.

13. Cited, Radziwill, *Taint of the Romanovs*, 179–80.
14. Buxhoeveden, 104.
15. Vyrubova, 16.
16. Gilliard, *Thirteen Years*, 205.
17. Mossolov, 29–30.
18. Longford, 235.
19. Mayre, 394.

Chapter 22

1. Massie, *Peter the Great*, 56.
2. Ibid, 63.
3. Cited, De Jonge, 32.
4. Cited, Salisbury, 137.
5. Vyrubova, 151.
6. Kokovstsov, 449.
7. Pares, *Fall of the Russian Monarchy*, 133.
8. Alexander, 183.

Chapter 23

1. De Jonge, 14.
2. Fullop-Miller, 14–15.
3. Ibid, 16.
4. Wilson, 38.
5. De Jonge, 35.
6. Wilson, 31.
7. Pares, *Fall of the Russian Monarchy*, 145.
8. Wilson, 33.
9. De Jonge, 48.
10. Ibid, 13.
11. Massie, *Nicholas and Alexandra*, 190.
12. Wilson, 11–12.
13. De Jonge, 94.
14. Paléologue, 1:141–42.
15. Vyrubova, 81.
16. Ibid, 81.
17. Gilliard, *Thirteen Years*, 40.
18. Mossolov, 53.
19. Gilliard, *Thirteen Years*, 38–43.
20. Radziwill, *Taint of the Romanovs*, 199.
21. Vorres, 138.
22. Ibid, 142.
23. De Jonge, 139.
24. Almedingen, *Empress Alexandra*, 127.

Chapter 24

1. Massie, *Nicholas and Alexandra*, 160.
2. Vorres, 130.
3. Vyrubova, 39.
4. Ibid, 100.

5. Buxhoeveden, 126.
6. A to Princess Bariatinsky, BA, 28 October 1910.
7. Radziwill, *Nicholas II*, 194–95.
8. Vassilli, *Confessions*, 147.
9. Buxhoeveden, 166.
10. Essed-Bey, 191.
11. Vyrubova, 30.
12. Ibid, 23.
13. Botkina, 8.
14. Paléologue, 1:229.
15. Ibid, 1:229.
16. Vyrubova, 35.
17. Dehn, 49.
18. Vyrubova, 29.
19. Pares, *Fall of the Russian Monarchy*, 127.
20. Massie, *Nicholas and Alexandra*, 160.
21. Vyrubova, 395.
22. Mossolov, 246. The *Standart* ended her days as a Soviet minesweeper in the North Sea.
23. Donaldson, 45.
24. Buxhoeveden, 122.
25. Heckstall-Smith, 77.

Chapter 25

1. Paléologue, 1:161.
2. Fullop-Miller, 206–7.
3. Iliodor, 202.
4. Rodzianko, 27–28.
5. Rivet, 40.
6. Iliodor, 108.
7. Cited, De Jonge, 169.
8. Iliodor, 111.
9. Ibid, 116.
10. Ibid, 233–34.
11. Cited, De Jonge, 154.
12. Moorehead, 72.
13. Kokovstsov, 300.
14. Fuhrman, 91.
15. Botkin, 123.
16. Vyrubova, 162.
17. Massie, *Nicholas and Alexandra*, 213–14.
18. Fuhrman, 53.
19. Ibid, 55.
20. Kokovstsov, 266.
21. Pares, *Fall of the Russian Monarchy*, 143.
22. Kokovstsov, 272.
23. Youssoupov, *Lost Splendour*, 146.
24. Kokovstsov, 281–83.
25. Ibid, 291.

26. Rodzianko, 33–34.
27. Almedingen, *Empress Alexandra*, 124.
28. Rodzianko, 38.
29. Ibid, 53.
30. Kokovstsov, 12.
31. Ibid, 454.
32. Ibid, 470.
33. Kilcoyne, 248.
34. Pares, *Fall of the Russian Monarchy*, 150.
35. Massie, *Nicholas and Alexandra*, 213.
36. Kokovstsov, 295–96.

Chapter 26

1. Cited, De Jonge, 198.
2. N to MF, 274.
3. Spiridovich, 2:202.
4. Vyrubova, 90–91.
5. De Jonge, 213.
6. Gilliard, *Thirteen Years*, 40.
7. Ibid, 28.
8. Vyrubova, 92.
9. Gilliard, *Thirteen Years*, 29.
10. Vyrubova, 92–93.
11. N to MF, 276.
12. Ibid, 276.
13. Buxhoeveden, 132.
14. Massie, *Nicholas and Alexandra*, 183.
15. Buxhoeveden, 132.
16. Vyrubova, 93.
17. Gilliard, *Thirteen Years*, 29–31.
18. Ibid, 29.
19. Ibid, 31.
20. Vyrubova, 93.
21. Ibid, 94.
22. Paléologue, 1:148.
23. N to MF, 278.
24. Vyrubova, 97.
25. Gilliard, *Thirteen Years*, 37.
26. Vassilli, 394.
27. Cited, De Jonge, 139.

Chapter 27

1. Cowles, *1913*, passim.
2. Rodzianko, 75–77.
3. Buchanan, *Dissolution*, 87.
4. Buxhoeveden, 175.
5. Buchanan, *Dissolution*, 36–37.
6. Vorres, 130.
7. Kokovstsov, 361.
8. Vassilli, 399.
9. Paley, 15.

10. Buxhoeveden, 153.
11. Botkin, 65.
12. Kobylinsky, in Wilton, 220.
13. Buxhoeveden, 155.
14. Gilliard, *Thirteen Years*, 76.
15. Hough, *Louis and Victoria*, 265.
16. Gilliard, *Thirteen Years*, 76–77.
17. Mossolov, 247.
18. Vorres, 53.
19. *Munsey's*, 3.
20. *Good Housekeeping*, 455–56.
21. Buxhoeveden, 180.
22. Vyrubova, 26.
23. Botkina, 9.
24. Cowles, *1913*, 111.
25. Almedingen, *Empress Alexandra*, 132.
26. Lincoln, *In War's Dark Shadow*, 377.
27. Paléologue, 3:122.
28. *Daily Mail (London)*, 23 May 1913.
29. Cowles, *1913*, 76.

Chapter 28

1. Cited, Cassels, 176.
2. Ibid, 179.
3. Mansergh, 219.
4. Pares, *Fall of the Russian Monarchy*, 182.
5. De Jonge, 237.
6. Ibid.
7. Paléologue, 1:14.
8. Ibid, 1:24–25.
9. Ibid, 1:27–28.
10. Mansergh, 345.
11. Pares, *Fall*, 181.
12. Ibid, 184.
13. Buchanan, *Mission*, 1:200.
14. Ibid, 1:202.
15. Cowles, *Kaiser*, 339–40.
16. Sazonov, 201.
17. Vyrubova, 105.
18. Buchanan, *Mission*, 1:204.
19. Paléologue, 1:48.
20. Pares, *Fall*, 188.
21. Vyrubova, 104.
22. Cited, De Jonge, 228.
23. Ibid, 228.
24. Ibid.
25. Simanovich, 196.
26. Gilliard, *Thirteen Years*, 165–66.
27. Marie Pavlovna, 162.
28. Paleologue, 1:45–46.
29. Cantacuzene, 15.

Chapter 29

1. Cowles, *Last Tsar*, 154.
2. Golovine, 53.
3. Ibid, 45–50.
4. Ibid, 34.
5. Ibid, 205.
6. Pares, *Fall of the Russian Monarchy*, 198.
7. Paléologue, 1:107.
8. AF to N, 24.
9. Knox, 103.
10. Pares, *Fall*, 211.
11. Knox, 189.
12. Ibid, 194.
13. Ibid, 249.
14. Golovine, 214.
15. Pares, *Fall*, 230.
16. Massie, *Nicholas and Alexandra*, 313.
17. Golovine, 98.
18. Ibid, 145.
19. Ibid, 237.
20. Ibid, 98.
21. Paléologue, 2:34.
22. Golovine, 127.
23. Knox, 255.
24. Ibid, 270.
25. Pares, *Fall*, 232.
26. Paléologue, 1:58.
27. Almedingen, *Empress Alexandra*, 137.
28. AF to N, 37.
29. Buxhoeveden, 186.
30. Gilliard, *Thirteen Years*, 109.
31. Lockhart, 102–3.
32. Knox, 515.
33. Kerensky, *Murder*, 55.
34. Almedingen, *Empress Alexandra*, 143.
35. Mossolov, 87.
36. Knox, 334.
37. AF to N, 91.
38. Ibid, 87–88.
39. Ibid, 89.
40. Ibid, 97–98.
41. Ibid, 100.
42. Ibid, 110.
43. Vyrubova, 123.
44. Paléologue, 2:68.
45. Vyrubova, 125.
46. Ibid.
47. Cited, Lincoln, *Armageddon*, 167.
48. Cantacuzene, 69–70.
49. AF to N, 113–16.

Chapter 30

1. AF to N, 20.
2. Buxhoeveden, 192.
3. Marie Pavlovna, 196.
4. Buxhoeveden, 192–93.
5. Vyrubova, 109–10.
6. AF to N, 11.
7. Ibid, 12.
8. Ibid, 24.
9. Ibid, 25–26.
10. Ibid, 31–32.
11. Ibid, 41.
12. Vyrubova, 110.
13. AF to N, 33.
14. Ibid, 53.
15. Marie Pavlovna, 194.
16. Ibid, 196–97.
17. AF to N, 394.
18. Ibid, 103.
19. Ibid, 366.
20. Ibid, 368.
21. Ibid, 391–92.
22. Cited, Grabbe, 163.
23. AF to N, 2.
24. Ibid, 3.
25. Ibid, 10.
26. Ibid, 11.
27. Ibid, 14.
28. Ibid, 90.
29. Ibid, 248.
30. Ibid, 267.
31. Ibid, 310.
32. Ibid, 43.
33. Ibid, 334.
34. Ibid, 318.
35. N to AF, 6.
36. Ibid, 18.
37. Ibid, 38.

Chapter 31

1. Fullop-Miller, 236.
2. Mossolov, 153.
3. Ibid.
4. Fullop-Miller, 183.
5. Ibid, 185.
6. Ibid.
7. Ibid, 187.
8. Ibid, 199.
9. Ibid.
10. Ibid, 200.
11. Ibid, 185.
12. Ibid, 188.
13. Ibid, 199.

14. Ibid, 189.
15. Ibid, 190.
16. Mayre, 446.
17. Pares, *Fall of the Russian Monarchy*, 140.
18. Cited, De Jonge, 213–14.
19. Lockhart, 125–26.
20. Paléologue, 1:321.
21. Lockhart, 126.
22. Pares, *Fall*, 225.
23. Cited, Salisbury, 271.
24. Quoted, De Jonge, 253.
25. AF to N, 105–6.
26. Vyrubova, 118.
27. Ibid, 119.
28. Gilliard, *Thirteen Years*, 167–68.
29. AF to N, 182.
30. Ibid, 225.
31. Ibid, 192.
32. Vyrubova, 127.
33. Gilliard, *Thirteen Years*, 155–56.
34. Vyrubova, 169–70.

Chapter 32

1. Pares, *Fall of the Russian Monarchy*, 280.
2. AF to N, 86.
3. Ibid, 153.
4. Ibid, 114.
5. N to AF, 71–72.
6. De Jonge, 249–50.
7. Kilcoyne, 279.
8. Cited, Salisbury, 237.
9. AF to N, 110.
10. Ibid, 441.
11. Quoted in Radziwill, *Nicholas II*, 242; see also, Buchanan, *Dissolution*, 128.
12. AF to N, 86.
13. Ibid, 87.
14. Ibid, 186.
15. Ibid, 379.
16. Ibid, 62.
17. Ibid, 94.
18. Ibid, 291.
19. Ibid, 117.
20. Ibid, 86.
21. Ibid, 94.
22. Ibid, 453.
23. Ibid, 454.
25. Ibid, 305.
26. Ibid, 453–55.
27. Pares, *Fall of the Russian Monarchy*, 397.

28. AF to N, 97.
29. Ibid, 121.
30. Ibid, 143–44.
31. Ibid, 145.
32. Rodzianko, 36.
33. AF to N, 120.
34. Ibid, 256.
35. Paléologue, 2:166.

Chapter 33

1. De Jonge, 259.
2. AF to N, 171.
3. De Jonge, 257.
4. AF to N, 283.
5. Ibid, 91.
6. Ibid, 297.
7. Ibid, 260.
8. Ibid, 290.
9. Ibid, 297.
10. Ibid.
11. Knox, 415.
12. AF to N, 156.
13. Ibid, 210.
14. Ibid, 130.
15. Ibid, 135.
16. Ibid, 156.
17. Cited, De Jonge, 287.
18. AF to N, 394.
19. N to AF, 256.
20. Billington, 500.
21. Kerensky, *Crucifixion*, 218.
22. AF to N, 428.
23. Rodzianko, 214.
24. Fuhrman, 184.
25. AF to N, 438.
26. N to AF, 297.
27. Ibid, 298.
28. AF to N, 439.
29. Ibid, 441.
30. Ibid, 442.
31. Mossolov, 168–73.

Chapter 34

1. Paléologue, 3:26.
2. AF to N, 211.
3. Ibid, 221.
4. N to AF, 202.
5. Ibid, 78.
6. Ibid, 203.
7. AF to N, 411.
8. Ibid, 385.
9. Ibid, 382.
10. Ibid, 411.
11. Ibid, 413.

12. Alexander, 271.
13. Kerensky, *Murder*, 51.
14. N to AF, Editor's Note, 203.
15. Kerensky, *Crucifixion*, 220.
16. Cited, Kurth, 345–47.
17. AF to N, 376.
18. Vyrubova, 111.
19. Buxhoeveden, 223.
20. Kerensky, *Crucifixion*, 244.
21. Shulgin, 90–101.
22. For more information, see Salisbury, 296.
23. The evidence implicating the dowager empress and other Romanovs in the plot against the tsar is difficult to establish. Nevertheless, many members of the family themselves believed that this was the case. My information comes from G. Nicholas Tantzos, a writer who had access to certain documents in the Archives of the October Revolution in Moscow, including letters of the imperial family not yet published.
24. Cited, Salisbury, 299.
25. Alexander, 275.
26. Cited, Alexandrov, 119–20.
27. AF to N, 433.
28. Cited, Salisbury, 297.
29. Paléologue, 3:158.
30. Marie Pavlovna, 248–49.
31. Youssoupov, *Lost Splendour*, 193.
32. Cited, Salisbury, 299.
33. Gilliard, *Thirteen Years*, 181–82.

Chapter 35

1. Pares, *Fall of the Russian Monarchy*, 376.
2. Ibid, 396–97.
3. Paléologue, 3:153.
4. Purishkevich, 74.
5. Vorres, 98.
6. Youssoupov, *Lost Splendour*, 19.
7. Ibid, 55.
8. Ibid, 70.
9. De Jonge, 296.
10. Youssoupov, *Lost Splendour*, 62.
11. De Jonge, 296.
12. Youssoupov, *Lost Splendour*, 65.
13. Ibid, 86.
14. Ibid, 174–75.
15. De Jonge, 297.

16. Youssoupov, *Lost Splendour*, 218–19.
17. Ibid, 213.
18. Ibid, 214.
19. Ibid, 225–26.
20. Vyrubova, 174.
21. Pares, *Fall of the Russian Monarchy*, 399.
22. AF to N, 466.
23. Youssoupov, *Lost Splendour*, 232.
24. Ibid, 233.
25. Ibid, 236.
26. Youssoupov, *Rasputin*, 150.
27. Youssoupov, *Fall of the Russian Monarchy*, 235.
28. Ibid, 240.
29. Purishkevich, 142.
30. Ibid, 145.
31. Youssoupov, *Lost Splendour*, 242.
32. Purishkevich, 146.
33. Ibid, 146–47.
34. Ibid, 147.
35. Ibid, 149–50.
36. Ibid, 152–55.
37. Ibid, 155.
38. Ibid, 158.

Chapter 36

1. Vyrubova, 181.
2. Ibid, 180.
3. Paléologue, 3:171.
4. AF to N, 461.
5. De Jonge, 324.
6. Cited, De Jonge, 325–26.
7. Massie, *Nicholas and Alexandra*, 380.
8. Vyrubova, 183.
9. Paléologue, 3:164.
10. Dehn, 123.
11. Kerensky, *Murder*, 106.
12. Paléologue, 3:126.
13. Ibid, 3:191.
14. Kokovtsov, 478.
15. Pares, *Fall of the Russian Monarchy*, 414.
16. Rodzianko, 251.
17. Paléologue, 3:119.
18. Vyrubova, 186.
19. Dehn, 137.
20. Almedingen, *Empress Alexandra*, 381.
21. Cited, Salisbury, 325.
22. Alexander, 283–84.
23. Ibid, 184.
24. Mossolov, 79.

25. AF to N, 280.
26. Paléologue, 3:157.
27. Rodzianko, 246.
28. Ibid, 252.
29. Ibid, 214.
30. Ibid, 249.
31. Cowles, *Last Tsar*, 183.

Chapter 37

1. Rodzianko, 261.
2. Cited, Salisbury, 331.
3. Kerensky, *Crucifixion*, 261.
4. Massie, *Nicholas and Alexandra*, 398.
5. Salisbury, 344–46.
6. Harcave, *Years of the Golden Cockerel*, 453.
7. Ibid.
8. Massie, *Nicholas and Alexandra*, 399–400.
9. Harcave, *Years*, 454.
10. Salisbury, 354.
11. Pares, *Fall of the Russian Monarchy*, 442.
12. Salisbury, 359.
13. Ibid, 359–60.
14. Cited, Salisbury, 361.
15. Pares, *Fall*, 443.
16. Buchanan, *Mission*, 2:58.
17. Paléologue, 3:214.
18. Buchanan, *Dissolution*, 164.
19. Cited, Salisbury, 368.
20. Pares, *Fall*, 451.
21. Salisbury, 384.
22. Cited, Salisbury, 384.
23. Pares, *Fall*, 450.
24. Ibid, 458.
25. Botkin, 139.
26. Kschessinska, 169.
27. Paléologue, 3:259.
28. Ibid, 3:265.
29. Knox, 558.

Chapter 38

1. Salisbury, 356.
2. Dehn, 147.
3. Ibid, 148.
4. Ibid.
5. Ibid, 149.
6. Ibid, 152.
7. Benckendorff, 5.
8. Gilliard, *Thirteen Years*, 211.
9. Benckendorff, 5.
10. Gilliard, *Thirteen Years*, 211.

11. Kerensky, *Murder*, 79.
12. Ibid, 86–87.
13. Pares, *Fall of the Russian Monarchy*, 459.
14. Dehn, 155.
15. Benckendorff, 6–7.
16. Dehn, 158.
17. Gilliard, *Thirteen Years*, 212.
18. Buxhoeveden, 256.
19. Benckendorff, 9.
20. Buxhoeveden, 254–55.
21. Dehn, 156.
22. Ibid, 158.
23. Vyrubova, 209.
24. Benckendorff, 14–15.
25. Dehn, 160.
26. Cited in Salisbury, 400.
27. Dehn, 162.
28. Buxhoeveden, 262–63.
29. Dehn, 163.
30. Buxhoeveden, 256.
31. Cited, De Jonge, 333.
32. Kerensky, *Murder*, 90–92.
33. Paléologue, 3:233.
34. Mossolov, 27.
35. Kerensky, *Murder*, 93.
36. Paley, 61.
37. Dehn, 165.
38. Buxhoeveden, 261–62.
39. Gilliard, *Thirteen Years*, 213.
40. Vyrubova, 209.
41. Dehn, 174.
42. Buxhoeveden, 264.
43. Pares, *Fall of the Russian Monarchy*, 467.
44. Ibid.
45. Ibid, 468.
46. Dehn, 176.
47. Benckendorff, 30–35.
48. Bulygin, 190.
49. Gilliard, *Thirteen Years*, 214–15.
50. Ibid.
51. Dehn, 185–87.

Chapter 39

1. Vyrubova, 212.
2. Almedingen, *Empress Alexandra*, 209–10.
3. Benckendorff, 65.
4. Ibid, 59.
5. Kerensky, *Murder*, 123.
6. Benckendorff, 55–56, 59.
7. Kerensky, *Murder*, 126.
8. Benckendorff, 75–76.

9. Vyrubova, 223–24.
10. Buxhoeveden, 279.
11. Vyrubova, 225
12. Dehn, 215.
13. Buxhoeveden, 286.
14. Ibid, 286.
15. Vyrubova, 218.
16. Buxhoeveden, 284.
17. Dehn, 192.
18. Buxhoeveden, 284.
19. Ibid, 285.
20. Dehn, 199.
21. De Jonge, 340.
22. Kerensky, *Murder*, 105.
23. Buxhoeveden, 298.
24. Vyrubova, 212–13.
25. Benckendorff, 71.
26. Buxhoeveden, 299.
27. Gilliard, *Thirteen Years*, 230–31.
28. Vyrubova, 222.
29. Buxhoeveden, 300–301.

Chapter 40

1. Lloyd-George, 507.
2. *Times (London)*, 21 April 1917.
3. Nicolson, 299.
4. Ibid.
5. Waters, 245.
6. PRO/FO 371/2995.
7. Paléologue, 3:258.
8. PRO/FO 371/2998.
9. PRO/FO 371/2998.
10. PRO/FO 371/3008.
11. Kerensky, *Murder*, 118.
12. PRO/FO 800/205, File 63.
13. PRO/FO 800/205, File 65.
14. PRO/FO 800/205.
15. PRO/FO 800/205.
16. Quoted, FOT, 250.
17. PRO/FO 800/205.
18. Lloyd-George, 514.
19. FOT, 251.
20. Kerensky, *Murder*, 118.
21. Buchanan, *Dissolution*, 192–93.
22. Quoted, Lambton, 389.
23. Quoted, FOT, 253.
24. BBC Interview, quoted in FOT, 245.

Chapter 41

1. Pares, in Introduction to Kerensky, *Murder*, 17.
2. Kerensky, *Murder*, 120.
3. Vyrubova, 222.
4. Buxhoeveden, 305.

5. Massie, *Nicholas and Alexandra*, 468, 472.
6. Kerensky, *Murder*, 128.
7. Bulygin, 194.
8. Kerensky, *Murder*, 130.
9. Gilliard, *Thirteen Years*, 239–40.
10. Ibid, 240.
11. Buxhoeveden, 311.
12. Gilliard, *Thirteen Years*, 242.
13. Bykov, 43–44.
14. Massie, *Nicholas and Alexandra*, 477.
15. Bykov, 45.
16. Massie, *Nicholas and Alexandra*, 479.
17. Vyrubova, 303.
18. Ibid, 316.
19. Ibid, 298–99.
20. Ibid, 300.
21. Ibid, 305–6.
22. Ibid, 313.
23. Ibid, 302.
24. Buxhoeveden, 316–17.

Chapter 42

1. Botkina, 50.
2. Trewin, 82–83.
3. Wilton, 198.
4. Vyrubova, 334.
5. Massie, *Nicholas and Alexandra*, 482–83.
6. Vyrubova, 326, 329.
7. Buxhoeveden, 323.
8. Vyrubova, 334.
9. Kerensky, *Murder*, 25–26; also quoted in Trewin, 87, in a slightly different form.
10. Bulygin, 198–99.
11. Ibid, 198.
12. Bykov, 57.
13. Bulygin, 216.
14. FOT, 260.
15. Trewin, 88–90.
16. FOT, 255–56.
17. Ibid, 256–57.
18. Ibid, 259.
19. Windsor, 131.

Chapter 43

1. Bulygin, 202.
2. PRO/FO 371/3310.
3. Deterichs, 1:78.
4. Cited, FOT, 278.
5. Ibid, 279. The "German Princesses" referred to here are likely to have been Alexandra and her sister Ella

rather than the tsarina and her daughters.

6. PRO/FO 371/3310.
7. Bulygin, 201.
8. Bykov, 62.
9. *Krasnaya Niva*, no. 27, 1928, 17.
10. Bulygin, 201.
11. Vyrubova, 340.
12. Botkina, 56.
13. Massie, *Nicholas and Alexandra*, 492.
14. Vyrubova, 338–39.
15. Bulygin, 208.
16. Wilton, 205.
17. Gilliard, *Thirteen Years*, 260.
18. Buxhoeveden, 329.
19. Gilliard, *Thirteen Years*, 261.
20. Buxhoeveden, 329.
21. Gilliard, *Thirteen Years*, 261.
22. Botkina, 56.
23. Botkin, 194.
24. Wilton, 249.
25. Bykov, 68.
26. FOT, 264.
27. Levine, 130.
28. Bulygin, 212.
29. Ibid.
30. Bykov, 72.
31. Levine, 131.
32. Bykov, 72.
33. Levine, 133.
34. Bykov, 72.
35. Wilton, 206–7.
36. Bulygin, 232.
37. Vyrubova, 341–42.

Chapter 44

1. Grey, Marina, 19.
2. Kobylinsky, in Wilton, 216.
3. Bulygin, 232.
4. Gilliard, *Thirteen Years*, 269.
5. FOT, 45.
6. Wilton, 179.
7. Ibid, 164.
8. Wilton, 148, 180.
9. Sokolov, 124.
10. Wilton, 34.
11. Ibid, 129.
12. Ibid, 149.
13. Ibid, 180–82.
14. Sokolov, 144–45.
15. Vorres, 243.
16. Bykov, 76.
17. Levine, 138.
18. Ibid.

19. Ibid, 140.
20. Ibid.
21. Ibid, 133.
22. Ibid, 139.
23. Ibid, 133.
24. Ibid, 139.
25. Cited, O'Conor, 81.
26. *Chicago Daily News*, 6 November 1919.
27. Radzhinskii, in *Ogonek*, no. 2 (1989), 27.

Chapter 45

1. Trotsky, 80.
2. Quoted, Pipes, 747.
3. Cited, Salisbury, 611.
4. Ibid, 581–82.
5. Pipes, 765.
6. *Times (London)*, 3 July 1918.
7. Melgunov, 365.
8. Deterichs, 1:31.
9. Trotsky, 81.
10. Melgunov, 402.
11. Alexandrov, 229.
12. Radzhinskii, in *Ogonek*, no. 21, (1989), 30.
13. Levine, 141.
14. Sokolov, 122–24.
15. Levine, 134.
16. McCullagh, 129.
17. Sokolov, 192–93.

Chapter 46

1. Wilton, Medvedev testimony, ch. 6.
2. This account of the murders is drawn from the recently published memoirs of Jacob Yurovsky, in both *Ogonek* and Radzhinskii, *The Last Tsar*.
3. For more information, see Radzhinskii, *The Last Tsar*, 391.
4. Radzhinskii, *Ogonek*, no. 21 (1989), 29.
5. Ibid, 30.
6. Ibid, 28.
7. Sokolov, 221.
8. Ibid, 205.
9. Wilton, 325–26.
10. Ibid, 322–23.
11. Bykov, 82.
12. For more information on the conduct of the various investigations, see O'Conor.

Chapter 47

1. Ryabov account, videotape testimony, distributed by the Holy Archangels Center in Washington, D.C. I obtained my copy courtesy of Mr. James Blair Lovell.
2. *Times (London)*, 15 April 1989.
3. Ibid.
4. Ryabov videotape testimony.
5. Kurth, *Vanity Fair*, 120.
6. *New Republic*, July 1991.
7. Kurth, *Vanity Fair*, 119.
8. Ibid, 120.
9. AP wire story, 29 July 1992.
10. See Radzhinskii, ch. 16, for further information.
11. Mr. Radzhinskii related this to me during an interview in July 1992.
12. The question of Alexei's possible survival is raised in Radzhinskii, 420–24. Mr. Radzhinskii details the story of a man who claimed to be the tsarevich while imprisoned in a Stalinist camp. My impression is that he believes the man was Alexei. "I think it's much easier to believe that he was Alexei than that [Anna Anderson] was Anastasia," he told me recently. The only other claimant to be Alexei, a Polish defector by the name of Michael Goloniewski, never produced any evidence to support his assertion.
13. *Times (London)*, 11 December 1992.

Epilogue

1. Pipes, 788.
2. Bulygin, 255.
3. Wilton, 362–63.
4. Bulygin, 256.
5. Vorres, 169.
6. For more information, see Pauline Grey, *Grand Duke's Woman*.
7. When she left Russia, Grand Duchess Vladimir carried with her a fortune in jewels, much of which was sold after her death. Queen Elizabeth II today often wears her famous diamond loop tiara. For more information, see Leslie Field, Suzy Menkes, and Hans Nadelhoffer.
8. Kurth, *Vanity Fair*, 123.
9. For more information, see Dobson; see also Bryan and Murphey.
10. Airlie, 231.
11. FOT, 170.
12. See Duff, *Hessian Tapestry*, for more information.
13. Yeltsin, 80–82.
14. Kurth, *Vanity Fair*, 123.
15. *New York Times*, 2 November 1981.
16. *Time* 14 November 1981, 15.
17. S. Massie, Pavlovsk, 179.
18. Ibid, 188.

Bibliography

Airlie, Mabell, Countess of. *Thatched With Gold*. London: Hutchinson, 1962.

Alice, HRH the Princess. *Letters*. London: John Murray, 1885.

Alexander Michailovich. *Once a Grand Duke*. Garden City, N.Y.: Doubleday, 1932.

Alexandra Feodorovna. *The Letters of the Tsarina to the Tsar, 1914–1917*. London: Duckworth, 1923.

Alexandrov, Victor. *The End of the Romanovs*. London: Hutchinson, 1966.

Almedingen, Edith Martha von. *The Empress Alexandra*. London: Hutchinson, 1961.

———. *An Unbroken Unity: A Memoir of the Grand Duchess Serge of Russia*. London: Bodley Head, 1964.

Bainbridge, Henry. *Peter Carl Fabergé*. London: Batsford, 1949.

Balfour, Michael. *The Kaiser and His Times*. New York: Houghton Mifflin, 1964.

Battiscombe, Georginia. *Queen Alexandra*. London: Constable, 1969.

Benckendorff, Paul. *Last Days at Tsarskoe Selo*. London: Heinemann, 1927.

Benson, E. F. *Queen Victoria's Daughters*. London: Cassell, 1939.

Bergamini, J. *The Tragic Dynasty: A History of the Romanovs*. London: Constable, 1970.

Bernstein, Herman, ed. *The Willy-Nicky Correspondence*. New York: Knopf, 1918.

Billington, James. *The Icon and the Axe*. New York: Knopf, 1966.

Bing, Edward J., ed. *The Secret Letters of the Last Tsar: Being the Confidential Correspondence Between Tsar Nicholas II and the Dowager Empress Marie*. New York: Longmans, Green, 1938.

Bogdanovich, [Madame] A. V. *Journal de la général A.V. Bogdanovich*. Paris: Payot, 1926.

Botkin, Gleb. *The Real Romanovs*. New York: Revell, 1931.

Botkina, Tatiana. *Vospominaniia o Tsarskoĭ Sem'ye*. Belgrade: Stefanovich, 1921.

Bovey, Kate Koon. *Russian Coronation, 1896.* Minneapolis: privately printed, 1942.

Bryan III, J., and Charles Murphey. *The Windsor Story.* New York: William Morrow, 1979.

Buchanan, George. *My Mission to Russia.* London: Cassell, 1923.

Buchanan, Meriel. *Dissolution of an Empire.* London: Murray, 1932.

———. *Queen Victoria's Relations.* London: Cassell, 1954.

———. *Victorian Gallery.* London: Cassell, 1956.

Bulygin, Paul. "The Sorrowful Quest." In *The Murder of the Romanovs,* London: Hutchinson, 1935.

Buxhoeveden, Sophie. *The Life and Tragedy of Alexandra Feodorovna, Empress of Russia.* New York: Longmans, Green, 1928.

Bykov, Paul. *The Last Days of Tsardom.* London: Martin Lawrence, 1934.

Cantacuzene, Princess. *Revolutionary Days.* Boston: Small, Maynard & Co, 1919.

Cassels, Lavender. *The Archduke and the Assassin.* New York: Stein and Day, 1984.

Charques, Richard. *The Twilight of Imperial Russia.* Fair Lawn, N. J.: Essential Books, 1959.

Corti, Egon. *The English Empress.* London: Cassell, 1957.

Cowles, Virginia. *Edward VII and His Circle.* London: Hammish Hamilton, 1956.

———. *The Kaiser.* New York: Harper & Row, 1963.

———. *1913: An End and a Beginning.* New York: Harper & Row, 1967.

———. *The Romanovs.* London: Collins, 1971.

———. *The Last Tsar.* New York: Putnams, 1977.

Crankshaw, Edward. *The Shadow of the Winter Palace: Russia's Drift to Revolution, 1825–1917.* New York: Viking, 1976.

Dehn, Lili. *The Real Tsaritsa.* London: Thornton Butterworth, 1922.

De Jonge, Alex. *The Life and Times of Gregorii Rasputin.* New York: Dorset Press, 1982.

Deterichs, Mikhail. *Ubiistvo Tsarskoi Sem'i.* Vladivostock: Military Academy Press, 1922.

Dillon, E. J. *Eclipse of Russia.* London: Dent, 1918.

Dimond, Frances, and Roger Taylor. *Crown and Camera.* London: Penguin Books, 1987.

Dobson, Christopher. *Prince Felix Yusupov, The Man Who Killed Rasputin.* London: Harrap, 1989.

Donaldson, Frances. *Edward VIII.* New York: Random House, 1974.

Duff, David. *Hessian Tapestry.* London: Frederick Miller, 1967.

———. *Victoria in the Highlands.* London: Taplinger, 1969.

———. *Victoria Travels.* London: Taplinger, 1970.

Edwards, Anne. *Matriarch: Queen Mary and the House of Windsor*. New York: Morrow, 1984.

Eilers, Marlene. *Queen Victoria's Descendants*. New York: Atlantic International Publications, 1987.

Epton, Nina. *Queen Victoria and Her Daughters*. New York: Norton, 1971.

Essed-Bey, Mohammed. *Nicholas II: Prisoner of the Purple*. London: Hutchinson, 1936.

Field, Leslie. *The Queen's Jewels: The Personal Collection of Elizabeth II*. New York: Harry N. Abrams, 1987.

Fischer, Louis. *The Life of Lenin*. New York: Colophon Books, 1965.

Florinsky, Michael T. *The End of the Russian Empire*. New York: Collier, 1961.

———. *Russia: A History and an Interpretation*. New York: Macmillan, 1964.

Fuhrmann, Joseph T. *Rasputin: A Life*. New York: Praeger, 1990.

Fulford, Roger. *Dearest Child: The Letters of Queen Victoria to the Crown Princess Victoria of Prussia*. London: Evans, 1964.

Fullop-Miller, Rene. *Rasputin, The Holy Devil*. Garden City, N. Y.: Doubleday, 1928.

Gilliard, Pierre. *Thirteen Years at the Russian Imperial Court*. New York: Doran, 1921.

———. *Le tragique déstin de Nicolas II et de sa famille*. Paris: Payot, 1921.

Golovine, N. N. *The Russian Army in World War I*. London: Oxford University Press, 1931.

Grabbe, Paul, and Beatrice von. *The Private World of the Last Tsar*. Boston: Little, Brown, 1984.

Grey, Marina. *Enquête sur le massacre des Romanovs: Vérités et légendes*. Paris: Librarie Académique, 1987.

Grey, Pauline. *The Grand Duke's Woman*. London: Macdonald and Jane's, 1976.

Hamilton, Frederick. *The Vanished Pomps of Yesterday*. New York: Doubleday, 1934.

Harcave, Sidney. *1905*. New York: Macmillan, 1964.

———. *Years of the Golden Cockerel*. London: Robert Hale, 1970.

Harrison, Michael. *Clarence: Was He Jack the Ripper?* London: W. H. Allen, 1972.

Haslip, Joan. *The Lonely Empress*. New York: Doubleday, 1970.

Heckstall-Smith, Anthony. *Sacred Cows*. London: Anthony Bland, 1965.

Hough, Richard. *Louis and Victoria: The First Mountbattens*. London: Hutchinson, 1974.

———. *Mountbatten*. New York: Random House, 1980.

Izvolsky, Alexander. *Memoirs*. London: Hutchinson, 1920.

Iliodor, [Sergei Trufanov]. *The Mad Monk of Russia*. New York: Century, 1918.

Jagow, Kurt. *Letters of the Prince Consort*. London: John Murray, 1938.

Judd, Denis. *Prince Philip*. New York: Atheneum, 1981.

Katkov, George. *Russia, 1917: The February Revolution*. London: Longmans, Green, 1967.

Kennett, Victor and Audrey. *The Palaces of Leningrad*. New York: Putnams, 1973.

Kerensky, Alexander. *The Catastrophe*. New York: Appleton, 1927.

———. *Crucifixion of Liberty*. New York: Day, 1934.

———. *Murder of the Romanovs*. London: Hutchinson, 1935.

———. *Russia and History's Turning Point*. New York: Duell, Sloan & Pearce, 1965.

Kilcoyne, Martin. *The Political Influence of Rasputin*. Unpublished Ph.D. diss. Seattle: University of Washington, 1961.

Kleinmichel, Marie. *Memories of a Shipwrecked World*. London: Brentano's Ltd. 1923.

Knight, Stephan. *Jack the Ripper: The Final Solution*. London: Harrap, 1976.

Knox, Alfred. *With the Russian Army*. New York: Dutton, 1921.

Kochan, Miriam. *The Last Days of Imperial Russia*. New York: Macmillan, 1976.

Kokovstsov, Vladimir. *Out of My Past: The Memoirs of Count Vladimir Kokovstsov*. Stanford University Press, 1935.

Kschessinska, Mathilde. *Dancing in Petersburg*. Garden City, N. Y.: Doubleday, 1961.

Kurth, Peter. *Anastasia: The Riddle of Anna Anderson*. Boston: Little, Brown, 1983.

Lambton, Anthony. *Elizabeth and Alexandra*. New York: Dutton, 1986.

Lee, Sidney. *Queen Victoria*. London: Smith, Elder, 1902.

Levine, Isaac Don. *Eyewitness to History*. New York: Hawthorn Books, 1973.

Lincoln, W. Bruce. *The Romanovs*. New York: Dial, 1981.

———. *In War's Dark Shadow*. New York: Dial, 1983.

———. *Passage Through Armageddon*. New York: Simon & Schuster, 1986.

Lloyd-George, David. *War Memoirs*. Boston: Little, Brown, 1934.

Lockhart, Robert Bruce. *British Agent*. New York: Putnams, 1933.

Longford, Elizabeth. *Queen Victoria: Born to Succeed*. New York: Harper & Row, 1964.

Lovell, James Blair. *Anastasia: The Last Princess*. Washington, D.C.: Regency Gateway, 1991.

McCullagh, Frances. *Prisoner of the Reds*. London: John Murray, 1921.

Magnus, Philip. *King Edward VII*. New York: Dutton, 1964.

Mansergh, Nicholas. *The Coming of the First World War*. New York: Longmans, Green, 1942.

Marie Louise. *My Memories of Six Reigns*. New York: Dutton, 1957.

Marie of Battenberg. *Reminiscences*. London: Allen & Unwin, 1925.

Marie Pavlovna. *Education of a Princess*. New York: Viking, 1934.

Markov, Serge. *How We Tried to Save the Tsaritsa*. London: Putnam, 1929.

Martin, Theodore. *The Life of the Prince Consort*. London: Smith, Elder, 1874.

Massie, Robert K. *Nicholas and Alexandra*. New York: Atheneum, 1967.

———. *Peter the Great*. New York: Knopf, 1980.

———. With Jeffrey Finestone. *The Last Courts of Europe*. New York: Vendome, 1981.

Massie, Suzanne. *Pavlovsk: The Life of a Russian Palace*. Boston: Little, Brown, 1990.

Mayre, George Thomas. *Nearing the End in Imperial Russia*. Philadelphia: Dorrance, 1929.

Mazour, Anatole. *The Rise and Fall of the Romanovs*. Princeton, N. J.: Van Nostrand, 1960.

———. *Russia Past and Present*. New York: Van Nostrand, 1951.

Melgunov, Sergei. *Sudba Imperatora Nikolaiia II Posle Ostrecheniia*. Paris: Payot, 1951.

Menkes, Suzy. *The Royal Jewels*. London: Grafton Books, 1988.

Michael of Greece. *Crown Jewels*. New York: Crescent Books, 1986.

Milford-Haven, Victoria. *Reminiscences*. Unpublished, Broadlands Archives.

Moorehead, Alan. *The Russian Revolution*. New York: Harper & Row, 1958.

Mossolov, Alexander. *At the Court of the Last Tsar*. London: Metheun, 1935.

Mouchanow, Marfa. *My Empress*. New York: John Long, 1918.

Nadelhoffer, Hans. *Cartier: Jewellers Extraordinary*. London: Thames & Hudson, 1984.

Narishkyn-Kurakin, Elizabeth. *Under Three Tsars*. New York: Dutton, 1931.

Nicholas II. *Letters of the Tsar to the Tsarina, 1914–1917*. London: Bodley Head, 1929.

———. *Journal Intime*. Paris: Payot, 1925.

Nicolson, Harold. *King George V*. London: Constable, 1952.

Noel, Gerard. *Princess Alice: Queen Victoria's Forgotten Daughter*. London: Hutchinson, 1974.

O'Conor, John. *The Sokolov Investigation*. New York: Robert Speller & Sons, 1971.

Oldenburg, S. S. *Last Tsar: Nicholas II, His Reign and His Russia*. Gulf Breeze, Fla.: Academic International Press, 1977.

Paléologue, Maurice. *An Ambassador's Memoirs*. New York: Doran, 1925.

Paley, Princess of Russia. *Memories of Russia*. London: Herbert Jenkins, 1924.

Pares, Bernard. *The Fall of the Russian Monarchy*. New York: Vintage, 1961.

———. *A History of Russia*. New York: Knopf, 1960.

Payne, Robert. *The Life and Death of Lenin*. New York: Simon & Schuster, 1964.

Pipes, Richard. *The Russian Revolution*. New York: Knopf, 1990.

Pobedonostsev, Constantine. *Reflections of a Russian Statesman*. Ann Arbor, Mich.: University of Michigan Press, 1965.

Poliakoff, Vladimir. *The Tragic Bride: The Story of the Empress Alexandra* New York: Appleton, 1927.

———. *The Empress Marie of Russia and Her Times*. London: Thornton Butterworth, 1926.

Ponsonby, Frederick. *Recollections of Three Reigns*. New York: Dutton, 1952.

Pope-Hennessy, James. *Queen Mary*. New York: Knopf, 1960.

Preston, Thomas. *Before the Curtain*. London: John Murray, 1950.

Prideham, Francis. *Close of a Dynasty*. London: Wingate, 1956.

Purishkevich, Vladimir. *The End of Rasputin*. Ann Arbor, Mich.: Ardis Press, 1985.

Radzhinskii, Edvard. *The Last Tsar: The Life and Death of Nicholas II*. New York: Doubleday, 1992.

Radziwill, Princess Catherine. *Secrets of Dethroned Royalty*. New York: John Lane, 1920.

———. *The Taint of the Romanovs*. London: Cassell, 1931.

———. *Nicholas II, The Last of the Tsars*. London: Cassell, 1931.

———. *The Intimate Life of the Last Tsarina*. London: Cassell, 1929.

Rasputin, Maria. *My Father*. London: Cassell, 1934.

———. *Rasputin*. London: John Long, 1929.

Richards, Guy. *The Hunt for the Czar*. London: Peter Davies, 1971.

Rivet, Charles. *The Last of the Romanovs*. London: Constable, 1918.

Rodzianko, Michael. *The Reign of Rasputin*. London: Philpot, 1927.

Rose, Kenneth. *King George V*. London: Weidenfeld & Nicolson, 1983.

Ross, Marvin. *The Art of Karl Fabergé and His Contemporaries*. Tulsa: University of Oklahoma Press, 1965.

Rumbelow, Donald. *The Complete Jack the Ripper*. Boston: Little, Brown, 1975.

Salisbury, Harrison. *Black Night, White Snow*. New York: Doubleday, 1977.

Sazonov, Serge. *Fateful Years.* New York: Stokes, 1928.

Shulgin, V. *The Years: Memoirs of a Member of the Russian Duma.* New York: Hippocrene Books, 1984.

Simanovich, Aron. *Rasputin i evre; vospominaiia lichnago sekretaria Grigorii Rasputin.* Riga: no publisher, no date.

Sokolov, Nicholas. *Enquête judicaire sur l'assassinat de la famille impériale russe.* Paris: Payot, 1924.

Spiridovich, Alexander. *Les dernières années de la cour de Tsarskoie Selo.* Paris: Payot, 1928.

Sulzberger, Cyrus Leo. *The Fall of Eagles.* New York: Crown, 1977.

Summers, Anthony, and Tom Mangold. *The File on the Tsar.* New York: Harper & Row, 1976.

Taylor, Edmund. *The Fall of the Dynasties.* New York: Doubleday, 1963.

Trewin, John. *The House of Special Purpose.* New York: Stein & Day, 1975.

Trotsky, Leon. *Trotsky's Diary in Exile.* Cambridge, Mass.: Harvard University Press, 1953.

Tuchman, Barbara. *The Guns of August.* New York: Macmillan, 1962.

———. *The Proud Tower.* New York: Macmillan, 1966.

Tyler-Whittle, Michael. *The Last Kaiser.* New York: Times Books, 1977.

Ular, Alexander. *Russia From Within.* London: Heinemann, 1905.

Vassilli, Paul [Princess Catherine Radziwill]. *Behind the Veil of the Russian Court.* London: Cassell, 1913.

———. *Confessions of the Czarina.* New York: Harper, 1918.

Victoria, Queen of Great Britain. *The Letters of Queen Victoria.* London: John Murray, 1907, 1932.

———. *Advice to a Granddaughter.* ed. Richard Hough. London: Heinemann, 1975.

Vorres, Ian. *The Last Grand Duchess.* New York: Scribners, 1965.

Vyrubova, Anna. *Memories of the Russian Court.* New York: Macmillan, 1923.

Warwick, Christopher. *Two Centuries of Royal Weddings.* New York: Dodd, 1980.

Waters, Hely-Hutchinson Wallscourt. *Potsdam and Doorn.* London: John Murray, 1935.

Wheeler-Bennett, John. *Brest-Litovsk.* London: Macmillan, 1963.

Wilson, Colin. *Rasputin and the Fall of the Romanovs.* New York: Farrar, Straus, 1964.

Wilton, Robert. *The Last Days of the Romanovs.* London: Thornton, Butterworth, 1920.

Windsor, HRH the Duke of. *A King's Story.* New York: Putnams, 1947.

Witte, Serge. *The Memoirs of Count Witte.* New York: Doubleday, 1921.

———. *Vospominaiia.* Moscow: Lenin State Library, 1960.

Wolfe, Bertram C. *Three Who Made a Revolution*. New York: True Books, 1964.
Yeltsin, Boris. *Against The Grain*. New York: Summit Books, 1990.
Youssoupov, Felix. *Rasputin*. New York: Dial, 1927.
————. *Lost Splendour*. London: Cape, 1953.

Russian Periodicals

Krasnaiia Niva. no 27. (1928), 17.
Radzhinskii, Edvard. *Ogonek*, no. 21, (1989), 4–5, 30–32.
Ryabov, Geli. *Rodina*, nos. 4 and 5, (1989).

English Language Periodicals

Coudert, Amalia Kussner. "The Human Side of the Czar," *Century*, October 1906, 847.
"The Czar and His Family," *Munsey's*, vol. 51, no. 1, (February, 1914), 3.
Fletcher, Richard. "Royal Mothers and Their Children," *Good Housekeeping*, vol. 54, no. 4 (April 1912), 455–56.
Illustrated London News. Various issues; dates referenced in Source Notes.
Kurth, Peter. "The Mystery of the Romanov Bones," *Vanity Fair*, vol. 56, no. 1 (January 1993).
Morris, Fritz. "The Czar's Simple Life," *Cosmopolitan*, vol. 23, no. 5, (September 1902), 487.
New Republic. July 1991.
Oustimenko, Vladimir. "The File on the Romanovs: Nicholas and Alexandra," *Royalty Monthly*, vol. 11, no. 3. (December 1991).
Pelham-Clinton, Charles. "The Russian Coronation," *Strand*, vol. 11, 1897, 487–93.
The Lady, July 1894.

Newspapers

(dates referenced in Source Notes)
Times (London)
Chicago Daily News
London Daily Mail

Other Media

New Findings. Videotape interview with Geli Ryabov, 1989, distributed by the Holy Archangels Center, Washington, D.C.

Index